Nia's Rose

By Lance Dakota

ISBN: 978-1-968970-56-7 (sc)
ISBN: 978-1-968970-57-4 (e)

Rev. date: 09/01/2025

Acknowledgments

As eyes are windows to the soul, writing is a window to be opened for the Will of God... With all my love for my mom, who always believed I could do anything, whispering in my ear when I was a child that she hoped all my dreams would come true, and the most important one did, having her as my mother. She came to see me everyday when I was in Lady of Lourdes Hospital when I was three-years-old after having a tracheotomy in which I almost died. Each morning, while recovering, I leaned over my crib, awaiting her appearance down the hallway.. and each morning she did, walking toward me with courage, faith, and hope. I could not ask for anything more than that in this world from God. In my mom, He gave me everything.

My friend Sharon, where can I begin? You were inspirational to me through the many years working on this novel and I couldn't have done it without you. Not only did you help me with the story but you also gave me insight into its purpose. To my sister, Pattie, the best writer I know, don't give up...just never give up. Veronica Pavez Varela - What a beautiful painting for the cover of this book, amazing, just phenomenal. To the doctors who saved my life so that this book could be written, to my family and friends I have made along the way, thank you for never giving up on me. My heart has grown learning of this world, and I hope that I have made it a better place than when I entered it. In the Book of Revelation 11:15 it states, The seventh angel sounded his trumpet, and there were loud voices in heaven which said, 'The kingdom of the world has become the kingdom of our LORD AND OF HIS MESSIAH, and He will reign for ever and ever...'"

For Jesus and Mary

Prologue

August 2005. When he got up and walked into the bathroom, he briefly glanced at the reflection of himself in the mirror. Confused, he saw an archangel staring back at him.

Frightened, he quickly turned away and went back into his room and sat down on his bed. Reaching over to a table next to him, he turned on a radio. Trying to keep his leg still from shaking, he wondered about his father and brother. Did they forget about him? It had been three years as he ran his hands slowly across newspaper articles that were upon it like he had seemingly done a thousand times before.

"Pinning is winning for Kahn Brothers." "Kahn Bothers Do it Again."

Something was peculiar, though, as the newspaper clippings were all covered in a yellowish tint. He knew, though, that everything around him was strange, even himself and how he acted. Was he really chosen by God for some divine purpose like an angel told him? Were there really dragons, fair maidens to defend? Deep within, he believed there were.

Yet, he did not like reflections, especially those shimmering through the passage of time.

Often, he made his own images of himself, who he was, who he is, and who he could become within the world around him—such as within a waterfall falling down into a crystal pond, cradled in woods, hidden in the deepest part of his mind. It was a place he liked to go when no one understood or seemed to care for him. His dreams by this pond, though, seemed like distant stars, flowing through his fingertips of his cupped hand, attempting to grasp them gently from the rippling water's surface, only to reappear back in the middle of the pond, encircling reflections within a mysterious moon draped in an unusual color of a mysterious bleeding color of red...

In a distant sea of time, he envisioned a seven-headed-dragon, rising up out of the sea with a turning of a page from and Ancient Bible - The Book of Revelation - *The Seventh Angel*.

Chapter 1

Christmas Eve, 1987. Carrying Joshua, her three-year-old son, in her arms, Elizabeth walked over and placed him tenderly in a chair in front of an open window beneath a full moon with an archangel weathervane atop the roof high above them barely moving in a gentle wind. The old Victorian house, alone, high on the mountainside, overlooked bright city lights in the distant valley below. Cradled in darkness, held in the shadows of the night, their home seemed abandoned except for the lit colors of a Christmas tree, just past the staircase, adorned with an array of medieval ornaments: one, a white winged horse glistening with green sparkles; another, an angel, right above it.

Joshua was a silent son, diagnosed as autistic, with crystal-like blue eyes, and as of yet, not speaking a word. With the different colors of the lights from the tree reflecting upon his brow, he clasped in his right hand a small, *closed rosebud* close to his chest as his mother reached over and placed a snow globe on the table next to him. She shook it. Snow fell on a woman and man dancing in a gazebo inside. "It's going to snow," she said as she opened a stained glass music box and knelt down beside him. Half asleep, Joshua heard his mother softly singing, "Oh, holy night holy night the stars are brightly shining. It is the night of the dear Savior's birth...fall on your knees, hear the angels' voices..." The song faded.

Elizabeth got up and followed a small ray of light appearing before her, coming from her husband's slightly ajar bedroom door. As with her life, the door was only partially open, the light only partially upon her. Hesitating, she stood before it, remembering just a few hours earlier

1

when her husband stood in the shadows behind her. She slowly began to cry softly. Her tears caused her makeup to run, revealing the bruises and scratches under her eyes, as she remembered his hand reaching out to grab her shoulder in the dim light. He pulled her into the darkness, caressing the back of her neck with his lips, slowly, as he bit her shoulder. With the smell of alcohol hitting her face, she dropped her hand and submitted while she watched the shadow of her open hand on the wall.

"I have to get ready. I have to be at the church soon," she said to him barely in a whisper with a downward cast of her eyes.

Brushing away this painful memory, she pushed the bedroom door open. She saw the bed with its massive and high wooden headboard, containing the carvings of dragon, swirling waves of antiquity. The bed practically took up the entire room. She squeezed past it to get to the basement door. The light was on as she peered down the stairs. The two bikes for her sons, Christmas presents, still lay in pieces next to an empty bottle. It was as if the bottle of whiskey had taken their place. Alongside the partially assembled bikes was an opened tool box, the tools apparently having been angrily thrown about. Her husband was gone.

She raised her hands, closed her eyes in thanks, and briefly touched her chest. Walking back into the living room, she paused to touch a picture of a young soldier in his uniform, her husband's brother, which was next to her diploma—Elizabeth Prather Kahn. Master's Degree, Medieval Literature, resting on the mantelpiece above the fireplace.

"God bless you, Michael," she said. She looked up, "Wherever you are," she added. She wondered how her life would be different if she married her husband's brother, Michael, instead. She loved her husband and her sons Tim and Joshua with all her heart. So, turning back, being more thankful for her husband and sons, she pulled the bedroom door slightly closed, though leaving it partially opened.

The moonlight was unusually bright, shining through the window down on Joshua curled up in the chair. It was as if the moonlight had secretly followed them home after the Christmas play. Wanting to put Joshua to sleep, Elizabeth took a small book off the Christmas tree that had a picture of a dragon on its cover. As she picked him up and cradled him in her arms to read to him, he clasped onto a small heart-shaped crystal draped around her neck. She opened the book and read as the moon's rays blended with the colors of the lights from the tree.

"This is a story, a story that happened a long, long time ago, when knights slew dragons for fair maidens, carrying them away into the night, and riding white winged horses off into the sky..."

As she read on, her voice became musical as if playing upon hidden sounds of the night. He gazed up at her as if she were an angel reaching down from heaven, lighting up his soul with a thousand dreams that can come true. Then, slowly, dark clouds passed before the moon as the front porch screen door began to swing open and shut in the wind of an oncoming storm.

"Look, Joshua, the dragon is eating the moon," she whispered to him while pointing out the window. At the bottom of the hill in the oncoming storm, a man rode a white horse upward toward the house. Elizabeth and Joshua both watched as the clouds blanketed their light.

Suddenly, the shadow of a man crept up behind them. He had a riding crop clutched in his left hand as his soiled stained riding boots crossed over the fading of the moonlight on the floor. A young white horse, tied to the porch post, whinnied loudly in fear, the reflections of the coming storm in his wide eyes. The words of her story faded and became silent in the growing wind as Joshua's eyes gently closed with the passing of the moon.

"Rest, my son, rest for the day you shall be a knight..."

The man, he placed his hand upon her... "No, I can't. It's Christmas Eve. Joshua..." she pleaded. But the man gripped her tighter into her shoulder with each bang of the slamming screen door. Hesitantly, she arose and placed Joshua back down in the chair, covering him with a blue blanket, already knowing from many times before, what the man's orders would be. Violently, the man grabbed her by her neck, dragged her by the collar of her white blouse, and kicked open the bedroom door as the light emanating from the room washed out the magical lights of the tree.

"No, please. Christmas!" she screamed out.

He had never been this rough, this fierce, before. Throwing her onto her back hard on the bed, he tore her white blouse completely from her as she fell. She tried to get up.

"Please..." she continued to plead.

With one swift blow of his hand, he slapped her face, cutting her bottom lip with a ruby ring on his left index finger. She gasped, but knew this time to stay quiet on the bed. Reaching into his long, gray, soiled coat, he took out a knife with a dragon handle and began to cut away her remaining clothes until she was completely naked. She lay like cold stone on her back, her legs spread out, submitting in silence before him, staring into the void blackness of his eyes. As he raised the knife upward toward the ceiling, she exploded abruptly in fear and tried to squirm out from beneath him. She could not escape, for he was much too strong.

He flipped her over hard onto her belly. Clasping the back of her head by her hair, he made a cut with the knife aside her neck as he lunged with his gaping mouth upon it, sucking her blood, as if a wolf upon its prey. She writhed ferociously in the struggle to break free as the white horse bound to the porch frantically reared up on his hind legs. The man pressed her face down hard into the metal rim of the bed with the anger in his eyes, a *reflection* in the turning of the blade. "Never tell me no, my sweet whore of Babylon. You are mine to use... It is my right."

Taking his unwilling victim from behind, the metal frame beneath the wooden bed felt exceptionally cold and hard as he slowly, yet forcibly, entered her bare, exposed vulnerable soul. She tried not to scream with each thrust joined by a slam of the screen door. Pulling her head by her hair, as if pulling back on the reigns of a horse, he forced her eyes to gaze upward at the carvings in the high headboard above her, tears flowing down her cheeks. The swirls were violent, as if sculptured by a storm, carved without reason or purpose, cutting deep and far to every edge. Not a single part of her remained untouched from the cut, from the tossing swirling winds of this artist's hands.

Humiliated, she tried to hold back even her gasps as her tears mixed with the sweat falling from her brow. Longing to escape, reaching deep within herself, she ran from the sounds of the slamming screen door and cracks of thunder against the sky to her memory of the light of day when the shadows were not alive and did not toss in the carved images of the bed...

"Joshua! Joshua!" Elizabeth remembered calling out, standing on the front porch with Joshua's angel wings clutched in her right hand. It was earlier in the day, a few hours before the play, and Joshua and his older brother, Timmy, were playing knights, dueling with toy swords in the front yard. Abruptly, Timmy tackles Joshua.

"Joshua! We have to get ready! Timmy, get off of him!" She called out.

"I'm teaching him to wrestle!" Timmy called back, tossing aside his toy sword.

"Oh, great, now he's going to be covered in mud, and I wanted him to be my lead angel," she said. Timmy helped Joshua up and led him over to his mother.

"What's this?" she asked while trying to wipe away the painted colors on Joshua's cheek. "That's war paint," Timmy said as he retrieves his sword, adding, "We're knights." "Well, tonight he's going to be an angel. So are you. Go upstairs and get your wings." "But I'm a knight, like King Richard the Lion Hearted." "So you can be a knight angel, the lion hearted. You can stand in front of the entire church with your sword in one hand, and a candle in the other. But you are still going to wear your wings. Now go!"

Timmy ran into the house as she gently took Joshua by the hand and led him through the doorway. She stooped down and positioned the wings carefully on his back.

"Now, you're going to be out in front, the lead one. I want you to raise your candle high to the sky and then call out Jesus' name as loud as you can," she said, hoping he would speak his first word tonight.

As she reached up to blot away the remaining paint from Joshua's forehead, the memory of the light of day faded to the colors from the Christmas tree reflecting on Joshua asleep in the chair before the open window...

Her soul naked, his cold soiled hands wrapped around her, clutching her tight, he ravaged her in rage with the fullness of the darkened moon. His eyes appeared to turn yellow, like a wolf. "Please stop. You're hurting me," she cried out as she looked into the eyes of the wolf.

Dismounting her, reaching underneath, grabbing her, he said, "You're mind to hurt. Say it! Raising his head like a wolf howling out into the night, she *felt* the final slam of the screen door.

"Yes. Yes. I understand," she moaned with her eyes closed, her head reaching upward in agony, through a wish, somewhere off to a distant hope of peace, somewhere off to where the horizon meets the sea...

Lightning struck and hit a branch of a tree atop a cliff overlooking the sea. Suddenly, Joshua appeared standing in the bedroom doorway. "Mom?" Joshua whispered his first word.

Opening her eyes, she cried out, "Run, Joshua! Run!" as she tried to break free.

But the man held her down tight.

"I give the orders! Benedictus es..." He whispered, crushing her with his strength. "Who do you think you are giving an order? A queen? Well, where's your crown?

Where's your crown, my lady?"

He grabbed the back of her head and slammed it into the carvings of the headboard. It left a mark, her blood trickling down.

"Mom," Joshua cried again, still clutching the unopened rose to his chest, swaying back and forth, between darkness and light.

"Stay back!" the man shouted to Joshua. Blood was flowing from her mouth as she felt herself slowly drift out to an open endless sea.

"Well, there's your crown." He used her own blood to paint a crown with his finger, encircling it around her forehead. "Oh, hail the queen of heaven! Of earth! You shall not rule over me!" The man lifted his head and bloodstained hands toward the ceiling. Joshua ran to his mother's side.

"Mom!" Joshua called out, trying to help her.

With one fling of the man's arm, he tossed Joshua against the bureau beside the bed. The move slammed the back of Joshua's head against a metal knob on one of its drawers. Dazed, Joshua fell to the floor.

"No. My son. My son," Elizabeth whispered, awakening with her blood flowing down her throat. The man raised the knife.

"Joshua," Elizabeth whispered with one final breath, reaching out her bloodstained hand toward her son *in that color of red.*

The man took his knife and made one quick slash... Joshua saw his mother's tongue cut off. The unopened rose from Hope fell from his hand... into the darkness. He reached back down and picked *it* up.

Joshua ran away as fast as he could, tripping over his own feet, through the living room, back through the reflections of the colored lights upon the tree, and fell into the shadows at the bottom of the staircase. On his hands and knees, he crawled, shaking uncontrollably to the top. Collapsing at the top of the stairs, he clutched the last rung of the banister and listened to his mother's final struggle echoing below. The Christmas tree lights faded. *The colors disappeared.* Then there was silence, as Joshua felt his mother's death.

He gazes down at his hands. There are holes, blood. He cries out. The screen door flies off. The gust of strong winds cover the echoes of his cries. The man's shadow appears at the bottom of the staircase. Joshua tenses, turns in fear...

Chapter 2

A cross with a statue of Jesus hung at the front of a small chapel in Lady of Lourdes psychiatric hospital in Los Angeles: "The City of Angels." Twenty-three-years had passed since Joshua had witnessed the violent tragedy of his mother's death as rays of sunlight shined through the stained-glass windows similar to passages through time. Along the side of the chapel, candles were lit beneath statues of archangels as a small group of women, kneeling in the front pews, began praying aloud the rosary.

Joshua sat quietly upon a stool in one of the hospital rooms on the second floor, drawing on a large sketch pad in front of him. Twenty-one years old, his crystal-like bright blue eyes still had a look of innocence, his wrists, though, scared from his suicide attempt a couple years ago.

Sitting back down, he continued drawing, *but only in images of black and white,* the colors of life, as if trapped in a glass, still not seen. With his right hand clasped shut, he sketched a beautiful young woman with exotic looking eyes and long flowing dark hair. She was kneeling, naked, clasping upon a rose while gazing upward toward the sky.

A Diana Ross song, "Ain't No Mountain High Enough," was playing on the CD player over the radio on the small table by his side.

His bags were packed and the bed carefully made as Joshua began staring, as if mesmerized, at the picture of the young woman he drew, who seemed to be coming to life before his crystal blue eyes. It was as if he had known her all his life, as if they shared the same destiny, the same hope, the same fate. Joshua reached out quietly and ran his finger gently across her lips.

Destiny's Dance Club. "I'll be there... Ain't no mountain high enough..." Nia, who looked like the young woman in Joshua's picture, softly sang the Diana Ross song playing over the radio in the dressing room of Destiny's Dance Club in another part of town. Nia, nineteen years old, was a mixture of races, part black, part white, and Cherokee Indian. She had long dark hair, beautiful brown eyes, high-cheek bones and an olive complexion. She was wearing only a white lace thong with a small red heart as she sat on a stool, leaning over a long table before a spanning mirror to put her makeup on. The large mirror's reflections encapsulated several other dancers, who were also getting ready to go out and perform. The heel of Nia's bare left foot rested on one rung of the stool. She raised her other foot to another rung as she sat up, tossed her hair back, and lifted her chin to sing out louder.

Still taped on the walls of Joshua's room were the newspaper clippings, old and tattered, and even more yellowish. "The Kahn Brothers Do It Again," "Pinning Is Winning for Kahn Brothers," "Kahn's Look Toward NCAA Wrestling Championships." Joshua was doing push-ups on the floor.

"Do you think my brother is ready?" Tim asked as he walked briskly alongside a doctor, a woman, with shoulder-length dark hair. Tim briefly looked down at her long, white lab coat, her legs, as they passed psychiatric patients along the way down the hospital's hallway toward Joshua's room.

"Yes. I think he's ready. That's all he's been talking about, going home with his brother," the doctor affirmed, catching herself looking longer than she should have into his eyes with her reply.

Tim was handsome, in a movie star sort of way, having a rugged, confident look and a perfectly sculptured face with thick dark hair above, though, soft eyes of brown. He was about six feet tall with a lean but sturdy build, good leverage for wrestling. As he walked, he projected a romantic magnetism as female patients in the hallway, and even in their rooms, looked up and at him as he passed. Several of these women, both young and old, smiled at him. One even blew him a kiss, an old lady with bright crystal green eyes, wearing a white hospital gown, tied to her wheelchair.

He's coming! He's coming! Jesus is coming!" she shouted to them as they passed. She struggled to break free from her bonds. An old man shuffled to her side to try to calm her down.

"They'll find out, Silvia. You don't have to scream it now," he said to her. Tim and the doctor paused as if to help her, but continued on.

"How long has she been here?" Tim asked.

"A while. Her family abandoned her. The only friend she has is that old man, Mr. Jeffreys. He thinks he is her prince. He told me that all he has to do one day is kiss her and they will be young again, walking off into the sunset. It's sad. They don't know they'll never leave here. But your brother, he's getting another chance." They stand in front of Joshua's room, looking in at him through a glass window of the door. Joshua was struggling, practicing sit out and turn ins, wrestling moves, across the floor. It looked like he was wrestling an invisible opponent from long ago.

"Are you sure he's alright?" Tim asked.

"He's made a lot of improvement," she responded, adding, "It's been a year, now, and I believe he's finally ready to go home. We've come a long way in treating his type of schizophrenia."

"So he's still crazy," Tim said.

"He's not crazy. His memory, the frontal lobe of his brain, is locked somehow in another time period associated with when he tried to kill himself."

"What time period?" Tim replied.

"Apparently, Medieval. Don't know why. He said, he keeps seeing a dragon, imagines himself as some kind of warrior. We haven't found a way to unlock what's inside of him, yet, that part of his brain to bring him psychologically fully back into our reality."

"What's all this supposed to mean?" Tim asked.

"He believes he's a angel, not just any kind of angel, but an archangel. He goes by Oriel." "Oriel?" Tim quivers with his voice.

"Yes, Oriel. I looked him up. He's a recognized archangel in post-exilic rabbinic and some Christian traditions."

"Really. Wow. How did Joshua come upon that?" "Oriel is cited in Medieval Literature.

Didn't you say at one of our therapy sessions, your mother..."

"This is all too much for me, doc. I mean, how do you know all of this?"

"He told us, not when he is calm, but when he's in one of his states, like a trance or something. He said when he looks in the mirror, he sees himself as Oriel. That's why he never looks too long. It's as if his brain has set up a defense mechanism to keep the illusion alive, like living in a fantasy in an attempt, we believe, to run away from his pain. If your trying to defeat demons, why not become an archangel, right?"

"As strange as that sounds, it makes sense. So, what should I do?" Tim asked. "Just be a brother," the doctor replied.

"Easy for you to say," Tim replied sarcastically, watching Joshua through the glass, flipping around on the floor, still wrestling an invisible opponent.

"He's not going to be doing that all the way home? I just got a new truck." Tim paused. "Does he know I've come for him?"

"I told you. That's all he's been talking about. Going home with his brother." "Did you ever find out why he tried to kill himself?"

"We're not sure. But it had to do something with what he witnessed with your mother when he was three."

"Why did it take so long to affect him like this, you know, believing he's an archangel?" "Those impacted by trauma often bury them deep within themselves their tragedy. Then,

years later, the pain sometimes explodes, causing people to take on defense traits, to cope." "So, you're really sure he is ready to go home with his illusions and all?"

"Yes. I'm sure. Joshua is—special, different. He's much stronger than he thinks." "He doesn't try to fight his... demons, does he, I mean, physically?"

"Only at sunset," the doctor replied with a smile, opening the door...

Tim and Joshua drive in Tim's truck upon a bridge, over a bay, leading to a mountaintop in silence as Joshua gazes out the window.

"Are you alright?" Tim asked, adding, "You look like you're seeing something."

Joshua didn't answer. Suddenly, an eagle flies past the windshield.

"Oh man. Wow. Did you see that? That eagle, it almost flew into us," Tim said. Joshua turned and said, "It wasn't an eagle."

"It wasn't? It sure looked like one... Oh." Tim said, beginning to notice Joshua getting agitated. "It's okay. Doesn't matter what it was, right... That's strange," Tim said, tapping the clock on the dash of his truck.

"What's strange?" Joshua asked, still gazing out the window toward the colors of the sunset, as if clawing to be seen through the images of black and white before being blanketed by the finality of a night in Joshua's mind, those woods, the secret part of his heart.

"The time. It says 1:11," Tim said.

Joshua turned away from the window and said. "Do you believe in angels?"

Tim took out a cigarette, bit down on it, and reached for the truck's lighter in the dash. He lit it and took a deep puff, then another.

"I thought you stopped smoking," Joshua said.

"Well, I've started again," Tim replied, taking another deep puff. "When?" Joshua asked.

"Just now," Tim said, then attempted to remain silent. "Because me?" Joshua pointed at himself. Tim did not respond.

"You still think I'm crazy, don't you?" Joshua asked. "Well, I'm not, you know. I'm better now." Joshua paused. "It's taken me a while to figure everything out, but my faith in God, it has grown stronger. And I believe that He has chosen me to do something, something important. You don't believe me, do you?"

"I don't know what I believe anymore, Joshua," Tim answered, flicking his cigarette ashes out the window. I saw dad the other day quoting Shakespeare as King Richard the Third."

"Do you believe in God?" "Sometimes."

"How can you sometimes believe in God? You either believe in Him or you don't.

You know, I learned a lot while I was in there. Everything makes sense, now. Time, space, other dimensions; all intersect on levels that no one really understands. That eagle was a coincidence, a sign. But, it wasn't an eagle." Joshua smiles at Tim. Tim breaks a smile back, tosses the cigarette.

"It's going to be great having you back home, Joshua" Tim said, adding, "I believe you," patting his shoulder as they rode over the bridge with a sunset in the distance across the bay...

Destiny's Dance Club. The door opens to the back dressing room of Destiny's Dance Club. A beautiful young woman, Christine, with shoulder-length blonde hair, green eyes, and long legs walked in and noticed Nia, sitting on her stool, singing, preparing to go out into the club. Nia was singing softly to herself a song about an angel.

"You're a good singer," Christine said.

Christine, dressed in jeans, a tee-shirt, and jean jacket, holds a small bag in her hand. She places it on top of a table next to a glass of rum and coke. It spills. She tried to clean it up.

"Don't worry," a lot of things spill out from around here, from the darkness," Nia blurted out, adding, "Are you our new waitress?"

"Yeah. Hi. I'm Christine," she said, extending her hand.

Nia reached out and shook it. Christine, eyes down, turned away and slowly, as if hesitantly, began taking off her clothes, kicking off her sneakers, first.

"Christine," that's a beautiful name," Nia said.

"It means, 'Believer in Christ,'" Christine replied, standing in just her bra and panties. "Nice physique," Nia responded as she turned and opened a drawer of the long table, taking out a small, gold, circular container with an emblem of a dragon on it. "What's that?" Christine asked.

Nia opened it, white powder- cocaine. She took a couple deep sniffs, glancing at herself in the mirror between each one.

"It looks like snow," Christine said, gazing at the cocaine. Nia remained silent. She took a third sniff, appearing to be drifting off, visualizing images of a distant war upon a cliff, angels and demons fighting; a large dragon rising up out of the sea... a sword.

Nia placed the container of cocaine far back into the drawer and took out white lace stockings. Swaying a bit, she began to slip them on.

"I never did this before," Christine said, slightly covering herself, standing before the mirror naked. "I don't know if I can do this," she added.

"Then why are you?" Nia asked, taking a sip of what was left to the rum and coke, turning to face Christine.

"Because I need the money," Christine responded, letting her arms drop to her side. "Don't we all," Nia replied. Pausing, Nia took out a locket necklace from the drawer.

"Can you help me with this?" "Sure." Christine stood behind Nia, helping her clasp on the necklace. The locket was brilliant, a shiny silver, with a bright reflection of the sun shining through an open window, with swirling, carved images of outstretched vines holding roses.

"What's inside?" Christine asked, gently patting the locket in place on Nia's neck.

"Don't know. I never opened it," Nia said, adding, "My father gave it to me a long time ago." Nia briefly turned, seeing the sun's rays begin to fade, the locket appearing to become suddenly rusted and old, like an old suite of armor of a knight.

"Do you have any kids?" Nia asked, turning back.

"A daughter. She's three," Christine replied, adding, "Single parent. Just us." "So, you're doing this for her?"

"Yes," Christine replied with a sigh.

"Alright. Then let's do this. What do you have in your bag?" Nia asked while opening it. Nia takes out skimpy white lace panty and bustier.

"Well, I see you got the uniform." She tossed the outfit to Christine. Nia looked at her sternly and said, "Put them on." Christine nodded.

Christine took off her bra and panties. A back door opened as a couple of dancers came in from outside. Christine, turning, could see men standing in the parking lot. With the outside door briefly opened, the men in the parking lot glanced in at Christine, naked. With a rush, Christine felt vulnerable and exposed from a dark place she wanted to remain hidden.

One young man called out, "Christine?" The door closed. Christine turned toward Nia, appearing to be in shock.

"Oh my God, I know him," Christine simply said.

"No you don't," Nia responded, adding, "In here, we don't know anyone. We have to not associate our live out there with what happens in here. First Rule. Second Rule. Come up with a new name for when you're working. That way you can assume a different personality. It's all about creating a new reality in which you can survive while we do what we do. I think we should call you... Blaze."

"Blaze?" Christine asked. "Yeah, Blaze. It's action oriented, like get out of my way, kick ass type of thing. You're definitely a Blaze. Out there, you can be Christine. But, in here, you need something that can keep you flying under the radar, like me," Nia said. "Do you have another name?" Christine asked.

Nia paused. "No. I'm just Nia, in here and out there. I have nothing to hide. If you think about it, I don't think anyone really cares who I am...or what I do."

"Girls, hurry up, your shifts started," the manager, Ms. Gongel in a dark suit with blonde hair in a tightly wrapped bun called into the dressing room to Nia and Christine. Ms. Gongel stood tall, statuesque, projecting strong confidence in a commanding tone.

"Yes, ma'am. We're coming," Nia responded, adding to Christine, "Come on. Let's get you ready." Christine put on her thong but had trouble with her bustier. Nia helped her. "I've never worn one of these before," Christine said, adding, "I was told I had to or they wouldn't hire me."

"There," Nia said, making an adjustment. "Now let's see," Nia added, going over to the drawer of the long table. Nia took out another pair of white lace stockings. Christine took them, sat down on Nia's stool, and slipped them on.

"Did you bring heels?" Nia asked. Christine remained silent, sitting on the stool with her arms nervously folded over her legs, one leg shaking, up on her toes. "That's alright. I think I have a pair that will fit you," Nia said as she went over and reached underneath the table. She took out a pair of white high heels and handed them to Christine.

Christine hesitated again, then asked, "How long have you been doing this?"

"Too long," Nia replied. "Look. Don't be afraid. Once you get used to it, it's not a big deal. Just keep thinking about your daughter. What's her name?" "Crystal." "You've waitressed before, right?" Nia asked. Christine nodded. She rose from the stool and stepped into the white high heels. They fit. Nia found a pair of heels for herself, along with another bustier. She put them on then reached out and handed Christine a drink. "Here. Take a sip of this. It will help."

"I don't drink." Christine said, turning away. "You will," Nia replied, turning back.

Nia briefly glanced back into the mirror. She tossed back her long dark hair and adjusted the locket on her chest, momentarily holding it, rolling it in her fingers. From the open window, she heard church bells ringing. She went over and looked out across the parking lot to a large stone cathedral, Saint Michael's, its high tower seeming disappearing above the clouds. The sun was setting. Colors of the sky in the horizon were painted in radiant and yet different shades of red. She continued to clasp the locket, holding it close to her chest.

Nia turned back and face the entrance to the bar full of men. Taking a couple of deep breaths, she reached out to push the door open - walked in followed by Christine.

Cigarette Smoke. Loud Pounding Music. Silhouettes of partially clad women swirling within Darkness. Out in the bar, dancers were swinging around poles and dancing atop stages in a large smoke-filled room packed with men. In the shadows, some dancers where curled up on laps upon men in the images of their sins, not able to arise nor turn away, succumbing to a silent demonic presence, unseen to the human-eye in the smoke-cast veil of another dimension...

Nia, trapped in darkness, her long hair flowing back as she arched upward, stoned on cocaine and alcohol, danced on a small circular stage overlooking the bar, swinging around a brass pole as dancers danced in various sections of the club to echoing sounds of men cheering them on and calling out, raising their glasses seemingly in unison as if an orchestrated planned performance within itself. Christine leaned over to serve a large, heavyset trucker in a plaid red shirt and wearing yellow snakeskin cowboy boots. He gave Christine's bare bottom a slap. The slap stunned Christine, appearing embarrassed and shocked.

"So, why aren't you up there dancing, hon?" The trucker asked.

Composing herself, Christine responded, "I don't dance." She turned and attempted to walk away. The man grabbed her wrist.

"Why? Are you gay, cute cheeks?" The man said, gripping her wrist tighter. "Are you my alternative," Christine responded, adding, "And my name's Blaze."

The man laughed in a bellowed sort of way, releasing Christine's wrist, letting her go. As she began to walk away, he then suddenly pulled her back by the arm. Christine appeared angry. He slipped her a hundred dollar bill in her thong. "You have a cute butt, Blaze," he said, pushing it further. She remained still - gave a hesitant nod, feeling used.

Nia continued dancing, running her hands slowly down her thighs, lightly covered in sweat, this time going all the way down to her knees. Reaching out and taking hold of the pole with one hand, she tossed her head far back, stretching her body upward. Sliding her knees farther apart, her long hair brushed back and forth gently upon the stage. In the background, the large TV screen came back on with clips of collegiate wrestling. One wrestler on the screen was also on his knees, like Nia, with his head far back, his chest covered with sweat, gasping for air, as he reached out his hand, trying to escape *his opponent*. Ms. Gongel watched her with an alluring inquisitive gaze from a corner in the shadows...

Palos Verdes mountaintop above the City of Los Angeles. Waves were beginning to break far out in the distance across the sea with cloud's moving rapidly through the night's sky. An angelic woman's voice could be heard softly upon the wind. "They were looking intently up into the sky as he was going, when suddenly two men dressed in white stood beside them. 'Men of Galilee,' they said, 'Why do you stand here looking into the sky? This same Jesus, who has been taken from you will come back in the same way you have seen him go..." (Acts. 1:11).

Atop the old Victorian house on the mountainside, Joshua's home was encircled by a swirling wind of a new oncoming storm as an archangel weathervane atop the roof spun counterclockwise - The angel's sword raised high, pointing out across the sea... Dangling next to an old paint chipped wooden porch post, wind chimes sounded out accompanied by distant rumbles of thunder from across the sea within arising strong swirling winds - the weathervane spun faster... One one side of the mountain, city lights flickered as candles in the valley far below, on the other side; looking like glass, lay a spanning azure of a tumultuous rippling sea lit by a hidden vestigial of a once embryonic harvest moon.

Over a radio, a song by the band, "Journey" began playing, "When the lights go down in the city and the moon shines on the bay..." "Joshua!" Tim called out into the powerful wind and over the music as he wrestled to hold down a large canvass draped over a secret project he was working on. He was in the driveway in front of the house, just beyond the echoing slamming screen door of the front porch. One arm was weak, lame it seemed, as he raised his head once more and called out, "Joshua!"

Lightning bolts cracked across the sky as an ancient appearing large old oak tree stood at the edge of a cliff, undaunted by the wind, overlooking an open, endless sky where the horizon meets the sea. Its lifeless branches seemingly reached far off to a distant dream as a wolf's labored breaths echoed along a moonlit path. Shrouded by a mist, a wolf ran up a dirt path as reflections of stars gently fell down from the sky upon a waterfall into a crystal clear blue pond- the one nestled in Joshua's secret part of his woods. Mirroring the eyes of the wolf, Joshua in cuffed jeans ran bare footed, wearing a tee-shirt, "Believe," along a parallel moonlit path, carrying an echo of a voice calling out to him from long ago. Holding onto the memory of his mother's death, still bleeding within his heart in a color of red, he ran in colorless images of gray and black through the woods as shadows beneath the oak tree reached out across the darkening sky above the sea.

With his right fist clenched by his side, shedding his clothes, Joshua ran to the side of an old, abandoned stone church secluded in the deepest part of these woods, the most secret part of his... heart. As branches parted above him, a ray of moonlight reached out and shined upon a large statue of Jesus hanging upon a cross on the church's outside stone wall. Drawn to the cross, standing in partial moonlight, Joshua's face becomes visible; his pain filled eyes. Remembering the story his mother told him about a quest to slay a dragon that had been placed in his hand those many years ago, naked before the cross, he slowly reached out his clasped hand toward his mother's grave laying just beyond the church, just beyond his grasp; barely marked, her name already fading with a single dying rose upon it. "Mom," he whispered in a gentle wind...

Amidst the strong winds of the oncoming storm, Christmas carols began echoing in the distance as the moonlight faded into the past through the church's stained-glass windows, turning into the colors of an unusual light, reflecting through a small child's hopeful heart into a last vestige of faith as Joshua finally reached out his soul to an opening moon. The clouds parted. The curtain opened. The moon's full glow was seen upon his pond. With the memory of his mother's hand reaching out, *the First Act of a Play* was about to begin...

Joshua, three-years-old, silently stood inside the stone church at the altar, holding up a lit candle with children by his side, singing, "Silent Night," echoing through the excited crowd.

Elizabeth, Joshua's mother, in a back room of the church, frantically, attempted to get a group of children in costumes ready to go out and perform their parts in the Christmas Play.

"Elizabeth, I need to see you a minute," one woman called out as she approached her while clutching donkey ears in her hand.

"Agnes can't be Mary. Her mother just called, extremely upset. She said, Agnes is really sick with a high fever." The woman elevated her voice at the end so she could be heard over the children singing louder in the church.

"Great... Who did we have as her understudy?" Elizabeth asked. "David," the woman replied.

"David?" Elizabeth responded, a bit surprised.

Children began lining up dressed as angels, each picking up a toy sword and a candle. "He wanted to be Mary," the woman simply added, handing Elizabeth the donkey ears while shrugging her shoulders.

"David?" Elizabeth asked perplexed.

"He wanted to be Mary," she simply added, handing Elizabeth the donkey ears with a shrug of her shoulders. Elizabeth looked over at David gazing into a full length mirror, holding up Mary's robe to himself, smiling.

"Alright, go get him dressed," Elizabeth responded while signaling to the children encircled around her, the next shift of angels, to move toward the doorway and prepare to go out onto the stage. "Irvin, get Maribel. Maribel! Come here. Here hold this. It's the donkey ears.

After they finished their *third* song, take these over to Clarence and put them on his head. Quickly, now go!" Elizabeth shouted as the first shift of angels with Joshua began filing off the small platform in front of the church and into the side room. The second shift of angels, including Clarence, walked out onto the stage, each holding a bell.

Joshua walked up to his mother, still holding his candle up in the air, remaining silent...

"That's very good, honey. You can put the it down now," Elizabeth told him, gesturing to the candle, adding, "Why didn't you call out his name?" Joshua, slowly, lowered the candle, remaining silent. A little girl, Hope, came over and tugged on Elizabeth's skirt. "Ms. Kahn. Why doesn't Joshua talk?"

"What, Hope?" Elizabeth replied but did not answer as she struggled to adjust cow utters taped to the belly of another blonde haired little girl.

Maribel, holding the donkey ears, came back. "Now, Ms. Kahn?" Maribel asked. "What?" Elizabeth replied, adjusting the wings of a couple supporting angels.

"Now?" Maribel repeated. "Yes, yes, go ahead," distracted, Elizabeth said, giving the go ahead to Maribel to put the donkey ears on Clarence's head. Suddenly, awakened by the echo of Maribel's words, Elizabeth dashed off after Maribel, realizing what she was about to do. "Maribel! Wait!" Elizabeth called out after her. Too late. The next set of angels were already lined up and had begun singing, "Hark, the Herald Angels Sing," and it was only their *first* song.

"Why don't you talk?" Hope, still awaiting an answer, asked Joshua. But Joshua remained silent as the singing of the second shift of children in front of the church grew louder. Hope, with her soft eyes of brown, quietly looked up at Joshua into his enchanting eyes of blue. With the stained-glass windows along the church lit up in all the colors of God's glory, the parents of the children stood proudly in the pews, enthusiastically singing along with the music, mysteriously echoing seemingly through the orbed vestibules of time, down the mountain, into the city lights, dissipating within the valley far, far below... Maribel cautiously creeped behind the angels, singing, in search of Clarence with the donkey ears, tightly, clasped in her hand as Elizabeth frantically pursued her, on her hands and knees, in an attempt to hide behind the rows of children singing. Hope was still captivated by Joshua's eyes. His eyes reminded her of a secret crystal ball, held by an angel from another realm within a vague, distant memory of a fireplace within an old, weathered home. When the fire burned within it, the crystal danced with a fascinating, powerful, blue light... reminiscent of a gentle and magnificent soul. Hope reached out and took his hand, a powerful wave of emotion came over her, a magnetic energy pulsed through her fingers as she quickly pulled away.

As a boy unknowingly created a diversion by hitting the back of the head of another angel with his bell, Maribel went for it - She put the donkey ears on Clarence's head. Clarence, stunned and embarrassed, became enraged - especially since he was trying to act cool in front of Lydia, on whom he had a crush. Lydia was only a couple of rows down and immediately noticed. She broke out in laugher, seeing Clarence wearing the donkey ears. A skirmish then broke out among all the children dressed as angels, similar to the battle in heaven between archangels.

Elizabeth tried to break up the fight with the children angrily swinging and tossing their bells.

It was then, with the full moon reaching down through the stained-glass image of a white winged horse flying off into the night that Hope, still facing Joshua, reached into her pocket and pulled out a small rose bud. Slowly, she reached out, opening her hand.

"Here. You can have this. I was going to give it to my mom for Christmas. But you can have it. I picked it myself from my secret garden."

Joshua reached out and took hold of it. Their hands momentarily touched. Hope flinched, then grasped upon it, saying, "I hope you call out his name someday." Hope had overheard Elizabeth. She turned and walked away... as if a mist of a passing moonlight, a white horse dauntingly above them - within the stained-glass, another realm that holds the secret of angels...

The winds of time rippled over the clear blue pond in a cascading light of a full moon, scattering the reflections of stars from the sky as Joshua alongside his mother, back up the hill toward their house, dressed as an angel, tightly holding onto her hand. Yet, for some strange reason his mother's hand felt cold. The slamming porch screen door in the powerful wind of an oncoming storm sounded out in harmony with the dangling wind chimes... "Joshua!" Tim cried out again, struggling with the arising canvas in the wind, raising his head toward the sky - Lightning... strike upon the branch of the oak tree... Joshua awakened from his trance before the cross on the outside stone church's wall. Turning away, he ran back through the woods toward his brother's call as the branch from the oak tree atop the cliff fell toward flashes of shimmering lights upon the rising barren sea... reflecting the hope held images of rippling stars upon the surface of the pond beneath the fall...

A candle was lit beside a single mattress on the floor of a small room over top of the Victorian house's garage. The window was open. The candle flickered with the wind as a pen rested next to Joshua's unfinished poems by the side of the mattress. The poems were gently lifted by the wind as the wolf continued to run along the path with his heavy breaths, between darkness and light, with only the reflections in his eyes being seen. Mirroring the eyes of the wolf, Joshua ran in despair, lost in the shadows of his soul with sharp branches scraping the back of his neck as he passed through the woods, trying to pull him back into the past, back into that color of red, his mother's blood cast out upon that night...

On the back porch, Joshua and Tim's father, Gabriel sat in his usual wooden chair, staring out into the inked shadows of the night. His face was drawn and tired; his hair was just about all gray. His body was still, completely motionless it seemed in contrast to the tossing winds and trees of the oncoming storm. Yet, in the stillness of his hand, there was a glass that gently churned with ice by the handle of his chair by his side. As he looked upward at a rope running up a flag pole, tapped against its metal high above him, the POW flag was outstretched, flapping more rapidly in the wind. Through *the glass,* inside the house, it appeared abandoned and dark except for pieces of moonlit dust, distant memories, aligning cobwebs up a dragon carved banister to the top of a staircase. In the shadows was a picture of Joshua, a collegiate wrestler - his arms and head raised, standing at the center of the mat before a large crowd as if *calling out.*

Joshua silently stood naked at the edge of the woods staring at Tim, swaying between images of darkness and light as he had in the bedroom doorway, watching his mother's murder. "Why are you naked?" Tim asked, barely holding onto the edge of the canvas in the strong wind. "I'm standing naked before the Lord," Joshua replied, adding, "And the Lord said, "Even as My servant Isaiah has gone naked and barefoot three years as a sign..." A bolt of lightning cracked across the sky above them.

What are you waiting for!" Tim shouted to him as the rising canvass in the strong wind began to slip from his grip. "Come help me!" Tim cried out.

Gripped with fear, Joshua, still trapped in the numbness of his father's glass, wrestled with his past through transcended time as if grains of sand slipping through one's fingertips. In the motion of his *breaths* within the arising winds, seeing his brother struggle, Joshua ran over and tried to help as he had once done running over to his mother's side. Taking hold of an edge of the canvas, crossing with his memory of his mother reaching out with her bloody hand, Joshua lets the canvas slip through his grasp as part of it flies high into the air amidst flashes of lightning cast across the sky.

"What are you doing! Hold on!" Tim called out.

Joshua tried to re-take hold of the canvas. However, with a strong gust of wind, it flew even higher as Joshua fell to the ground. With Tim struggling alone, the canvas flies out of his hands, briefly revealing with flashes of lightning, a sculptured horse. With another strong wind, the canvas and sculptured wooden object, roll away together in a swirling powerful wind...

"Great... Just great. Look at what you did!" Tim shouted.

Joshua, appearing distant and confused, responded, "It's going to snow." "What? What are you talking about? We live in L.A." Tim responded, angered.

"It's going to snow. She told me," Joshua replied, standing defiantly in the winds of the on-coming storm. "Who?" Time asked. "Mom," Joshua replied, looking upward.

"You're still crazy, Joshua! You know that!" Tim shouted, charging Joshua.

Tim wrestled Joshua to the ground, hitting him on the side of the head. Joshua continued to shout, "The snow is coming!" while covering his face with his arms, trying to protect himself from his brother's blows. Taking Joshua by the throat, Tim slid him on his back toward the edge of a small cliff, trying to suffocate his breaths, the panting breaths of a wolf - pushing Joshua's head, dangling it over the edge - far above the valley, far above the city lights in the valley below.

"She's dead! Say it!" Tim screamed into Joshua's widening fearful eyes.

"No," Joshua whispered back, barely able to breath with his brother's hand tight on his throat. As Joshua turned his head, struggling to break free, he looked over the cliff. The city lights swam before his eyes.

"She's dead, Joshua," Tim said in a softer tone. Joshua remained silent, unable to breath. Tim suddenly frightened by what he was doing and let go. He got up and started to walk away.

"You're still crazy," Tim said. "Snow." Tim laughed. "It would take a miracle for it to snow here. Miracles don't happen anymore, Joshua. This isn't the Bible. Those days are over."

"I'm not crazy. It's true," Joshua said, beginning to get up, regaining his breaths.

"You're crazy, Joshua! You've always been crazy! Can't you see? Nothing can change that! Nothing!" Tim shouted, turning his back, moving toward the canvas and sculpture.

Joshua, angered, rose to his feet, ran, and tackled Tim from behind. As they wrestled, Tim's project was carried off by the winds, off the side of the cliff, and crashed into the night, down upon jagged rocks in the darkness below as Joshua tried to keep Tim down, but Tim was too quick, too strong, even with his lame arm. Tim flipped Joshua over onto his back. Joshua rolled over struggling to his side.

"Open it!" Tim shouted trying to grab Joshua's clasped hand. "Open it!" "No!" Joshua cried out as a loud crack of thunder was heard.

"Open your hand!" Tim grabbed Joshua's wrist, pulling it away from his chest. "No!" Joshua cried out again.

Joshua pushed his hand into the dirt, digging into the soil as if into his very soul, trying to reach out beyond the pains of the night, to his mother's outstretched hand. Then, with an unknown hidden strength, Joshua arose with his brother on his back. He escaped. With his hand still clasped shut, Joshua stood facing his brother, eyes of blue to those of red, with thunder and lightning sounding and flashing across the sky.

"Alright. Come on," Tim spoke barely above a whisper as Joshua, frightened, tried to turn and run. But Tim was quickly upon him; as a snarling wolf going for the throat. "Let me go!" Joshua screamed. "You want to fight! Come on! Fight!" Tim punched Joshua in the back of the head. Blood began to spill out as it did from his mother's mouth, mixing with the dirt, the soil from the man's hands staining the ground in red. Tim grabbed the back of Joshua's hair as the shadow of the man had done to their mother long ago. With the image of his mother's head being slammed against the headboard, his brother pushed Joshua's face into the dirt again and again, muffling his calls of her name and that the snow is coming, finally breaking the clasp of Joshua's fist. *It* fell out of his clasped hand and into the dirt... as Tim lashed out with one final blow to the back of Joshua's head.

With one last breath, one last gust of wind felt upon his chest, Joshua clenched both his fists and raised himself up into the clouds of the passing sky. Joshua lunged, this time throwing Tim to the ground. Tim's eyes now widened as Joshua's fingers began to clasp with his forearms across Tim's throat, choking him. "She's alive," Joshua whispered into his brother's ear with the thunder and lightning of the storm began to migrate back to the horizon's edge, back across that open endless barren sea.

Letting the past briefly go, Joshua got up as Tim rolled over onto his side, coughing and gagging. Joshua staggered to his feet and fell against the old wooden porch post which was brittle with chipped paint, seemingly only to exist with no support nor purpose. Joshua slowly turned back and gazed out to the city lights in the valley below. The wind chimes tinkled as he wondered if he would find his *destiny* somewhere down within the shimmering lights.

Listening to his brother's gasp, Joshua heard it in the form of a whisper, and upon its echo, he heard a laugh. Tim lying on his back, with his arms outstretched overhead as if trying to gently touch the fast retreating clouds of the opening sky, laughed out while slowly drawing back his breath.

"We're too old to be doing this. You know that?" Tim coughed out, adding, "Where did you ever learn that move?" Joshua did not answer. Closing his right hand tighter, as if his secret was still clasped in it, Joshua drew back his own breath and walked into the house. Standing in the darkness of the room in which his mother had once filled with so much light, telling him stories of white winged horses and knights slaying dragons for fair maidens by the window of a bright full moon, her chair was now empty, with only pieces of moonlight passing through the window upon it. The warmth that once seemed so close, as if it were something that could be touched, something that could be forever held in his hand, was gone. His father sat now before him, much older, much more distant, on the back porch, with the coldness of the glass still clasped in his hand, gazing out into the woods. Joshua stood motionless before him as if suspended in time, apprehensive to take that step, to reach out, to move toward what he felt inside was destined for him to become. Focusing again on his breathes, taking rhythmic centered meditated strength, he took a step. "Dad," he whispered, cautiously moving toward him...

Standing by his father's side, their father remained unmoving, still staring into the woods of the backyard, into the tossing shadows of the trees swaying, dancing in the wind. Next to Gabriel there was a small T.V. that had a news station on showing a war on the other side of the world. One woman in tears, held her little girl. The child's face was covered in patches of blood.

Tim suddenly appeared next to Joshua.

"Why can't he hear me?" Joshua asked, appearing distraught.

An empty bottle of liquor was beneath the glass, beneath his father's dangling hand. Tim remained silent as Joshua turned and walked back through the living room, with the sounds of war from the T.V., past the mantlepiece above the fireplace with his uncle Michael's army picture and their mother's diploma from college. The rest of the mantle was empty. Joshua passed by a few other pictures hanging on the walls of him and Tim growing up with their father. In one picture, their father was teaching them how to fly a kite by a lake, the kite beginning to fly.

Joshua vanished up the staircase as Tim sat down by his father's side. After turning off the T.V. with another story about terrorism, Tim took hold of a yellow tattered old letter clasped in his father's hand. The letter was dated March 27, 1968. Tim began reading to their father aloud, as he had lately when he discovered his father was suffering with dementia and reawakened memories about his brother, surrounded by the recent images of war.

Joshua went into his room over the garage. Still naked, he looked at himself briefly in a full length mirror in his room. He was very muscular, lean. He then knelt down in front of the lit candle beside the pages of his unfinished poems by the mattress he had hidden long ago. Joshua looked toward the open window as the passing wind from the storm flickered the candlelight on the pages of his poems. As if in a prayer, Joshua lifted up a pen and began to write, *In the light of the moon, I shall await your call; henceforth I shall come…*

Tim read aloud Uncle Michael's letters to their father. *"My Dear Brother. The days have been so hot. The insects swarm around us, everyday. I wish I could rest somewhere on an island, then come back and fight. I'm so tired. Death now is becoming common. We passed through a village the other day. My Lai. You'll probably hear about it. There were many children, many of them were…"*

Vietnam. March 27, 1968. It was Michael's eleventh month leading his unit as their captain. It was night, in a thick swamp with heavy fighting. Michael and fifty-seven American soldiers of the U.S. Army Rangers Wolf Battalion struggled in shadows amidst anger and pain. The helicopters and gunfire lit up the sky above the swamp to the ridges of the mountaintop.

"Captain Kahn!" Private David Matthews, U.S. Army Rangers, cried out while wading in water up to his waist toward Michael. Michael was standing in the center of the swamp up to his chest, holding a dying soldier up over his head, trying to place him into the waiting arms of those reaching down from a hovering helicopter. Other helicopters shined lights down over the swamp. Gunfire intensified with shouts of soldiers calling out. Michael's hands were stained with the young soldier's blood, eighteen-years-old, his right hand clasped tightly in a fist upon the young man's chest with the blood from the chest wound pulsating down Michael's arms. The young man almost completely pale, drained from much of his blood, looked down in fear at Michael as if he knew. With a last gasp of breath, his eyes closed. The young man went limp, sagging into Michael's arms raised above him. Gunfire hit the hovering helicopter above Michael. The helicopter began to rise. Michael stood momentarily in silence, still holding the young man's dead body overhead, looking upward to the sky, watching the chopper's lights fade into the darkness of the night. Explosions erupted around him... flames.

Michael slowly lowered the young man, letting him sink into the swamp. Just as the head started to fall beneath the surface, Michael took the dog tags off his neck and clutched them in his right hand, as Joshua with his secret.

"Captain Kahn!" David, wading through the swamp, finally reached Michael. "Corporal Marian said, they want to talk to you on radio command!" Gunfire continued to pass overhead. Michael looked down at his hands stained in blood. He placed the dog tags into David's hand. "Make sure this gets back to his family!" Michael called out.

"Yes, sir," David replied.

David went over and took hold of a dangling cord from one of the other hovering choppers. Soldiers inside the chopper pulled him up and aboard. He gave a final salute to Michael before Michael's image disappeared into the shadows of the swamp. All the other choppers vanished together into the night's sky. When Michael reached the side of the bank, he lifted himself up, ducking the gunfire that was hitting the trees around him, and quickly took out the radio from the box Tommy securely held, who was crouched down behind a tree.

"This is Sea Hawk. You copy?" A voice over the radio blurted out.

"This is Romeo! I read you!" Michael shouted while trying to wipe away the young man's blood still flowing warmly down his arms.

"You are to proceed to the west alternative. Repeat. Your target has been changed." "What! West?" Michael asked, shouting even louder.

The gunfire echoed loudly around them... then, suddenly, silence.

"Sea Hawk? Do you copy? West side? Repeat. West side?" Michael repeated, tossing down the radio. Ed, Sergeant Conway, approached and sat down next to Michael. Ed was Michael's best friend. A large black man, Ed's shadow passed over Michael's angered eyes.

"Was that Jerk Hawk?" Ed asked with a smirk, adding, "You know what I mean." "Yeah. I swear, sometimes I think he's doing it while I am talking to him." Michael said, reaching down and picking back up the radio.

Ed, nicknamed professor because he carried small books, took off his boot and shook it. A small snake that had been hiding beneath his foot during all the fighting began to slither out. "Come on, little guy. It's safe to come out now. Let's see," Ed said. Ed started to point and count the soldiers in their platoon coming toward them through the swamp's mist. Charlie's shadow, the enemy, had retreated into the far edges, disappearing into the mist. The retreating soldiers on both sides, fired back a few last rounds. With the befalling silence, the flickering of gunfire echoed away into the distance... into the parting mist, dissolving upon the mountaintop.

"We started out with fifty, no... fifty-seven. Right? Now we have..." Ed said to Michael as he started to count the remaining soldiers. Ed added, "Well, Jerk Hawk is probably jealous. Not everybody is a man of the world like us. All we have to do is smile and we'll have a beautiful vixen fall at our feet, and in my case, hopefully a blonde..." Ed began to smile.

"They want us to go west, professor," Michael said. "I knew a blonde Lisa once. Man, she was built, smart too. When she walked down the street, every head would turn, including mine," Ed replied, adding. "I think I liked her the best."

"Did you hear me?" Michael asked, "They want us to go west. You know..." "Yeah. West. I know, right into the middle of everything," Ed's smile faded, adding,

"Pretty soon we'll be all the way into Cambodia. What about Karese? I thought he was heading east? Isn't he our target."

"I don't know. They're up to something. I think they're mounting some kind of offensive to keep Charlie out of Saigon," Michael said, appearing concerned.

"If we're a part of it, shouldn't they tell us?" Ed asked. Michael nodded.

"You would think," Michael replied, standing up and gazing out into the jungle. "Why do I feel everything is going to happen even without a plan," Ed said, standing too,

adding, "We wander this jungle seemingly with no ultimate goal other than to flex our muscle. Our numbers keep falling, an equation of a jungle... There's no plan."

"Maybe it's part of God's plan, something bigger," Michael turns with a smile, adding, "Vietnam. No place like it... Bruce! Get everyone out! Now!" Michael called out to another young soldier, Private Bruce Manning. Michael waded back into the middle of the swamp. "Tommy! Over there! Not there! There! Bring it with you! That's where the drop is! Hurry!" Tommy, a soldier with a young face but hardened hands, gripped a box, moving to Michael.

As Michael got the rest of his men safely out of the swamp, they attempted to regain their breaths, their heads down, becoming more visible with a brighter moon... Michael began leading his unit out of the shadows of the swamp and up a hill as pieces of moonlight cascaded in rays of hope down upon them, cutting away the remaining fleeting mist. As they stood atop the hill, the swamp was, now, far beneath them. Ed finally returned Michael's smile.

"You're right. Maybe all of this is somehow God's plan," Ed said, adding, "Although I don't quite understand why He allows all of this suffering and pain."

"Look at His son..." Michael nodded, adding, "Vixen at our feet? You're reading those books again aren't you?"

"Those books?" Ed replied, adding, "You mean literature?"

"All I know is that when I tried to read them, I got lost in the poetic narrative. Moon? Stars? Give me a break. You probably could move a lot faster without them," Michael said. "Move faster without the moon or the stars?" Ed replied.

"Your books. When do you have time to read them, anyway?" Michael asked.

"At night, like I did as a kid sneaking under my covers to read Playboy." Ed explained, adding. " And I only carry two; one small book of poetic verse by Shakespeare, my mother gave me, and the other, a comprised work of medieval literature novelettes my handed to me from my father. I think he wanted me to be a knight," Ed replied with a laugh, raising up his rifle. "My sister-in-law loves Shakespeare. King Richard the Third is her favorite play. She's a high school English teacher. Many of her students ended up here." Michael paused. "He was just eighteen... that boy who died in my arms. I promised his father I would bring him back. Now, I don't know if that's the right thing to do. This place has jaded my judgment, the inner peace of my soul."

A plane flew over their heads and dropped napalm into the swamp. There was a large explosion. A series of flames ignited the jungle beneath them, lighting up the hills to the mountaintops, shooting off treetops. Reflections of red were seen in their eyes.

"Well, that's great, just great. Now I feel bad," Ed said.

"About the boy?" Michael asked?

"About the snake. I told him it was safe to come out." Ed said, gazing below.

In the days that would follow, it would still be Michael and his men against anything else that moved in the jungle... and with each village they passed, the horrors of war would reflect in their eyes in the same color of red in the flames far below...

Tim continued reading aloud to his father, "We are constantly being shadowed by Charlie. Patrols are always around us. I have been able to save some of my men, others... Ed is starting to concern me. He thinks he's some kind of English professor or something. He's always quoting medieval literature and Shakespeare. He has become very hardened to death, like me, and everyone else here. One guy, we call him, Ears," has become a collector of sorts. He wears a belt around his waist, having collected about thirty ears so far. That's what Ed says anyway."

"Ed likes to count, since our unit is getting smaller. I don't think we will be receiving any replacements. I'm starting to believe that they will just keep moving us around this place until we slowly fade away into the jungle, into the mist... like in one of Ed's medieval novels. Yet, I will fight, my brother, to not let them do that. Don't worry. I will come back home as I promised. I will be coming back soon..."

Tim stopped reading to his father and reached down to pick up an old *Life Magazine,* covering the Vietnam War. On the cover was a naked little girl screaming, running out of a village that was just napalmed. Her back was severely burned from the flames. She was in agony. Tim placed the magazine on a stack of others by his father's chair, upon pictures of war, pictures everyone was trying to forget. Tim paused. He then hesitantly picked up another issue. Opening it, he briefly leafed through pages of pictures of the soldiers that *Life* had published to show who and how many had died in Vietnam in just one week. At the top of each page was a large marked "X." Their father had gone through each page many years ago searching for his brother. The ice churned in the glass within his father's hand as he gazed out into the *dark shadows* of the woods.

Joshua put down the pen by the side of his mattress next to his poems, got up, and headed back into the *dark shadows* of the hallway. As he stood before his brother's slightly ajar bedroom door with a translucent ray of light appearing to cut Joshua's face in half, he watched Tim, in the corner of his room, sitting at a table, hesitantly take white power - and inhale it up his nose.

"Eloi," Joshua whispered through the cracked door, his face becoming fully visible in the light. "Dad," Joshua repeated in English. Startled, Tim put the cocaine down and partially turned. "Dad taught me that move," Joshua added.

Tim walked over in silence and gently shut the door, leaving Joshua standing in the hallway, completely naked and alone in the darkness. Feeling abandoned, Joshua went over and sat down at the top of the stairs, clutching the last bannister rung. He got up and started to walk back down the staircase, back into the *shadows* of the past. With each step he took, passing through linear dimensions of time, he became younger, until he was three. He remembered pausing at the bottom of the staircase, hearing nothing but silence except for the scraping of branches outside against the side of the house from the retreating wind of the storm. Walking toward the center of the living room, he remembered a tree; how it swayed back and forth with images of its shadow passing across his face...

The clouds parted. The moon's light upon him, he looked up, and remembered. His mother was hanging by her neck, her feet dangling just out of his reach above him... The wolf ran up the mountain path with labored breaths to atop the cliff, gazing up at the large old oak tree then out across the ocean of time to where the horizon met the sea, listening to the sound of an ancient wind... The wolf raised his head and howled out.

33 AD. In the wind, sounds of Roman soldiers nailing Jesus to the cross could be heard with women crying out, wailing, in Aramaic as an angelic voice from across the sea echoed an eternal pain, whispering upon a gentle wind, "Carrying the pains of our sins upon him, with the image of a shadow of a tree bound upon his back, to a hill, Golgotha, they drug him through the streets, his head bleeding with thorns. Thrown up onto the cross with the echo of nails being hammered into his flesh, his mother's cries echoed with his pain, out into the valley below. At one moment he called out for his father, 'Eloi, Eloi, lama sabachthani?' 'My God, my God, why have you forsaken me?' Then with His last breath..." The wind stopped...

The scraping of branches against the house became silent as Joshua stood alone, naked to the pain of his past, gazing upward to where his mother once hung, inches from his grasp. With the sight of her hanging, the pain tossed him to being fully grown, the image of her death fading back into the past.

He used his pen to trace over his scars on his wrists, a wish once of wanting to die. Yet, he turned, seeing the shadows on the branches of trees dancing through the room. Her chair was empty. The moon was gone. His tears... in the form of the rain of the storm was finally heard.

He walked over and stood by the side of the chair - gazing out the window... as if entering a distant dream of his mother's stories, from a long, long time ago... A crack of lightning, thunder, heavier rain hitting the house from all sides... the full brunt of the storm. *Flashes of Lightning... Cracks of Loud Thunder... Sounds of Pouring Rain, Heavy Wind...*

Chapter 3

Joshua awoke the next day with the sun shining brightly into his second story bedroom. He heard the sound of his brother's hammer along with a song from the radio playing loudly by the driveway outside. Tim was just beneath Joshua's window working again on his secret project. The sounds of the hammer were familiar ones. Brushing his hands back over his eyes, drying them completely from the rain of the night that had fallen down upon him from his open window, he sorely sat up, rolling over on his side. Taking a deep breath, he got to his knees and leaned over the pane, looking out the window. The night before seemed only to be another nightmare; the fight with his brother, the distance of his father, the turbulent winds of the storm, all just part of dreams echoing in some distant forgotten past, envisioned with the panting of a wolf's breaths, culminating in a howl... or so it seemed.

"Timmy!" Joshua called out, hitting his head on the window.

After Joshua bumped his head, hundreds of small bugs fell on him, sticking to his sweat from the turbulent night. Covered in bugs, Joshua walked back down through the hallway with rays of daylight passing through large aligned windows hung with torn laced white curtains.

Cobwebs with chipped paint were along the baseboards at the bottom of the walls; the carpet, covered in dirt, was a faded red. Joshua paused again at his brother's room. He cautiously entered still hearing his brother hammering outside.

Tim's room was unlike the rest of the house. It was furnished in a bizarre fashion. There were many light fixtures, each one decorated with a distinctive statue of a beautiful naked woman in various positions. A dancing beer can sat in a corner, and next to it, a naked fat lady with a clock in her belly just beyond a laughing bear holding up a cigar. Next to Tim's bed was a small table. Joshua looked down and saw the remnants of the white powder, the cocaine, he had seen in his brother's hand the night before. Concerned, Joshua reached up his hand to a map taped to Tim's bedroom wall. "New York" was circled in red - The hammering stopped.

Turning around, appearing confused, Joshua went into the bathroom. He leaned in and turned on the shower by alternating one handle back and forth between two spigots. The other handle was missing. Mist began to fill the bathroom. As he stood in the shower, letting the water cleanse him, a couple of old tiles fell from the walls. Joshua pushed them aside with his feet.

Turning the shower off, he stepped out of the tub. The mist was heavy as he closed his eyes and stood naked to a ray of bright sun shining through the window. Wet, he aired dried, drops of water flowing down upon him. There were no towels. The drops of warm water moving down his side and upon his chest made him feel cared for; as if all his sins were slowly washing away.

Opening his eyes, with the water dripping onto the floor from upon him, he suddenly looked up and gazed into a mirror covered in mist. He reached up and wiped it away - stunned, he gasped, and took a step back. There, looking back at him from the mirror was an archangel. In shock, he ran down the staircase, through the living room and his father's room to a rickety door leading to a basement staircase. Opening it, barefooted, he cringed with each step toward the bottom of the stairs to a dusty, cobwebbed old basement.

To his right, there was a large, wooden, medieval-appearing door with a large, heavy, black iron latch - bolted shut. He walked up to it, and noticed a peculiar Knights Templar appearing seal carved in the door. Shaking his head, he turned and went left, away from this strange appearing door, following rays of light emanating from small aligned windows along the edges at the top of the basement walls, toward a large pile of disheveled clothes, lying on a wooden table next to a washer and dryer. In the sun's light, cascading in through the windows, glistening with the remaining moisture dripping down upon his chest, he pulled out his clothes.

"Samson! Come here!" Joshua heard as he walked over to one of the aligned windows and raised up on his toes to see. Samson, a half wolf, half malamute dog, was scampering about playing as Joshua's father was frantically trying to put him back on his chain. Joshua turned back, again sorting through the large pile of clothes.

Reaching up his hand, feeling for another light, Joshua felt a bulb. Sliding his hand down he felt a small chain. Pulling it, there was more light. He looked over to a wooden wall with pencil marks on it. At each recorded height, there was a name, "Tim 45 inches, Joshua 33 inches." Tim's heights continued up the wall. Joshua's recorded height stopped at 33 inches.

Pulling his shirt over his head, "The Lion of Judah," Joshua walked out onto the front porch. Tim was still working on his secret project, but, seeing Joshua, paused, wiping the sweat from his forehead with the bottom of his shirt, "Carpenters Union Local 12."

Joshua approached Tim, staring, stopping a few feet away.

"I'm glad you're wearing the shirt I got you," Tim said while wiping his sweaty brow. "Didn't plan to," Joshua simply replied.

"I guess it was meant to be then," Tim said, hammering into his project. "What are you making?" Joshua asked.

Tim briefly looked up but did not answer as the sunlight reflected brightly upon the driveway, cemented in white, as sweat continued to pour down Tim's brow. Tim's face glowed with the reflection off the driveway as his one lame arm struggled with each swing of the hammer, using his strong arm to keep his project from moving.

"Sorry about your project," Joshua said. Tim paused, looked up. "Forget it." Tim nodded, "I had to start over again anyway. It wasn't right."

"When you gonna be finished?" Joshua asked.

"Don't know. It's not something I planned," Tim smiled, adding, "Like your shirt." Joshua looks down at his shirt. "The Lion of Judah," Joshua read it aloud.

"Yeah, I thought you'd like it. Not sure what that means and all, but I know you like lions," Tim said.

"Thanks. Sorry I didn't wear it before," Joshua replied.

"Well, it's never too late to do something, right?" Tim responded, adding, "Can you hand me that screwdriver, there... not the wrench, the screwdriver." Joshua gave Tim the screwdriver.

"Hey, I have to go into town and pick up my paycheck if you want to come?" Tim said. "Sure," Joshua replied, looking down at the lion on his shirt.

Joshua walked off the porch and followed Tim to his truck. They got in. Tim started the truck. Joshua turned, glancing out his open side window.

"Wait a minute," Joshua said, seeing their father coming toward them, swaying a bit, appearing unsteady on his feet.

"Is dad alright?" Joshua asked. Tim paused.

"Yeah... Why you asking?" Tim asked as they watched their father getting closer. "He acts like he's in another place, space, time" Joshua simply said.

"You're a physicist, now?" Tim asked. Joshua turned toward him and said. "You're a part of it, too."

"A part of what?" Tim asked.

Joshua turned back. Their father stood by them, by the open window. He appeared distant, as if still staring out into the inked woods of the night before, those within the woods of the past. Tim gave a glance to Joshua before acknowledging their father, a concerned glance, a glance that answered Joshua's question in a subtle soft way to that of, "Is dad alright?"

"Are you going into town?" Their father asked, looking past Joshua.

"Yeah, dad. I have to pick up my paycheck. Joshua's going with me," Tim gestured toward Joshua. Joshua bowed his head, again, their father looked past him, handing Tim an envelope.

"I might not be here when you get back," their father said, adding, I may be gone for three days, business. Make sure someone feeds Samson. But keep him on the chain. He was running loos all night. God knows where he went. A dog like that, part wolf and all, can tear someone up." Their father glanced - staring at Joshua. Joshua looked up, meeting his father's glance with the "eyes of wolf" from the night before.

"The usual?" Tim asked as he put the envelope into the glove compartment by Joshua.

Their father just nodded and walked away, back toward the house, back toward the shadows of dangling wind chimes upon that old chipped paint post. As Tim drove away, Joshua watched his father pass a blossoming cherry tree, colors of various shades of red.

The image of the cherry tree on the truck's windshield passed away from the glass with the image of his youth, the rising marks of the height measurements penciled in upon the basement wall, the one on the other side of the medieval imposing large iron bolt locked door. As Joshua watched his father's image pass away from the glass, he felt his path toward him was bolted shut in a cast iron darkness held on that other side of the mysterious basement... Tim floored his truck, peeling away - arising dirt.

"You in a hurry or something?" Joshua asked, as they drove fast down the mountain road. "I'm always in a hurry. You shouldn't waste time, right? You know, the precious time

God gave us." Tim replied as Joshua looked down at the glove compartment. "So, what's in the envelope?" Joshua asked.

"You ask a lot of questions," Tim responded, adding, "You shouldn't ask questions you don't want to really know the answers to..."

"What's that supposed to mean?" Joshua asked, adding, "Is dad ashamed of me?" "Case in point," Tim said with a smile, adding, "Just give him time. You know how dad is..." Tim replied, pausing. "Dad's been struggling with stuff, lately, Joshua. His mind, it wanders. He has difficulty, now, let's say, living in the moment."

Joshua turned and looked ahead as they drove toward the valley below. He felt a sensation of peace, being able to look out to the newness of the day with his brother by his side, imagining shiny reflections of leaves turning golden brown, an autumn before a winter's snow.

"I guess there's a lot we don't know... So, where's Dad going, for three days?" Joshua asked, his hands beginning to shake, his eyes turning lost as if seeing something in the distance. "Got me. That's his business," Tim replied. Joshua did not answer. He glanced over at Joshua, pinning a tag with his name on it to his shirt - just above the lion - *Joshua.*

"What are you doing?" Tim asked, where did you get that tag?" "I made it, in the hospital. Soldiers used to do this in the Civil War before they went into battle..." Joshua calmly said, adding, "So, if they died... people would know who they are. I want people to know who I...am, after I'm gone."

"And who's that, Joshua?"

"Oriel... The Seventh Angel in the Book of Revelations."

"Oh, God." Tim said, pausing, then adding to himself, "The Eagle has landed."

Joshua continued. "He held a little scroll open in his hand. Setting his right foot on the sea and his left foot on the land, he gave a great shout, like a lion roaring. And when he shouted, the seven thunders sounded. Then the angel whom I saw standing on the sea and the land raised his right hand to heaven and swore by him who lives forever and ever, who created heaven and what is in it, the earth and what is in it, and the sea and what is in it: 'There will be no more delay, but in the days when the SEVENTH ANGEL is to blow his trumpet, the mystery of God will be fulfilled, as he announced to his servants the prophets.'"

"We're just going into the city, Joshua. We'll come back alive... I hope," Tim said rolling his eyes, staring at Joshua's tag, adding, "Don't worry, bro. I'll pick up your medications... I should have gotten them for you already."

"All of us will be in the war, when it comes," Joshua responded, blankly staring ahead. "I have no idea what you're talking about, bro." Tim responded, appearing concerned. "Armageddon." Joshua simply said, turning to look at him in the eyes.

"Maybe what you're thinking, it's all just dream," Tim said.

"You could say that," Joshua replied, adding, "But this dream? It has a face."

"Who? What are you talking about? Armageddon has a face?" Tim asked. Tim rolled his eyes again, reached past Joshua, and picked up a pack of cigarettes off the dash. As Tim lit one, he turned the radio on. "The road is long..." The song, "He Ain't Heavy, He's my Brother," by the Hollys began to play. Tim changed the station.

"I like that song," Joshua said, adding with a smile, "We need a theme song as we ride into Armageddon."

Tim smirks, begins to smile, "Are you messing with me? You're messing with me, right?

That's what you're doing. Man, you had be going for a minute, Joshua." "It's Oriel," Joshua said with a nod and slight smile.

"You're a genius. You had all those docs confused," Tim said with a puff of his cigarette. "You played them all out, didn't you? To get out of there?"

"Did I? Reality is not all what it seems. It depends upon who's. I prefer to live in mine," Joshua said, adding, "I saw her last night, by the pond, just like I did over twenty years ago."

"Who?" Tim asked.

"That Woman in White. Remember?" Joshua replied, gazing back out the window. "Are you still messing with me?" Tim asked, taking deeper puffs of his cigarette.

"She said we have to repent and come to Him. She said, our time is running out. You're right, we shouldn't waste the precious God has given us. It's time..." Joshua said.

"Time? Time for what?" Tim asked, tossing his cigarette out his truck window. "Jesus," Joshua said, envisioning Jesus's passion within the glass, Roman soldiers pushing Joshua back into the crowd as Jesus carried his cross through the streets of Jerusalem in 33 AD. Atop a hill, a deer looked down upon Him as nails hammering into the cross were heard.

"Jesus!" Tim cried out, swerving his truck, suddenly, as a deer ran out of the woods. They hit the deer with the Tim's truck, tossing it to the side of the road - *bleeding*. "Stop!" Joshua cried out as Tim slammed on his brakes. Joshua darted out of his side up to the side of the deer, struggling to breath, gasping for air on his side. Joshua places his hand, gently, on the deers head, bleeding from his mouth as Tim walked up, standing behind him.

"You can't help her, Joshua. She's going to die," Tim said as the deer's eyes closed.

Joshua leaned further in, breathing softly into her mouth. *A flash of light from the mountain's edge.* The deer's eyes opened. The bleeding stopped. She regain her breaths, arose, and walked off, away into the woods. "What the... How did you do that?" Tim asked.

"You shouldn't ask questions you really don't want to know the answers to," Joshua said. Atop the hill, the deer stood looking down toward them as the deer atop Golgotha, staring up at Jesus...

She then turned and vanished into a mist as a shroud was torn in two - *THUNDER*. As they continued driving down the road, initially in silence, Tim reached out and opened the glove compartment. Moving the envelope aside, he took out a plan and paper, handing them to Joshua.

"What am I suppose to do with this?" Joshua asked, raising his pen like a sword. "Make me a tag," Tim simply replied.

"A tag for what?" Joshua asked.

"A tag like your's. Oriel's brother," Tim added.

"Ah, Benedictus es," Joshua quipped, creating a quizzical look upon Tim. "Benedictus es?" Tim asked.

"Yes," Joshua replied, appearing saddened. "It's latin, from a long time ago," He added. "Meaning..." Tim began to say.

"You are blessed," Joshua said, raising his clenched hand up against the glass.

In the distance, hawks hovered, floating upon a wind blowing upward as if mirroring the sea with small ripples of waves upon it as in the distance a horizon of unusual colors began to form at the outer edge of the earth's crust, silently, softly, unseen to a visible sense, yet there, beating, living, arising beyond a mist...

Chapter 4

As Joshua and Tim drove through Los Angeles, they noticed large groups of homeless, sitting on hot pavements by raggedy tents alongside a few emaciated dogs that looked like they were starving, searching through fallen trash containers. Some people danced in the sunlight, although held in darkness, appearing to be high on drugs, as sex workers in booty shorts, short skirts, and six-inch heels pranced up and down the city's street with their naked souls exposed.

Joshua, appearing concerned, turned away and looked up, seeing a silhouette of a mass of oncoming protestors marching down the street toward them, fists, flags raised, chanting loudly, their voices echoing, parting the city street's grayish wave of pain, dodging in an out of shadows.

"It's all happening," Joshua said.

"What's happening?" Tim replied, slamming on his breaks for a stop light.

A man on a corner, held a large sign, "Repent! For the Kingdom of God is at Hand!" Joshua's window was down. He approached them. Through the window the man said, "It's you."

"Do you know him?" Tim asked Joshua.

"I hope not," Joshua replied. Tim smiled. The light turned green. Tim pushed his foot on the accelerator, driving away.

When they arrived at the construction site, dirt blew across the front of the truck as they came to a stop, creating a haze before Joshua's window. Joshua turned to Tim. "Are you going to ask him? He said. Tim remained silent.

Joshua looked up as Tim got out of his truck and walked up a hill toward a trailer in the center of the construction site, heavy machinery, loud noice, men in hard hats seemingly moving recklessly, balancing upon beams of a high skeleton structure for an arena, U.C.L.A.'s Apollo.

The trailer door flew opened. A large, obese gray haired man in suspenders; chewing a cigar barreled out. "Hey! There he is!" The foreman shouted to Tim, approaching him from up the hill. The foreman shoved the cigar in his mouth, clinching it in his teeth while reaching out to shake Tim's hand, now standing before him. Tim looked up toward the sky, at the high skeleton, releasing his grip shaking the man's hand, partially covering his eyes from the sun.

"When do you think you'll be finished?" Tim asked. "We're supposed to be done by nationals. They're scheduled to be here this year," The Foreman said, adding, "Are you going?"

"Don't have a reason to," Tim said, looking away from the sun. "I just thought with you being a former wrestler and all..." The Foreman began to say as he turned away, gazing at Joshua looking up at them from he truck, "...you'd want to see the national championships. Is that him?" The Foreman asked, looking at Joshua in the truck.

Tim paused. "Yeah, that's him... my brother. Tim looked the Foreman in the eyes. The Foreman, turning away from the glance of Joshua, stared at the ground.

"So, when do you think you'll come back to work?" The Foreman asked Tim, as bulldozers began moving large mounds of dirt.

"Don't know. I guess when my arm is completely healed," Tim replied.

The Foreman looked at Tim's arm, partially curled, shaking. ""All this because of something that happened years ago."

"You look like you could still wrestle heavyweight, Larry," Tim smiled and said, patting the man on his large stomach. The bulldozers stopped. The air cleared momentarily from the swirling dirt. "He wanted me to ask you if he could work here, again," Tim said.

The Foreman paused, looked back down at the truck, Joshua peering through the glass. "Is he still crazy?" He asked.

"Just forget it," Tim replied.

"I'm sorry. I would. But, it took us a week to fix that wall he wrecked the last time. I can't believe he ripped it down with his bare hands. Half that wall was made of steel and concrete. It's like he has Samson genes in him, or something."

"I get it," Tim said, adding, "Do you have my paycheck?"

The foreman reached into his pocket and handed it to him. All of a sudden, from high above, upon one of the beams on the skeleton structure, a worker cried out, "Look out!" Both the foreman and Tim looked up, shading their eyes from the sun. The top of the structure mysteriously began being lifted up with a strong gust of wind. Three workers grabbed hold of a rising beam, holding onto it, tight. Finally - it was in place.

Tim got into his truck. Slamming the door, he started it up, trying not to make eye contact with Joshua, who was intently staring at him, hoping for a signal, a direction in his life.

"So, what did he say," Joshua asked, adding, "Can I work here? I really need a job."

Tim turned, looked at Joshua and said, "This doesn't mean anything. It just means, you're meant to do something else." Joshua appear saddened, turning back and staring out the window, watching the structure being built in the reflection of glass; images of reflections of stars passing through his vision of his cupped hand trying to grasp upon them, within that moon, that pond held in the secret part of his woods. Joshua ran naked through the woods within the images of his mind toward the crystal blue pond, the cascading waterfall; a memory of a full moon, long ago.

The foreman watched them drive away, puffing on his cigar with a frown and clenched teeth, both his hands gripped tightly, holding onto his suspenders. Another construction worker came and stood by the foreman's side.

"Was that Tim's brother in the truck, the one in the hospital everyone's been talking about?" The worker asked.

"Yeah, that was him," The Foreman said, taking a puff on his cigar.

"Is he okay, now, after trying to kill himself like that?" The worker asked.

"Don't know. His brother didn't say. Just said he needed a job," The Foreman said, turning to walk away.

"I heard he found his mother stabbed or something, when he was a kid," The worker blurted out. The Foreman paused, turned back. "Hung. The poor bastard found her hanging from a beam in the living room," The Foreman said, looking up at the beams of the skeletal structure, adding, "He was only three. They said, she killed herself, even bit off her tongue when she did it. They found him curled up in a chair, just staring out the window, mumbling something about a knight. His hand was clasped shut, like this." The Foreman made a fist, continuing. "It took a while before they could pry it open." The Foreman tossed his cigar and began walking back up toward the trailer.

"What was in his hand?" The worker cried out.

The Foreman turned back and said softly with saddened eyes, "Her tongue."

As Tim and Joshua drove back through the city, Joshua continued to stare blankly out the window with his clenched hand up against the glass of the truck's window. Tim finally turned to him and said, "Hey, I know a place we can go..."

"Where?" Joshua asked, lowering his hand, his reflection turning away from the window.

Tim paused and smiled, patting Joshua on his shoulder. "A place where you can begin your journey toward your true *Destiny*," Tim replied, nodding with a wider smile.

A beautiful female singer sang out on a stage of the dance club, her voice echoing through the smoke filled room with flickering lights shining down upon her as dancers danced in the shadows of the club, silhouettes of movements amidst large T.V. screen depicting graphic images of war. One veteran, appeared drawn to a news story with a reporter in the Middle East. He paused before taking a sip of his beer. A woman, in a see-through short dress, leaned down from the stage, distracting him.

As Tim and Joshua pulled into the parking lot, Joshua gazed up at the sign, *Destiny's Dance Club*. "See, Destiny. This is where it all begins," Tim said with a smile. "All what begins?" Joshua asked. "I'm not sure. Let's just go check it out. Come on," Tim said, getting out the truck. Joshua hesitated, yet followed. They paused, seeing the old lady with a green eyes in her white hospital gown, holding a long stem rose.

Joshua walked up to her. She just stared at him into his bright blue eyes. Without a word, she reached out and handed him the long stem rose. "What's this?" He asked. "A miracle rose," She replied. Joshua, clasping upon the rose with his left hand, turned toward Tim. Tim looked at him and shrugged his shoulders. When they both turned back, she was gone. They looked at each other again, appearing confused. Joshua looked at the rose...

The door of the club opened to the sounds of booming music as they passed from sunlight into darkness with only remnants of light, encircling the bar and seated intoxicated cheering men at tables spanning a large room with offshoots of corners where women entertained them.

"Let's sit down!" Tim said, loudly, over the music, guiding him by the arm.

There were two other stages, in addition to the third that was now empty, with young women dancing upon them in g-strings and small lace tops. A large bar in a semi-circle spanned halfway around the large room, encircling several dancers, dancing seductively upon it their six-inch heels weaving in and out of half-filled glasses of drinks among beer bottles and laid out cash. As Tim and Joshua found seats at a high table, the singer finished her song and left the stage. Gazing through the smoke, Joshua was drawn to the empty third stage before them.

"I'm, Blaze. I'll be taking care of you," Christine said, standing next to Tim. "Hi Blaze. I'll have a Bud. And my brother, here, will have…" Tim said. "Just a coke," Joshua interrupted, adding, "Is your name really, Blaze?"

"You have nice eyes," Christine surprised herself, saying to Joshua, drawn to him with a mysterious rush. "Excuse me," she added, feeling embarrassed, walking away.

"I think she likes you," Tim said in a slight whisper as the music became louder.

Joshua watched the dancers move around them in varying twists and turns like vectors of a mathematical equation within his confused mind of crossing dimensions of time. After a while, he said to Tim, cutting through the noice of the loud music, "Didn't John the Baptist get his head cut off because of this kind of stuff?" Joshua placed the rose down upon the table before him.

"I don't know what's floating around in your abstract mind, little brother. But, we're just here to have a good time, find your destiny," Tim said, attempting to get Joshua to focus on the dancers. "Look at her. She's really hot. Why don't you just try to relax, and enjoy the ambiance."

"You know, the dance of the seven veils when the daughter of King Herod's wife danced for him. He lusted so much toward her, he said he would give her anything. Because John the Baptist had called out her mother for adultery, she leaned toward the king and asked him for…"

"Here's your beer and here's your coke," Christine said, leaning in and placing the bottle of beer and glass of coke onto the table before them, adding, "Do you want anything else?"

Tim and Joshua paused. "No, this is good," they both said.

Christine became captivated, looking into Joshua's eyes as Joshua reached out his hand and touched a small gold cross hanging from her neck. She gently took hold of his hand as his touch seemingly touched her soul. She felt there was something different about him, an intense passion, an unconditional love that she had never experienced before. She quickly turned and left. Strangely, she could still feel his touch deep within her, deep within her soul, the small cross warming upon the top her chest, just beneath her neck, she reached up and grasped upon it as she walked away.

"So, what do you think... about John the Baptist?" Joshua asked, turning toward Tim. "I don't know. You're the Bible expert... I haven't read it in a while," Tim responded, distracted, focused on watching Christine, her reaction to Joshua, moving through the bar as if parting the smoke of darkness like a small version of the miraculous parting of the Red Sea... With an unusual light upon her with her hand clasped upon her small golden cross as high atop the cathedral's tower of Saint Michael's, bells rang out above the clamor of the city's streets.

Inside Saint Patrick's Cathedral, a small group of people were singing "Amazing Grace." Inside Destiny's Dance Club, Joshua whispered, "Believe, Christine," while gazing over at *Blaze,* taking her cross to her lips and kissing it as *Christine.*

"Who are you talking to?" Tim asked, noticing Joshua staring at Christine.

"A Believer in Christ," Joshua replied as a light illuminated upon the third stage.

Another waitress came up to Christine as she spilled a beer, picking up drinks from the bartender. "Are you alright?" The waitress asked Christine. "Yes. I'm fine." Christine paused. "For some reason, all of a sudden, I miss my daughter. Can you do me a favor and cover my tables? I want to give her a call." "Sure," the waitress replied.

Christine hurried over to a pay phone behind the bar near the rest rooms. She picked up the phone, put coins in, and called home. Genny, the babysitter answered. "Hi. Genny. Could you put Crystal on? Thanks... Hi, Crystal. I miss you." "Hi mommy. Can you take me on a horsey ride?" "Sure, honey. When I get home." "When will you be home, mommy?" "Soon, Crystal.

Soon. I love you..."

Upon the third stage, Nia emerged in her white thong and skimpy top. Yet, on her back there were large angel wings. The music died, became totally silent with all eyes upon her in an unison aura of respect throughout the club, including Joshua's, appearing drawn with an elevated energy of awareness beneath the bright stage light. This light changed to varying colors as she danced with only the soft classical notes of a piano being heard; her beautiful olive-skin, her long flowing black hair, her deep-set eyes of brown, Joshua became one with the lyrical music within his soul, as each beat of the piano note coincided with each beat of his yearning heart.

Beneath the colors of light, the dimness of the colors that faded upon the Christmas tree the night of his mother's death came back to life with each lit color down upon Nia, each beat of a note, casting out an illuminated awakening toward his shadowed, gray and black painful soul.

Joshua gazed up toward her, unable to take his eyes off of her. She turned - their eyes locked. Immediately, an intense power, an unmitigated passion was felt. She paused in mid motion as if suspended within two dimensions of time... It was as if they were intimately and secretly bound to each other by some unknown force upon an ancient wind; like that of which was within the old Oak Tree atop that jagged cliff, overlooking the tumultuous sea toward the horizon's edge... sharing the same destiny, same fate as if they had known all their lives - She moved toward him, dancing, drawn, captured by an emerging *path of light before her* - as if taking a step of faith, walking off the cliff out across the sea; Joshua gazed at her, floating upon the sky... Reaching out, their hands touched and... he handed her a miracle - the rose...

As Joshua gave her the rose, a shade over one of the windows fell. Rays of sunlight cascaded down upon his hand. She clasped upon it, *her Destiny,* and with their touch, the last piano note was heard. Applause. Time *fast forward*. Motion of the club resumed. Crowd cheered.

Tim was gazing at Joshua, wondering, confused, taken back, getting up off his chair and standing, watching Joshua standing, reaching out to her. Nia turned away. Carrying the rose, she left the stage. Joshua turned toward Tim. "Well, I think you found your destiny, bro," Tim said as the lights faded and the darkness of the club emerged, covering the light as the clouds covering the moon, "Look, Joshua. The dragon is eating the moon..." Joshua remembered his mother...

Tim and Joshua left the strip club. They stood momentarily, looking up at the sky, at the high church tower before them on the other side of the parking lot as Nia had. The bells were ringing with a sudden gust of wind. Tim took out his keys and started to walk toward his truck with a bottle of liquor underneath his arm for their father. Joshua headed directly for the church, drawn by the sounds of the bells. Seeing this, Tim put the bottle of liquor in the truck and followed Joshua.

Joshua had already entered the church. When Tim entered, he saw Joshua walking toward the altar with his arms extended outward. Joshua fell down on his knees before the cross. Tim remained standing in the back, watching. The church was empty with the walls adorned in an array of beautiful stained-glass windows of archangels fighting dragons. They appeared to be telling a story of some great battle of the past, or one to come. Tim, gazing at the stained-glass, sat down in a back pew as Joshua remained on his knees in the front of the church, praying, transfixed upon the cross. Tim glanced over at a large statue of Mother Mary. Before Her were rows of unlit candles. Joshua brought his arms in to his chest and, suddenly, began calling out the Lord's Prayer in Ancient Aramaic.

"Abba (*Father*), Yətqadaš šəmak (*May thy name be holy*), Teṭe malkutak (*May thy kingdom come*), Tehəwe raʿutak (*May thy will be done*), Pittan də-ṣorak hav lan yoməden (*Give us today our needed bread*), wa-Švuq lan ḥovenan (*And forgive us our debts / sins*), Hek ʿanan šəvaqin lə-ḥaivenan (*As we forgive our debtors*), wə-La taʿel lan lə-nisyon (*And lead us not into temptation*)."

The candles in front of the Large Mother Mary Statue, one by one, on their own, mysteriously lit up. Tim appeared shocked, confused as Joshua rose up from his knees, nodded his head toward the cross, turned, and walked back toward him, now, standing by a large church door with iron handles. "How did you do that?" Tim asked. "Do what?"

Joshua responded, clasping upon one handle, turning it, and pushing the large door open into bright cast sunlight.

Nia, in the backroom of the club, holds the rose to her lips as other dancers begin changing back into their *alternative lives* of regular clothes adorned in garb of contemporary thought and norms.

"He is different. Isn't he?" A dancer said, getting changed, next to Nia. "Who?" Nia asked.

"That guy who gave you that rose. I felt it when I got close to him, something different, like he didn't belong here," the dancer added. Nia gazed at herself in the spanning mirror, holding the rose... "Yes, something different," Nia said, bringing the rose to her lips...

An old blue corvette drove into a gravel driveway of a sky-blue Cape Cod House. The engine cut off with the loud sound of a backfire as Crystal stepped out, wearing her high-heels and fishnets, covered slightly by a short tee-shirt. She slammed the car door.

Nia gently put down the rose and turned, appearing fearful...

Crystal entered her home within a dimly lit foyer and opened up her arms to her three- year-old daughter, Crystal, running into them. Picking her up and kissing her tightly on the cheek, shouting emanated from the house next door of a couple arguing. Loud music then resonated from this house, drowning out the sounds of the argument.

"You're home early," Genny, a teenaged babysitter said, standing by a toy castle in a tiaras while holding a princess sword.

"I just needed to see my daughter, not sure why," Christine said, gently placing her down.

Crystal ran over to Genny, taking hold of the toy sword.

"We're playing princess warrior," Crystal said, raising the sword. "Am I going on a horsey ride, now, mommy?" Crystal asked.

"A horsey ride?" Genny asked with a quizzical look.

"Yes. I promised her," Christine replied with a nod and fake smile, taking off her heels and tossing them into the corner. "You wouldn't know where I could find one."

'A...' Genny began to say. "Horse," Christine simply said.

"Is everything alright?" Genny asked Christine.

"Yes. Everything's fine," Christine said, brushing back her hair and taking off her tee- shirt, revealing her skimpy top. Genny gave her a slight smile. "Part of my uniform," Christine said, returning a smirk. The loud music became silent...

You stupid..." A crash was heard coming from the house next door. A window broke. The front screen door slammed open as a young woman with a black eye, her shirt torn, fell out onto a wooden porch; her hand being cut by a rusted nail embedded in the rotting wood. A young man followed her out, dirty, drunk, angry. He stood over her, looking down at her. "All you do all day is get high!" He gave her a slight kick in the side.

"Leave her alone, Martin! Christine said, approaching the porch. Martin paused, appearing taken back by what Christine was wearing. "What do you want?" Martin said, adding, "Stay out of it, Chris." Christine walked up onto the porch and shoved him back.

"Just leave her alone," Christine said, turning, helping the young woman up. "This has nothing to do with you," Martin told Christine.

"Are you alright, Miriam?" Christine asked, attempting to console her. Miriam nodded and began to wipe away her tears.

"All she does is smoke crack and whore around," Martin said, attempting to regain his breaths and calm down. Christine turned back and shoved him again.

"Keep your hands off her," Christine said. Christine helped Miriam off the porch as Genny and Christine's daughter watched from the distance. Putting her arm around her, Christine walked her toward her car. Helping Miriam by her arm, Christine noticed that she was on drugs, barely able to walk as she gently tried to guide her away. As they got closer to Christine's car, Genny came over to help her get into it. However,

Miriam pulled away and said, "No, I'm sorry...I can't." "Why not?" Christine asked.

"I just can't," Miriam replied.

"Then I'll call the police," Genny said.

"No. No. Don't... I just need a second," Miriam said, leaning up against the car. Crystal walked up to Miriam, tugged gently on her torn shirt. "It's okay. He loves you." "Who?" Miriam asked. "That man, that man right over there," Crystal pointed toward a hill. Everyone turned. No one was there. Crystal looked up to Christine.

"I saw Him. He was standing right over there," Crystal said, pointing again. "Genny, can you take Crystal inside? I'll be there in a minute," Christine said. "Come on, Crystal," Genny said, guiding Crystal into the house.

"You're both whores!" Martin shouted from his porch toward Christine and Miriam. "Okay, let's just go inside my house and figure this out," Christine said, trying to hold her up. Genny came over and helped.

"Don't come back! You hear me, whore!" Martin called out again. "Ignore him. Come on," Christine said, guiding her into her house.

"You know, if you weren't such a creep maybe she wouldn't do drugs!" Christine shouted back said while holding her tight, struggling to help her walk.

"Aw! You're all bitches," Martin said with a wave of his hand, adding, "I'm out of here," leaving the porch and, angrily, getting into his old pickup truck and racing away.

"Good!" Christine shouted, "Stay away!"

"My babies, my babies where are they?" Miriam suddenly said, pushing off the car, turning back toward the house. Both of Miriam's eyes were swollen and bruised.

"Your kids..." Christine sprinted toward Miriam's house, up the porch steps, bursting through the door. There was a musty odor, remnants of cocaine upon an unclean kitchen table, a half eaten sandwich, smashed lamps, dishes, and broken glass strewn all throughout the living room. Christine, abruptly, stood still and listened. A soft angelic voice, "Do not be afraid. Stand still, and see the salvation the Lord...And the Lord said to Moses, 'Why do you cry to Me? Tell the children of Israel to go

forward. But lift up your rod and stretch out your hand over the sea..."
The voice faded. Christine then heard crying coming from a closet. She
opened the door - two little girls were huddled behind hanging clothes,
shaking in tears, consoling each other, holding each other tight. They
appeared fearful. "Come," Christine said, reaching out to them. "It
will be okay, Amy, Lillian," Christine added in a reassuring stronger
tone. The clothes parted as a sea as the children passed through the
darkness of the closet toward light and Christine's hand...

The waterfall flowed into the crystal clear blue pond as shadows of
birds passed upon the surface in a bright sunlight while in the distance,
on the other side of the sea, ships horns could be heard approaching
the land, the mountain, the cliff, that Tree. Hawks hovered over it,
joined by others. A few rested down on the branches, gazing out. The
others scattered at a loud sound of a ship horn bellowing out as the
waves to the sea appeared to flicker, as a candle, higher in the distance
of the horizon's edge.

Inside Christine's blue house, Miriam was on the coach, holding
ice packs on her eyes with her daughters sitting next to her in silence
without even the slightest smile. It was as if the world had cast out
innocence toward a dimensional time without hope.

"That's it. If she won't do it, I'll file a complaint against that creep,"
Christine said to Genny in a low voice in the kitchen, looking at Miriam
through the adjoining doorway.

"No. You can't," Miriam said, pulling icepacks away from her eyes,
hearing her, and sitting up. She added, "If you do, he will hurt me even
more. He will hurt.. us more," Miriam pleaded, wrapping her arms
around her daughter. Christine and Genny walked over to Miriam's
daughters. Christine stooped down and looked them in the eyes.

"That's why I never see them smile," Christine said, reaching out
and gently stroking their hair. On the top of their shoulders, Christine
noticed bruises. Christine glanced back at Genny beginning to call
someone. Christine shook her head at Genny. Christine mouthed, "I'll
do it." Genny put away her phone.

"Are we going for horsey ride, now, mommy?" Crystal asked.

"In a little while, honey," Christine said, turning to Genny. "Here. Could you hold Crystal?" Christine walked back toward the kitchen. Taking out her phone, she hit 911..

"What are you doing!" Miriam cried out, attempting to stand. "I'm calling the police. I've had it with all of this," Christine said.

"No! Please! You can't! Please..." Miriam pleaded again, getting up and moving toward Christine. "911 What's your emergency?" Miriam frantically grabbed the phone from Christine. "You know him! The police can't stop him! You know him!" Miriam cried out. Miriam, clapping upon Christine's phone, fell to the floor. She placed down the phone and raised her hands up over her swollen and bruised eyes. "You remember what happened the last time," Miriam said.

"You can't let him keep doing this to you, Miriam. Think of your daughters," Christine answered, gesturing to her daughters, fearful by the couch.

"I know. I know. You're right. But let me do it. Please. I'll tell him that he has to leave, tonight, when he comes back. But no police. That will only make him madder."

"You're going to tell him that he has to leave for good?" Christine asked.

"Yes. I promise. When he comes back. I'll take care of it. But let me do it. Just let me do it," Miriam said, stretching out on the floor. Christine reached down and gently took back her phone. She got a blanket and placed it over Miriam.

"Can you stay?" Christine asked Genny. Genny nodded. "Good. You can help me with the kids."

"Are you going to call the police?" Genny asked. Christine paused, remained silent.

Genny glanced over at the high-heels. "Nice heels. Where did you get them?" "A friend," Christine replied.

Crystal and the two other little girls, Amy and Lillian, stood by the window, looking out. Atop the hill, they saw a Middle Eastern man in a brown robe with long black hair and powerful eyes. All three of them were drawn to him, unblinking, as if in a trance. He vanished.

At Destiny's Dance Club loud music boomed with dancers upon stages and people shouting, calling out. In the dressing room, Nia was staring out the window, as if in a trance, toward the church's steeple with a cross, across the parking lot.

"What are you looking at?" One of the dancer's dressed as Minnie Mouse asked.

"Nothing," Nia said, turning away from the window.

"What was with that guy that gave you the rose? Did you see how he was staring at you?" The dancer asked. Nia shrugged her shoulders. "Really? A guy was staring at me?" Nia sarcastically replied, walking away. Nia picked up the rose on the table in front of the spanning dressing room mirror and placed it carefully into her backpack.

"He seemed different," the dancer added. We all saw it. He kept looking at you, like he was your long lost love or something." "Yeah, right," Nia simply replied.

"Really," the dancer barked back, adding, "Do you know him? You must. I can't believe he gave you a rose and not cash."

"Look. I don't know the guy, okay? Nia angrily began changing back into a tee-shirt and jeans.

"Then why did you take the rose?" Another dancer, dressed as an Arabian princess, asked while adjusting her costume.

"I don't know," Nia replied, dressed in her tee-shirt and jeans, gazing at herself in the mirror, reflecting the large defined rectangular mirror, spanning many dancers in various kinds of costumes; fairies, baby dolls, wizards, elves, and princesses.

Nia picked up her things, including the dragon container of cocaine inside the dressing table drawer, and put everything into her backpack. She began to leave. She paused. Angry, she turned back toward the dancer dressed as Minnie Mouse.

"You really think guys get turned on by what you're wearing?" Nia asked.

"Honey, I'll get dressed as any character as long as they give me cash and not a rose," the dancer replied, gazing at herself alluringly in the mirror, adjusting her look as Ms. Gongel entered the dressing room. "Girls, come on. Stop all this gabbing, get out there and perform,"

Ms. Gongel commanded. Angered, she turned toward Nia, noticing her dressed in her tee-shirt and jeans. "And where do you think you're going, love?"

"I'm leaving," Nia replied, tossing her backpack over her shoulder, starting to walk away.

Reaching out, Ms. Gongel grabbed Nia forcibly by her shoulder, firmly pulling her back as she attempted to pass.. "No, you're not going anywhere, love. I've already had two dancers call out on me and your shift isn't over, yet. I told you when you begged me to hire you, you need to stick to the schedule and mind what I say. Remember?"

"Sorry, ma'am. I've got to get to my class," Nia meekly replied, pulling gently away from Ms. Gongel's grasp.

"When are you going to stop pretending to be a college student and accept who you are?" Ms. Gongel asked, placing her hand on her hip as Nia paused at the exit.

"I'll cover her shift," the dancer dressed as Mini Mouse said. "Thanks. I owe you one," Nia replied, dashing through the exit.

Ms. Gongel gave the dancer's exposed bare bottom a hard frustrated slap, immediately turning it red similar to the shape of a Blood Moon. "Ow!" The dancer, stunned, shrieked. "What was that for?" The dancer added with a wince.

"For interfering in my business," Ms. Gongel snipped in an authoritative manner, adding, "Make sure it doesn't happen again. Just do your job."

"Yes, ma'am," the dancer meagerly replied, bowing her head in the mouse ears.. "Now, go out there and make me money, "Ms. Gongel snapped in a stricter tone. The dancer obediently complied, scurrying out while rubbing her bottom and adjusting her mouse ears while being absorbed, overcome by a wave of darkness and pain, trapped within arising fear, exposure, and vulnerability.

Ms. Gongel like a Drakaina (female dragon) who had just lost her prey, turned back toward the exit in a gaze of determination and dominance. With a deep angered breath, she followed the path Nia took, through the door and out into the parking lot, approaching Nia with an unyielding spirit. Nia was getting on her white motorcycle with *Destiny* written in red on its side. Catching up to her, Ms. Gongel stood over her, casting a shadow over *Destiny*.

"I told you, you're shift isn't over, yet," Ms. Gongel said, looking down at her. ' "I'm sorry. I told you, I have to get to class," Nia said, starring her motorcycle.

Ms. Gongel reached out and grabbed Nia by the back of her hair, pulling Nia off her motorcycle. Leading her back toward the club, clapping her hair, tightly, *Destiny* fell in the parking lot as Nia attempted to pull away. Ms. Gongel tugged back.

"We both know what you are. I don't care who your father is. I gave you this job because you begged me. You work for me, here inside this club and outside when I send you out on your discrete missions. Do you understand? I own you."

"Let me go," Nia said, trying to pull away more frantically.

Ms. Gongel slammed Nia up against the door. "Do you understand!"

"Yes, yes. I understand," Nia said as people in the parking lot began looking over at them. "Good," Ms. Gongel, noticing the looks, said, releasing Nia. Nia and Ms. Gongel turned. They both noticed a priest staring at them from across the parking lot. Nia turned away, bowed her head, and went through the door, back into the club. Ms. Gongel gave the priest a stern look. The priest just watched, unmoving. He walked over, and stood the motorcycle back up, and walked away back toward the church.

"Hey, can we stop by the place?" Joshua, suddenly, asked Tim, seeing a hidden road emerge as they drove up a mountain overlooking Los Angeles toward their home.

"Sure, Joshua," Tim sympathetically replied, making a sharp turn down the small narrow dirt road into a deeper, denser part of the woods cradled within Joshua's mind. Tim was slow to answer. But looking over to Joshua with only a glance, catching a glimmer of his own reflection upon the glass, Tim nodded, as if reaching out to an image of his soul clasped hidden upon the past. Tim added in a whisper, "I know... the place." Tim didn't like to talk about it much. He never did. Like Joshua, he hadn't accepted their mother's death. He, too, had been wrestling with the pain for years, but in his own way, silently building a secret project, a piece of the puzzle that Joshua was searching for. Joshua, however, didn't know that his brother still cared or even could feel pain. He believed his brother Tim had conquered pain long ago, along with giving up on love, seemingly not real as if an imaginary white winged horse in their mother's stories of fairytales..

When they got to *the place,* Tim parked off the side by the small church hidden in Joshua's deepest part of his woods. Joshua got out and *walked fully clothed, his naked soul hidden,* hesitant in a way, toward the large cross upon it's outside wall. As Joshua stood silently before the cross with his head bowed, Tim sensed a coldness of frost in the stillness of a swirling wind; watching Joshua standing before the cross, near their mother's grave beside the abandoned old stone church. The sun was almost down, just beyond the mountain's ridge. A tree with blossoming flowers hung over Joshua's head. Pedals began to fall down upon him...

Joshua whispered, "I love you, Mom," briefly seeing momentarily colors of fading lights upon a Christmas tree. Turning away from the past, Joshua walked back, passing through an old rusted black rod iron gate that hung open, dangling from its last bolt. With the colors of the past faded, Joshua glanced over at all the graves beyond the iron gate. He wondered what all their dreams had been and if they had ever come true. As Tim and Joshua drove away, the reflection of the cross from the outside wall of the stone church slowly passed in a reflection across the windshield. The sun set, as if a page turning to night, back into the images of a lifeless black and white...as Joshua gazed, once again, out the passenger side window, thinking of Nia. He put his hand up to the glass, reaching out from the most in the inner part of his soul.

Booming music. Nia swinging on the poll, lights upon her dancing on the stage, her long black hair flowing back, she arched as a puppet on a string backwards... trapped within that darkness of the numbness of churning ice within a frozen glass.

"Morality," a bishop whispered over the booming loud music, adjusting his glasses and gazing out an open large church window of his office toward the club. The bishop turned. The priest who watched Nia, stood just inside the doorway. "Do you think young people, today, understand what it is, Father Gabe?" The bishop asked as Father Gabe approached the bishop, standing by his side by the window, gazing out. "I believe it's a primary role for us to participate in young people's lives so that they will ultimately follow the right path. There are just too many diversions, today, that lead them..."

"It's part of a bigger battle, isn't it?" Father Gabe said. "Yes, yes, a bigger battle," the bishop replied, appearing to see something that looked like a shadow of a dragon, hovering above the club. The bishop took off his glasses and wiped them off. Putting them back on and looking out, the image was gone.

"Are you alright?" Father Gabe asked.

"Yes. I'm fine," the bishop said, facing Father Gabe. "I'll just come out and say it. I'm looking for a leader, someone from our church who can lead young people..."

"Down the right path?" Father Gabe asked.

"Yes. Exactly. Are you interested?" The bishop asked.

"I'm just passing through. I never really connected with young people. I'm more adept in helping...well, soldiers, fighters, guards, people of that lot" Father Gabe said, adding, "I follow commands. But, I thought it was good that you know my talents."

"I've heard of your talents, rumors anyway," the bishop said, adding,

"I haven't gotten your paperwork, yet. Do you know when they will be arriving?"

Father Gabe paused turning back. "Soon. They will be arriving soon."

"Well, good, then. We're happy to have you...Father Gabe, no matter how long you're planning on staying with us. With that said, I believe that our youth ministry would be good for you, particularly for those who have mental and physical disabilities. We have quite a few of them, you know. I don't know if they really have much fellowship other than their therapists. A ministry would be especially good for them. They're a feisty group. We have gone through several youth ministers. But, you, a leader of, what did you say, soldiers, should not have any problem."

The bishop smiled and turned back toward the window, adding, "I'll keep you advised as when you can begin. Thank you." Father Gabe nodded. Father Gabe walked down a red carpeted high ceiling hallway of the church aligned with statues and paintings and spanning stained-glass windows. He paused before a giant sized statue - Archangel Michael, standing holding a large spear, his foot on the head of a dragon. "Well, it will all begin soon, Michael," Father Gabe said, gazing upward at the statue. "And we'll be fighting together, once again, my old friend.

The bishop opened his bible, standing once again by the window. He began to read aloud. "Revelation 12. A great sign appeared in heaven; a woman clothed with the sun, with the moon under her feet, and a crown of twelve stars on her head. She was pregnant and cried out in pain as she was about to give birth. Then another sign appeared in heaven, an enormous red dragon with seven heads and ten horns and seven crowns on its heads. It's tail swept..." He then heard a loud powerful wind...

Later that night, almost midnight, Nia exited the club, dressed only in a tiny white crop top, flip flops, and tight denim short, shorts, exposing her bottom cheeks, as Ms. Gongel stood by the exit, smiling, watching her, as if controlling her walking across the parking lot toward her motorcycle. In Ms. Gongel's hands were Nia's tee-shirt and jeans. There was a strong wind, blowing back her long hair. Nia momentarily paused, turning back toward her. She smiled, gave an affirmative nod, and gently closed the door. Nia stood before her motorcycle beneath a flickering dimly lit streetlight, searching for her keys in her backpack. "Come on, I know you're in here," Nia said to herself, frustrated.

"Can I help you," Father Gabe said, seemingly appearing out of nowhere.

Nia, slightly, gasped, dropping her backpack. "You startled me," Nia said, quickly bending down to pick it up. Glancing upward, Nia paused, noticing the flickering of the streetlight had stopped, remaining still, illuminating Father Gabe in a steady pulse of light before her as she rose to her feet, clasping her backpack. "Who are you?" Nia asked, adding, noticing his collar, "Are you a priest?"

"For now," Father Gabe replied with a smile. "But, you never know what life will bring.

We often have different personas, don't we, Nia? Are you a dancer?"

"For now," Nia replied in a somewhat sarcastic tone, getting onto her motorcycle, attempting, again, to find her keys in her backpack.

"What are you searching for?" Father Gabe asked, his image in the light appearing to become larger. "My keys. I can't seem to find them," Nia replied. "Maybe you're searching for the wrong key," Father Gabe said, reaching out and handing her the keys. "Where did you find them...Wait, how do you know my name?" Nia asked.

"You should come to church, sometime. Maybe...you'll find what you're really searching for," Father Gabe said as the flickering of the street light returned. Father Gabe was, suddenly, gone.

Nia, appearing confused, shook her head, started her motorcycle and rode off. Ms. Gongel watched her, standing outside the club in the shadows, smoking a cigarette. Taking a puff of her cigarette, Ms. Gongel turned, looked up. She saw the bishop looking down at her, watching her from the church window. The bishop pulled the window shut as if closing a curtain to the *Second Act of a Play*...Darkness... Heavier sounds of winds - the flickering light of the lit cigarette in

Ms. Gongel's hand accompanied by the street light within the echo of the winds, a dragon's soft howling breaths...

A large white horse in an array of straps, attached to a buggy, whinnied through it's nostrils as Christine, Crystal, Genny, and Miriam's two daughters, Amy and Lillian, appearing fearful, were about to get into the buggy's seat. The sun was bright, hardly a breeze amidst the bustle of the busy city's street. "How much for once around?" Christine asked the buggy driver, standing by the side of the large white horse attempting to steady him.

"It's alright, Bud. It's alright. They're friendly," the driver said to him, gently patting him on the side while clasping, tightly, to his reins. "Fifty dollars," the driver quipped with an unknown accent. "Fifty dollars?" Christine responded, nodded, searching for the money in various pockets as Genny helped the children into the carriage. Finding forty dollars, mostly crumpled up fives and ones, Christine turned toward Genny and asked, "Hey, do you have ten bucks?"

Bud started to buck, rising up. "You can pay me after the ride," the driver frantically said, trying to hold onto Bud, pulling him back down with the children aboard.

Christine put the money back into her jeans pocket and climbed in with them, helping Genny up into the carriage, taking her by the hand. The reins slipped from his hands.

"Wait, Bud!" The driver shouted as Bud began to try to take off without him. He jumped in, climbing up, and took hold again of the reins. "Bud! It's not a race." The driver said. Turning to Christine, he added, "Bud is the oldest but the strongest and fastest of the horses from our stable."

Bud took off, galloping...passing cars, going through red lights, weaving in and out of traffic, racing ahead of traffic. Christine and Genny appeared concerned. The children were laughing.

"Is he supposed to be doing this?" Christine asked the driver, appearing frightened, trying to slow Bud. "No. He's not. Don't know why he's doing this...Come on, Bud, slow down! Slow down, boy!" Bud blew by other horse and buggies with the drivers shouting, "Go, Bud!" "Not funny!" Bud's driver called back.

"Are you having fun?" Christine asked the girls. They nodded, looking out as they moved along the city's streets at a quick pace. "Of course we get that special horse," Christine said to Genny, holding tight in the ride. "That's because we're special," Genny replied as Bud began prancing at a slow pace. "Finally," the driver responded. relieved.

"We want him to go fast again," Crystal blurted out.

"Give Bud a break, honey, then he can do it," Christine replied.

"No! It's not a break. It's supposed to be like this. Not a break," the driver said, turning back. Christine and Genny smiled at teach other as the driver added, "Fifty bucks is not worth my life." "Drama queen," Christine said, reaching into her bra, suddenly, remembering. "Oh, yes..." She took out and handed the hundred dollar bill to the driver. "Okay. Maybe Bud is done his break. Come on, Bud! Let's go!" The driver shouted, placing the hundred dollar bill inside his shirt. Bud started again in a gallop.

"So, where did you get that hundred dollar bill? I thought you were broke." Genny asked Christine.

"Got it from a woman, a woman named... Blaze," Christine replied, looking down. "Who's Blaze?" Genny asked.

"Someone with courage," Christine said, looking back up toward Bud.

The driver had no control over Bud as he blew by all the other horse and buggies, traveling at a leisurely pace as if pulling an Egyptian Chariot racing toward Moses's destiny within the Red Sea. Crystal was laughing and, for a brief moment, Amy and Lillian began to smile, no longer appearing fearful, more secure in the images of a wild horse, encompassing an indomitable spirit, attempting to break free and reach his destiny, unseen by the human eye, un relinquished to the human soul.

When the ride ended, Genny helped the children down off the buggy as Christine handed the driver another fifty dollars. "Bud's tip,"

Christine said with a smile. The driver nodded and said, "Thanks. I'm sure he will appreciate it... By the way, do I know you?"

Christine turned away and caught up the Genny and the girls walking down the street.

The driver continued to stare at Christine. She briefly turned back. "Aw yes, the waitress from the club," the driver said. Suddenly, other horse and buggy drivers pulled up. The drivers got down off their buggies and approached Bud, pulling him hard by his reins. One whipped him as Bud arose on his hind legs. Another hit him again. Christine paused. The children began to turn back. "Genny, I'll meet up with you and the kids home." Christine marched back. The driver of Bud's carriage, stopped her from intervening. "No. Don't," the driver said getting in front of her as she watched the other drivers pulling him forcibly away. "What are they going to do to them?" Christine asked. "It's okay," Bud's driver said, "The Lord will fight for you, and you shall hold your peace."

The men pulled Bud into a trailer and slammed the door shut. "What?" Christine asked Bud's driver. "What? I didn't say anything," he replied. Christine reluctantly turned away.

As Christine walked listlessly down the street, she heard someone call out to her.

"You have a beautiful daughter." The old lady with bright green eyes, wearing the white hospital gown, said to her, coming out of the shadows. "Thanks. Who are you? How do you know my daughter?" Christine asked, guarded.

"She will make a great leader," the old lady followed.

Appearing confused, concerned, Christine said, "Were you...watching us?" "I only see what the Lord let's me see," the old lady responded.

"Oh," Christine said, adding, "I see..." Christine reached into her pocket for money.

Taking out a ten dollar bill, she reached it out toward the old lady. The old lady gently pushed Christine's hand back. "There is much more in life than money my dear. Search within your heart and you shall find the answer. For the Truth is always within your reach." Christine stood with her hand outstretched toward her. A truck blasted its horn. Christine turned. Turning back, the time had passed. The old lady had vanished. Christine appeared stunned, looking around.

The old lady with green eyes sat in her wheelchair by a window at Lady of Lourdes Hospital, looking out. Next to her was a vase full of eleven roses along with a picture of Padre Pio, a saint who was attributed with being able to utilize the phenomenon of "bilocation." Gazing at the picture then out the window, the old lady said, "Now, I understand how you did it, Father Pio. Now, I understand... But, what do I know. I'm just an old woman." She gave a sly smile.

Joshua opened a pot cooking on the stove, cautiously peering in. He saw something that resembled some kind of burnt piece of meat. Finding a pewter dish, he lanced the piece of meat with a rusted knife and slid it onto the dish, then went into the dining room, sat down at the table, and stared out the window, remembering, just remembering, transcending time, space...

Their father stood by a red SUV, opening the passenger door. "Joshua!" His father called out. Joshua, five-years-old, stumbled off the front porch with Tim holding his hand. Together, they both walked toward the SUV, pausing, looking up at their father. Tim reached into his gym bag and began helping Joshua put on wrestling headgear, adjusting it to make it fit.

"Come on. We're supposed to weigh in by three. You can finish that when we get there," their father said to Tim while staring at Joshua. Tim nodded and took off the headgear.

The large gymnasium had three large wrestling mats, spanned across the gymnasium floor with hundreds of screaming parents in the stands. One by one, small children went out upon the mats to wrestle. Joshua, still not speaking his first word, stood in fear in the corner of one mat with Tim helping him put on his headgear back on as parents from the stands shouted out.

Once the headgear was fitted, Joshua ran out to the center of the mat. Appearing fearful, Joshua glanced back to his father for help. His father sat poised in a chair by the corner of the mat with a bottle of water in his hand, signaling for Joshua to go ahead. Joshua turned back to his opponent, shook hands and began wrestling. Joshua was slammed immediately onto his back with his headgear becoming twisted around his throat, causing him to have trouble breathing.

"Don't give up! Don't give up!" His father called out to him from the corner of the mat. "Bridge up! Joshua! Bridge!" Tim shouted. *The referee slapped the mat…*

Joshua found himself biting into the burnt piece of meet, his teeth clenched, coming to a consoling self-acceptance encompassing where he was in this dimensional "burnt piece" of time.

Headlights suddenly appeared through the dining room window, making his eyes wince at the brightness, illuminating through the darkness of the dining room. It was an Uber. Joshua's father got out, carrying a large red gym bag. Joshua swallowed the sharp gristle of the meat and remained seated at the table as, without a word, his father entered and passed by him.

A phone rang. It rang again… "In that day there will be inscribed on the bells of the horses, *Holy to the Lord.* And the cooking pots in the Lord's house will be like the bowls before the altar," Joshua said, as if in a trance - staring out the window, adding, "Zachariah 14:20." His father immediately went into his bedroom, tossed the gym bag on the bed and answered an old black rotary phone, sitting atop a marble bureau, partially closing the door of the bedroom that connected, directly, to the dining room. Joshua attempted to listen, remaining motionless, paused in the shadowy images of encircling orbs of time…

"Hello… Oh, hi, coach Fanelli. Really? That's great. Thank you so much. Yes. I'll bring him by. We really appreciate everything you've done. Hold on." The orbs stopped spinning as the partially ajar door opened and Joshua's father stood, looming in a large shadow in the doorway.

"Joshua," his father said in a deep, resonating tone. Joshua slightly turned, unwilling to rise up from his chair anchored, now, in the center of his *perception* of his universe. "Yes," Joshua simply replied with a slight turn of his head. "The call is for you," his father responded. "Me?" Joshua replied, knowing, but acting as if he didn't understand. His father did not respond, he just opened the door wider with a slight push of his hand.

Joshua got up and saw the black receiver of the phone resting upon the marble table. He hesitantly walked in and picked it up. His father stood towering over him, handing him a pen and piece of paper. Joshua tried to untangle the cord of the phone's receiver.

"Hello?" Joshua said while looking at pictures atop the bureau in front of him.

Joshua looked up on top of the bureau in front of him. There was a picture of his mother on a balcony dressed as Juliet for a college play. Joshua placed the pen and paper down before it.

"No. I can't. I won't be coming back for a while. I will. Bye," Joshua said. As he slowly reached to hang up the phone, gently letting the receiver fall, his father angrily swatted the phone from his hand, causing it to fall onto the floor.

"What are you doing!" His father shouted at him. Picking up the phone off the floor, he shoved it into Joshua's chest. "Here. You call him back and tell him you'll do it."

Joshua sat down onto the bed, bowed his head. "I'm not ready yet," Joshua whispered. "When will you be ready? Call him back. Tell him you're coming. He went out of his way to get you back into U.C.L.A. And you have to register before everything closes," his father said, his shadow appearing to grow larger. Sensing the darkness closing in on him, Joshua got up and tried to pass. But, his father pushed him back. "You're not going anywhere until you call Coach Fanelli back and tell him you're going back to school." Samson, tied to a chain in the backyard, began barking. "So, you're going to blow this opportunity too?" His father quipped.

"I told you, I'm not ready yet," Joshua got up again and gently pushed his father aside to move by him. "What's going on?" Tim asked, suddenly, standing in the doorway.

"Nothing," Joshua replied, adding, "Dad and I were just talking." Joshua walked away and went outside.

"Dad, what are you doing? He just got out of the hospital and you're already pressuring him to go back to college?" Tim said, adding, "What the..." "Stay out of this," he replied to Tim, adding, "Not your fight... not your destiny."

Flash of *lightning*. Rumbles of thunder in the distance. In the backyard Joshua met Samson and hugged him, calming him down. Unhooking the chain, together they ran into the woods, down a partially, moonlit path toward the crystal clear blue pond beneath the waterfall. Standing on the side of the white sandy bank of the pond, gazing upward, he saw that the moon, half full, surrounded by stars with the sounds of the distant thunder getting closer. Approaching With Samson approaching to his side, Joshua knelt down on one knee and put his arm around him while gazing up at the waterfall with reflections of stars glistening, cascading down upon into a reflective image of the half moon seemingly floating upon the surface of the rippling pond.

With images of stars flowing from his heart, Joshua began speaking from his own prose, as if the love of his life was just on the other side of the pond, "Oh Lady Blue, where art thou upon this night, upon this dusk of thine heart? Tis your soul unseen with the visions of a virtuous cast? Shall you not come to save me from my own misgivings; the inner reaching of my dream, the hope for my love? Where art thou my Lady Blue, my sweet Mother of the night, my sweet heart of a virtuous hue?"

Joshua turned to Samson. "Samson. Who am I talking to? It feels like, someone is speaking through me. I remember what my mom taught me, what she taught me about love, about always holding onto my dreams and becoming a knight." Joshua looked up. "Who am I?" Joshua looked back down and into Samson's loving eyes. "Do you know, Samson?" Joshua reached out to his own reflection within the pond. Stirring the stars, gently, upon the surface with his extended hand, the rippling moon began to disappear behind the covering of passing clouds overhead as the stars, encircling the half moon, began to move - slowly changing to lit candles before a large statue of Mother Mary in a church with Father Gabe knelt in prayer before Her.

April 7, 1968. Vietnam. Michael and his men headed toward the west ridge. A mountain was in the distance as they walked through a large, open field that was once rice patties but now burnt down. The jungle surrounded them about five hundred yards off on each side. As they marched in single file, Michael and Ed were in the front. It was high noon.

"I can't believe that they killed him," Michael said.

"I can. The government had been after him for many years," Ed replied.

"The government?" Michael asked. "Who else do you think did it? James Earl Ray?" Ed said. "There will be neither rest nor tranquility in America until *Blacks are granted citizenship rights*. The whirlwinds of revolt will continue to shake the foundations of our nation until the bright day of justice emerges." Ed paused. "My father took me to see him that day in Washington, Dr. King. I'll never forget it. August 28, 1963. It made me feel proud to be a black man. Up to that point, I had just been called various derogatory names throughout my so called education. I was a sophomore in high school, and my father took me to the greatest class I would ever attend. We were close too. I could see the fire in his eyes, as if *God was truly speaking through him*. And he ends up being gunned down in Memphis, defending my father and other garbage men. My uncle, you know, was one of the ones who got crushed in the back of one of those trucks. Blacks weren't allowed to ride in the garbage trucks. They had to ride back with the garbage. And someone turned on the switch. My father was there. He heard the screams when his brother and the others got..."

Ed paused. "I think the government did it. Probably the same ones who killed JFK." "Maybe Jerk Hawk didn't get the story right. Maybe he wasn't killed," Michael said.

"He was killed," Ed replied. "How do you know?" Michael asked. "Because I can feel it," Ed answered as they walk across the open field, toward the jungle, toward the mountain.

"It's like a piece of the world has fallen away, only to be remembered upon torn faded yellow pages of history books, as if he was never truly alive, but now, only a part of our past, a past that may never be recovered or changed."

Ed looked up toward a *mountaintop.* "I hope those in the future remember him. I know, I always will."

"Shakespeare once said, 'When to the sessions of sweet silent thought I summon up remembrance of things past, I sigh the lack of many thing I sought...'" Michael replied, gazing upward at the blue cast mountaintop with a hawk, hovering in a timeless rising wind...

March 28, 1968. Dr. Martin Luther King leads a march of approximately six thousand protestors to support the striking sanitation workers in Memphis.

April 3, 1968. Dr. Martin Luther King delivers his final speech at the Bishop Charles Mason Temple. "And they were telling me, now it doesn't matter now. It really doesn't matter what happens now. I left Atlanta this morning, and as we got started on the plane, there were six of us, the pilot said over the public address system. 'We are sorry for the delay, but we have Dr. Martin Luther King on the plane.' And to be sure that all the bags were checked, and to be sure that nothing would be wrong with the plane, we had to check everything carefully. And we've had the plane protected and guarded all night.'"

"And then I got to Memphis. And some began to say the threats or the talk about the threats that were out. What would happen to me from some of our sick white brothers."

"Well, I don't know what will happen now. We've got some difficult days ahead. But it doesn't matter with me now. Because I've been to the *mountaintop.* And I don't mind. Like anybody. I would like to live a long life. Longevity has its place. But I'm not concerned about that now. I just want to do God's will. And He's allowed me to go up to the *mountain*. And I've looked over. And I've seen *the promise land*. I may not get there with you. But I want you to know tonight. I'm not worried about anything. I'm not fearing any man. *Mine eyes have seen the glory of the coming of the Lord!*"

April 4, 1968. Gunfire is heard. People call out. A news reporter on a black and white T.V. reports Dr. Martin Luther King is assassinated. His wife walks behind his casket...

June 5, 1968. Bobby Kennedy is shot. More cries of agony, calling out, and disbelief.

Both wives, Bobby Kennedy's and Dr. Martin Luther King's walk behind his casket. Ted Kennedy gives a speech about his brother in Saint Patrick's Cathedral in New York City.

August 26-29, 1968. Democratic National Convention. Antiwar protestors erupt in violent clashes with police. Hubert Humphrey is nominated for president at convention.

November 5, 1968. Nixon defeats Humphrey.

July 20, 1969. Neil Armstrong steps onto the moon. "One step for man, one giant leap for mankind..."

Joshua reached down and touched the fading reflection of the moon among the stars. Touching the passing moon, he whispered in his own words, "My love, my dream upon this night of a lonely cast, reach out thy hand to the bareness of my chest, and run your touch upon the inner hopes of my heart. For thou art my mercy, my sweet longings of my soul."

Joshua glanced across the pond. "Please believe in me, my love. Please feel me and awaken to the knight who I am. For inside my armor, inside my heart there beats my love for you in the form of a rose..." Joshua gazed upward, toward the stars... He rose up and stood, gazing across the other side of the pond, envisioning Nia, standing in a gentle breeze, her long hair, a white sheer gown. The pond rippled in a gentle wind with images of the past beneath the surface fold, as if a mirror, reflecting cast images of one's own soul. Hidden within the surface, deep down in a cradle of truth, these images arose within the mind, to become alive in a reality of spinning time, in a rapture of explosive sounds of illumination of sight and imagination...

Reaching out his hand, he said, "In the light of the moon, I shall await your call.

Henceforth, I shall come upon my white stallion to carry you off into the arising sun still draped in the colors of the dawn. For thou art more beautiful than an envious moon, more radiant than the sun. And unto thine heart, deep lies an impenetrable hope, a wish, cast across a star filled sky, alas upon the wind, above the sea, beating softly and silently in the form of a red rose for thee..."

April 7, 1968. Michael's men were still walking across the burnt down field that was once rice patties toward the mountain, the jungle's indistinct *edge* of its entrance getting closer.

"Do you think there will ever be another Shakespeare?" Ed asked Michael, who was gazing toward the edge of the jungle before them.

"I doubt it. Who talks in Iambic pentameter, anymore?" Michael responded. "Ah. You have an Literature background," Ed added.

"I told you. My mother was..." Michael began to say. "A Spanish whore," Ed interrupted.

"What?" Michael had a puzzled look, continuing to gaze at the tree line in the jungle ahead of them - *that edge.*

"A Spanish whore was the vixen at my feet," Ed replied as if in a trance in another time. "Oh," Michael said, noticing, adding, "Where did you find a Spanish..." Michael added,

but paused, raising his gun a bit as Ed kept talking. "Last stop. Back in Saigon. She dressed me up as her bull and clanged her castanets while digging her toes into my back. We gave a new meaning to running of the bulls that night."

"How can that be?" Michael asked peering more intensely into the tree line.

"I was her conquered bull. She danced her victory celebration on my back. I think she lanced me hard though." Ed reached his hand behind to feel his butt.

"Down!" Michael screamed, raising his arm. His men immediately fell to the ground, firing rounds into the jungle. Michael and his men stopped firing. There was silence except for a few birds, flying off, aroused by the gunfire.

"What the... What are we doing?" Ed asked while on his belly next to Michael, both their guns aimed toward the jungle. "Do you see something?" Ed added, wincing.

"Those three trees, at the edge, aren't moving," Michael said pointing. "So?" Ed asked. "All the other ones are," Michael replied. "Oh... The wind," Ed said figuring it out.

Michael and Ed fired again at the trees. The rest of the men joined in. They stopped. "What do you think?" Ed asked.

"I don't know. They're still not moving," Michael said. "Maybe we killed them," Ed said.

"Then they would be moving. Don't soldiers fall from trees once shot?" Michael said. Turning to his men still on the ground, Michael signaled for another soldier to come to him.

"Tommy! Sergeant Marina!" Michael shouted.

Corporal Tommy Marina, Hispanic, crawled on his belly up to Michael. "Sir?" Tommy asked.

"You're the youngest. Can you see anything at the tops of those trees?" Michael asked, pointing. He added, "The ones that are still."

Tommy peered at them. "No... Sorry, sir."

"I could have told you that," Ed said, adding, "Wouldn't they be firing back by now?" "Take another good look, Tommy," Michael said.

"I still can't see anything, sir. You're right though. They're not moving," Tommy said. "Maybe they're sturdy trees, a hundred, a thousand years old. How long are we going to stay here, like this?" Ed asked.

"I guess until one of us decides to get up," Michael said as they all remain poised on their bellies with their guns pointed toward the trees.

"You're the captain. We're waiting for you to give us the order," Ed responded. "Well, I'm not giving it. I believe they're still in those tree," Michael replied back. "How do you know?" Ed asked.

"I can feel it," Michael said, turning with a smile, adding, "Just like you."

Ed replied, "Oh. You're probably right, then. So, do you want one of us to stand up to draw their fire? How about Ears? He's been getting on my nerves lately." Michael smirked.

"Well, he has." Ed continued. "Tommy told me that he's thinking about expanding. I like my ears."

"Ears did say he wanted to add American ears to his collection," Tommy said to Michael. Michael started to reply, "Look, no one..." Just then, Ears, overhearing the conversation,

tossed down his rifle, got up, and started walking fully upright across the field toward the trees. "What is he doing?" Michael gasped.

"Maybe he heard us," Ed said.

"Ears! Ears, get down!" Michael called out.

Ears continued walking toward the trees with his arms up, screaming in Vietnamese that he was the Messiah and that he had returned.

"Get down you!" Ed shouted to him. Nothing. Ed turned to Michael. "What do you think now, Captain? Can we get up?" Michael didn't say anything, measuring in his mind what was ahead. "Well, if they are up there, maybe they're too busy laughing. Look at him," Ed said as Ears began spinning in circles waving his cut off ear trophies over his head. "He looks like a moron," Ed added.

Michael reached for the radio in a duffle bag. "What are you doing?" Ed asked.

"I'm calling it in," Michael said. Ed grabbed the radio from him. "You know we can't do that, Captain. If we call in air cover, Karese will know we're here. It will be like ringing a doorbell when we're trying to break in."

"Just once I wish we could make a move without wondering what Karese would do," Michael said, putting away the radio.

"You have to look at it as a game. Like the game of chess," Ed said. "I hate chess. Too slow," Michael answered.

Suddenly, a barrage of gunfire cut into Ears; so much that it kept him from falling.

Michael and his men fired back. Michael got to his feet amidst all the gunfire, shooting at the tops of the three trees, running toward Ears, who was still tossing in the barrage of gunfire. A couple more of Michael's men were hit, one wounded, one killed. Three Vietnamese soldiers fell from the trees. There was silence except for a large flock of birds flying off to the distant horizon of gray that was above the mountain's ridge.

"Fast enough for you?" Ed called out to Michael as he rose and walked over to join him.

Michael waved his hand. The rest of his men slowly got to their feet with their weapons poised. Tommy and Bruce attended to the wounded soldier. Michael went over to Ears and then over to the other soldier who was also dead. He took dog tags off of both of them. Michael handed Ed the tags.

Ed asked, "Shouldn't we bury them?" Michael replied, "We just did."

Michael and his men continued their march toward the jungle. Tommy, having finished bandaging the shoulder of the wounded soldier, walked by his side, with Bruce covering the rear.

Ed said to Michael, leading in the front, "If I die here, can you do me one favor?" "What?" Michael asked.

"Make sure my body gets back. Not just my dog tags," Ed responded. When they came to the jungle, Michael entered first. He stood looking up, before North Vietnamese soldiers. Blood was still flowing out of them, hanging helplessly upside down from the branches of the trees, entangled within their own equipment, just out of the reach, dying, but still alive. One was on the ground, attempting to frantically crawl away. Tommy grabbed him and calmly took out his knife.

"Tommy! Wait!" Michael called out as the Vietnamese soldier on the ground before them started screaming out something in Vietnamese.

Tommy slit his throat as he screamed out in agony. With the blood gushing from his neck, the screams turned to gasps, the gasps turned to wisps of breath, the wisps to silence.

Michael said in shock. "What did you do?"

"What did he say?" Tommy asked, covered in blood. "Something about the end of the world," Bruce said.

"He was right," Tommy responded, turning and walking away.

Michael reached down and touched the warm blood running from the neck of the Vietnamese soldier Tommy just killed. "Alright. Let's help the others," Michael said, adding, "Bruce, get up that tree."

"The others are dead, now, Captain," Ed responded, looking up at the North Vietnamese lifeless bodies, adding, "Tommy's still feeling it, what they did to his brother in that cage by the river. His legs were eaten up by rats when Tommy found him, his eyes gouged out, too." Tommy dropped his knife, walking farther into the jungle.

"Go get him," Michael ordered. Bruce went off to retrieve Tommy.

Michael gazed upward toward rays of sunlight shining down through the jungle's canopy. There was a platform nailed to three trees, resembling a balcony. "How about some Shakespeare, Professor?" Michael said to Ed. "Hamlet?" Ed asked, hesitantly. "Romeo and Juliet,"Michael said. Ed did not respond. "What? You don't know verses from that one?" Michael asked.

"I didn't get that far yet," Ed replied, adding, "In my book of poetic prose." "And here, I thought you were a Romantic," Michael said moving, closer, to just underneath the platform within the tree trees.

"Only when a red cape is being waved before me by..." Ed began to reply. "Your Spanish whore," Michael said while continuing to gaze upward the rays of sunlight. Bruce had Tommy by the arm by Michael's side. "Tommy..." Michael said.

"Yes, sir," Tommy said as Michael looked down at him.

"Next time...Next time, just let him live," Michael said in a deadpan facial expression. "There won't be a next time, sir," Tommy said, grabbing Bruce's handgun and shooting himself in the head. "What the!" Bruce shouted, covered in Tommy's blood.

Michael remained unmoving. He stooped down, pulled off Tommy's dog tags, gazed at them, and handed them to Ed.

"Let's keep moving," Michael said, turning, looking back up.

"Romeo and Juliet, professor One of my favorite plays. I'm surprised you aren't well versed in that one. That perch, up there, it kind a looks like a balcony, doesn't it?" Michael said.

"What's wrong with the captain?" Bruce whispered to Ed.

"Captain. Michael, Mei Lee and her village will be alright. I think headquarters is wrong.

Karese must be heading East. Why would he come back to her area? But, even if he does, I know, I just know she will be alright."

"How do you know, professor? Do you *feel* it?" Michael asked sarcastically. "Remember when I told Mei Lee's daughter, Hoa Sung the story about the goose the last time? How even though all the other animals were being slaughtered, they still spared the goose because she could lay golden eggs?" Ed said to him, placing his hand on his shoulder.

Michael glanced at the dog tags gripped in Ed's hand. Ed pull his hand away.

"So, that's why Karese will spare them? Because Mei Lee will lay golden eggs of obedience and servitude? That's a great thought. The woman I love with Karese," Michael angrily replied, looking back down to Ed away from the tree line.

"She won't do it, you know. She's more headstrong than me. She gave her life to the Lord." "No, not like that. I mean they're special. God will spare them because they bring beauty into the world. Like poetry. God always spares poetry," Ed said with a smile.

"I'm going to kill her," Michael replied.

"You're going to kill the woman you love?" Ed asked.

"No. Your *pernicious* Spanish whore," Michael returned the smile.

"Ah, Hamlet," Ed replied, adding, "Did you every read Revelation Seventeen?" "No, I didn't. To busy keeping everyone alive," Michael responded.

"Well, it talks about the Whore of Babylon and how she will rule.

It's right here," Ed said, taking out his small Bible, continuing, "I saw the woman, drunk with the blood of the saints and with the blood of the martyrs of Jesus..."

Michael nodded, looking back up at the North Vietnamese platform in the trees, dancing in the wind, back and forth through rays of cascading light from the sun.

"So, God spares poetry. Well, let's see if I can remember, if I can remember what she tried to teach my brother, Richard." "Who?" Ed asked.

"My sister-in-law, Elizabeth. She was into Medieval Literature, wrote some of her own stuff, shared with my brother and... me. Michael paused, teary eyed, then continued. "Where are you from my lady? What star cast out such brightness, without fear of loss of its own shining? 'Tis you my lady? And what is this time of which you speak? How can you see the bareness of my soul? For it is your beauty that beholds my sight. It is in your heart that I see that star. For you are all that I feel, all that I am, and I shall always hold your memory close and pray for a touch such as this." Michael looked down at his hands, blood.

"For thou art my beauty; cast upon a stillness of a shallow wound, full of light, and carried by all the stars of the sky." Michael gazed up, trying to see beyond the rays of sunlight falling through the jungle's canopy. "The stars are up there, professor. We just have to look."

Michael gazes toward the canopy, sensing an arising wind. The trees moved in an unusual sway, dancing in synchronization to a universal touch, a movement, a reach into some distant future. He gave a slight smile, knowing that God was upon them, His Will spanning any darkness cast upon Light. "For He is greater than forces of darkness," Michael whispered to himself.

Nia walked through a sheer, curtain through the winds of time, out onto a balcony, wearing a very short, sheer, white lace nightgown, holding Joshua's long-stem rose to her chest. She gazed upward, with a gentle gust of wind, out across a star filled sky, seeing a shooting star. She closed her eyes, pressed the rose close to her chest, took a breath, and made a wish. With her breath, a slight wind arose across the mansion grounds.

Joshua stood before the reflections of the stars falling into the pond with his right hand outstretched upward toward the shooting star. He turned away and ran with Samson back through the woods. He went around to the front of the house and with Samson's help, found in the dirt what he had lost in the fight with his brother. He clasped it tightly, again, in his right hand.

Chapter 5

Christine was bent over sitting at her kitchen table both arduously and meticulously clasping upon a pen in her right hand while looking over her bills. The three little girls, Amy, Lillian, and Crystal, were watching Disney's, "The Sword in the Stone" in the other room.

Christine saw through the window Martin return and Miriam approach him. Miriam did not resist as Martin took her into his arms and kissed her. Christine got up, went over and pulled down her blinds. Lillian came up to her and said, "I have an earache." "Oh, I'm sorry, honey." Christine tenderly looked at it, opened a pantry door, reached in, and gave her an children's aspirin.

Christine went back to the table and opened her Anatomy and Physiology book, over top of the bills and shut-off notices, shook her head, and began to study...

In a barn, Bud was tied to a post as the horse and buggy driver placed cash inside his shirt. Standing in the doorway, watching, the buggy driver bowed his head and walked away.

With shadowy, demonic infused images of men around Bud, they began to whip him, again and again from all sides, cutting into his flesh, leaving streaked marks, open slashed bloody wounds. Bud's whinnies of pain with each hit, as he frantically attempted to rise up and break free, seemingly echoed along the mountainside through an aura of a red mist above the tree tops.

Nia's bedroom door opened. A man walked in. The rose fell from her hands into the shadows of a red aura beneath the balcony. She turned and attempted to stealthily move back into her bedroom. Pulling down the bottom hem of her nightgown, she saw him standing there, by the side of her bed, as he always would in a overly confident, commanding manner. He had a gray business suit on, and in his hand was a riding crop that he moved back and forth, up and down, sliding it through the palm of his other hand. She approached him, submissively standing before him, looking up at him. Without a word, in silence, with the wind blowing the curtains from the balcony back toward them, she laid down on her stomach upon the bed, drew her arms in close, bowed her head, and closed her eyes as he slowly slid the bottom of her short nightgown upward toward her shoulders...

When Joshua entered the Victorian Home, his father was lying drunk across his bed with a bottle of liquor in his hand just above the phone on the floor. A dial tone was heard. The light in his father's room cast Joshua, again, halfway in shadows and light as he stared in through the partially open bedroom doorway...

He saw his father half conscious, coughing, trying to clear his throat. Joshua pushed the door all the way open and walked in. Picking up a pen and piece of paper before his mother's picture, the one of her playing Juliet, Joshua wrote down, "I'll go back, and do the best I can.

Thanks for trying to help me. Joshua." He placed it in his father's hand.

Atop the cliff, the old oak tree moved slightly in the wind as clouds passed through the night across the sea; an angelic voice sounded out barely above a whisper... "Immediately after the suffering of those days the sun will be darkened, and the moon will not give its light; the stars will fall from heaven, and the powers of heaven will be shaken...

Then the sign of the Son of Man will appear in heaven, and then all the tribes of the earth will mourn, and they will see 'the Son of Man coming on the clouds of heaven' with power and great glory. And he will send out his angels with a loud trumpet call, and they will gather his elect from the four winds, from one end of heaven to the other."

A grand mansion sat upon the mountainside, a light emanating from Nia's balcony. "That was really stupid. What were you thinking?"

Nia's mother asked her, sitting curled up out upon the balcony. Nia just stared straight ahead into the darkness of the mansion grounds as her mother was trying to arduously wipe away blood stains from Nia's bedroom floor with white carpeting, using a wet rag, dipping it into a bucket of water, becoming shaded in red.

"Did you hear me!" Her mother cried out.

Nia turned but did not answer. Her Irish mother, Melinda, very slender and attractive, was wearing a red silk dress, conservatively cut with a single pearl button just below her neck, fitting snugly with the hemline just below her knees, and had on red high heels. She walked out onto the balcony and grabbed Nia by her arms, pulling her up and back inside. "Come," Melinda spit out.

"Look at what you did," Melinda said to her, gesturing toward blood stains in the white carpet by the side of her bed. Nia's wrists were slit with the blood just about dry. Wearing four bracelets with diamonds and rubies on her own wrists, Melinda reached over to a small dressing table and placed icepacks on her daughter, Nia's wrists. "Here. Keep this on them," she said.

Melinda got back down on the floor and continued to try to wipe away the stains.

"I don't know what gets into you sometimes. I just don't. I hope your father doesn't find out about this. Look how you ruined his new carpeting...Ugh."

"He's not my father," Nia snipped, sitting down on a small white wooden stool in front of the dressing table. Nia looked into the mirror. Bringing her hand up to her eyes, she tried to rub off the makeup that ran down her cheeks from crying as her mother continued to scrubbing.

"I told you to keep the ice on them," Melinda quipped, clenching the bloody rag.

Nia turned away from the mirror. With her feet bare she sat cross-legged on her stool, pulling down her nightgown, putting the icepacks back on her wrists by holding them between her thighs. She had nothing on underneath her gown as she hunched over with her head bowed. She glanced to atop her bed, seeing her white lace thong panty with the small heart upon it.

"To embarrass your father like that, after all he did for you, and with his election just two months away. We do not need this kind of drama," Melinda explained while cautiously scrubbing so as not to ruin her dress. "He's not my father," Nia repeated again in a softer tone.

Melinda paused, looking up at Nia curled up on the stool. "Your father, young lady, is Senator Justin Stanworth the Third. And you will treat both him and his house with respect. Do you understand?" Melinda replied squeezing the rag.

"My father is a priest, a black man of God, not some white lying politician," Nia said. "But your white mother is the one who kept you. Remember? And the white politician is

the father who takes care of you. Your so called, Black man of God won't even acknowledge that you're his," Melinda hissed.

"He's a priest. He can't..." Nia started to say.

"He can't? He can't what? Tell everyone that you're his daughter. Tell everyone that he slept with me when I was just eighteen," Melinda said, tossing the rag down into the bucket at the foot of the bed. She paused. "Maybe you should start becoming more thankful to Justin for being your father, your real father, and for taking us into his home, a mansion no less, and allowing us to become his family." Melinda grabbed the rag from the bucket. "Here." Carefully, so as not to stain her own red dress, Melinda tossed Nia the rag. Bloody water splashed onto Nia's white nightgown. "You can clean up your own mess," Melinda said, beginning to leave, adding, "You need to get your act together, Nia. Others won't do it for you..." Melinda paused, turned back, and said, "I heard about you dancing at a club. But, you know what, Nia? You're nineteen, now. You're old enough to make your own decisions. If you want to be that kind off dancer, that's great. It's your life. All I'm asking is that you show some respect while we're in his house." Melinda stormed to the bedroom door and placed her hand on a golden dragon handle.

"Mom." Her mother paused. "Did you love him?"

Melinda only partially looked back. "Yes. I did... your man of God." She turned all the way around, facing Nia. "And, in a way, I will always love him, even through all the pain."

"Then what happened? Why didn't you..." Nia started to say.

"Why didn't we what?" Melinda asked. "Run off together? He's a priest, remember.

When they found out I was pregnant they tried to cover everything up. They tried to make me give you up for adoption; pretend the whole thing never happened. Someone even suggested an abortion. But I wouldn't let them take you away from me or let you end up in the bottom of some..." Melinda briefly glanced down at the bucket of bloody water. She looked back up at the white curtain by the balcony moving with a gentle breeze.

"But I will always remember him that day he left. He was standing there by the fountain within a garden of a small chapel with the most beautiful sunset I've ever seen, looking so strong and confident, as if he could make all my dreams come true. I always thought that I'd see him there at that garden again some day. And we would fall in love again. I often wonder what would have happened if I didn't get pregnant, if Philip and I would be..." She paused, looking over at Nia. "But of course, you wouldn't be here."

Melinda approached, standing over her, looking down at the ice pack covered in blood upon her wrists. Nia put the icepacks on her dressing table. The bleeding had stopped, or so Nia thought. "And look at you, Nia. Just look at you. Well, why should I be surprised. Your conception was tainted, why not your life. And it's ironic. I rejected having an abortion, and now you try to kill yourself." Melinda regained her composure. She said again sternly, "Make sure you get all the stains out." Melinda glanced at Nia's nightgown, a circular stain in the side.

Melinda left without another word, closing the bedroom door behind her. The white lace curtain became still, hanging motionless, as if trapped in time, waiting for another breeze to bring it back to life. "I'm sorry I'm tainted," Nia said, curling up her legs underneath the short nightgown, hearing her mother slam the front door, get in her car and drive away down a gravel driveway.

After putting the rag on the dressing table, Nia stood up and untied her nightgown, letting it fall to her feet. Naked, she stepped out of it. She picked up her nightgown, got on the floor and put it underneath her bed. Picking up the rag, now naked, she began scrubbing the bloodstains in the carpet. Strangely, one stain looked like the image of a rose, like the one Joshua had given her. She touched it with a brief smile, pausing, glancing toward the balcony remembering his touch... The door of her bedroom suddenly opened. Her stepfather, still wearing his gray business suit, stood in the doorway. She did not hear him come in as she continued scrubbing. He quietly locked the door behind him as he entered and smiled. Nia's bare bottom was raised in the air, her legs wide apart, on her hands and knees on the floor as she scrubbed by the side of her bed..

She felt a stinging slap and turned her head looking up. "You've been a bad girl," he said softly, standing over her. He pulled her back toward him by the back of her hair. She did not struggle. She slide back, remaining on her knees, with her head back, clutching the bloody rag.

"Please. No. Not now, not again," Nia pleaded.

"Never tell me no, my sweet whore of Babylon. You are mine to use... It is my right," her stepfather, the senator said, caressing her with his ruby ring on his left index finger, leaving small scratches as if marking a path, continuing, moving deeper into the woods.

Glancing back from beneath her long dangling hair, she fought nausea as she looked at her attacker's body. All she could do was close her eyes and clench both her fists, one hand strangling tighter the bloody rag as Joshua did with his *clasped hand*. Feeling his rage, she let out a gasp followed by a louder one as the *attack* became more vicious, more threatening to the soul.

"Ow! You're hurting me! She cried out as he *bar armed* her arms behind her back. He then took hold of her wrists, pulling them father up behind her back. Licking her dried blood on her wrists, he began ravaging her as a predator its prey. The eyes of the wolf, the panting breaths, the charge up a moonlit path...

Nia struggled to break free, momentarily squirming out from beneath him as he let go, frantically attempting to crawl away. It was if he was toying with her; as he quickly dove again upon her, pushing her face into the bloody carpet, into the image of the bloodstain resembling Joshua's rose. As she continued to squirm, briefly glancing back, she saw his eyes, a fierceness not of this world, a darkness swallowing light. Pulling her wrists back farther up behind back, her deep gasps slowly turn to high pitched; shallow groans as he reopened her clotted wounds on her wrists with his teeth, rubbing his face in her blood as it oozed out. It tasted metallic, as he tried to suck up every drop, engulfing his thirst for domination over her.

She could feel each beat of her heart, the pounding of her chest. The smell of her blood permeated around them, staining the air as a darkened perfume blended with lust and desire. He raised his head up; it was smeared in her blood as the victorious predator after the hunt. The fear of his power made her body quiver as her gasps for breath, the taste of her blood; all gave him a greater sense of control over her that exhilarated him, empowering him with an aura of darkness. Time seemed to be endless with the white curtains blowing back as Nia remained on her knees, her legs spread apart, feeling his *panting* breaths upon her neck. With a slight turn, he softly and meticulously began to daub her blood around her neck with his tongue.

Suddenly, she heard her mother's car return up the gravel driveway, followed by the opening and slamming of the front door. "Justin!" Melinda called out for the senator from a marble foyer below, making her way up a long circular staircase beneath a large illuminated crystal draped chandelier.

With his hands squeezing Nia's breasts, he shouted, "I'm up here!" "No." Nia pleaded, struggling again to break free. The golden dragon door handle began to move...

"It's locked," Melinda said, adding appearing confused, "Justin? Are you in there?" "Yes. I'll be there in a second," he said, deep inside her, still riding her as she crawled frantically a few feet from the side of the bed. After two final violent thrusts, he withdrew, letting her go with her blood appearing more visible upon his face. "Coming," he said, pulling his pants back up.

Nia was horrified, still naked upon the floor, as he wiped her blood off his face with the bloody rag and went over, beginning to unlock the golden dragon handle. Nia crawled back to her bed and retrieved her nightgown underneath it. She didn't have time to put it on, so she just covered herself with it, curling up on the floor as her mother shoved open the bedroom door.

"What's going on?" Melinda asked, bursting in, noticing Nia curled up in the corner on the floor, shaking, her wrists clotting again, oozing a little with tiny bits of pieces of blood.

"We were just having a talk," he said as Melinda entered further. "I was trying to help her," he added, holding up the wet rag. Melinda went over to her, bent down, and looked at her wrists. "They're still bleeding?" She reached up on the dressing table. The icepacks were still cold. She took them and angrily put them on Nia's wrists. She got up and walked back to the senator.

"Do you want to take her to the hospital? See a doctor? I was worried about her. When I came up here, I found her like this. I told her to get dressed. But, she refused," He said, as Nia attempted to cover herself, along with her emotions, with just her skimpy nightgown - silent.

"Is that true, Nia?" Melinda asked.

"Yes," Nia hesitantly said in a whisper, looking blankly away. "What?" Melinda followed.

"Yes," Nia said more clearly, adding, "He found me here, like this."

"So, you decided to prance around naked in front of your stepfather? How could you, Nia. What were you thinking?" Melinda began pacing, running her fingers up her forehead and through her hair. She scratched her cheek and bit a nail. She paused, then answered, "With your election almost here, I don't want your campaign to get hurt by my daughter's mental issues. No. She will be fine, just fine. I'll make sure of that. No need to take her to a hospital."

Melinda looked down at the bloodstains still on the carpet and then back at Nia. Nia covered herself more with her nightgown.

"I'm sorry about all this, Justin. It's just that she's been going through some rough times lately. You know. Adjusting to living here and with school and all."

"I understand. That's what we were talking about. Weren't we, Nia? I think we both understand each others' position now, our roles in this house," he said smiling, looking down at Nia as she raised her nightgown further up, covering her chest while trying to balance the icepacks on her wrists. Nia's eyes looked back down, away from his mocking grin. "Don't worry. I won't let her ruin the election or this house," Melinda said to him. She turned back to Nia. "I thought I told you to have everything cleaned up. Look at the rug. And look at your nightgown." Her mother walked over and shockingly ripped the nightgown from her.

"Mom!" Nia cried out, thoroughly embarrassed, curling up even more, completely naked before them, trying to cover herself up with her arms.

"I thought you wanted to show off," Melinda snipped with a toss of her head.

The senator did not leave but continued smiling and staring. Melinda took the wet rag from the senator's hand and tossed it over into the bucket.

"Clean it up! Now! This instant!" Melinda shouted, pointing to the stains. "You're going to respect the senator and this house!"

"Can't I get dressed, have my nightgown back?" Nia pleaded.

"No!" Melinda commanded, shaking the nightgown. "Maybe this way you'll finally learn," Melinda replied, looking back to the senator, adding, "You embarrassed us. Now, we'll embarrass you." The senator nodded and said, "So, approved. Here, here Melinda. Well said."

A maid appeared standing in the bedroom doorway. "Ma'am, do you need help?" The maid asked Melinda as she looked over at Nia still curled up, refusing to move in her misery.

"No. Thank you, Maria," the senator said, adding, "We have things under control, here." He nodded again his approval to Melinda while keeping his eyes on Nia. "Wait. Maybe you can come in and tell Nia how to do it, how to get the stains out." He gestured for Maria to come in.

Bewildered, Maria, a mature Hispanic woman, walked over and stood by Nia with the senator and Melinda watching.

"Well. Are you going to get started or what?" Melinda said coldly to Nia.

"But Mom," Nia said again, not wanting to get up. "No. No. This is good. Maybe some humiliation will teach you a lesson," Melinda replied.

"You heard your mother," the senator sternly said. "Tell her, Maria," the senator added. "But is she alright?" Maria asked hesitantly, adding, "Is all of this this child's blood?" "Just tell her!" The senator tersely commanded. Frightened and angered, Nia got back onto her hands and knees and took the rag out of the bucket.

"You have to move in circles. It helps to dilute the stain," Maria said softly as Nia scrubbed the floor, naked, with the three of them watching. Maria looked concerned and embarrassed for Nia. But Nia's mother's face was set cold and firm, like the icepacks cast aside on the floor.

"You're doing very well, Nia," he said with a grin.

Nia finally threw the rag into the bucket, got up, ran out of the bedroom and down the hall past a butler carrying a tray of food into a bathroom. She shut the door, locking it. With her back leaning against the door, she slid down to the cold bathroom tile floor, degraded, sobbing.

"Maybe I shouldn't have..." Melinda started to say.

"You did what was right. Remain firm. She will come around," the senator responded.

Melinda turned away from the senator and went after Nia. The senator, shaking his head with his mocking grin, walked back down a long, spiraling staircase. Portraits of eighteenth century noblemen aligned the walls, intricately decorated, arising high to a golden dome surrounded by a white marble of the vast foyer. From the dome hung a large chandelier with many pieces of crystal, as if tinsel, painstakingly but beautifully placed upon a Christmas tree.

As she stood, leaning up against the closed bathroom door on the other side of Nia, Melinda remembered Christmases of the past the past when they sometimes didn't have enough money even to buy a tree, when it was just her and Nia. Nia had always found a way, though, to give her a Christmas gift, even if she had to make it herself. Her mother touched a small pin on her dress of an angel; one Nia had made for her.

"Nia, I'm sorry," Melinda spoke to her through the door. Nia was still crying on the other side, sitting up against it, her knees curled up to her chest, her wrists still marked in seeping red.

"Leave me alone. Why can't you all just leave me alone," Nia said.

"I'm sorry," Melinda said again. "It's just that you get me so mad sometimes. I'm always looking for something, something that will, help. I guess it's the Irish in me. My temper. You have a temper too. Right?"

"Mom," Nia said wiping away her tears. "You went too far this time. You know? I mean, I love you. But you don't know what you've done this time. The senator..." Nia started to say, trying to control her shaking voice.

"What about the senator?" Melinda asked.

"He's not the man you think he is," Nia said, touching her wrists. The blood clotted, bleeding stopped.

"Look. I don't know what came over me. I guess, I thought, by embarrassing you like that it might help in some way. I'm sorry. I'm just sorry. I don't know what else you want me to say."

"Why don't you believe me?" Nia asked.

"The senator... He's a fine man, Nia. An upstanding man."

Resigned, Nia gave in. "Just leave me alone, for now. Alright Mom?"

"Alright. I'll be downstairs if you need me, in the study. I'm sorry, Nia. I really am."

In the study, the senator was sitting in a high back brown leather chair reading a book. He looked at Nia's mother entering over his reading glasses.

"Well. I really screwed that up," Melinda said to him.

"Nonsense, Melinda," he replied, adding, "Give her time. She will come around. Just continue to be firm."

"I really embarrassed her. I shouldn't have done that, in front of you and all," Melinda said.The senator slammed the book shut in his hand. "End Times" was the title. He remained silent a moment, then briefly looked over at the large stone fireplace. It mysteriously became lit; first with a flicker of a small flame, then with a blaze that quickly engulfed three logs within it. "That's strange," Melinda responded to the arising fire, the glow flickering across her face.

The senator looked back to her with the reflection of the fire in his eyes and said, "I don't think she really wanted to kill herself. Do you? She probably did it to just get attention."

"It seemed more real this time," Melinda answered staring at the fire. "I hope she forgives me. Maybe she should see a doctor," she said again.

When Melinda turned around, the senator startled her, standing before her. Without a word, he began unbuttoning the pearl button at the neck of her dress. For a moment, they remained in silence as he continued unbuttoning the others that followed. Melinda was learning her role in the house, a submissive one, as she gazed up at him waiting for him to take control.

"Nia is a young woman. All women like attention, being desired, being wanted," The senator said, drawing her close, caressing her hair.

"What do you mean?" Melinda said with a gasp, reaching up gently to pull his hand away. Regaining her composure, looking away from the fiery reflections in his eyes, she added, "I changed my mind. I want her to see a doctor. I think it would be best."

He ran his finger across her lips. "Alright. I'll find her one. It will be alright," he replied, gazing back into her eyes, kissing her, tasting her neck... As he continued undressing her, Melinda collapsed into his control; sinking into the vast darkness of his strength. Suddenly, she looked up, attempting to point over toward the open door of the study leading to the marble foyer. But he continued whispering, "It will be alright," as he raised her dress further up from the hem beneath her knees, taking it off of her over her head. Lifting her up, her feet slipping out of her red heels, he carried her over and placed her down on top of a piano near the open doorway. Undoing the pearl button of her blouse, slowly removing all of her clothes as the fire burned in the large stone fireplace. Completely naked, he began kissing her lips, slithering his tongue deep into her mouth, stretching her out atop the piano... Masterfully, as if a musician, he caressed her, moving his ruby ring back and forth across the nipples of her breasts; up and down her exposed body. Totally vulnerable to his touch, she began to gasp for breath, each time more feverishly, her feet striking the keys of the piano, hitting eery notes that echoed out into the foyer.

Suddenly, she heard the front door of the mansion slam shut. Concerned, with a blaze of panic, she attempted to get up. Yet, he pushed her back down, relentless in his pursuit, the fire arising higher, as she began to wrench and writhe, her toes hitting more rapidly the keys on the piano, sounding off rapid notes. Barely able to keep her eyes open, she struggled and looked over at the ajar study doorway. There, discretely watching was the butler, holding a tray, giving her a demeaning smile. Balancing the tray, he reached in and gently closed the study's door.

A few days later, Nia, wearing gloves to cover her bandages and a jacket with "UCLA" monogrammed on it, approached Father Gabe's car in the parking lot next to the church. She momentarily looked up at the cross atop its bell tower, reaching upward into the night's sky. It began to ring. She saw Father Gabe's marked parking spot. She walked over and placed a note on his car beneath the windshield wiper. She turned. Ms. Gongel was standing right behind her.

"Did you come back to work?" Ms. Gongel asked. "Ms. Gongel," Nia paused. "I really appreciate you giving me a job and everything; to help me pay for school. But I don't think I want to strip anymore. I don't feel right...being naked... in front of people." Nia wrapped her jacket tighter around her adding, "I'm sorry."

Ms. Gongel let out a loud laugh. "You don't feel right being naked in front of people? You've been a slut for two years and now you all of a sudden don't feel right being naked?"

Nia turned to walk away. Ms. Gongel grabbed her by the arm and pulled her back.

"A couple of phone calls and I can bring down you and your whole family. I'm sure your father won't be pleased when he finds out about your life as a stripper. And I'm sure it will make good news footage, especially since your dear father has become known as the 'voice of morality.' I can see it now. A picture of you swinging around a pole in your G-string on the front page of every news site and the lead story on every news show in town."

"He's not my father," Nia whispered. Ms. Gongel let go of her arm. Nia looked down, confused, then back up at her. "Why do you need me so much? You have other girls."

Ms Gongel reached up and stroked back her long black hair, exposing her downward eyes. "Oh honey, you're are one of my girls now, one of my favorites. I don't let go too easily. You know how I like to take care of my girls..." Ms. Gongel pulled her hand away. Nia looked back down, her hair falling partially over her eyes.

"Tomorrow night a friend of mine is having a private bachelor party. I'd like you to come with me. I'll drive. They put in a special request for you do it. We can make a lot of money," Ms. Gongel said, reaching back up and gently brushing back Nia's hair away from her eyes as Nia looked back up at her.

"They?" Nia replied, adding, "Who are they?" Ms. Gongel just smiled.

Father Gabe, inside the church, walked down a long corridor with marble walls and red floor carpeting, past a large statue of the Pieta. He paused, before it, then fell to his knees.

Ms. Gongel watched Nia drive away. She sensed someone behind her. She turned. "What's your problem," Ms. Gongel said. The old woman who gave Joshua the rose stood behind her, staring at her with an angered look. "Why can't you leave that child alone," she said.

"Don't you have some trash cans to dig into or something," Ms. Gongel said to her as she passed the old woman, forcibly brushing up against the old woman's shoulder. The old woman turned, and without fear or malice, stared into her eyes. "Woe to those who try to take a way a child from God," The Old Woman said. The church's bells rang out.

Ms. Gongel shook her head in disgust and turned. Taking a few steps away, she stopped, and turned back. The old woman was gone, nowhere to be seen as Father Gabe's image appeared coming toward her, forming it seemed, from a crossing haze.

"Did you see an old woman? She was right here, a second ago," Ms. Gongel said to him.

Father Gabe looked lovingly into her eyes with a smile, "You mean, Mary? He nodded and went toward his car, noticing the note on his windshield.

"You know her?" Ms. Gongel asked.

"Many people do," Father Gabe replied, lifting up the note, adding, "You should, too, if it's not too late." Ms. Gongel, appearing confused, silently walked away... Father Gabe, hesitantly, read the note, *Need your help. I can't seem to find the right key.* He looked down and saw Nia's locket had fallen on the ground. He picked it up, brushed it off, gazed over at the club, then up at the bell tower of the church. It sounded out as inside the club, Nia swung half-naked around a brass pole in a smoke-cast room of sin.

Chapter 6

"There he is! College student!" Tim called out in the driveway, standing by his secret project as Joshua walked out onto the front porch with notebooks, pens, and pencils in hand. On his tee-shirt was still "You've Got to Believe." Their father sat waiting for Joshua behind the steering wheel of Tim's truck. The passenger side door was open.

Tim put down the hammer and walked over to the open door to meet Joshua as he started to get in. "This is it, Joshua. Your day has come," Tim said to him with smile. Tim shut the door. "Now, remember, you're going to school for one thing, to meet nice babes." Tim paused. "Tim glanced over at their father nervously clutching the steering wheel, staring straight ahead. He looked back to Joshua. "Now don't let Dad go four wheel driving or anything."

"Make sure you take it slow. Please, Dad. I'm still paying for this truck," Tim added. "You act like I haven't driven in years," their father replied.

"You haven't," Tim answered, then raised up his hand. "Dad. How many fingers am I holding up?" Tim laughed. Their father didn't.

"You have everything?" His father asked. Joshua nodded, looking down at his notebooks, pens, and pencils.

"God bless you and good luck!" Tim cried out.

Joshua gave the thumbs up sign as they drove away. With reflections of the red cherry tree passing across their windshield, Joshua and his father both felt this turning point in their lives. Not a word was spoken, though, as they drove down the mountain with images of the leaves turning to the color of an imaginary golden brown of fall—just before winter, just before they go to sleep. Joshua and his father were almost to the bridge before the silence became as apparent as the glare of sunlight partially blinding them upon the glass. Driving over the bridge, spanning high above the river, the sun's rays reflected out to an seemingly endless horizon. For a moment, the sun's rays passed through the rungs of the steel bridge and appeared to change into colors as Joshua almost opened his clasped right hand. His father looked over to him, at his tee- shirt. "Do you really believe, Joshua?" His father asked him at the highest point of the bridge.

Joshua turned to him and said, "Sometimes."

"Because I believe you can do anything. Any dream you wish for can come true," his father said to him, adding, "If you just believe." As they drove over the bridge, the bright sun's rays faded to that of a lamp turned down a notch. In that one brief moment that had passed high atop the bridge, it was if heaven had opened up and miraculously drawn Joshua and his father closer. Joshua would always remember this moment, and each time passing over this bridge, at the highest point, he would pray while looking to the sky.

"U.C.L.A." A large banner was draped over the city's street. They passed under it as they both saw the Apollo being built down the road in the distance, reaching upward as if almost touching the sky.

"Look at that. They have the roof up finally," his father said, adding, "Nationals are supposed to be here this year." Joshua remained silent. His father pulled the truck over to the side of the road and parked next to a lunch truck. Joshua began to get out.

"Your brother said that he would pick you up in front of Pierson Hall after work. Here.

This should be enough for your books," his father said to him handing him money. Joshua got all the way out. "If you have time, Coach Fanelli would like to see you..." his father began to say through the open door as Joshua shut it. Joshua just nodded and walked away. As he stopped and turned, watching his father drive away, he looked ahead toward the Apollo. Looking across the street there was Pierson

Hall, a large building looking like two that were connected. In front of it was a large statue of two gymnasts; a naked man holding up a naked woman by one hand over head. Her feet were pointing toward the clouds with his arm outstretched, pushing her closer.

They seemed to be trying to touch the sky as Joshua looked back to the Apollo's large dome, seemingly even higher than the skyscrapers of the city. Strangely, the rays of light that he had felt atop the bridge appeared to have set the golden dome ablaze. He looked back down. His father was gone.

A few yards away from the lunch truck there was a tall black man wearing a long red leather coat in spite of the warm day in front of a small table display of watches and jewelry. The man was arguing with an older black woman whose only color was a scarlet colored scarf tied around her head. The man was hovering over her with gold watches up his wrists and gold chains around his neck, reflecting the red color of her scarf. The woman was in rags. The man, in gold, raised his fist.

"I want my watch back!" The lady screamed.

"I don't have your watch, lady! Get out of my face!" The man screamed back, towering over her.

"You have my son's watch, the one he gave me, and I want it now! It's all I have left! He died in Vietnam!"

The man measured his fist on her chin. He hit her. She fell to the ground. She didn't say another word as the man calmly turned, resuming his business as if nothing had happened.

Joshua ran over to her as she struggled to get up. Bending down, taking her by the arm, Joshua gently helped her to her feet. The woman got up but remained silent. Her eyes looked stunned as Joshua picked up her bags and gently placed them back into her hand. She only gave Joshua a slight glance as she shuffled away, dabbing at her bleeding lip. The man in the long red leather coat approached Joshua. "You got a problem? Who do you think you are helping that woman."

Joshua put down his notebooks, pens, and pencils, and slowly raised his fists. "You want to fight, punk? Alright. Come on then sucker," the man said to Joshua.

Taking off all his gold watches and, carefully, his red coat, the man turned with his fists raised as a small crowd formed around them. The man started to dance as a boxer on his toes, faking jabs in the air. The woman turned and looked. The man swung at Joshua's head. Joshua ducked, grabbed him, lifted him up, and with one swift throw, slammed the man to the city's pavement. The small crowd applauded. The woman stared out and up to the golden dome of the Apollo. She thought she heard an echo of a resonating hallow voice above it.

"Lucky shot," the man said, wiping away a small amount of blood trickling from his mouth, trying to arise.

"I'm sorry," Joshua said, going over and helping him to his feet.

"Man. You're some strong dude, alright," the man said to Joshua, brushing off his clothes and putting his red coat back on. Taking something from the table, he tossed it to Joshua.

"Joshua caught it and ran after the woman with the scarf. Catching up to her, Joshua gave her what the man, destiny, had thrown to him. It was her watch. "To Mom. Love Always, Ed," was visible as she held it up for him to see.

"Thank you," the woman said. Crying, she added, "His body was never returned. They said he was missing. But I know he died. Vietnam. It was a horrible war," The woman said.

"My uncle fought in that war," Joshua replied as the woman nodded and walked away.

Joshua turned and went past a series of lunch trucks, all in a line according to an ethnic group, Chinese, Japanese, Italian. He noticed a young man, appearing like him, wearing jeans and a tee-shirt, "Oklahoma Wrestling." The young man, although large and muscular was being pushed out of his place at the head of a line in front of one of the lunch trucks.

"Could I have that, please? That one over there! Excuse me! Could I have a pretzel, please! Excuse me!" Everyone kept ignoring him, shoving him aside until he finally was pushed all the way to the end of the line. As Joshua passed, they bumped into each other. Joshua's pens and notebooks fell from his hands.

"Sorry," the young man said to Joshua as he helped Joshua pick them up. The young man noticed Joshua's name written on top of one of the notebooks—"Joshua Kahn."

"Well, hello, Joshua Kahn. My name is Mike. Are you a teacher?" "A student," Joshua replied and began to walk away.

Mike followed. "Hey, wait up. I'm a student too. Are you going to register?" Mike called out, catching up to him. Joshua nodded.

"Nothing like waiting until the last minute to register. You mind if I tag along? I have to register too," Mike said.

"Alright," Joshua replied.

"Good. I don't know anyone yet. I just got here. It was between here and Oklahoma. I got a wrestling scholarship at both places. But I decided on here because of Coach Villecco." Mike paused then continued. "Joshua Kahn. I know about a Tim Kahn who used to wrestle here a while ago. I don't suppose..." Joshua looked at him. "Are you related to him?" Mike asked.

"My brother," Joshua responded.

"How about that. Tim Kahn's brother. Man, two more seconds and he would have won Nationals. That was U.C.L.A.'s best shot to have its first National Champ ever. It's a shame about his arm breaking like that in those final seconds. How is he doing after all these years?"

"Alright. I guess," Joshua replied, trying to walk away. "Are you a wrestler?" Mike asked.

"Used to be," Joshua replied, walking faster. But Mike kept up with him. He reached out his hand to shake Joshua's. "All my friends call me Mikey, because they think I look like that little kid Mikey. You know, the one on the coral box. I eat a lot of Life too," adding with a hearty laugh, "That is when I'm not cutting weight."

Joshua shook his hand. "I'm Joshua." "So are you a senior?" Mikey asked.

"A freshmen," Joshua replied as they stood before Conwell Hall, a large stone building with many cement steps arising toward the front doorway of two large, arched, medieval- appearing wooden doors with black iron handles.

"It looks like a castle," Mikey said. "This is where we're supposed to register," Joshua replied as he and Mikey began their quest, climbing the high stone steps.

"What have you been doing, before coming to college?" Mikey asked. "Trying to reach the top," Joshua said.

"Of what?" Mikey asked.

"A mountain," Joshua said as they stood at the top of the high steps.

Inside at a counter of the bursar's office, Nia gazed at her tuition bill. "Three thousand two-thousand dollars?" Nia asked a woman on the other side of the glass. The woman with glasses at the end of her nose through a small window nodded and added, "You have to pay that within ten days, or you will be washed out of all your classes." Nia, upset, took the bill and walked away, running her hand up her brow and her fingers back through her long hair, appearing distraught and confused, the high-arched ceilings swirling above her. "How am I going to pay this?" She asked herself, barely above a whisper. She folded up the bill and stashed it inside her jean jacket.

Mickey and Joshua stood just inside the Conwell Hall beneath a stone vestibule. On the walls on each side were coats of arms adorned with lions and dragons. Beneath the dragon coat of arms was a suit of armor about Joshua's height and size. They looked out, gazing down at all the long lines of students waiting to register. Music was playing softly over an intercom.

"You know what we're supposed to do now?" Mikey asked. "I guess get in a line," Joshua answered.

Mikey and Joshua walked down the marble steps and stood confused in the middle of the hall. A female student with long red hair and a pin on her lapel, "Welcome to U.C.L.A." approached them.

"Hi. You're new, aren't you?" She said to Mikey. "So is he," Mikey replied, pointing to Joshua.

The young woman looked at Joshua and said, "Do I know you? You look familiar." Joshua shook his head. The young woman continued. "Here. You have to fill out these cards using the registration number, section number, and course code from this book." She handed them the registration cards and booklet. "Your advisor should have mailed you the list of classes.

After you fill out this card, take it to line three, then take the card that they will give you to line two along with this one. The one you will get after you turn in that one you will have to get validated by your advisor, who, for freshmen, is in line seven. Then take everything back to line one. After all of that, you have to go down to the basement to get your registration confirmed.

And if they tell you downstairs that it is not confirmed, you have to come back up here and start all over again. Once confirmed, you'll get your bill at the bursar's office. Make sure you pay within ten days. They're pretty efficient on washing you out of your classes. Got it? Good." She turned away and approached another group of students. "Hi. Welcome to UCLA..."

"I didn't get all that," Joshua said.

"Surprisingly, I did," Mikey said. "My father has a photographic memory. I inherited the audio part." Mikey said, adding, "I guess that's good. It took me a while, once, to get that old song, *Don't Stop Believing*, out of my head." *Don't Stop Believing* played over the intercom from an oldies radio station as Joshua and Mikey began filling out their cards with their schedules and walking through all the lines. Mikey took a look at Joshua's cards.

"Chemistry, calculus, statistics, electrical engineering, and physics? Are you some kind of genius or something?" Mikey asked.

Villecco, U.C.L.A's wrestling coach, muscular, overly confident, walked toward them. Villecco also had blond hair and blue eyes, in his twenties, with a a shadow of beard's growth.

"Hey, there's coach," Mikey said with a slight wave. Villecco walked over and stood before them. Joshua turned away.

"Did you get that list of classes we sent you?" Villecco asked Mikey, taking the registration cards out of Mikey's hands and looking them over.

"Yes. Oh, do you know Tim Kahn's brother? You must. That's when you wrestled, right, coach?" Mikey pointed to Joshua. Joshua slowly turned back but kept his head down.

"After all this time, you're back," Villecco said, adding while looking at Joshua, "You really let yourself go." Villecco paused, then said, "You shouldn't hang around losers Mikey. Losing's contagious." Villecco handed Mikey back his cards. "Practice begins at two, Mikey," Villecco said angrily, walking away.

"Is he mad at you or something?" Mikey asked Joshua.

Joshua didn't answer. He just continued filling out his cards. When Joshua and Mikey got at the front of line number two, a female student was sitting down at a long table in front of them. "May I help you?" She asked Joshua. Joshua handed her his cards.

"Let's see. Well, chemistry is closed. Calculus is closed. I'm sorry, but the only class out of these we can get you into now is physics," she said to him, handing back his cards.

"But I have to take those classes. I want to be an engineer... like my father," Joshua said to her. "I'm sorry. You can pick other classes," she replied.

"Come on, Joshua. I'll help you pick out some other ones," Mikey said to him as they got out of line. Concerned for Joshua, Mikey didn't even give her his cards to register. "We'll be back," Mikey simply replied to her.

"My father was an engineer. I want to be like him," Joshua said to Mikey as he led Joshua over to a small table by a tall, circular, marble stone post reaching upward to the high ceiling of the large hall. Mikey leafed through the course booklet on the small table as Joshua leaned up against the marble post.

"I failed physics three times. Why couldn't that one be closed?" Joshua said.

"Don't give up. Hey, your Tim Kahn's brother, remember. Here, Joshua. Here's a class you can take," Mikey said to him. Joshua looked down at the booklet where Mikey circled with his pen. "History, 'The Vietnam War.'" Joshua slid off the post thinking of his uncle, Michael. He had overheard his brother, Michael, read his letters from Vietnam to their father.

"You alright?" Mikey asked. Joshua nodded. "Is that a good one?" Mikey asked. Joshua nodded again. Mikey flipped to another page. "Here's one."

"Disco Dance?" Joshua asked.

"It's making a comeback in Oklahoma," Mikey said, adding, "We're on a roll." Mikey smiled. "Let's pick two more," he said while flipping through the registration book. After Joshua and Mikey got done registering, they paused outside at the bottom of the steps of Conwell Hall.

"Do you want to come watch wrestling practice?" Mikey asked Joshua, adding, "I should have been there a half hour ago."

Joshua shook his head. "No. I have to go to the bookstore."

"Well. It was nice meeting you, Joshua Kahn," Mikey said adding, "If you have time later, why don't you stop by practice? We'll probably still be there. I heard Villecco likes to have his team practice up to seven hours a day. I guess he has a Dave Gable complex."

Joshua nodded, turned, and walked away as Mikey ran toward Pierson Hall where the wrestling room was. When Joshua entered the bookstore, he walked to the back and stood behind a student who was being waited on by a young woman, Sarah, with short brown hair and brown eyes behind a counter. Maureen handed the young man in front of Joshua his books.

"Alright. That's organic chemistry, nuclear physics, and advanced statistics," Sarah said to this student. She then called out, "Next!"

Joshua stepped up and handed her the list of his classes.

"Let's see. Physics 101, History 211 'The Vietnam War,' Disco Dance," she smiled, continuing, "Fencing, and Male Anatomical Figure Drawing. You like posing nude?" She asked, looking briefly back up at Joshua as she began shuffling through an index.

"I thought I was going to draw," Joshua replied.

"Oh, right," Sarah said, still smiling, adding, "Ms. Dominique, the art professor, I think you'll like her. You look like her type of... student."

"What's that supposed to mean," Joshua replied with a quizzical look.

Another young woman, Maureen, laughed, adding, "Yes. He appears to be, her type. Sarah. Do you need help? Maureen approached from behind the counter with long black hair braided in the back and looked over Sarah's shoulder at Joshua's cards. They laughed, smiled at each other, and then briefly looked at Joshua, checking him out.

"Yes. Ms. Dominique will definitely like him," Maureen said. "We're both in that class.

She will probably want you to model, not just draw. Right, Maurine," Sarah confirmed. "Most... definitely," Maurine replied, still checking him out. Sarah left, going far back behind the counter to rows of books.

Joshua turned away from Maurine's leering eyes. He saw a key ring—"U.C.L.A. Father"—hanging on a small copper rack behind him. He lifted it off, turned back around, and placed it down on the counter to buy. Sarah returned.

"Alright. Here are the two physics books, one text, and one lab book. And this is your text for your history class," Sarah said. On the cover was a picture of a Vietnam soldier holding a dying little girl. Sarah added, "You'll also need a sword for your fencing class, but your professor will probably provide you with one. We don't sell them here." Sarah let out a gasp of a laugh while glancing over at Maurine, who joined in with a laugh too. "But of course, you don't need a book for Disco Dance." Sarah paused and then finally said, "I suppose you want to be a disco dance knight or something?"

Joshua glanced behind her on the wall at a poster of a knight riding a white horse and slaying a dragon. He paid for his three books and the key ring. "Thank you," Joshua said.

Sarah smiled, put everything into a small white plastic bag and handed it to him. After Joshua left, Maurine leaned on the counter and asked Sarah. "So do you think he will do it?"

"It's possible," Sarah replied, adding, "Yes... I think he will."

"It will be fun watching what Dominique does to him," Maurine said, adding, "You remember what she did to the last one? The one that seemed crazy."

"I remember. He went through a lot. Didn't he end up transferring out or being admitted to a psychiatric hospital or something?"

Gripping his books, Joshua headed toward Pierson Hall. He walked between two tall stone buildings that together changed a gentle breeze into a savage wind, creating a wind tunnel. Blowing his hair all the way back and the books in the bag almost from his hands, Joshua leaned forward into this seemingly ferocious wind, feeling as if a forbidden valley was closing in on him. The key ring fell out of the bag. Joshua reached down to pick it back up, clasping it in his right hand that he briefly opened again. When Joshua got to Pierson Hall, he momentarily stood before the image of stone looking up at the statue of a male gymnast holding up an equally grand female gymnast overhead with her feet pointing to the sky. The artist seemed to have captured a victorious moment in time. Upon entering, Joshua walked down a long, dark hallway. He could hear Villecco's calls echoing from the wrestling room, as if the lifeless stone images of the past in his mind coming to life. Passing by a series of team pictures lined up on the walls, Joshua stopped and looked at one that captured his past. In the picture he saw his brother and on the other side, Villecco. Looking at Villecco's stone imaged stare, it was as if nothing had changed, nothing was ever gone. Tim had just moved through a parallel wind as quickly and quietly as the one that had erupted between the two buildings. Inside the wrestling room, Villecco paced at the front of young men engaged in wrestling on four large red mats spanning the room. The slams of bodies echoed out into the dark hallway. Outside the room, two small windows were covered with a mist from the humidity, heat, and sweat of the wrestlers. Temperatures in the wrestling room were often over a hundred degrees to help the wrestlers dehydrate themselves to cut weight. Inside, with all the sweat, the mist created was only allowed to escape when the doors opened to the cool green hallway from the room of red. With the thunderous sounds of bodies slamming, groans of pain echoed across time as Joshua peered in.

Two wrestlers fell up against the door, causing Joshua to take a step back. Suddenly, the doors of the wrestling room flung open with the mist from the room barreling out as if carrying a prehistoric breath from another time. Joshua found himself, struggling not to be sucked in, standing tightly with his back up against a wall, that moment we must decide. A large wrestler, Tony Mantella, walked out of the haze into the hallway before Joshua, remaining motionless, as if suspended in time. Tony staggered toward the water fountain. Hovering over it, clasping his massive arms around it, he inhaled all the water he could.

"Tony! Get back in here!" Villecco screamed hanging out the doorway. He saw Joshua. He paused, taken back, and said, "What are you doing here." Mantella lumbered back inside. Villecco slammed the door, leaving Joshua standing alone in the hallway. Joshua slowly walked up and cautiously looked again through the small windows. The glass was still clear, but mist had begun to gather back on the panes. "Tony. Go with Carmel. He keeps dogging it. Ready.

Wrestle!" Villecco shouted. Villecco glanced back at Joshua looking in through the windows.

Carmel's grandparents were from Italy, but he had thick, dark hair cut straight across his forehead and brown slanted eyes that made him look a little Asian. He was slightly larger than Tony Mantella, the 177 lb. Wrestler. Carmel wrestled at 190 lb. He was smiling, as he often would, while wrestling Tony. But, of course, it could have been anyone. That's just how Carmel was. He never took wrestling too seriously even though he was one of the best in the country. He liked wrestling. It was just that he felt there were many more important things in life, like family. That's what his grandparents had taught him. And his smile, it always made Villecco mad.

"You're dogging it, Carmel! My grandmother moves faster than that! Come on! You wear underwear or panties? Come on! Move! Move!" Villecco called out.

"Come on, grandmom," Carmel said to Tony with a smile. Tony shot in. Carmel, with one graceful move, countered, throwing Tony to the mat.

Joshua walked back down the long, dark hallway and paused before the team picture from years ago, another dimension. He looked again at Villecco as back in the wrestling room Villecco was squared off about to wrestle Carmel. "Hey, Douglas! Pray for me!" Carmel jokingly shouted to a middle weight wrestler taking off his headgear, sweating profusely, sitting up against the wall on the mat next to him and starting to open his Bible.

"Keep your eyes on Jesus!" Douglas said, tossing his headgear down on the side as two wrestlers crashed down upon it. Villecco shot in and raised Carmel high over his head, throwing him down hard to the mat. Carmel was no longer smiling.

"The truth shall set you free!" Douglas called out as Villecco, on top, began to press Carmel's face further into the mat using his forearm on the back of Carmel's neck. Angered, Carmel started to wrestle more intensely. He escaped. He faced Villecco. It turned into a ferocious battle. As all the wrestlers in the room, all except for Douglas, began to wrestle at an intensified pace, Douglas read aloud from the Bible, shouting above all the body slams and groans. "It is I, Jesus, who sent my angel to you! I am the root and the descendant of David, the bright morning star! Let everyone who hears say 'Come!' Let everyone who is thirsty come! The one who testifies to these things say, 'Surely I am coming soon! Amen! Come, Lord Jesus!

Come!'"

A lightweight, Mitch, a 118 lb. Wrestler, African American, cried out to Douglas, as he momentarily escaped from his opponent, "Tell it like it is, brother!"

Mitch's opponent, a 134 lb. Wrestler, Cifanelli, also Italian, said, "We're probably the only team in the country with our own preacher." Douglas just smiled.

Another middle weight wrestler, Aikens, a 158 lb. Wrestler, very thin, but strong, appeared pale, seemingly lifeless. Yet, he had piercing blue eyes and a fiery reddish blond hair. Aiden was thrown up agains the wall, wrestling his opponent. He landed by Doug, still squatting up against *this same wall,* reading the Bible.

Douglas didn't even flinch as two bodies, one of them Aikens, crashed around him.

Remaining in a steadfast, unyielding aura of confidence, even though beneath them, Douglas just kept on reading silently to himself the Words of the Lord.

"Douglas. What are you doing?" Aikens, gathering himself, said to him. "You're in," he added as all three tried to uncoil themselves from the fall.

Aikens took the Bible from Douglas's hands, though, only briefly looking at it before putting it down. Douglas moved to the center of the mat and began to wrestle Aikens' previous opponent.

"What's a matter, Carmel! Can't beat an old man," Aikens called out.

Villecco had Carmel all twisted up with Carmel's legs spread wide apart, over his head.

"You look like my last date at Cif's party! You Yankees sure know how to throw a party!

All those girls wearing diapers and sucking liquor out of baby bottles."

Aikens laughed. Carmel returned a smile, adding, "Christine was so hot."

Downstairs in the training room, Coach Fanelli, a man with gray hair, in his late fifties, was showing an attractive female trainer with shoulder length blonde hair and green eyes, how to tape a knee of a male gymnast. She was wearing tight short shorts with her bottom cheeks partially exposed, having athletic, shapely, tan legs. It was Christine, Crystal's mother.

"Here, hon, it's like this? You have to leave enough room when wrapping the tape," Fanelli said to Christine, taping the gymnast's knee. Christine took the tape and followed Fanelli's lead as Joshua stood, unnoticed, in the doorway, watching.

Watching the athletes from other sports who were also in the training room, Joshua noticed that they didn't have bags under their eyes from dehydration and torture that could be seen on a wrestler's face. Even though some were covered with sweat, it seemed a pleasant form, not one of a disguising blood.

"You see? You have to leave enough room for circulation. You're doing fine. It just takes practice. You just have to do it again and again." Fanelli said to Christine as she continued to tape the gymnast's knee. The male gymnast gave Christine a smile and a wink. Christine rolled her eyes at the gymnast and responded to Fanelli, "Thanks. I think I've got it."

"You still work at the 'Doll House?'" The gymnast asked, adding, blowing her a kiss.

Christine, appearing embarrassed, put down the tape and walked away, passing Joshua standing in the doorway. Fanelli turned. "Joshua? Joshua. You've returned. Come on in." Joshua hesitantly entered the training room. "I've been speaking with your father for the past few months. It took some doing, however, we were able to get you back in. Did you have any trouble registering?" Fanelli asked. Joshua shook his head no. "Good. I'm sorry I didn't meet you over there, but I've been really busy breaking in new trainers. You get all the classes you wanted?" Joshua nodded.

"Your father said that you might want to help out with the team, maybe be a trainer," Fanelli said sympathetically. "I don't know..." Joshua started to answer.

Christine returned, brushing up against Joshua as she passed by him again. She reached up and softly touched his chest. "I'm sorry. Excuse me," she said to him, continuing by. Villecco abruptly entered the training room, aggressively pushing Christine aside, nearly knocking her down. She caught her balance by falling against one of the training tables.

"Hey!" Christine shouted toward Villecco.

"I don't want him here, Coach!" Villecco shouted at Fanelli, pointing toward Joshua. "It's not your decision," Fanelli replied, adding, "It's Joshua's and his father's."

Villecco moved closer, standing nose to nose with Fanelli.

"You're no longer the coach running this team," Villecco said to him.

"I went out of my way to get Joshua back in. And you're not going to stand in the way. If he wants to be a part of this team, he will be."

"And I went out of my way to get you a job as head trainer. And it wasn't easy, the way you screwed up," Villecco snapped back.

"That was five years ago. And you know that suspension was unfair. That kid hid that injury from me."

"Like Tim Kahn, twenty-seven years ago?" Villecco asked. Fanelli remained silent.

Joshua backed up into the doorway. Fanelli took the tape that was in his hands and threw it in the trash. "Look. For the thousandth time, when his arm broke, he wanted to go on. So I let him. There were only two more seconds left and..."

"He would have been U.C.L.A.'s first and only national champion," Villecco finished.

They both glanced simultaneously over at the doorway. Joshua was gone.

Fanelli turned back to Villecco. "Why are you so obsessed with Tim Kahn's injury anyway, two decades ago? And what's with you hating on Joshua?" Fanelli asked.

"Joshua Kahn is a loser. He gave up. It cost us the title that year. And I don't want him back in any way on this team. It's that simple," Villecco blurted out, rambling.

"That's not it. I know what it is. It's because of his brother. Tim defeated you, pushing you out from qualifying for the Easterns. And you think, probably in some bizarre way, that he stole your destiny. So, if I had stopped him from wrestling, because of his injured arm, you would have gotten your chance, your dream. Well, I won't let you take your anger out on Joshua. Joshua will be a part of this team. I promised his father. It's that simple... And if you ever touch one of my trainers like that again..."

Villecco defiantly moved closer toward Fanelli. "You'll what?"

"He'll kick your ass," Christine jumped in, said to Villecco. Fanelli nodded to Christine.

Villecco backed off. Just as he was about to leave, he turned back. "We both know the truth, though, don't we Coach? You knew about his arm. So, who cared the most?" Villecco left.

"He has issues," Christine said to Fanelli.

"He's right," Fanelli replied as he started to tape the ankle of a female gymnast. "About what?" Christine asked.

"Something that happened a long time ago, "Fanelli answered, signaling to another trainer to finish taping the ankle. He walked to the back of the training room and into his office.

Christine followed. His office was small with a large desk. Pictures of wrestlers from years in the past were on the walls. One was of Tim wrestling in the finals of the NCAA Wrestling Championships. Fanelli lifted the picture off the wall, momentarily gazed at it, then looked up at Christine. "Villecco is right. I knew. I knew his arm was fractured, at first, just a stress fracture." Fanelli looked back at the picture. "It was his last year, his last chance. So I let him wrestle. He made it all the way through the Easterns and all the rounds of Nationals until the finals. It finally gave way in the last match, breaking clean all the way through in those final seconds of the third period. The bone pierced right through his skin. I can still remember his scream; through all these years I can still remember his scream..." Fanelli looked back up into Christine's green eyes. "I knew it might happen. And I didn't do anything to stop it."

Fanelli carefully put the picture back on the wall. He sat down in his chair behind his desk with his head down. Fanelli opened the desk drawer. He took something out.

"What's that?" Christine asked. In Coach Fanelli's hand was a Miraculous Medal of Mother Mary. It was silver, slightly rusted. He held it up to show her. "This was Tim's. Before each match he would give it to me to hold while he wrestled. After the last one... He told me to keep it. He never gave up, Believing." Fanelli placed it carefully back into the drawer.

Joshua passed through a large, black iron gate across the street from Pierson Hall. On his right was a stone Baptist Church. As he passed, he looked up. High atop the Baptist church, there was a tower that looked like a castle's. Joshua looked back down. He saw U.C.L.A.'s Bell tower about a hundred yards ahead of him as he walked through the cobblestone courtyard with other smaller stone buildings on each side. The Bell Tower rose high into the sky like the Washington Monument. It stood in front of the library, the largest of all the buildings, almost taking up the entire city bock.

The library had marble stone pillars that could have been in another time where Samson was chained with his outstretched arms; as seemingly, just as strong, just as spiritually anointed, beneath the Bell Tower there was a young black man, a student, an evangelist, enthusiastically shouting scripture while raising the Bible up in his right hand. As students and faculty passed him by, some smiled, some shook their heads with other students lounging on the spanning grass, studying underneath nature's rationing shade of sparse trees adorning four concrete paths, each one leading to the tower.

It could have been any college campus on a bright sunny day with hardly a wind in any direction. There were students dashing off to class or stopping to talk with some male students and even a couple of professors carrying backpacks, giving a quick, discrete glance over at the young female students sunbathing. These students, either lying on their backs or stomachs, all had pulled their shorts up high upon their thighs to expose as much as they could to the sun.

One young woman sitting on the grass, soaking up the bright rays far from the shade of the trees; she had a book open in her lap with it resting on her crossed legs. Intermittently, she glanced up at those passing by. Another young woman wearing sunglasses, was lying on her stomach in shorts that she had tucked farther up her legs than any of the others, sunbathing with one foot raised. This young woman was smiling at the reactions of those passing by and at those sitting on benches as the young Evangelist confronted them upon the campus in this bright day's sun. "People think Jesus is just cool! A prophet! Had a prostitute as a friend! But he is the Savior! Buddha, Muhammad, they weren't God! They were great prophets, Holy men of God!

But, Jesus! Jesus is God! Be perfect in him! He died for us!" The young evangelist outstretched his arms like Jesus on the cross. He lowered them back down and continued to point the Bible at those passing by. "His blood was shed for us! We can be Holy all the hours of a day! We have to turn from sin! Evil likes it when young people want to commit suicide! When they have no faith! When they hate the world! God wants us to believe! Believe in Him! All of you have no self esteem! You fornicate! You commit sins! And evil knows that! It knows that we are weak! But God is calling you to be strong! To believe in Jesus! So, BELIEVE!"

Joshua glanced down at his tee-shirt, BELIEVE.

Music. A small rock band with folk guitars began singing near the Bell Tower. Two attractive young women came up and hugged the young preacher. He momentarily stopped shouting and talked to them in a normal tone. He nodded as they hugged him again and left. He resumed his preaching with some of those passing, smiling, and laughing deridingly.

The rock band began to sing a song from "The Who," during the

1960's. "See me...Feel me...Touch me...Heal me...See me...Feel me... Touch me...Heal me..."

August 15-17, 1969. Woodstock Music Festival. A year had passed with Michael and his men fighting in the jungle, moving from village to village. Michael and his men's uniforms were more worn and tattered; projecting a resonating *coldness* within their eyes. At Woodstock, "The Who" were singing on stage, "See me...Feel me...Touch me...Heal me... Listening to you I get the music, gazing at you I get the heat. Following you I climb the mountain. I get excitement at your feet. Right behind you I see the millions. On you I see the glory..."

Young people were before them in the thousands; a sea of people, a sea of hope. Some held children, some bathed naked in a lake, and some made love in the grass.

Joe Cocker appeared on stage. He paused, looking out. He sang, "With a little help from my friends," telling the large crowd to remember the song...

On the other side of the world in the Vietnam War, there was fighting in a small village. Mostly women and children ran carrying terror, surrounded by gunfire between the Vietcong and Michael's men, who fired back into the surrounding jungle as they ducked and ran through the small village. A mother lunged after her little girl who was standing in front of a hut as it burst into flames. The child was screaming with tears running down her cheeks, frozen, her bare feet, toes digging, curling into the soft soil. Just as her mother reached her, her mother was gunned down and died atop her feet, blood flowing, expanding, turning the rich soil into stains of war.

Michael, noticing the child calling out, charged toward the little girl, firing his weapon at the edge of the jungle toward the unseen enemy, hiding within the shadows. With gunfire exploding around him, Michael lifted up the little girl, cradling her in his arms, and carried her off. Yet, Michael fell with a nearby explosion. The child slipped from his hands.

"No!" Michael shouted, trying to quickly arise and pick the child back up. As he reached out, blood splattered on his face, partially blinding him. Wiping it away, no longer hearing her cries, the little girl's head was gone; her arms lying lifeless by her side with the soil stained mixed with her mother's blood on the bottoms of her bare feet.

1969. Woodstock. A young man was on the stage with the microphone, talking to the spanning crowd before him. "Hey, man. I've just got to say that you people have got to be the strongest bunch of people I've ever saw. Three days, man. Three days. We just love you. We just love you..." Another voice, "Ladies and gentlemen, please welcome with us, Crosby's Stills, and Nash." Crosby's, Stills, and Nash appeared onstage. They began singing, "Sweet Judy Blue Eyes." "It's getting to the point where I'm no fun anymore. I am sorry. Sometimes it hurts so bad that I must cry out loud, I am lonely..."

Joshua paused looking up at the Bell Tower ahead of him. He could hear the young preacher as he sensed an unusual wind forming high above him, somehow knowing that some magnificent destiny and challenge lay ahead of him. But he was not sure what it was. He did not know how it would happen or when. He only knew that it was something that he had always carried with him, deep in his heart from the time he was only three, placed within him from his mother's story. He clasped his right hand tighter and walked on through the campus...

1969. Woodstock. Crosby, Stills, Nash, and Young were still on stage. They were singing, "Well, I came across a child of God. He was walking along the road..."

The young preacher shouted by the Bell Tower, "Be on guard so that your hearts are not weighed down with dissipation and drunkenness and the worries of this life! For it will come upon all who live on the face of the earth! Be alert at all times, praying that you may have the strength to escape all these things that will take place, and to stand before the Son of Man!"

1969. Woodstock. Country Joe and The Fish were on stage. "Listen people. I don't know how you expect to ever stop the war if you can't sing any better than that. There's about three hundred thousand of you fuckers out there. I want you to start singin. Come on." Everyone sang. "And it's one, two, three, what are we fightin' for? Don't ask me, I don't give a damn. Next stop is Vietnam. And it's five, six, seven, open up the pearly gates. Well, ain't no time to wonder why. Whoopie, we're all going to die..."

Atop the cliff, the old oak tree moved slightly in the wind as clouds passed through the night across the sea; an angelic voice cried out, "Immediately after the suffering of those days the sun will be darkened, and the moon will not give its light; the stars will fall from heaven, and the powers of heaven will be shaken. Then the sign of the Son of Man will appear..."

1969. Vietnam. In the village, with the little girl lying beside him on the ground, her lifeless limbs beginning to cover with a mist of soil, Michael rose up and screamed out, firing back into the jungle. He stood defiantly amidst the return gunfire erupting around him as he and his men were out numbered. Dodging explosions, Ed ran up to Michael, grabbed him, and pulled him away. Michael and his men retreated back into the jungle, returning fire.

1969. Woodstock. "I want to, I want to, take you higher! Take you higher, girl..." Sly and the Family Stone were on stage singing.

1969. Vietnam. Michael and his men struggled, making their way through the jungle with sporadic sounds of gunfire slowly fading to the distance. One of his men screamed out, holding his leg. He had stepped into a sabotaged camouflaged hole with bamboo spikes. The soldier's leg was gushing with blood as two others tried to help him, pulling it out. Another soldier screamed out as he was pulled by his foot with a boogie trap rope around his ankle toward an arising wall from the brush composed of spiked bamboo. With his final scream, his lifeless body hung upside down, the spikes cutting all the way through his chest, the blood flowing down to his lifeless, wide, fearful eyes. Michael screamed out as Ed joined in with his rage, both kneeling side by side, firing through the jungle with the rest of their men as gunfire suddenly rained down upon them from the surrounding trees. One by one, Michael's men began to fall with their chests exploding with blood as *"Sly and the Family Stone" continued to sing "Take me higher!"*

Janis Joplin was on stage. "How are you all? Ah. I mean, how are you out there? Are you okay? You not, ah, you're staying stoned and you've got enough water and you've got a place to sleep and everything?" Janis Joplin started singing.

1969. Vietnam. Michael and the rest of his men fired their weapons into the Vietcong hidden in the trees... Finally - SILENCE. Michael signaled to stay down in the brush with their weapons poised. Twelve of Michael's men had been killed, their bodies covered in blood amidst the thirty or so in Michael's unit that remained. "Are they still out there?" Ed asked in a whisper.

The soldier that had stepped on the bamboo spikes was still crying out.

"Shut him up," Michael ordered. "Shut him up," Michael said, again, slightly louder. Bruce tried to calm the screaming soldier down, finally putting his hand over his mouth. "What are we doing..." Ed began to ask.

"I'm trying to hear them," Michael said, adding, "Just listen. Listen." "So, what do you think?" Ed asked.

"They're possibly setting us up," Michael replied, adding, "Not sure."

"I think we got them all," Tommy, Sergeant Marina, answered. Michael paused, then nodded, Slowly, Michael's men arose. Bruce helped up the young soldier with the injured leg.

"Can you make it, buddy?" Bruce asked him. The young soldier nodded, wincing. "I'm alright," the young soldier said, grimacing in pain with blood still flowing from his leg.

Bruce leaned down to try to stop the bleeding. Then another explosion of red. The young soldier's chest was blown apart. Bruce was covered in the blood, as if someone had dropped a bucket of red paint on him. Michael quickly turned, seeing the Vietcong's face through the trees, ending his look in a returned painting of red.

"An eye for an eye," Michael whispered, glancing back at the bloody body of the soldier that had fallen on top of Bruce. Bruce screamed out, tossing the body from him of the young soldier, firing ferociously into the trees. Tommy ran to Bruce's side to calm him down.

"It's alright! It's alright!" Tommy shouted to him as Bruce continued firing while Michael and Ed peered through the jungle for any more faces, any more eyes of lurid death.

Slowly, Bruce stopped firing and let his weapon fall down to his side. He fell to his knees. Gently cupping the headless boy in his arms, he held him as he looked up to the sky, to the blue through the tops of the trees. Michael and his men moved forward, seeing red in the trees, the bodies of the Vietcong dangling from the branches as those before, caught in their final fall. The bodies slowly moved in the wind, this time, as if wind chimes of war. This time, no sorrow, no remorse. Michael's unit became shadows of the jungle, continuing on, sharpening the coldness of the horrors of war captured within their eyes...

A flagpole stood high above the Bell Tower, holding a large American Flag as remnants of time played upon pieces of echoes in the wind. 1969. Woodstock. Jimi Hendrix was on stage. He began playing the Star-spangled Banner on his electric guitar.

Joshua paused before the young preacher. They stared at each other, just staring. The young preacher appeared moved and said, "The Seventh Angel...There will be seven angels. In the hand of the seventh there will be a book. There will be a rainbow over his head with his right foot on the sea and his left on the land. He will shout out like a lion..."

Joshua looked up into the bright sun as the Bell Tower sounded out over the preacher's voice. Joshua saw the American flag flickering as a candle in front of the stunning sunlight.

1969. Vietnam. Back in the village where Michael and his men had fought, by the little girl's headless body were many others; many children with their arms outstretched, as if reaching out with a final breath for their once cherished dreams. One child clutched a tattered, bloody, teddy bear. Another was lying beside her mother, cradled as if in a final wish by her side. And still, another was lying at the edge of this village atop a hill with colors of a sunset above her.

The echo through time of Jimi Hendrix playing the Star Spangled Banner faded.

On November 15, 1969, three months later after Woodstock, two hundred and fifty thousand anti-war demonstrators marched in Washington. On Nov. 16th, the My Lai massacre of hundreds, including women and children, became known in news reports. American soldiers killed four hundred and seven people in only two hours. One hundred and seventy, including children, were gunned down into a pit. One South Vietnamese man, after the killing, went into the pit to look for his family; his father, wife, and two sons who were only eight and twelve- years-old. He went through body after body. He eventually found them all. He and his surviving brother carried them over their shoulders several hundred yards away. They dug a hole for each of them. "The thing I always felt worst about is my father," the man said. "I felt I should have done something good for him while he was alive."

As Michael and his men moved through the jungle, he kept remembering the echoes of the children's screams. Michael and his men fought to save the children during the My Lai massacre, carrying as many of them as they could in their arms, passing these children to the awaiting arms of other American soldiers in helicopters. Michael, covered in the blood, saved as many of the children as he could. He thought about how strange it was soldiers on the same side could turn against one another and could become so brutal, so cold.

Walking down the city streets a few blocks away from campus, Joshua stopped and gazed at a long line that was not moving in front of a Welfare Office. There were many children crying, clinging to the bottom of their mother's skirts. Some of the children became quiet as they looked up into Joshua's eyes as he passed. Joshua glanced to the other side of the city's street. There were homeless people sitting against buildings, begging or lying drunk on the concrete as women, prostitutes, passed in spike heels, boots, and various forms of revealing clothing adorned with leather and lace. "They've all given up on their dreams," Joshua heard behind him.

Joshua turned. An old man dressed in a white robe, the man Joshua saw when he first came into the city with his brother, still had the sign. As he stood behind Joshua looking up at him, the old man was completely gray with a few days unshaven gray bristle on his face. "They've all given up. That's why they do what they do," the old man said.

Joshua looked across the street at the prostitutes and those lying in despair on the pavement. He gazed back at those in front of the Welfare office, at the children who were now eerily silent. "You have to help them believe. So many are depending on you," the old man said. He paused, then added, "Where is your robe?"

Joshua, not knowing what the old man was talking about, saw the children who were clinging to their mothers staring at him, as if ghostly images of children from another time. The old man passed with his head down, not speaking another word. The images faded as the turning of colored leaves with a gentle wind on an autumn day, a distant past in another dimension of time, flowing upon the wind around him within a wave particulate of a quantum realm.

1969. Vietnam. Michael and his men arrived at another small Village. They were still in the jungle, on the side of another hill from where the child's body lay, miles away from the last village, yet beneath the same sunset. Looking down over this village, only a couple hundred yards away, they heard sporadic gunfire within it.

"What do you think is going on?" Ed asked Michael, pushing away a large branch hanging over a bush shielding them.

"I don't know," Michael replied, taking hold of the same branch, keeping it down so they could both see.

"You think it's Karese?" Ed asked.

"No. There would be screams. He likes screams. Remember? I knew we should have brought them with us," Michael added.

"Don't worry. I'm sure Mey Lee and Hoy Sung are oaky," Ed asked. "I hope so," Michael replied.

"She loves you, you know, Mey Lee," Ed said, adding, "And her daughter."

Michael did not answer, continuing to stare down at the village, listening to the gunfire. Michael raises his hand, signaling to his unit to cautiously follow him down the hill, through the brush as the distant gunfire began to fade.

In Mey Lee's village, a Vietnamese boy sat alone on a swing by the side of a small chapel. The little boy watched as twenty-five North Vietnamese soldiers passed by him. He began to swing slowly, back and forth. As they one by one they passed. One of the soldiers kicked a blue soccer all. Jumping up off the swing, the little boy ran after it as rolled toward the chapel's gate. Inside the chapel many eyes were hidden, peering out from the shadows; women trying to cry out to the boy the danger in whispers from the darkness. The boy reached down, picked up the ball, and threw it back to the passing soldiers. With a brief flurry of shots, the boy was gunned down. The ball continued to roll. Muffled cries broke out from inside the chapel. A couple of soldiers stopped and turned, appearing to hear them, but continued walking. Gunfire erupted coming from the edge of the village. Michael and his men charged into the village.

Huddling down with the children behind the pews, the women heard the fighting explode outside. A Vietnamese priest tried to comfort them as the fighting continued. Then silence. A few moments passed as all they could hear were the children crying from under the pews. Suddenly, the chapel doors were kicked open, allowing fading sunlight to shoot across the chapel's floors to the altar. Soldiers walked in. A Vietnamese woman jumped up and cried out, "Michael!"

All the women, children, and a priest rushed out from their hiding places. The windows, with blankets over them, were uncovered and the dimming sunlight shined through. Michael entered as if a conquering angel. A beautiful young Vietnamese woman wearing a gold necklace of a cross with long, soft black hair and brown eyes ran into Michael's awaiting arms along with her daughter, three-years-old.

"I've missed you, Mey Lee. You too, Hoa Sung," Michael said to them. The rest of the children ran to Ed, who was standing in the chapel doorway. "Eddie! Eddie!" they cried out.

The children's chants faded. Ed held the dead little boy in his arms, who chased after the ball, blood upon Ed's arms. Ed carried him and placed him gently down before the altar.

"What is his name?" Ed asked the priest.

"Matthew, after his father, who was an American," the priest answered.

The priest knelt down and lit a candle as the women, except for Mey Lee, who was still in Michael's arms, joined the priest in a prayer. Ed left. The children followed.

"Oh, Father. We thank you for being our Father, oh Lord. We thank You for sending us Michael. We thank You for his return," the priest said, with Mey Lee looking up into Michael's eyes and Hoa Sung clinging to Michael's leg.

"Come. Hoa Sung has something she wants to show you," Mey Lee said, looking up to Michael. Hoa Sung took Michael's hand and led Mey Lee and Michael outside the chapel toward their small hut. The children led Ed to the center of the village by the side of a stone fountain that no longer worked. The children, speaking in Vietnamese, said to Ed, "Do it again! Do it again!"

"How come you guys don't ever get tired of this?" Ed replied to them surrounding him. "Alright. Get back. You have to give me room." Ed did a trick with his thumbs that made it look like one was cut off. The children carefully stared at Ed's hands each time, trying to figure out how he did it. One little girl said to him, "Now do your head." Ed just looked at her.

Another little girl, who was missing a toe on her right foot, asked in English, "American Santa Claus coming? The rest of the children joined in, saying in English, "Santa! Santa!"

"I should have never told you guys about that," Ed said, then in Vietnamese added, "Yes.

Santa is coming soon. He's going to bring lots of gifts." The children cheered.

By the side of Mey Lee and Hoa Sung's hut, Michael looked down at what Hoa Sung wanted to show him. A rosebud was just beginning to open with Hoa Sung pointing toward it.

"It should bloom soon. She wanted to give it to you when it did," Mey Lee said to him.

Hoa Sung, speaking in Vietnamese, said to Michael, "Father, I grew it for you. I grew it for you." Michael picked up Hoa Sung in his arms and hugged her. He turned and kissed Mey Lee. The Vietnamese children chanted around Ed. "Eddie! Eddie! Eddie!"

The children's chants faded as Ed reached out for a small child in the middle of the pack who was silent. She only had on a small skirt, her feet bare, nothing above the waist. Ed placed her on his lap and looked at her bare back. It was welted with ugly scars. "Fire in the sky," one child said to Ed in Vietnamese. The child lifted up his shirt to show all the burn scars covering him.

One by one, each child revealed their scars. "Fire in the sky," they all cried out in Vietnamese. Ed slowly appeared by the Mey Lee's hut. Michael and Mey Lee were kissing.

"Don't we have to keep moving? Especially after our grand entrance?" Ed asked Michael. "Tell Marina to get the others ready to move out," Michael replied.

"They've been ready. We're the only ones who have anything here," Ed replied. Michael's men were poised at the edges of the village just beyond all the fallen dead North Vietnamese soldiers with their rifles aimed toward the jungle.

"Alright," Michael said to Ed. Ed discretely left. "Wait here," Michael told Mey Lee and Hoa Sung. Michael walked over to where Ed was standing, waiting.

"We can't leave them, not now. What if Charlie comes back," Michael said to him. "Are we moving out, sir?" Tommy called out, still poised, looking out toward the jungle with the others.

"What do you want to do? Take them with us? Look. I don't want to leave either. If I had it my way, I'd take them all home to the states, dress up as Santa, and then hand out the gifts. But we're in a war. Remember? Their war," Ed replied to Michael.

Mey Lee approached Michael. She fell back into his arms. "Go. We will be alright. God will protect us. He has so far," she said to him. They parted with a final kiss as Hoa Sung reached down and touched the rose bud. With Michael and his men disappearing back into the jungle, the women and children dragged the dead soldiers' bodies from the streets, hiding them in the brush at the edges of the village. The children then returned to the dried up fountain, each trying to do the thumb trick.

After sunset with stars emerging in the night's sky, Michael and his men were deep in the jungle when they heard explosions back at the village. With fiery light raining down on them in the ominous darkness, like the stars cascading down the waterfall into Joshua's pond, the children ran, as they always had, screaming for cover. Michael screamed out, "Hold up! Hold up!" to his men. He turned to go back, but Ed grabbed him again. "We have to keep going!

They'll be alright. We have to keep on going, Captain," Ed said to him.

"Tommy! Keep everyone moving! I'll meet you up on the north perimeter!" Michael called out to Tommy in the front.

"I'm going back. I have to," Michael said to Ed. He pulled away from Ed's grasp and disappeared back through the brush.

"Wait! So am I," Ed said, following him into the night.

Tommy signaled to the others to keep going. As Michael and Ed moved swiftly through the jungle, with more explosions filling the sky ahead of them, Ed shouted, "They're ours!"

"What?" Michael shouted back. "They're ours! They don't know we're this far North!"

When they reached the village, the explosions continued as the children's screams became louder. One little girl, naked, ran with her arms high over her head, tears running down her face, toward Ed just entering the village. Another explosion. Ed fell down by her side. She was lying face down in the dirt when he awoke, brushing the smoke away from his eyes. He picked her lifeless body up in his arms and he saw that her face was gone. He looked down at her feet. One toe on her right foot was missing. She was the little girl who asked if the American Santa Claus was coming. With the "Fire in the Sky" moving into the distance, the burned children's cries echoed. Ed still held the little girl in his arms, whispering to her, "Santa is coming. Santa is coming," into the night, until there was silence. The silence resonated through a mist, rippling back through time upon dimensional folds, connected, yet separate.

Joshua, as he walked down the city's street at sunset, came upon a small church. He paused. It was six o'clock and the church bells had just started to ring, "Ava Maria."

"That's really beautiful," a Jewish man remarked coming up and standing next to Joshua's side. "Do you know what that song is?" He asked. Joshua didn't answer. A Muslim man also came up and stood by their sides. "You're right. It's beautiful," the man said as people on the city's street paused to listen to the bells. The three of them prayed together, bowing their heads. With the finality of night upon him, Joshua sat alone on a bench in front of Pierson Hall. The city streets seemed empty and desolate with all the lunch trucks having vanished. He looked up with a sound of a horn and saw headlights of his brother's truck coming toward him. Tim pulled over to the curb and waved. Joshua got in.

"Hey. Thanks for picking me up," Joshua said.

"No problem, bro. So, how was your first day? Did you meet any hot babes or anything," Tim said with a smile. Joshua smiled back.

"You did?" Tim asked. Joshua nodded, staring out the window at a mountaintop in the distance. "Cool. Well, this is a new beginning for you. Just follow your dreams, bro."

"Thanks," Joshua simply replied, adding, "How was your day?"

"Well, we're finally putting the roof up on the Apollo. It looks like a dome. It isn't easy, but it's going to be one fantastic arena when it's done."

As they drove over the bridge, the sky became again clear and the reflections of the city lights in the bay returned. Joshua looked down to boats passing below. Tim watched, too, as they left the bridge, the lights becoming smaller, fading in the distance in his rear view mirror.

"I'm proud of you," Tim said, patting Joshua on the shoulder, adding, "It takes a lot of courage to try to get your life back on track. You know, with going back to school and all."

"Thanks," Joshua replied, adding, "I wish dad was proud of me."

"Give dad time. I am sure he's proud of you in his own way," Tim said, gazing at the mountaintop. He turned back to Joshua with a smile. "You know, what Joshua? I'm proud of you." "Really," Joshua appeared surprised. "Yes. I am..."

They turned together... Gazing upward at an unusual red cast sky above the mountaintop.

Chapter 7

When Nia arrived back home, she entered the foyer of the mansion. She shut the door and noticed her mother sitting curled up in the senator's high-back leather chair inside the study with a book open in her lap. Her mother looked up, appearing ashamed, saddened.

"Well, I guess I owe you an apology," she said to Nia, standing silently in the doorway of the study.

"It's alright," Nia answered, hesitantly, moving further in.

Nia stood before her wearing a pink sun dress; her arms, shoulders, and back exposed, seemingly anxious about something, finding with a white bow of the dress snugly fit around her waist. Her mother gently reached out, helping her adjust the bow, giving it a couple final pats.

"So, how did you make out registering for school?" her mother asked.

"Mom, I need three thousand dollars for the classes," Nia blurted out. Her mother pulled her hand away from the bow. "I thought your father was taking care of that?"

"I don't want to have to depend on him anymore," Nia said, turning away, pushing down the bottom hem of her dress. Her mother put down the book, got up, let out a forced laugh, and walked over to straighten flowers in a vase atop the piano.

"Oh, so it's alright then to depend on me," her mother replied sarcastically back, adjusting the flowers, taking hold of a red rose.

"I'm sorry I asked," Nia said, beginning to leave... "Wait." Her mother let the rose she was holding fall down into the vase beneath the water line.

"Why don't you just ask, the senator, your father, this one last time? It will give you maybe enough time to save money from your... job, you know to pay for your classes."

"I don't know if I want to dance anymore," Nia said with a downward turn of her eyes.

"I love watching you dance," the senator said, approaching from the foyer, startling Nia. "Justin..." Melinda said, moving the vase atop the piano, accidentally striking a note.

Nia attempted to leave. But, he stood solidly in the doorway, unmoving, tall, imposing. "So, what is it that you wanted to ask me?" He asked, blocking the doorway. Nia wondered how long he had been listening. Melinda approached and stood next to Nia, readjusting the bow wrapped tightly around Nia.

"She looks cute in this dress? Doesn't she?" Melinda said, adding, "Oh, she just wanted to ask you about...support for school. She wants to make you proud of her. She's been doing quite well with her grades and all."

"Oh. I see," the senator answered, entering the study, giving a slightly lustful glance at Nia in her sundress, brushing up against her as he passed. "So, you want money..." He abruptly turned. "A life lesson, Nia, nothing is for free..."

"Madam, the cook needs to see you in the kitchen," The butler said, interrupting, standing in the doorway. Melinda appeared embarrassed, envisioning herself naked, stretched out across the piano top with the butler discretely watching from this doorway. He gave her a slight smile as knowing, what she was thinking.

"Okay...Uhm. Yes. Thank you, Maurice," Melinda said in a soft, submissive tone, turning away from his coy leering smile, reaching up and fondling the pearl button atop her blouse. Melinda was embarrassed, more like humiliated. It was the first time she had seen the butler since she caught him staring at her and the senator making love on top of the piano.

Slightly shaken, she closed the top of her white ruffled blouse, clasping upon the pearl button, and answered again, "Very good, Maurice. Thank you," not remembering what she said.

The butler stared at her for a second too long with the smile playing on his lips.

"Excuse me," Melinda said, leaving, "I better see what Darlene needs."

The senator moved closer to the piano. Nia backed up, her hands hitting the keys. "Sir," the butler addressed the senator as the senator leaned in closer to Nia. "The

governor's office called. They want to know if you can entertain the Chinese consulate tonight." "Why don't you take care of that, Maurice. Like you did the last time," the senator replied while asserting power, staring downward at Nia pushed up against the piano.

"Very good," the butler answered, exiting, leaving Nia's fearful glance, looking up at the senator against the backdrop of a new awakening blaze.

"So you need money for school. Well, you know what you have to do for it," the senator said in a commanding tone, untying strings of the sundress on Nia's shoulders. Turning from the piano, Nia pushed his hand aside. Holding her sundress up, she hurriedly left the study, bumping into the butler just outside the doorway, seemingly guarding it. Nia, upset and confused, ran to her motorcycle, got on it, and rode away with a haze of dirt arising from the long gravel mansion driveway. With the butler gone, Melinda, apprehensively, approached the study doorway.

"Where did Nia go?" Melinda, appearing concerned, asked the senator. The senator moved toward her, placing his arms around her as she gazed upward, captivated by his eyes.

Tim and Joshua pulled into their driveway. A light was on in the dining room. "Now what?" Tim asked.

The dining room didn't have a light that worked for a while. They both got out of the truck, but Joshua entered the house first. When Tim entered, he saw Joshua standing just inside the entrance of the house, looking into the dining room with a shocked expression.

"What's going on?" Tim asked. As Tim walked further in, he saw what Joshua was shocked by. The dining room had been set up as if for a Thanksgiving Dinner. There were dishes, though cracked, laid out on a white tablecloth along with mismatched utensils, a couple of them rusty and bent. Alongside the plates, were crystal glasses. Antique chairs surrounded the table, two high-backs at each end.

"Has dad flipped?" Tim whispered over to Joshua as their father entered from the kitchen, carrying a large cooked turkey on a silver tray.

"Well, don't just stand there, sit down!" Their father called out, placing a turkey down at the center of the table. Joshua and Tim sat down next to each other, as their father continued bringing out food; corn, mashed potatoes, stuffing, even gravy. Joshua and Tim looked nervously at each other. Their father sat down across from them, smiling.

"This is a surprise," Tim said as his father reached over for Joshua's plate, filling it up with large pieces of turkey, a giant roll covered in butter, and a heaping pile of potatoes oozing in gravy. "We need our strength for our purpose," their father said, placing the filled plate down before Joshua. Tim's plate remained empty. He finally served himself.

"Shall we pray," their father said, reaching out with both his hands to his sons. Joshua took hold of his father's hand, and with his other reached over for Tim's. "Get out of here," Tim said to Joshua, refusing to grab his father's hand too.

"Heavenly Father, we thank you for being our Father. Lord, we thank You for the food we are about to eat, but most of all, Father, we thank You for Joshua's new path. We pray to You that You take care of him even though much time has passed, and that he does his best with school, Lord. Amen," their father prayed.

Tim repeated, "Amen," while already digging into the food on his plate.

Joshua, though, remained silent, not touching anything after letting go of his father's hand. "Come on, Joshua, dig in," Tim said while cramming a large piece of turkey into his mouth. "You have to build up your strength for wrestling, Joshua," their father added, also eating. Pausing to swallow, he asked, "Did you talk to Coach Fanelli today?"

Joshua stood up. "I don't think I can do this," Joshua said, slightly pushing his untouched plate back toward his father. His father stopped chewing, placing his partially eaten turkey leg down. "Why can't there be, just once, a nice, quiet moment in this house?" Tim said, shaking his head, continuing to eat. "I don't care what happens, I'm eating."

"I'm not like you, dad," Joshua added, sitting back down with his head bowed. "I don't have a purpose. I don't think I even want to go back to school, anymore. It's not me, not now."

Their father remained quiet, picked up a butter knife, and took a slice of butter for his biscuit. "Everyone has a purpose, especially you," he said, taking a bite of his biscuit with butter dripping down the side of his mouth.

"Can I have your stuffing?" Tim asked Joshua, trying to ease the tension.

Their father picked up the turkey leg, waving it, but not eating it. "You're ungrateful. You know that? You've been ungrateful your whole life. I give you a roof over your head. I give you food, and you've already given up?"

"Oh, here we go," Tim said in between chewing.

"What's the matter with you? I had big dreams for you. Did you know that? I had dreams that someday you would be a national champion. Your mother had dreams for you too. She hoped that you would graduate from college someday, maybe even go on and get graduate degrees. Your education was very important to her. Did you know that? She spoke of it from the moment you were born. And here you are wanting to quit again. What do you think she would say about all this, your mother? Do you think she would be proud of you? Huh? Well, do you.

Let me tell you something. You will go to school and you will finish. You're smart. God gave you talents. You just need confidence, that's all. Quitting? Now that's *not* you."

"I'm sorry, dad," Joshua got up and went out the front door, around the back of the house, through the woods with Samson following by his side back to the edge of the pond. He sat on the bank with his arms wrapped around his legs gazing up at the waterfall. Slowly, he closed his eyes and attempted to imagine, her... Nia, her long black hair, her beautiful eyes...

As Nia walked across the parking lot toward the strip club, Father Gabe called out to her, standing by a statue of Mother Mary next to the church. He approached her as she paused, appearing hesitant, as she waited for him. "I got your note. Oh, and I found this," Father Gabe said before her, reaching out his hand, placing something within her's. She felt a strange force from his touch. She shook her head.

"What's this?" Nia said, opening her palm, seeing her locket. "Your answer," Father Gabe simply replied.

"I thought, I lost it," Nia said.

"You did. But, now you have it back," Father Gabe said with a smile. "I have to go," Nia responded, nervously, turning away.

"You should open it some time," he said. Nia paused.

"How do you..." she whispered. Father Gabe smiled again. "The clasp. It looked like it hadn't been opened in a long time. Can I put it back on you?" He asked.

Nia softly replied, "Alright." She turned around and let Father Gabe place the locket back around her neck. She added, "Thank you," but could not look at him back in his eyes as she walked away. It was as if he knew her, her darkest secrets. She slightly waved as he watched her open the rear exit door and enter the dark club.

Inside the club, Ms. Gongel was talking to the bartender at a corner end of the bar, whispering something into his ear while looking over at Nia standing in the doorway. Nia appeared unsure, nervous, but walked over and sat down at the bar on a raised barstool.

Attempting to keep her eye on Ms. Gongel, Nia suddenly became distracted by a customer.

The bartender, making sure he wasn't being watched, looking around, began preparing Nia her *favorite drink, Sex on the Beach.* He then took five *e*-labeled green pills from his shirt pocket, dropped them discreetly in Nia's drink, and stirred until completely dissolved.

Once completed, the bartender approached Nia, causing her to turn away from the customer.

"How are you Nia? Working tonight?" the bartender asked while giving her the drink. "Sex on the Beach, just how you like it," the bartender added with a smile and a distant approving nod by Ms. Gongel on the other side of the bar.

"I don't know if I'm working tonight or not," Nia nervously replied, taking the drink in her hands. She brought it to her lips. She took a sip. The bartender smiled again

"How is it?" The bartender asked.

"Perfect. Thank you," Nia replied, taking another sip, holding a small green straw.

Ms. Gongel approached Nia and stood next to her by the side of the bar. "I knew you would come. So, are you ready to perform, make some money?"

"When will we be going?" Nia asked with the drink poised to her lips.

"Go ahead. Finish your drink," Ms. Gongel gestured authoritatively to Nia as the bartender obediently nodded to Ms. Gongel and walked away. Nia finished her drink, continuing to sip the rest of it, using the straw. Ms. Gongel towered over her until the glass was empty except for some ice at the bottom. Nia sucked on the ice and crunched down on them with her teeth, feeling drawn further in, into a swirling arising warm, moist darkness."

"Good girl. That's enough..." Ms. Gongel said, taking *the drink* out of her hands. As soon as Maribel shows up, we'll go. She has your costume."

"Costume?" Nia asked.

"Yes, costume," Ms. Gongel said, taking hold of her arm, seeing Nia begin to sway a bit. "For your role," Ms. Gongel added as Maribel walked in, wearing sneakers, a black sweatshirt, and black sweatpants. Maribel was slightly taller than Nia, having long blonde hair and light complected skin in contrast to Nia's long dark hair and olive skin-tone. Maribel walked up to them carrying a small bag.

"Hi. Sorry I'm late," Maribel said to Ms. Gongel. To Nia, she said, "Did Ms. Gongel tell you?"

"Tell me what?" Nia asked, surprisingly beginning to feel *the kick* of the drink so soon. "We'll talk about it in the car. Let's go," Ms. Gongel said, taking Nia firmly by the arm.

Maribel followed.

"Are you coming with us?" Nia, looking back, asked Maribel.

"Yes," Ms. Gongel replied. Maribel noticed Nia staggering a little, appearing concerned.

As they drove away out of the city with Ms. Gongel at the wheel, Nia was in the front seat and Maribel was in the back. There was silence as Maribel and Nia stared out the windows.

It began to rain. Ms. Gongel turned on the windshield wipers. Thunder sounded out in the distance. "I didn't know a storm was coming," Maribel said. She glanced into the frontseat. Nia appeared distant, staring out the window, just like the thunder of the oncoming storm.

"I need you girls to be on your A-game tonight, got it," Ms. Gongel said enthusiastically with an air of discipline in her tone. "This is a big night. You girls can each earn at least three- grand tonight. That's if you both perform well," Ms. Gongel said to them as Nia shook her head, feeling more disorientated, gazing through the glass. Feeling as if she was floating off into a distant dream, Nia allowed Ms. Gongel to reach over and slightly raise the bottom hem of her sun dress, exposing her bare, shapely legs. Maribel watched, confused. "You girls should feel honored that I chose you two for this important... performance,"

"I know this may sound strange, Nia. But I've been kind of looking forward to it," Maribel said, leaning in from the back seat, popping a couple of pills, jugging a water bottle.

"To what?" Nia asked, trying to keep her eyes focused. They didn't answer her. Maribel sat back in the backseat.

"I'm glad you're preparing," Ms. Gongel said with an orchestrated look, using the car mirror to glance back at Maribel. Maribel took another pill, another slug from the water bottle. "Good girl," Ms. Gongel affirmatively added.

Ms. Gongel turned down a dirt road, driving deep into dense woods in a secluded, upscale neighborhood. Ms. Gongel drove toward a house at the end of the dirt road. Lights from other houses in the distance could be seen emanating from their windows. Arriving at their destination, Nia looked up and saw a large dark house, new, modern, with only one light in one window, an electric candle. The house appeared ominous, shady, an aura of hidden darkness as Nia and Maribel cautiously got out, following Ms. Google toward a door with a lion knocker.

There were several black limousines in and around a winding dirt driveway with some parked on the grass. Two of the limousines had international license plates. These license plates appeared slightly blurry to Nia as she began to appear intoxicated, swaying.

"What's the matter with Nia?" Maribel asked, holding her arm.

"I'm fine," Nia said somewhat angry. "Drop the attitude, now, and behave," Ms. Gongel said to Nia taking hold of the lion knocker and giving one firm knock.

"Sorry," Nia said, turning toward Maribel looking down.

The door eerily opened. They heard men's laughter, talking, seemingly shouting, as hesitantly they walked in, following close behind Ms. Gongel. When they entered further in, down a dark hallway, there was a lot of cigar smoke spilling out into the hallway with Asian men in business suites, in a back room, sitting in a semicircle. Men's faces were lost in the shadows, peering over at them, as both Nia and Maribel glanced inside this room, pausing, passing by.

In the middle of this room there was an unusually large white marble table, about five by ten feet, three-feet high. It had a black light shining on it that was suspended from the ceiling.

One of the businessmen reached over and turned on another light. The table's legs had dragons carved into them. He looked over at Nia and Maribel and smiled. They turned away and continued down the hallway. Ms. Gongel pointed toward a bathroom. "You both can change in there. Hurry up. They're waiting," Ms. Gongel commanded. They nodded.

Inside the small bathroom upon a cold tile floor, the men's voices and their intermittent blurts of laughter echoed down the hallway toward them as Maribel reached into her bag, took out the costumes, a bunny and wolf. Maribel helped Nia strip down until she was naked and put the bunny costume on her.

"I guess I'm as nervous as you are. I feel like we're getting ready to perform in a play, Maribel said, making final adjustments of the bunny ears on Nia.

Kicking off her sneakers, Maribel took off her sweatshirt and sweatpants as Nia leaned, holding herself up against the wall. Maribel's long blonde hair flowed down over her shoulders over the gray fur of her wolf costume she pulled up that completely covered her in contrast to Nia's revealing bunny costume. Maribel's showed her fangs. She was the wolf. Ms. Gongel stood by the large marble table in front of the businessmen, the same man who had turned the light on reached back over and turned it off, allowing the black light shining down on the marble table to be the only light in the room as they sat, now, silently in the shadows waiting. "Gentlemen. For your entertainment tonight, predator meets prey, the wolf devours the bunny!" Ms. Gongel announced, calling out the signal.

Maribel led Nia out of the bathroom and down the hall as Nia stumbled along in white spiked heels. When they entered, Maribel bent down and helped Nia take them off so that she wouldn't slip. She then helped Nia up onto the white marble table where her bottom was completely exposed under the black spotlight along with her bare breasts underneath the sheer cover of the bunny costume. Maribel let go of her hand as Nia peered out into the smoke-filled room. With a sudden eruption of music, Nia intuitively started to dance as Maribel got up on the table and danced, too, completely stripping from her wolf costume. Underneath the black light, Maribel seductively danced around Nia, showing off her fangs, tickling Nia's neck, as if she was about to devour her. With their bare feet they danced slowly and cautiously upon the marble as cigar smoke rose up their bare legs, followed by the eyes of those sitting quietly in the darkness, watching. Maribel flirting, grabbed hold of Nia so she didn't fall. While securely holding Nia around her waist, Maribel gently guided her to a sitting position down onto the table.

Nia felt the cold marble. But, she also still felt the heat of the black spotlight on her as it penetrated her sheer cover, continuing to expose her. With a mist-like marsh of cigar smoke encircling them, Maribel danced as a predator over its prey, towering over Nia, with her blonde hair lighting up as if in the eclipse of a sun as Nia tried to look up into the spotlight, attempting to see her face, arching back on the marble table. Maribel reached down and pulled off the sheer cover of Nia's costume, tossing it aside. She then got off the table, positioned herself in front of Nia, and lowered herself, kneeling down in front of Nia as Nia reclined further back, leaning on her slipping hands; her long black hair flowing down across the white marble as her head began to sway. Reaching upward, with her mouth agape, Maribel moved her hands up Nia's bare body, caressing her, bringing her fangs to Nia's neck, tenderly embedding the teeth...

Hearing applause, the smoke momentarily cleared as Nia looked up and saw the butler, Maurice, between two Asian businessmen, watching. With the cloud of the drugs clearing, Nia had a sudden sense of reality - *what just happened*. Frightened, ashamed, she reached over and picked up Maribel's gray wolf costume by side of the table and quickly covered herself. She felt humiliated and sick as the applause continued, the sounds becoming sharper as another, brighter light was turned on. Trying to clasp upon some dignity, she got up, clutching the wolf costume close to her chest, and scurried, still wearing her bunny ears, briskly back toward the small bathroom. The butler watched, smiling, until she disappeared down the dark hallway.

"And where do you think you're going?" Ms. Gongel said to Nia, standing in shadows at the end of the hallway. "You're not finished your performance, yet." Ms. Gongel added, snatching the wolf costume out of her hands. "You'll wear this afterwards, as a symbol of your compliance to me and respect," Ms. Gongel said to her, grabbing her by her arm, leading her back down the hallway and into the smoke-filled room filled with the Chinese Businessmen.

"You know what you have to do," Ms. Gongel sternly said to Nia, tossing the wolf costume onto a red velvet high-back chair. Yet, defiant, Nia stood her ground, refusing to move.

Ms. Gongel suddenly gripped Nia's arm tighter and pulled her over toward the marble table. "What are you doing?" Nia blurted out, unable to pull away from her as the businessmen laughed. Ms. Gongel sat down upon the table and forcibly pulled Nia, face down, over her knee.

"Are you crazy? Let me go!" Nia shouted amidst louder laughter. "Someone's been bad!" One of them called out.

As Nia attempted to resist in vain due to Ms. Gongel's enormous strength, Ms. Gongel, angrily with an expression of focus and determination, raised her right hand and began spanking Nia's bare bottom in front of the Chinese businessmen. Squirming, kicking up her heels, her bare feet, it was no use as she writhed to break free, continuing to get spanked.

"Who's your daddy!" Another called out as the other Businessmen laughed out loudly and cheered. After a final affirmative spank, leaving a red hand mark on Nia's bottom, Ms. Gongel arose, shoving Nia to the floor to sounds of applause. Ms. Gongel jokingly bowed and gestured at Nia toward the marble table. "Now." Ms. Gongel commanded. Nia nodded, got back up, and stepped onto the table, rubbing her bottom, feeling conquered and denigrated, embarrassingly complying to Ms. Gongel's command. Maribel, appearing fearful, obediently leaned in toward Nia underneath the reasserted spotlight of the blacklight. They passionately embraced and began kissing each other as if musicians playing instruments upon the direction of the orchestra's Maestro, Ms. Gongel. Maribel, upon cue, slowly began moving her hands up and down Nia, playing her like an instrument, lowering her onto her back upon the cold marble table. On her back, widening and wrapping her legs around Maribel's waist, Nia became entranced, engulfed in the overcoming warmth of the *mist, beginning to writhe in pulsations of a spasm.*

In the wolf's costume, seemingly shackled in a sign of compliance and respect, Nia rode upon her motorcycle into the *mist* of the woods, deep into the brush, near the mansion, but away from the humiliation and subjugation she both accepted and endured. The butler's stare, his touch, resonated within her as an echo in a way that utterly surrendered any sense of dignity.

Confused, ashamed, embarrassed, humiliated to levels she did not understand in terms of at what she had become, she let her motorcycle slip from her grasp and fall onto the side of a dirt road as she took a deep breath and entered the woods, searching for answers, some kind of sign that would put all these pieces together for a meaningful purpose of some greater good. Yet, the deeper she went into the woods, blindly driven, the more confused and ashamed she became, feeling more naked than she *performed,* "My God, My God, what have I done?" She said to herself, unknowingly reaching into a pocket while stumbling over a fallen branch, pulling out a series of hundred dollar bills. She took another breath, sighed, and said, "I can pay the tuition." She began to cry, shoving the cash back into the pocket, feeling sold, used. Gathering herself, she tried to find humor in where she was, sarcastically blurting out, "I end up having sex with my girlfriend and now I'm hobbling through woods dressed up as a wolf. I'm so messed up." She attempted to smile, but paused. She could still hear an echo through the woods of the Chinese businessmen cheering, laughing, shouting as if that moment would never end in time. Solving one solution of paying her tuition had created a dark hole that she did not want to carry, rather forget, and more importantly, she had no idea of a way out. She felt lost, abandoned...

Joshua still sat beside the pond, gazing up to the sky with Samson by his side. Listening quietly to the waterfall, he could hear the gentle rustling of the branches of trees around him with an owl's distant hoot amongst the scattering of crickets calling for their mates. Joshua let nature embrace him as he walked over and lifted up a rock. Taking out pages of hidden poems beneath it, he sat down upon this rock and began writing in the stillness of the half moon without a single star in the sky. Joshua looked up toward the tree atop the waterfall. It's branches, though appearing lifeless and barren, seemed to move as remnants of shadowy miniature sculptures of the past, like frozen mysterious figures coming to life. Joshua wondered what lay within its soul, what secret of life did this majestic tree hold? He began to speak in his own poetry.

"What is that tree? What symbol lies within its soul? Who's hand is it reaching for?

Who's name is it calling out in the wind? For what soul doest not have a mystery, a hidden truth awaiting to be discovered, a hope of many somehow resting within a distant dream of a few? But if so, how can one reach for what cannot be seen, that which is within? Do we really have souls? Are there really mysteries, miracles, awaiting to be reached for and awakened?"

Joshua walked over and looked into the reflections of the pond. He looked up, continuing to speak in verses of poetry, imagining the fair maiden of his dreams standing on the other side of the pond. "Her beauty was that of an open heart, endless upon the vision, unending upon the touch. Where are you from, my lady? What star cast out such brightness without fear of loss of its own shining? 'Tis you, my lady? For thou art my beauty; cast upon a stillness of a shallow wound, full of light, carried by all the stars of the sky..."

Joshua envisioned the fair maiden of his dreams appearing out of the woods, walking to the water's edge on the other side of the pond just beyond his reach as Samson walked up and sat down next to him with a quizzical look, wondering who Joshua was talking to.

Joshua, as if in a daze, shed his clothes and walked up to his chest halfway into the pond. He looked down, as if peering through a glass, and saw the reflection of his face beside the half moon in the sky. Reaching down, but seemingly up, cupping the moon in his hand, he raised it to her, imagining his fair maiden still standing on the other side of the pond.

"I give you the moon, my lady... I give you the glorious moon!"

Suddenly, he heard a rustle from the bushes. Someone was coming... He got out of the pond and ran, naked, up the hill with Samson following and ducked behind a tree, pulling down a branch to see, looking out.

Cradling the feeling of being lost and abandoned, Nia came upon an opening, a nestled pond deep within the woods, seeing the reflection of a half moon within a pond. She walked to the side of it, dressed in the wolf costume, as Joshua peered out, further pushing down the branch to see. "A wolf?" Joshua whispered to Samson. "How could it be." Nia turned. He saw it was a young woman. "Oh, it's a woman," Joshua said to Samson. "I wonder why she's dressed like that?" Samson did not move.

"Screw being compliant," Nia said, taking off the wolf costume and tossing it to the side of the pond. Naked, she stepped into the pond, walking up to the water covering her chest, with the half moon before her. She reached down and touched it, cupping it in her hands. Going in deeper, reaching out with her arms, she began to swim, turning over, floating on her back with the moonlight shining upon her, attempting to wash away the memory of the pain. Joshua pushed the branch down even further, wondering if she was real as she flipped over; the moon glistening upon her bare back; with her submerging beneath the surface in a single breath of the wind within the image of the reflection of the half-moon.

Silence. A long moment passed with just the sounds of the forest as Nia swam deep under the water. Joshua could no longer see her. Nia swam to the bottom, momentarily wanting to die. Taking a few gulps of water, she coughed and swam upward, bursting through the surface with one deep gasp for breath.

"I'm sorry. I'm sorry," She said, looking up to the sky. Then, she noticed the tree atop the waterfall. She sensed something, something strange, like a strong force. She swam up to the ponds edge and walked out. She looked around, completely naked and wet, feeling vulnerable.

Yet, she heard a voice, a voice coming from that tree. She found a place to climb the rocks of the waterfall and made her way up to a path leading to the Tree. Joshua and Samson watched, walking out to the edge of the pond, white sand.

Making her way, climbing to atop the cliff, *naked* - she saw it, the Tree, and the ocean behind it as she felt a strong wind, a force blowing toward her, moving toward the cliff from across the sea. Walking up to the tree, she gazed upon it. She placed her hand gently on it and looked out across the sea. She stood in silence, in a reverence, she felt strange after what she had done. Still, the wind gained strength as if speaking to her, speaking to the essence of the most inner part of her soul. "My child, do not be ashamed. For I am the Omega and the End. I will be with you always and you always will be with me. Forsake not the darkness of lies, you are beautiful within the heart of My hope. Do not fear loss of her way, I am awaiting for you with open arms and all of My love. Do not give up. Darkness will not win. My love is greater than an evil this earth possesses for My Son has given His life, for you my child, to have your life."

Samson ran to Nia's side. Nia, startled at first, reached down and petted him. Samson walked out to the cliff's edge and howled out as Joshua raised his fist, standing by the fall.

Suddenly, stars emerged from the sky as Samson's echo sounded out far across the sea...

Nia turned. She saw Joshua approaching toward the cliff. Shaken, she ran back into the wood, cutting off the path and through the brush, shielding herself with her arms with Joshua closely following. Breaking free out into the open, she ran toward a black iron gate. It was open. She ran through it and frantically closed it, bolting it shut, behind her. Samson appeared, waiting for Joshua. When Joshua caught up to Samson, they both watched as Nia ran toward a large mansion, becoming seemingly a shadow, as if running into the clouds of the mansion atop a large hill. Joshua, hesitant, waked up and placed his hands upon the iron, cold, gate.

Inside Saint Michael's Church, Father Gabe was bowed in prayer inside a small chapel.

Candles lit up by an altar by his side. He smiled. "They're getting closer to their destiny," he said, gazing up toward the Cross. "They're hearing Your Call," he added.

The weathervane atopT's house spun in a direction pointing East as the wind chimes sounded out. Their father had his Bible open to ACTS 1:11.

Covering herself with her arms, Nia tiptoed around the side of the mansion naked, peering in through the library window. The senator was standing by the window, talking to the butler. The butler handed him a large roll of money. The senator smiled, followed by a nod. Nia, knowing that she couldn't just walk naked into the house through the front door, turned, looking to find another way in. She crunched down and continued, all the while hoping not to be caught, trying to remain in the shadows close to the side of the mansion, clutched hundred dollar bills.

"Got my tuition," She proudly said in a whisper, adding, "But, I won't be... compliant." Nia came to white wooden lattice arising up the side of the house toward the balcony of her bedroom with ivy woven on it. She climbed as she heard the senator's voice, now outside, a few yards away as Nia was only halfway up the lattice, clinging naked with her fingers and toes.

"What do we have here?" The senator called out. She froze, thinking he had spotted her. The senator walked out to the driveway. He picked up a pack of cigars on the ground by the side of the butler's car. He took one out, lit it, and smiled at the butler who was approaching. They talked with bursts of laughter as she watched them. She remained still, frozen, afraid to move.

Puffing on the cigar, the senator walked dangerously close to her, passing underneath the lattice right beneath her with the butler, Suddenly, she began to lose her grip with her fingers and toes. One foot slipped. She tried to hold back a gasp. The senator paused, appearing to hear a sound. The cigar smoke rose up to her. She tried not to cough.

"What's wrong?" The butler asked the senator.

"I don't know," the senator replied, looking like he was going to glance up.

Nia tried to hold on as her legs were tightening. Her chest and knees were pushing up against the lattice, feeling the splintered wood. The senator and butler let out a laugh and continued back around the house on the other side and, finally, inside. Nia heard the front door close. She took a relieved breath and continued her climb. After lifting herself over the side of the stone balcony, she paused to catch her breath. She glanced back out across the spanning mansion grounds, wondering about what she had just experienced. It seemed strange going from darkness to light so quickly. But the more she thought about it, the more sense it seemed. She had fallen and God had come after her, to help her, to give her that hope, that hand.

She smiled, looking out from the balcony and wondered what would happen next. Yet, this time, she had hope. She walked over to her small table by the side of the bed and secretly placed the money far within it's drawer, placing it in a small envelope, thinking, God in a bizarre way, had somehow taken care of her. She glanced back out her balcony and pondered upon the half moon. *Joshua and Samson made their way back through the woods down the moonlit path.*

She was drawn... back toward the balcony. Standing upon it, looking out, it was dark, only a single narrow stream of light, shooting off the front porch, joining bits of lights spilling out from the large windows below. She watched the tops of trees sway; the scattered bushes, the large garden with a maze of perfectly manicured hedges, and a fountain; the water rippling peacefully beneath the subtle rays of light. She smiled and turned, feeling a moment of peace.

Going back into her bedroom, she discovered her white gown,

cleaned from the bloodstains, laid out on her bed. Wondering, she pulled it over the top of her head and slid it down upon her as her bedroom door began to open.

Justin! I'm ready to go now! Melinda cried out up the stairs from the foyer below.

The senator, standing in the doorway, paused, and without a word, closed the door. Nia, still feeling an echoing effect of the drugs, swayed a bit, like the tops of the trees, as she finished putting on her gown, patting it in place, not seeing the shadow of darkness beyond her doorway. Yet, suddenly, sensing something unusual, startled, she went over and locked the bedroom door, continuing to wonder about what she had experienced. Was it real or, hopefully, just an illusion. She thought about the smoke, the leering eyes upon her, the laughter, and *the dragon table legs.*

As Melinda sat in the back seat of the limousine with the senator, the butler kept looking back at her with a demeaning smile through an open sliding window that separated them.

"Can we shut that?" Melinda asked the senator, gesturing toward the small window. "Why?" The senator replied, leaning over and kissing her on the cheek, sliding up the hem of her short black dress, placing his hand on the upper part of her thigh, exposing her white panties. "I don't like how he keeps staring at me. It's like he's waiting for me to do something," she answered with a slight gasp and downward cast of her eyes as the senator continued groping her atop her panties. "Maurice is a trusted employee. I owe him a lot," he said with a firmer grip.

"Please, Justin..."She placed his hand on his chest. She felt something inside his sports jacket. Partially. With her leopard panties partially exposed, she noticed a silver hand gun in the jacket of the senator. Fearful as to ask why he was carrying it, pushing him gently away, she sat back, pushed the bottom hem of her dressed down, and remained silent, becoming fearful.

"The luncheon is coming along nicely, you know, the one I told you about, for your fundraiser," she said, attempting to take some kind of control of the situation, she found herself in, in an attempt to bring it back to some type of normalcy. Yet, the butler continued to stare back at her with a leering anticipatory smile, looking into the rearview mirror, as if he knew. The senator nodded toward the butler as the butler reached through the small window and handed him a black leather riding crop, her eyes widening more in fear while pushing her legs together.

"What's that?" She nervously asked, pulling her bottom hem of her dress further down.

"Oh, this is just something that I used to train a wild horse, a long time ago," the senator said with a darkening look in his eyes, sliding the riding crop, slowly, back and forth in the palm of his hand as she felt his stronger grip. The senator tapped the riding crop on Melinda's knee.

"Oh, I got you something," he said with another tap on her knee. He reached behind the seat and took out a small wrapped gift. "Open it," he said, again tapping her with the riding crop.

Melinda, her hands shaking, began opening "the gift" while glancing up at the butler who she noticed was still watching her through the mirror. His eyes widened as she held up black lace stockings. "Thank you," she replied, putting them back into the box. Yet, the darkness from the box had escaped. A captivating display of power and seduction had just begun. "Put them on," the senator commanded. "Now?" She asked, still looking at the butler watching her with his exhilarated smile. The senator nodded, holding up the riding crop, twirling it in his hand as a masterful circus ringmaster. He watched, along with the butler, as she unraveled them and slowly pulled them up each bare outstretched leg. After slipping them on, she tried to push the hem of her dress back down, again. But, this time, the senator stopped her, raising it even more upward, almost to her hips - exposing her leopard skin thong-cut panties. "Now let us see. You have very nice legs. Doesn't she, Maurice?" The senator gestured with the riding crop at Melinda with an affirmative nod toward the butler. The butler nodded and smiled back. She turned and glanced out the window, attempting to run away deep within her mind as the senator started running the riding crop up and down the lace gripped tightly upon her legs, tantalizing her as she began envisioning a vast endless sea, waves rippling upon it with dark clouds approaching in the distance from an unusual reddish hue held within the horizon's edge.

The wind chimes on Joshua's front porch, five moons being held by an angel blowing a horn, sounded out in a strong wind. Joshua stood with Samson by his side, watching the city lights flicker in the valley below as Nia, in her bed, clasped upon her locket close to her chest. Joshua and Samson quietly watched as the flicker of lights became covered by the passing night. With Tim's truck gone and their house behind them remaining in darkness, Joshua leaned down and hugged Samson as Nia slowly drifted off to sleep while holding the locket upon her chest— *into a louder sounding chime of a distant wind of time from far off across the sea…*

The butler pulled up to the secluded house at the end of the dirt road on the mountainside, the one with the Chinese Businessmen. The other limousines were gone. "Wait here," the senator commanded Melinda. Melinda obeyed, waiting in the back of the limousine, peering out the crack of the partially open window by her side with her fingers clasping the edge of the top of the glass. She could see the butler walking sinisterly alongside the senator toward the house with small bursts of laughter and whispers. She couldn't hear what they were saying as they abruptly paused on the porch and glanced back at her gazing out through the crack. Quickly, she backed away, trying not to be seen, all the way to the other side, clinging to the door. Leaning up against it, as much as she could, she pulled down the hem of her short dress, pressed her knees together, and wondered what they had planned. When the limousine door flung open, she almost fell out. But the senator caught her, taking her firmly by the arm.

"Come, Melinda. I have a romantic birthday surprise for you."

Melinda was still a little drunk and staggered a bit, submissively clinging to the senator's arm, as they walked across the winding stone driveway and toward the house. Suddenly, the senator stopped.

"Take them off," he said, gesturing to her heels. "Take them off," he more sternly commanded with the spotlight upon her, being led into "the center ring."

Melinda reached down while balancing herself on the senator and did as he said. Yet, while holding her heels in her hands, she was afraid to move with her toes curling under, feeling the cold sharpness of the rocks. Violently, and without warning, the senator grabbed the soles, ripping the heels from her, tossing them in a bush, and stared deep into her once again with his fiery, commanding eyes. Bending her arm far up behind her back, he escorted her over the stones cutting through her stockings and into her as she tried to tiptoe on the balls of her feet. The senator, smiling, was enjoying watching her wincing as she gingerly skipped across the sharp edges of the rocks until she finally had to stop to rub one of her feet.

"Did I tell you to stop?"

Melinda continued on with the senator pulling her more forcefully by "the reigns," leading her into the dark house and toward the room with the dragon table legs, the same room where her daughter had entertained the Chinese Businessmen. Upon entering, she was stunned, mesmerized by forty lit candles surrounding the dragon leg white marble table. The butler was no where to be seen as, slowly, the senator began undressing her, as frightened, at first, she tried to resist but finally succumbed, quickly finding herself standing naked before him in the flickering candlelight. Keeping her head down with her hands obediently at there sides; her skin tingled in rising goose bumps as parts of her body swelled and hardened, feeling the cold air aura of the room. He gave her a nodding approving smile as he moved closer, kissing her neck. She started to gasp, drawing back breaths, her head falling back into the darkness as "a series of dark clouds moved across the sea towards land." Lifting her up into his arm, he carried her to the white marble table, sitting her down pin it, slowly, gently guiding her over onto her stomach.

Shockingly, she discovered leather straps and been placed onto the dragon table legs as she felt him, suddenly and swiftly, bound her wrists and ankles until she was firmly spread eagle, face down, unable to move upon the table. Petrified in her subservient role, and yet enthralled by his total control, feeling the coldness of the white marble rush through her, her goose bumps exploded as he asserted his uncompromising command.

"I told you I have a birthday surprise for you," the senator said as he tenderly placed a blindfold on her.

"Wait. I don't..." she started to say. "It's alright," the senator reassured her, snugly fitting it over her eyes. As she sensed the arising warmth of the candles around her, she strangely felt an "ancient darkness," awaiting to erupt as if in a battle upon and ancient, distant wind. The man clutching her... she began to writhe, so vulnerable, so at his mercy. Yet, the touch was not that of the senator. Upon her, caressing her, she felt elderly hands as she attempted to twist, kick, and buck free, the blindfold unmoving, snuggly fit. It was the butler. "Justin!" She screamed out. But he didn't answer her. He just stood in silence on the porch smoking one of the cigars, tapping the riding crop in his left hand and on the side of his leg, orchestrating the circus in which Melinda was the main event.

As the butler continued to ride her, like an old out of practice cowboy trying to break in a newly found wild horse, she continued struggling to break free. But the more she struggled, the tighter the butler's grip became with the tightening of the bonds that the senator had devised well with his carefully planned sailor slip knots, her hands and feet tied securely to the dragon legs.

Each dragon looked fierce, carved into the wood, *ancient antiquity,* appearing to come alive, the claws long, the teeth poised and sharp, and the eyes, the eyes of her tormentor even more fierce.

Melinda lay draped over the table, broken and tamed, finally giving up, her hands and feet remaining in stillness, limp, as if the life, her will, was drained from them. Sweat poured down the butler's face, his old body resting atop of her. She had accepted her cast fate, her role in the senator's house; her soul, identity, somehow ripped from her and thrown to the wind as the candles flickered upon the dragons' eyes with the senator, on the porch, looking out beyond the mountain, taking another puff on his lit cigar.

With the chimes sounding louder, the wind thundering much stronger, Joshua rose up from his front porch and walked out to the center of his yard. Looking upward, he raised his arms to the sky as Samson, after letting out a howl, met him by his side. With the wind almost blowing both of them away, as if magically, the canvass was lifted off of Tim's secret project, enabling Joshua to look over and be amazed at what he saw, what Tim had been building all this time.

Maybe Tim hadn't given up believing in their mother's stories, Joshua thought.

Far off at the edge of the mansion grounds, Nia, awakened from her sleep, wearing only her gown, was mysteriously drawn by a force and stood in the strong wind, gazing upward at the sky as if something was coming. Suddenly, she heard something, coming from an old barn she had rarely noticed, hidden far back behind the garden at the base of a small hill. Slowly, she walked toward it. When she came to the door, she reached out and started to open it. A piece of rotted wood fell off. She heard the sound again, something whinnying. Like her locket, she had never looked inside. She always thought it was some old barn of the senator's that he had used long ago. Peering inside, unable to see, with her feet bare, courageously she took a step, feeling damp straw beneath her. She could hear it breathing, struggling it sounded, inhaling with a lot of mucus. The manure suddenly overwhelmed her. The barn probably hadn't been cleaned in years. Getting closer, it whinnied again. It was a horse, standing all alone, in the corner, as if forgotten.

Nia's bare foot kicked into an old lantern. "Ow. That hurts," she winced out. She lifted her foot and rubbed out the ·pain. Picking the lantern up, feeling it in the darkness, she discovered a pack of matches wedged into its metal base. She blew off the cobwebs, lit it, and turned it up using a small brass ring on the side. As she did, she thought about the carousel her father had taken her on when she was a little girl, riding a grand stallion, feeling the ocean's breeze, his arms around her. It was then he gave her the locket. He told her that no matter where she was, he would always be with her and always love her.

Nia moved carefully over to the white horse and reached up her hands to a clear gel covering the horse's eyes, as if he had been crying for years and no one had cared to wipe it away. Startled, at first, the horse bucked a bit but calmed as Nia gently placed her hand upon him. She ran her hand tenderly down the side of his face, down his nose, to a metal bit embedded by growing into his mouth. The horse barely had any teeth left, his hooves long and unkempt.

Nia's heart sank. She looked down and saw only a half inch of water with floating insects in a rusted bucket with a little bit of scattered oats spread about the ground. She tried to break the chain, but she couldn't. As with her life, it was tied too strong, too tight, all knotted and twisted.

The butler joined the senator on the porch, staring out into the shadows of the night with Melinda still bound to the dragon-legged table, still swirling in the carved images of the wood. The senator offered him a cigar.

"How was she?" The senator asked. "Smooth," the butler replied.

Taking hold of the cigar, the butler lit it, sliding it back and forth in his mouth, and took a puff... Smoke encircled them, mixing with a dampened night's dew.

"Should we untie her?" The butler asked.

"You don't untie a wild horse you're trying to break, Maurice," the senator said, holding up the riding crop, adding, "After breaking it down, you don't let it right up. You keep beating it until it finally gives in. It takes time to tame a rebellious animal." The senator handed the riding crop to the butler.

After lighting another cigar, this time for himself, the senator continued. "No. Don't let her right up. Let her lie there and think about it. Let everything sink in, become a part of her, so she will always remember, realize her new role as... our girl." The senator gestured with her dress in his other hand. Taking it, he walked off the porch. "I'm going for a walk, Maurice." He turned back. "Oh. You'll see that our girl gets home?"

The butler nodded with a devious remaining grin as he proudly placed Melinda's leopard skin thong panties, the trophy of his conquest, into his pocket. He would use it to remind her of her place, he thought. The senator paused walking away from the porch. He then turned and said, "I want that church torn down." "Which one?" The butler asked. The senator just smiled, briefly gazing upward. "You know which one," the senator replied, walking onward into an arising unusual red-cast mist...

Nia lugged the rusted bucket she had filled with water across the mansion grounds toward the old barn, appearing confused, distressed.

"Now, I just need to find more oats," she said, raising the bucket higher up, by her side. She kicked the barn door open with her foot. The horse was no longer whinnying. He was silent. Filled to the brim, she placed the bucket down before him. He tried to reach down to drink, but he couldn't. The chain was too short. So she raised the heavy bucket, struggling, with water splashing on her silk white gown, so that he could drink. He drank it slowly, weakly, as she held it up with its metal edge resting on her chest, trying not to splash any more on herself. Finally, she had to put it down. It was too heavy. She reached back up and started petting his brow. Her touch seemed to soothe him as the churning winds outside began to calm.

Turning around, she knelt down and began gathering up some of the sparse scattered oats. It was then she saw the riding boots, his shadow over her in the flickering light of the lantern on the ground. *Fearfully, she slowly looked up. It was the senator.* The senator forcibly took hold of the lantern and held it close to her face, casting himself into a *further darkness as the lantern dangled from his fingertips.* Tossing the lantern, smashing it into a giant stone brazier, rekindling primeval ashes and coals, it awakened a fiery blaze... He then reached for a branding iron, and cast it into the fire as Nia's eyes widened with a gasp...

As Melinda timidly sat alone in the back of the limousine, she was curled up naked in the backseat, her knees raised tight up against her chest, her arms wrapped around them in a fetal position as a newborn demon to darkness. She appeared shocked, stunned, staring wide-eyed out the window, unblinking as the butler watched her from the mirror with a conquerer's look.

The butler lowered the limousine's back windows, pressing on the lock key as a sudden rush of wind overcame Melinda. She curled up more horrified as the butler slowed, riding down the street with passerby's looking in. Some laughed. Some pointed. Some appeared concerned. Some laughed and cheered. He continued to parade her around dense populated blocks, unable to break free from a dark cast of circumstances that began with a thought, a look, a touch, a simple sinister smile. The darkness had been locked around her, the windows remaining open to her soul as her sweat became tingling ice upon her skin, sinking deeper and deeper into her fate.

"Please..." she began to plead. "Please, I'll do as you say," she ended with an admission of defeat. The butler nodded with a wider smile, raised the windows, and drove into a rising mist.

Chapter 8

Underneath a partially lit moon, Joshua walked out onto his front porch, sensing something was changing, a transformation somewhere out there, hidden within the dense woods. The wind chimes were silent, dangling as if in a dream, as he walked toward Tim's secret project, carefully covering it back up with the canvass. Appearing concerned, he began to look around, feeling a darkness surrounding him, demons dancing, far off at a horizon's edge.

Suddenly headlights appeared, passing across Joshua's brow. Tim's truck pulled up in the driveway. Joshua approached the driver's side. Tim's window was done. He looked in. Glancing down, Joshua saw a small bag of cocaine wedged in between a half-filled McDonald's super- sized Coca Cola and partially eaten Big Mac. Tim's eyes looked glazed over.

"Are you alright?" Joshua asked.

"I'm fine. Are you alright?" Tim responded.

Angrily, Tim got out of his truck, slammed the truck's door and walked into the house. Joshua glanced up. He gasped. A demon, scaly, dark, folded wings, stood just out of the woods, staring at him. It quickly darted back within the trees. Joshua shook his head and looked down as Samson ran up to his side.

"It's alright, Samson. Just seeing things. That's all," Joshua said, adding, "They're just demons... We'll stay close to God and not fall into the darkness."

Inside the mansion, Melinda stormed into her bedroom, which was separate from the senator's, and tore off her clothes and jumped into the shower. Making sure it was hot, she grabbed a bar of soap and started to scrub, trying to get the old man smell off of her. She sunk down, sitting in the tub, the shower pummeling her while she cried. The petals of the miracle rose Joshua had placed in front of the cross, were mysteriously bleeding...

Nia was in bed, curled up underneath her covers wearing her gown. Putting her hand to her chest, then to her neck, she discovered that her locket was gone. She didn't know what had happened to it. She thought it might have fallen under the bed as she briefly patted around the covers and the sheets and then leaned over her bed looking for it. "Great. Now I can't find my locket," she said to herself.

Suddenly, her door began to open. She went back under the covers. "Nia," her mother said.

Nia looked out, bringing the covers down to just above her lips. She didn't say anything as her mother, dressed in sweats, walked over and got into bed under the covers next to her. They both lay there a moment, with their backs to each other, silent. Finally, her mother said, "You were right. I should have believed you. The senator isn't the man I thought he was."

They rolled over and faced each other.

"What are you going to do?" Nia asked.

"I'm leaving. I'm going back east, and I want you to come with me. I should have never brought you out here," her mother replied.

Nia turned over on her back, gazed up at the ceiling, and said, "I can't leave yet." "Why?"

"I have to save someone first," Nia replied. "Who?"

"A friend," Nia simply answered.

The old horse in the barn cried out before the flames of the brazier.

"But the senator...You can't stay here. He's too powerful, too deviant."

"He's much more than that," Nia replied, adding, "He's... something dark. He's a..."

In the barn, the senator stared into the brazier's blaze, as if he was a part of it, as Melinda drifted off into a sleep - envisioning his fiery, captivating eyes. Taking out the branding iron from the hot coals, the senator went toward the old horse. Frightened, breaking his chain with a sudden explosion of an enormous unseen strength, the horse tried to escape. But the senator grabbed hold of the chain tightly as he thrust the iron upon the faded mark of the horse, bucking whinnying loudly. Slowly, the horse began to moan, becoming softer, quieter, until he finally fell. Nia quietly got out of bed, turned on a small light atop her dressing table, and lifted her gown to look at her bare bottom in the mirror. And there, upon it, was a brand mark of a *DRAGON*.

1969. Vietnam. With the bombardment over, the "Fire in the Sky" finally succumbed to the reappearance of bright stars in the sky. Ed lowered the dead little girl that had asked if Santa Claus was coming, carefully and gently to the ground as women and children slowly came out of their hiding places. Children who were burned, cried out the most as the haze from the bombardment was clearing, as the mist over the pond after a rainstorm. Michael, with Mai Lee and Hoa Sung close by his side, walked up beside Ed. Gently brushing away blood off the dead little girl's cheek, Ed quoted Shakespeare, "'Good night sweet, princess, may angel's wings...'" Ed gazed up at Michael, into his eyes. Ed paused then asked, "If I die here, could you promise me that you make sure my body gets back home?" Michael nodded, "Yes," then gently raised Ed up by the arm, leaving the little girl where she lay lifeless and still.

The next day inside the large church next to the strip club, Father Gabe was leading a group of singing children in the balcony. He was signing for those who were deaf as the children sang the "Adoration of Sweet Jesus."

When Nia awoke, she was lying on top of her bed in a fetal position. Her mother was gone as the sunlight, strangely, was brightly shining down upon her. She got up and walked over to the balcony, gazing out across the mansion grounds. With the rising new day, sunshine permeated through artistically-designed stained glass windows, looking like dancing demons, into the marble foyer of the mansion as servants were bustling, trying to get everything ready for the Annual Republican Tea Party. The tea party was hosted each year by political officials and candidates' wives, and it was an event that Nia's mother had been thoroughly prepped for by way of her submissive sexual performance of the night before. As Nia's mother, struggled to forget, reaching out to the farthest edge of her memories, she would soon discover as she entertained at the tea party that she was still bound to the marble table, still a slave to the senator, gazing into the deep carvings of the dragon's legs, looking into the deep carvings of evil within its eyes.

"Now, this is going to be a very special tea party. All the women of my club will be here," Nia's mother said to a servant as Nia, dressed only in cheeky boy-shorts and a tank top, entered into the foyer of the mansion with *shadows of dancing demons.*

"Mom. What are you doing?" Nia asked.

"Just a second. Over there, Maria. We have to make sure every table is set," Nia's mother cried out.

"Mom. We have to talk," Nia said, attempting to get her mother's attention.

"Alright, dear," Nia's mother responded, adding, as Nia pulled her off to the side, "I'll help you in a minute, Maria."

"Mom."

"What? What's the matter?"

"What's the matter? I thought everything is a matter. That's why you're leaving, remember," Nia answered, "Do you remember, mom?"

Nia's mother paused, then whispered in her ear, "I'm not leaving now. I'm staying..." "What! You're staying? But the senator..." Nia said, appearing shocked.

"I'm not going to leave you here alone in this house. When you're ready, then I'll think about going too. But I'm not going to leave you in this house alone. I don't want anything to happen to you. You're my only daughter, and I love you."

Nia guided her farther away from the servants. "What did he do to you last night, Mom?" "Never mind. I don't want to talk about it.

I just don't want anything to happen to you." "Mom. What did he do to you? You look... different."

"Last night..." her mother paused, taking a breath.

"I know. Last night you were really upset. You were ready to leave," Nia said, interrupting, then letting her mother continue.

"Last night he just got carried away. It was kind of my own fault. To tell you the truth, I remembered later that I had told him a couple months ago, in passing, after a couple glasses of wine, over dinner, about a..." She paused again, waiting for a servant to pass, "...fantasy that I had, and he decided to give it to me for my birthday. That's all."

"What was it?" Nia timidly asked.

"Never mind. It's not something that I can share with my daughter. It's too embarrassing.

He apologized before he left this morning if he went too far. And I'm fine now with it. I really am. I mean, we all have fantasies, right? I just don't want anything like that to happen to you. Don't worry about me. I'm alright. I've accepted it. It happened and now it's over. A lot of people do things they are ashamed of, right?"

"Mom. What did he do to you?" Her mother remained silent as a small tear began to fall down her mother's left cheek. Nia paused, reaching up, brushing away the tear. "Mom. I have to tell you something and, I don't want you to get mad at me, alright?"

"Just tell me. They're starting to look over here," Nia's mother smiled, brushing away another tear, at a couple of servants who were looking over at Nia and her talking in the corner of the foyer near the library.

"Just don't get mad at me, alright?" "Please, Nia."

"The senator's been..." "Been what?"

"He's been raping me, Mom," Nia whispered.

"What knives should we set, Madam?" Maria asked, interrupting.

"The new ones, Maria," Nia's mother, stunned, answered. "The ones that cut far and deep."

"Very good, Madam," Maria replied as she went to set the tables that were meticulously aligned outside on the front yard for the tea party.

Nia began to cry as her mother took her into her arms, remaining stunned and silent. Nia continued. "I didn't tell you because I was afraid to. I was afraid you'd think it was somehow my fault and get mad at me."

"You should have told me, Nia," she replied with a forced fake smile at passing servants, trying to act like everything was fine. She waited until all the servants had passed and were outside setting the tables before continuing. "I can't believe that you hid this from me."

As another servant started to approach, she took Nia by the arm and led her into the library. After closing the door, she stood a few feet away from Nia as Nia, appearing confused, backed up against the piano. Her mother looked angry with her eyebrows tensed, arms folded across her chest, and right foot tapping.

"Look at me, Nia. Look at me. I have to know the truth. Did you in any way say or do anything to..." her mother paused. "...lead him on?"

"Mom!"

"To get back at me, to get attention? Anything?"

"So you think it's my fault? After what he did to you?"

"Well, you have been having emotional problems lately, and I know how your are sometimes."

"What do you mean, 'How I am?'"

"I mean, look at you. You're always half-naked in front of everyone and the other day I found in your bureau a check from Destiny's Dance Club. What's that all about?"

"You have no right going into my private things."

"What are you, a stripper or something? Is that something else that you didn't tell me about?" Nia lowered her eyes away from her mother's. "It's true, isn't it? You can't hide things from me Nia. I know my own daughter. And I certainly would know if my own daughter was raped." Her mother turned to leave.

"This isn't about you, Mom. I was the one who was raped," Nia cried out.

"Stop saying that!" her mother angrily replied, pulling at her own hair and turning back. "I knew you'd get mad and blame me!" Nia shouted, leaving the library, bumping into a servant with a tray as she stormed away up the staircase.

Her mother followed her up the stairs and into the bedroom. When she entered, Nia was standing, crying, as if in slow motion, with one knee upon her bed.

"I can't believe you think it's my fault," Nia said.

"It's not all your fault, Nia. It's partially my fault too. I should have raised you better."

"You're defending him?" Nia sank down; motion sped up. Sitting on her bed with one leg crossed underneath the other, she said, "I can't believe that you just said that. He raped me, Mom! He's the one! What is it that you don't understand? And who knows what he did to you last night, too!"

"Keep your voice down," her mother sternly replied, closing the bedroom door.

"You know what, Mom? You and the senator deserve each other. You know why? You're right. You probably really enjoyed whatever he did to you last night. Don't pretend to feel guilty or protective of me. You're just covering up your own feelings of guilt. You liked it, whatever it was that happened to you, didn't you, mom? That's why you're not leaving. It's not because of me. It's because you like being, what did Shakespeare say? Oh, yes, a pernicious whore..."

Her mother stormed over and slapped her face. "Don't you dare talk to me like that.

Don't you dare. And you're quoting Shakespeare? Really? What's your interest in poetry all of a sudden."

Unnoticed, the butler slightly opened the bedroom door a crack, watching...

"I'm sorry. But I don't know how to get you to believe me. You never believe me," Nia said, looking toward the white laced curtains of the balcony.

"Now you listen to me..." her mother began. "Do you think it's easy hearing that your daughter has been raped? Do you know what that means? Do you know how that feels? And who am I to believe, Nia? Who? I want to believe you, I really do. But you've been living here for three years, three years, Nia, and not once did you indicate in any way that you were being raped. You were never traumatized or anything. And when you strut around half-naked all the time, doing drugs..."

"I don't strut around half-naked all the time! Would you stop saying that?"

"But you still do drugs." "Sometimes."

"Well, were you on drugs the times he raped you?"

Nia envisions the senator reaching out to her, pulling her back through the lance curtains. "Oh. So now the truth comes out. How do you know what really happened when you were stoned?" her mother quipped.

"It's the only way I could take it. It's not my fault, mom. And for the last time, I don't strut around half-naked!" Nia shouted. "I don't!"

"Oh, really? Do you remember the time that night, when you used cocaine and you walked down the staircase and out onto the front lawn past everyone in just your panties?"

"I didn't know anyone was home."

"Yeah. Right. And being stoned had nothing to do with it. What were you doing anyway, getting the mail?"

"I wanted to see the stars. I already explained this! There were supposed to be shooting stars!"

"In just your panties? Oh. That's right. You did explain it. Now I remember. You thought it would be fun, like skinny dipping. You wanted to lie on the side of the hill and look up, see all the shooting stars with your bare body basking in the moonlight. You're always showing off, always. Well, here, show off some more!" Her mother shouted, opening the drawer of her bureau and tossing Nia a pair of glittery gold pasties and a g-string. "Go ahead. Put them on so you can strut down stairs and outside like you did before in front of everyone! I'm sure the guests of my tea party would love to see my daughter in her work uniform."

"I quit. I'm not stripping anymore."

"Like the drugs, right. You can't ever tell the truth! Ever! And now you're telling me this rape story..." Her mother started crying, pulling more intensely at her own hair.

"Mom, please. I'm sorry, alright. I'm sorry. Just calm down. I wasn't raped. Okay? I just made it up to get attention like you said," Nia pleaded, bringing her knees up to her chest. "And I'm sorry for whatever happened to you last night. I really am. I know you must feel ashamed. And I know, like you said—it must have really been embarrassing. I guess you'll have to either move on or confront it. I mean, I've been in... situations that I've wanted to forget."

"I'm sure you have."

"But last night is not my fault either, mom."

"Everything's you're fault, Nia! Everything! My daughter, the drug addict stripper. You know what, Nia—my precious... daughter—I think you're the one who likes it, the attention, all the sex. I really do. And now, for whatever reason, you're making up this rape story. But you are right about one thing, Nia. I don't believe you. I never have. You've lied too much to me. You've just hurt me too much. You're all life has been a lie, beginning with your birth." her mother ended, walking out as the butler backed away from the door, hiding, lurking in the shadows.

"I'm not the one who hurt you, mom," Nia whispered.

The senator intercepted Nia's mother as she walked down the staircase. "Melinda. Is everything alright?"

Melinda gathered herself. "Why, yes. I was just having a talk with Nia."

"I hope you're ready for your tea party and have reminded Nia about the important fundraiser here next week."

"Yes. I did. She said that she would be able to come and, more importantly, to behave and not embarrass you in any way. I made her promise. Don't worry. She'll be under control."

"And you reminded her that she has to dress conservatively?" the senator asked, taking her by the hand.

"Yes. I picked out an outfit for her, very conservative," Melinda replied, then timidly asked, "Justin. Can I talk to you?" She gestured toward the library.

He gestured back. "After you."

In the library, Melinda stood backed up against the piano as Nia had moments before. He stood, like Melinda had, as if becoming angry. "What do you want to talk to me about?" he asked.

"Did you rape my daughter?" Melinda blurted out.

The fireplace mysteriously became lit with a sudden eruption of flames as Melinda was startled with the loud crackling of the wood. "We've had sex," the senator answered as Melinda appeared stunned, shaking. Her voice began to quiver.

"Did you rape my daughter?" Melinda asked again.

"The senator paused, looking over at the flames, then answered. "Yes. Several times. In fact, I've been raping her repeatedly for the past three years."

The senator moved closer to her, running his hand down the side of her cheek. "You see, Nia is another one of my girls. But unlike you, I'm her only man. I'd kill anyone else who touches her." The senator paused with a smile, then continued. "Don't tell me that you didn't know? How could a mother not know that her own daughter is being raped?"

"If you ever touch her again, I'll..."

"You'll what? Kill me?" The senator asked gingerly wiping away tears from Melinda's eyes as she stood before him frozen in fear of what he would do next. He reached over and started to hit the piano keys one by one. "Have you ever killed anyone, Melinda? Seen the last gasp of breath, the cast of darkness, lifelessness across their eyes, their souls?" The sounding of notes stopped. "No, you haven't. Unlike me your hands are not stained with blood. They're pure, innocent. Instead of killing me, you'll try to turn me in, bring me to justice. Go ahead," he said with a deep, arrogant laugh. "But who will they believe, a respected senator or a former whore?" The senator paused. "Did you forget where you came from? I found you as a prostitute?

Remember? In that sleazy dive of a strip club back east. I saved you, took you from rags to riches. And this is how you repay me, with threats." He reached up and ran his fingers gently across her quivering lips as she trembled.

"If I tell...it will bring you down," she whispered out.

"How quickly we forget who our friends are," he said, more forcibly tapping the piano. "You know, maybe I should give you back to your pimp, the one who almost beat you to death that time. I think he's still looking for you, isn't he? He thinks you're still his property." The senator let out a laugh. "Oh, by the way, did you ever tell Nia what a slut you were? It would be interesting to see how she responds to finding out her mother was a prostitute."

"I have friends. I have standing. They'll believe me. I'm respected..." she started to say. "You have friends? I think you better remember your place, your role, your niche. On the societal food chain, I'd say you're a bottom feeder, sucking on algae and waste while flapping your gills. You have no friends, only the ones I allow you to have. You're a scaleless loner, like a catfish. Wouldn't you say? Don't worry. I won't blow your cover over being a whore. Of course, there is the threat of turning me in. And maybe you're right. They might believe you, someone with a disfigured face from an unfortunate, unforeseen accident, possibly from being burned."He grabbed her by the hair and turned her face toward the fire. He then ran his hand down the side of her face again, more slowly this time, as he continued. "Better yet, maybe they'll believe a grieving mother whose daughter was mysteriously murdered in the park or down by the beach. It might even get me more votes." The senator smiled as he started to tap the piano keys more rapidly in an evil melody never before heard, the flickering flames dancing in rhythm.

Suddenly, Melinda began to feel sweat building up beneath the ruffles of the blouse around her neck. Besides her dark-colored blouse, she was wearing flat black shoes and black stockings that could only be seen beneath the hem of a long navy blue skirt which hung down far below her knees; she appeared to be in mourning.

"I heard you hit a few high notes last night. Did you have a nice time? You were really bucking near the end on that dragon-legged table," the senator added.

"You bastard!" She finally cried out. Taking hold of a flower pot atop the piano, she tried to hit him with it. But he caught her wrist and the flower pot fell, breaking on the floor as the flames arose higher in the fireplace with an angered look in his eye.

"Still some fight in you, hmm? Maybe I'll summon your lover, Maurice."

"Please, Justin," she pleaded as he held her tight, twisting her wrist. "I just don't want you to hurt Nia anymore."

He brought Melinda closer to him, almost to his lips, as she felt his heated breaths from the arising flames. "I'll think about it. But you have to do exactly as I say, be my little obedient housewife, you know, play your role."

"I will. I promise. Just please don't hurt her anymore."

"When Maurice comes in here, I want to see what kind of encore you can give to last night's performance. If you prove to me that you are still...behaving, then I'll leave Nia alone. She will be safe. I'll never touch her again."

"You will?" Melinda asked.

"Yes. That's my promise," he whispered with a kiss on her lips, adding, "I never lie," with a smile. Then he paused while running his fingers slowly across her lips, sticking his first index finger briefly into her mouth, encircling it upon her tongue. After reaching in with his thumb, he took hold of her tongue and pulled it out.

"Maybe I should cut this off to be sure you keep your promise," he said.

She gasped, trembling, fearful of the touch of his threats, unable to move, frozen in the moment, still shaking, curled up naked in the backseat with passerby's laughter and shouting.

"No. I'll let you keep it for now," he said, letting go. "But, if you cross me..." He took hold of both sides of her cheeks with one hand and began to squeeze. "...in anyway, by attempting to leave or betray me, both you and Nia, wherever you go, will not be safe, will not have peace. I'm the one with friends. Do you understand?"

She began to open her mouth to say, "Yes," but he placed his hand atop her parted lips and said, "Just nod." She did as he ordered in silence.

"Good. Now I want you now to go over to the corner and get yourself ready." "May I speak?" she asked.

"Yes," he replied, appearing disgusted, taking his hand away from her. "How do you want me to get ready?" she nervously asked.

"I want you to take off all of this," he said, flipping up a ruffle around her neck. "Everything," he ordered.

"Then what?" she asked with her voice shaking more.

"After you're naked, I want you to go sit in that leather chair by the fireplace and spread your legs as wide as you can over the tops of the arms of the chair, put your hands up behind your head, close your eyes, and then wait. *We'll* tell you what we want you to do next. But if you don't follow these instructions..."

"But my guests, they will be arriving soon," she uttered out. "No. I don't think I can do this, not again, not with everyone here. No. I won't do this, not this soon, please," she pleaded.

"Not even for your daughter's sake?" he simply asked. Melinda paused, bowed her head, and whispered, "Alright."

The senator added, "*We'll* be quiet. No one will hear a thing. I'll take care of your guests." Leaving, he closed the door. She then heard him lock it with a key.

Melinda wanted to escape, but she didn't know how. She thought that she would go along one more time with whatever it was the senator had planned until she could get Nia out of the house and safely back east. She slowly began taking off her clothes, placing them atop the piano seat. Once completely naked, she walked over to one of the leather chairs, the one on the right facing outward toward the library's door, and sat in it, keeping her knees close together, gazing at the fire. A moment later, she thought she heard someone coming. So she quickly spread her legs, placing her one leg over one arm of the chair and her other leg over the other arm. As she put her hands up behind her head, her toes pointed and her legs tensed, she stretched them farther apart, trying to stay in position with her bare bottom barely touching the seat. Suddenly, she heard the key rattling in the door, unlocking it. She took a deep breath and closed her eyes. The library door opened - A group of guests for the tea party stood in the doorway.

"Oh my," one of the tea party ladies said as the rest of them stood staring in disbelief. A few laughed. Melinda opened her eyes and dove for cover, curling up behind the chair. "I'm sorry, ladies. My wife is still practicing her yoga. As soon as she gets dressed, I'll send her out," the senator said, closing the library's door. The senator remained in the library by the door while Melinda remained crying, "How could you?" while still hiding behind the chair.

The senator and butler entered the library as Melinda dug in further behind the leather chair. The senator locked the door with the butler smiling, standing next to the piano. He turned to the senator with a nod and moved toward Melinda. Dragging her out from behind the leather chair by her hair, he threw her onto the floor before him. She looked up and knelt on her knees, resting on the heels of her feet with her head down, drifting off to a distant place, a rippling peaceful sea.

The sense of taste seemed like spoiled seafood that was left on some dock at the side of a bay to rot, the pillars of the dock, weather beaten and worn, barely moving within ocean waves from an arising tide slowly beginning to break. Awakening from the sea, Melinda felt the butler grab the back of her head and rhythmically move it as she let out small muffled gasps for air.

With each gasp, the senator tapped the keys of the piano again in the evil melody. After a few moments, the sounding notes stopped as Melinda was curled up on the floor, gasping for breath, her chest rising and sinking deeply, her fingers and toes as if claws tried to dig into the floor. It was as if the senator and butler had reduced her to some type of species of animal, in a catatonic fetal position, borne from the womb of some ancient demon of darkness.

Upstairs above them, Nia sat in front of her dressing table gazing into the mirror. She reached down and over to the bottom drawer of her dresser and took out cocaine. After she began snorting it, she was eventually naked, too, curled up in a fetal position, as if borne from the same evil seed of darkness.

After she had gathered herself, the library door reopened and Melinda came out, conservatively dressed, wearing her neckline ruffled blouse, long skirt, and flat shoes as if nothing had happened. Playing her role, she walked out the front door, onto the grounds where the tea party was being held and, holding her head high, approached the group of women seated at the table who had seen her naked in the library. A few smiled. A few whispered. Bravely, Melinda reached out her hand.

"Why, Melinda," one woman said, "I must say you have a unique way of practicing yoga.

Please sit." Melinda sat down with them. "Yes. I took an enrichment class last semester at the university. Another woman asked, "You weren't naked in the class, where you?" All the women laughed.

Melinda forced a laugh too. "No. It's something that, up until now, I've done in private. It's very relaxing. It makes me feel, well, in a way..." Melinda glanced over at the senator across the grounds talking to other guests, "...free. I must apologize. My husband didn't know that I was in there. I'm sorry about all of that. I'm really embarrassed."

"Nonsense, dear," one elderly woman said. "You have nothing to be embarrassed about. For all I care you can practice yoga in your birthday suit right here." The ladies laughed again. "But wait until after we eat. Speaking of which, here comes the food."

"So, Justin..." a woman began to ask the senator on the other side of the grounds, "How is the fundraising going?"

"We're about three hundred thousand behind our last campaign at this time. But I have an idea how to catch up," the senator said with a smile, looking over at Melinda's table.

"Do I know you?" Melinda asked the elderly woman. Then, sensing a dark cloud coming toward her, Melinda saw the butler approaching, carrying a tray. He went up to Melinda's table first. "I thought Maria was serving," Melinda said to him.

"She was suddenly called away, madam. I'm taking over. Would you care for an appetizer?" "No, thank you," Melinda replied.

"Oh, go ahead, honey Eat something. From what I saw, you look to be in great shape," the elderly woman said.

A young Hispanic woman, who was wearing very high-heels and a mini-skirt with long brunette hair past her shoulders and shapely tanned legs which were crossed, confirmed, "Why, yes, Melinda, you are in great shape. Do you work out a lot... with yoga?"

Melinda did not answer. Instead, she remained silent as she reached out to take an appetizer off of the tray with the butler still poised over her.

Just as she was about to grab it, the butler teased her by pulling the tray away.

"On second thought," he said. "I don't think you've totally earned one yet," the butler disrespectfully added to Melinda with a laugh. "After all, you didn't finish your yoga workout. Perhaps you should have something less spicy until our next session."

"You help her with her *yoga*?" a woman asked.

"Why, yes. I coach her through many of her...positions. She's getting to be very good." "That's interesting," the woman replied.

"No. Maurice. I'll take one, thank you," Melinda replied, reaching out for an appetizer. "I'm sorry, madam. But I think you've had enough spice lately," the butler said.

"Oh, let her have one," another woman sarcastically said, taking an appetizer and handing it to Melinda as the elderly woman appeared to disappear.

Melinda started to chastise the butler. "Maurice, this is my tea party and..."

The butler then began to pull something out of his pocket. It was Melinda's leopard thong panties that he had removed from her upon the table the night before. Melinda briefly looked at the panties, gave a submissive nod, and continued. "...I'm very glad that you're lending a helping hand, Maurice. You're right. I've had enough spice lately."

"Thank you, madam. As you know, I'm always willing to give you a hand." Maurice smiled, putting the panties back in his pocket.

"Excuse me," Melinda said, getting up.

Nia walked out onto the front lawn wearing only her glittery g-string, pasties, and high- heels. Her mother quickly got up to intercept her as Nia was greeting a group of ladies at one of the tables, staggering a bit, appearing to be stoned.

"So this is the entertainment?" one woman asked with a smile, raising her glass. "Hi. I am Nia. I am a stripper," she said, reaching out her hand to her.

"What are you doing?" her mother asked, swiftly intercepting her and guiding her away. "You said, you wanted the ladies to see me in my uniform."

"Nia. This is not the time," her mother replied, leading her back into the house, passing servants and guests along the way who were staring, a bit stunned.

"Hi," Nia said to them, adding, "I am a..."

"Stop it," her said, pausing with Nia at the bottom of the stairs to take off Nia's heels. Her mother then helped her up the stairs and back into her room, sitting her down on her bed.

"So. How do you like my uniform, mom?" "How much did you have?" her mother asked. "A few snorts," Nia replied, collapsing on her back onto her bed. "Look, Nia. I'm sorry

for everything I said. I believe you now." "You don't believe me. You never did."

"You have to get dressed, Nia. I'm getting you out of here, back East." "No. I'm staying.

Leave me alone. I like the sex, remember?" Nia said, pushing her mother away. Nia left the bedroom and staggered back down the steps, removing her g-string and pasties with servants in shock. Some attempted to intercept her. But, Nia just pushed them away continuing back down the swirling staircase, a high chandelier shining an unusual bright light upon her.

"Nia. You must come back up here!" her mother shouted from atop the steps.

"No!" Nia shouted back, "I'm not leaving him." "Who?" her mother asked, appearing confused. Nia paused, gazed up the swirling staircase at her mother and said, "An old horse."

Totally naked, Nia walked confidently through the foyer, out upon the grounds, and into the tea party. As the crowd parted, the senator, tall, dark, imposing, stood before her in the way, towering over her. She paused, slowly glancing up at him, looking him in the eyes as reporters began to gather around them. "Get dressed," he said down to her, glancing around as reporters began taking pictures. "No," she defiantly said, unmoving with an unwavering stare upward toward him. He took off his suit jacket, covered her up, and led her back toward the mansion.

"I'm sorry, everyone... my daughter, she's not feeling well," he said, pushing the reporters aside. When he got her inside the mansion, he began to lead her to the study. But, Nia pushed him away. "No. I am not your's anymore," Nia cried out, taking off the suit coat jacket and tossing it at him. Maria noticed the brand mark of the dragon on Nia's bottom's cheek. She stared at it with a gasp, bringing her hand to her lips. "Very well," the senator said, keeping his demeanor, remaining calm in his "masked" presence as Nia stormed off toward another exit.

He turned and greeted arriving guests with subtlety and grace as if nothing had happened. "Is your daughter alright?" one reporter asked, pushing a microphone in his face. "Yes. She is fine," the senator said with a dismissive laugh. "You see, she often sunbathes in the nude on the mansion grounds and she was startled to see a tea party going on.

She told me to offer her apologies. She's really embarrassed by it all, which is understandable... But, as you see, everyone is here to have a good time. No harm. No fowl. And, please, do not publish those pictures of my daughter. Although this is a public event, in the tone of privacy, this is her home and it was, as I said, an understandable mistake. The reporters nodded in agreement.

Chapter 9

The weathervane atop the Victorian House spun counterclockwise. "Joshua!" his father called in to him through his bedroom door as he was getting dressed to go to school.

"Yes?" Joshua replied.

"Tim said, he's ready to take you to school."

On Joshua's bedroom walls were written, "My Dad. My Hero. Jesus…" Beneath these written words was a book, *The Annotated Works of Shakespeare*. Joshua ran his fingers over what was inscribed on the inside cover. "To my loving wife, Elizabeth. Congratulations on your Master's Degree. May your sons go as far."

"Do you have everything you need for school?" his father asked through the door. Joshua did not answer. Instead, he looked out his window and up to the sky and whispered Shakespeare, "But, soft, what light through yonder window breaks? It is the east, and Juliet the sun. Arise, fair sun, and kill the envious moon, who is already sick and pale with grief. That thou her maid art far more fair than she."

Joshua opened the bedroom door, passed his father without another word, and went into the bathroom. His father walked down the stairs and sat at the dining room table, waiting. When Joshua came down the stairs, he paused at the dining room doorway.

"I'd like to talk to you," his father said to him while pulling out one of the chairs. Joshua sat down. In his father's hand was a small wrapped gift.

"What's that?" Joshua asked. "It's for you. Open it," his father replied, handing it to him. Joshua slowly and carefully unwrapped the gift. It was a min I'Pad.

"I wanted you to be prepared for your engineering classes," his father said with a smile.

The smile abruptly faded as his father grimaced in pain and clutched his chest.

"Dad. Are you alright?"

"Yes. I'm fine," his father replied, looking better. He continued talking to Joshua. "Joshua. You're not stupid. You're a very bright young man. I know that I place a lot of pressure on you. But I've always believed that you can do anything you dream of. I don't think, though, you believe in yourself. But I do. You just have to believe, Joshua. *Believe.*" His father paused then added, "You don't have to go back to school if you need more time. You can go back when you're ready."

"I'm sorry if I've disappointed you and mom," Joshua said.

"You haven't disappointed me, son. I'm proud of you and love you. And as far as your mother..." He paused. "Your mother has been dead for a long time."

"She's just asleep. It says in the Bible, 'she's asleep,'" Joshua blurted out, adding, "When Jesus was taken by the leader of a synagogue to a little girl, the leader told Jesus that his daughter had just died. Jesus told him, though, that his daughter was not dead but sleeping. So, Jesus knelt down by the little girl's side and said, 'Talitha cum,' which means 'Little girl, get up.' And the little girl did. And so will mom someday. Right? Maybe when I graduate from college? It's my dream for her to see me march at graduation."

"Joshua...when you graduate, I'm sure she will be there," his father said to him with a gentle pat on Joshua's shoulder. "And if you ever wrestle again, I'll be there too. But we both know it's too late for that." His father then grimaced more with pain, clutching his chest.

"Dad. Should I call 911?" Tim asked, suddenly appearing. Their father waved his hand. "No," he said, as the pain subsided again. "You have to see a doctor about that," Tim said. "It's been going on too long."

"I'm not going to see any doctor," their father replied, regaining his breaths and taking his hand away from clutching his chest. "It's just a little indigestion from last night's dinner, that's all."

"Yeah. Well, you've been getting a lot of indigestion lately," Tim replied, adding, "You ready?" to Joshua.

"I don't think we should leave him," Joshua said.

"I'll be alright, boys," their father said, adding to Joshua, "Now, remember. They'll throw the book at you in the beginning. But you just have to hang in there, wear out the batards, and persevere. God is with you. You just can't see it now. But, he's there, right beside you."

"Okay, dad. We believe you. We're going to go wear out the bastards, now. By the way, if you have another heart attack, please, please call 911," Tim called back as they left.

"Okay. But, it wasn't a heart attack!" their father called after them.

As they drove down the mountain toward the city, Joshua turned to Tim and said, "I'm worried about Dad."

"I'm going to come back on my lunch break and check on him" Tim replied, adding, "I'm also going to talk him into seeing a cardiologist. We just did a job at a hospital, and I got to know a couple of them."

"I thought you're working on the new arena," Joshua responded.

"We are. But we had to work at the hospital too. The nationals are going to be there, at the arena we're building. It's amazing U.C.L.A. has never had a national champion."

"Maybe some day they will," Joshua said, staring out the truck window, seeing his reflection upon the glass.

"Yes, some day, they'll have their first champion," Tim said.

In the weight room, next to the wrestling room, a music video was loudly playing on a T.V. screen above the wrestlers as they were working out, strenuously lifting heavy weights between their classes. Carmel got up and started singing along with the song, mimicking a dancer in the music video on a motorcycle and chair by doing the same dance moves with a weight bench. The same song played over Tim's truck's radio as they drove over the bridge, across the spanning bay, going into the city.

Their father, making sure that they left, reached into his bureau drawer to retrieve and opened bottle of whiskey. In the drawer, next to the bottle, was a stack of letters from Michael in Vietnam. He picked up one letter and hesitantly, with his hand shaking, the bottle of whiskey.

Going to the back porch, he sat back down in his chair and stared out into the woods.

"This is all the medicine I need," he said, raising the bottle to his lips. It was not long before the bottle was empty. With his blurred eyesight and slurred speech, he attempted to read aloud Michael's letter with Michael's picture, in uniform, remaining steadfastly through all the passing years, unmoved upon the old mantle piece... as the clock ticked in unison with the weathervane spinning, dimensions of time encircling an orb like cast above the sea...

Dear Brother,

We've been ordered to abandon our mission. Something big is going on, but we don't know what yet. We just know that President Nixon is pissed and wants to mount some kind of grand offensive. I guess we'll find out when we get back to one of the bases. The closest one to us is so secret we hope we can find it.

Rumor has it that they are going to put someone else in charge of my unit for this offensive to relieve me, temporarily, of my command. I think about you, Timmy, and Joshua a lot. I miss the Christmas dinners and the exchanging of gifts. I also miss the ones we use to have with Mom. I can't believe how many years it's been and that she's gone. I guess death doesn't discriminate. I'm glad you rebuilt your life. Say hi to Elizabeth for me. Also, say a prayer for Mey Lee and Hoa Sung.

They are continually getting bombarded including by what the brass calls "Friendly Fire." They have been told to leave the village, but they have no where else to go. And besides, the village is their home. Like all the innocent here, they are caught in the middle. Many children were badly burned from the last bombing. Some died. At night I can still hear their screams of agony, their cries for someone to help them.

I don't know why God allows them to suffer so. I don't know why He doesn't hear their cries...

Keep the faith, Michael

1969. Vietnam. Michael and his men, twenty miles south of May Lee's Village, walked alongside the base of a mountain through the jungle, having just received orders to head toward the nearest base hidden the farthest north, "Point Bravo."

"Why is it, when we're already as far north as anybody, do they order us to come back south for a supposed major offensive that will bring us back up north where we were in the first place? Why don't we just stay where we are and wait for our gang to come to us?" Ed asked Michael as they led their unit.

"You're talking logic," Michael answered. "Yeah," Ed replied.

"We're in Vietnam, remember?" Michael said.

Suddenly, Michael and his men hit the ground with a barrage of gunfire. They fired back, upward toward the top of a hill, through the brush. Michael stopped firing, followed by the others. "Can you see where they are?" Michael shouted to Ed.

"No!" Ed replied back, continuing his firing with a hail of gunfire raining down upon them. One of Michael's men's head exploded. The blood splashed onto Michael's face, in his eyes.

"Bring it on!" Michael shouted, again firing back.

Tommy crawled on his belly toward Michael. "I think I can hit them from that hill, sir!" Tommy shouted amidst the continual gunfire, pointing to a small hill close to the enemy about thirty yards away.

"You see 'em!" Michael shouted to Tommy.

"Yeah!" Tommy shouted back, pointing again as Michael tried to wipe more blood out of his eyes. Michael gave a nod. Tommy, on his belly, disappeared into the jungle.

A couple moments passed as Michael and his unit continued to exchange gunfire. Then, there was an explosion atop the larger hill where the enemy was entrenched; a direct hit by Tommy. After the explosion subsided, along with the gunfire, Tommy's cheers were heard, though he remained hidden in the jungle after throwing the grenade. Silence. Tommy's cheers stopped.

"Tommy!" Michael shouted.

"Yes, sir!" Nailed the Gooks!" Tommy shouted back.

Some of Michael's men fired a few shots into the larger hill to make sure no one fired back as they arose and marched toward it after Michael's signal. Moving cautiously toward the top, they saw Tommy appear out of the jungle first, standing atop the hill as if he had just won a game of "King of the Hill."

"All dead, sir!" Tommy called out. Soon, the rest of the unit joined Tommy, standing along side of him, poised with their weapons. There were the remains of two North Vietnamese soldiers, their faces bloody, with one, although his detached, still clutching to his machine gun. Michael's unit panned farther out in a semi-circle looking for more Vietcong. The jungle was unusually quiet, except for boots crunching down through the brush, their knees pushing aside taunt branches with thorns scratching and piercing through their pants, a few whipping up and hitting their chests. As they gripped their weapons, peering out into the jungle, they were only able to see a few yards ahead of them.

"Captain!" Bruce called out, standing over a large hole in the ground on the other side of the hill from where Tommy was scouring, remaining at the top. Michael approached Bruce.

"One here, too, sir!" Tommy called out atop the hill about twenty yards away from Bruce, standing over another hole.

"Oh, here we go," Ed said, adding, "Rat men time."

"Do what you have to do," Michael said loud enough for both Tommy and Bruce to hear him as he waved to the rest of the unit to keep panning out into the jungle.

"You coming?" Michael asked Ed.

"Not yet," Ed replied, adding, "I want to make up for the last time."

Tommy, who was poised with a grenade over the hole he found, called out, "Who's got the time?" Ed answered, "I do!" taking out a watch. Bruce remained standing over his hole.

"Ready!" Tommy shouted, pulling the pin. "Fire in the hole!" Tommy added, dropping the grenade. Tommy, Bruce, and Ed, the last ones remaining atop the hill, dove for cover. There was an explosion. After the explosion cleared over Tommy's hole, all three ran back to Bruce's.

They stooped down, listening beneath the ground, hearing the Vietcong soldiers scampering like rats underground through their holes. Then, just as they heard the scampering coming closer to Bruce's hole, where they were still poised, Ed shouted, "Time!" Bruce then dropped his grenade and they all dove for cover again followed by another explosion. This time there were no more sounds of scampering underground, or anywhere else for that matter; just silence, like in a calm of wind before a storm.

"The official time is twenty-five seconds," Ed said, adding, "I guessed fifteen. What did you have, Tommy?"

"I had twenty. I guess I win," Tommy answered.

"No, you didn't. You were penalized ten seconds because of the Gook's head you shot off before. He popped out of your game hole, remember?" Bruce said.

"He's right," Ed replied. "Bruce. You had seventeen, right?" Ed asked. Bruce nodded. "You're the closest. You're the winner," Ed said, taking out from inside his boot three joints and handing them to Bruce.

"Captain! Captain!" Another soldier in Michael's unit called out at the base of the hill on the other side of where Ed, Tommy, and Bruce were, with a large part of the hill having just fallen away from the blast of the two grenades. Michael and the rest of his men came running back out of the brush to the young soldier's side. Ed, Tommy, and Bruce also came to see. They all looked in and saw what the two explosions had unearthed. It looked like an opening of a cave as they slowly walked in. Two dead Vietnamese soldiers were on their backs on the ground with bloody, bare feet. One was holding onto a dish with something that looked like a sandwich on it. With sunlight trickling, cascading in, the large, tunneled-out room looked like something the Lost Boys from "Peter Pan" would have lived in. It was even decorated with a few pictures, light fixtures, a table, and chairs. The openings to five other tunnels were also seen, but these were completely caved in. A few lamps were still lit next to what appeared to be bunk beds tunneled in the walls. Michael's eyes widened at what he saw lying in them.

"Oh my God," Michael said as Tommy, seeing something too, immediately fired into the bunks, into the shadows.

"Hold up!" Michael shouted as a bloody arm fell down out of one of the bunks.

Ed looked over by the two dead Vietnamese soldiers. One of them, with his arm outstretched, looked like he was reaching for something. Ed saw a white box with a large red cross on it, half open, with bandages unraveled from it and a large bottle of alcohol, open on its side, still emptying.

Michael grabbed onto the dangling arm as Tommy and another solider covered Michael with their weapons aiming them at the bunks. Michael then pulled on the arm. A dead American solider fell out.

"Man," Ed said, going over to help Michael.

One at a time, Michael and Ed pulled out five dead American soldiers from the bunks, the same number as each caved-in tunnel.

"The Gooks made this into a hospital for us?" Bruce asked, with his body passing before the sun's rays and his shadow falling over Michael and Ed as he walked deeper into the cave and away from the light.

Michael and Ed laid out the five dead Americans next to the two dead Vietnamese. In a way, they looked the same, all covered with blood, their eyes closed, their hands reaching up over their heads as if they had tried to call out something in their last gasps.

"Well, I really messed up this time," Tommy said, adding, "Sorry, sir." "Now what?" Ed asked. "We just leave them here? Fill in the hole?"

Michael bent down over the dead American soldiers to take off their dog tags. There weren't any. "You want to kill us! Then kill us!" Michael shouted, starting to randomly firing into the two dead Vietnamese. Ed stopped him as the blood from the dead bodies splattered on Ed's legs.

"You're wasting your ammunition!" Ed shouted, adding with a whisper, "You're wasting your anger."

Michael stopped firing and threw down his weapon. "We can't carry them back, not time," Michael said. "And if we bury them here, no one will ever know who they were." Michael reached down and picked back up his weapon.

"Close up the hole," Michael finally said.

With the sun's rays seemingly pulling back, Michael and his men disappeared back into the brush of the jungle as Tommy remained by the hill, ordering two other soldiers to throw grenades. With everyone cleared, there was a third explosion. The entrance to the cave became covered with earth and brush tumbling down over the large opening, as if an avalanche. With the rains that would come and new growth of the jungle that would sprout, the secret beneath this hill would never be known, and so, too, the identity of those five American soldiers.

"How would you like to live underground like a mole?" one of the soldiers in Michael's unit asked Bruce.

"Not me," Bruce replied. "I have to see the sun."

As Michael and his men marched into the fading sun with passing clouds before it, there were no more skirmishes. When they finally reached Point Bravo, the sun was setting as Michael stood at the edge of the camp in front of the sunset. An officer approached him, saluted, and then apologetically gave him the news that another captain, a West Point graduate, was taking command of his unit. Michael could remain with his men, but only as second in command along with additional soldiers - new recruits just out of boot camp.

On the other side of the world and time, with the sunlight shining brightly upon him, Joshua walked through UCLA's campus upon cobblestone.

Pausing, he looked over at the library, the spanning manicured grass and flowers surrounding it, and the Bell Tower. After entering a large stone building, he walked down a hallway looking for classroom number 212. Finding it, he went in with twenty other students who were casually entering. Joshua sat in the back with the graphing calculator that his father had given him next to his notebooks and physics books on the desk before him. Some students still stood in the doorway talking, many seeming to know each other. No one, however, said anything to Joshua. It was as if he wasn't there. When the professor walked in, an elderly man, bald on top with gray hair on the side, wearing thick, black-rimmed glasses, and with part of his shirt tail untucked and hanging out over the back of his pants, everyone got quiet.

Picking up a piece of chalk, the professor immediately turned to the chalkboard and wrote, "Physics is fun." When he turned back around, facing the class, no one was smiling.

"Dr. Johnson. Dr. Henry Johnson. Comprehensive Physics. Welcome," he said. Joshua replied, "Welcome."

Dr. Johnson held up a book and said, "Murphy-Bowman. This is the book we will be using. Lab book?" He reached over on his desk. "Also Murphy-Bowman. Labs will be conducted in room 111 every other Thursday except the third Thursday of every month. On the third Thursday of those weeks the labs will be held on the following Tuesday in addition to the Thursday of the following week. And if you understood what I just said, you automatically get an A." Dr. Johnson smiled, attempting to be amusing, as Joshua and the other students just remained quiet, appearing to be already totally confused. Dr. Johnson read off the roster as one by one each student raised his or her hand. Dr. Johnson then put the roster away and repeated each name again while looking at them. He had memorized each student's name. However, when he got to Joshua, he paused then said, "Joshua... Kahn?" Joshua nodded.

Dr. Johnson continued. "Linear velocities, in terms of constant accelerations including gravity, regarding all aspects of Newton's laws of motion will be our first challenge. How many of you know who Sir Isaac Newton was? Good. How many of you have never heard of

Sir Isaac Newton?" Joshua and a couple of other students raised their hands. The class laughed. Dr.

Johnson added, "Well, by the end of the first couple of weeks, hopefully, all of us will know about Newton's contributions to physics. In fact, some believe that Newton is actually the father of physics, even though he never married." Dr. Johnson smiled and paused. "He was once deeply in love, though." The smile faded. Dr. Johnson began writing a series of equations on the chalkboard with the students copying them down in their notebooks.

"Newton, Kepler, Einstein, all of these physicists, their works, their thoughts about motion we will be studying. That's what it's all about in the beginning, perfect, synchronized, harmonic motion," Dr. Johnson said, continuing to write equations on the chalkboard as the class in perfect, synchronized motion momentarily paused in unison, motionless, wondering how many of the equations they had to copy down. Joshua, though, continued copying, writing down the equations as fast as he could.

"There will be two major tests, a mid-term and final. You fail one, you the fail the course," Dr. Johnson said somewhat sympathetically, adding, "That's not my rule, that's the university's. Actually, the physics department. If it's any consolation, when I was your age and took my first physics course, I didn't pass the mid-term or final."

"Great. And he's teaching us," Joshua heard someone whisper.

"But don't worry. I've passed many an exam since," Dr. Johnson said.

"In physics?" Joshua heard the same person whisper.

"Yes, in physics," Dr. Johnson replied with a smile, continuing. "This course is calculus- based. So not only will we use trigonometry but also calculus to help us solve problems, particularly when we cover vector analysis. Well, how about if we get started?" He began writing on the chalkboard again. "This is a vector. A vector is a unit of measure that has both a magnitude and direction." He drew more arrows in different directions. "For example, if we are talking about velocities and the velocity is five meters per second and the direction is thirty degrees north of east, that would be a vector quantity..."

1969. Vietnam. The new captain who was put in charge of Michael's unit stood poised over a map that Tommy had spread out on the ground before him. With Tommy tautly holding the map, the new captain knelt down and drew an arrow with a pencil in the direction that they were ordered to go. "Alright. Thirty degrees north of east," the new captain said, adding, "That will bring us directly into position."

Tommy remained silent, folding up the map, as the new captain signaled for everyone to march onward down the side of the mountain through the jungle. It was the day after Michael and his men had left Point Bravo. However, Captain Reynolds, the new captain, was now in charge.

Forty of them, some soiled, some not, hesitantly moved down through the brush. The fourteen rookies, including Reynolds, all stumbled through the brush making loud sounds. Just flown in from the states, their eyes peered out beneath their unsoiled helmets in bewilderment as newborns from their bassinets. Their boots, rigid and tight, still had a shine upon them, and their pants even had slight creases as if they had just been issued from some company command supply post. As they moved onward, Reynolds appeared cocky. With his helmet slightly slanted, he gave orders with his hands on his hips as if he was trying to imitate a portrait of Napoleon.

With the rookies in the front, Michael, Ed, and the others were in the back, being told to "bring up the rear." Michael, in cut off shorts with no helmet and a bandanna around his head, smiled over at Ed, who was making vulgar gestures toward Reynolds. Ed had his helmet on, stained in blood, with the bottom of his pants shredded, barely covering his calves. Ed's boots looked like they were being held together by mud with gaping holes in the sides.

"The only rear I want to bring up is the one I left back in Saigon," Ed told Michael, adding, "You know, my Spanish vixen did have a nice ass. I wonder if my teeth marks can still be seen; something she can remember me by." Ed paused. "So who's the panty waist? The rookie in front."

"Captain Nathan J. Reynolds. A West Pointer," Michael replied. "I thought you would outrank a rookie," Ed said.

"I don't outrank a general," Michael said, adding, "He's the nephew of General Smithe, one of the strategic geniuses who planned this offensive, or so I hear."

"Jerk Hawk?" Ed asked. "Yes," Michael answered.

"If his uncle is a general, what is he doing up here with us when he could have a nice cushy job pushing paper with babe secretaries back in Saigon? Ed asked, adding, "I heard about some of those beach parties. It's supposedly just like being in Malibu."

"He needs a run in combat for a promotion. One of his relatives, apparently, thinks it will look good on a resume," Michael replied.

"Being dead," Ed said.

The ground slowly became softer, more moist, as they moved farther down through the brush toward the valley below while still being hidden by a canopy of the jungle overhead. With a slight gust of wind hitting them from behind, Michael and Ed tried to pause, as if sensing something with their grips on their weapons in a reflex action becoming tighter. Yet, the wind suddenly became stronger, nudging them along to a place where they didn't want to go. Being in Nam more than most, Michael and Ed had learned to rely on their senses, not ESP or the other five, but a sense that could only be learned by experience, a sense that Captain Reynolds didn't have as he blindly led them onward, stumbling in small pockets of mud along the way, leaving a print of a fresh new boot with each step.

Once down in the valley, Reynolds continued to lead them across an open field to the base of what appeared to be a blue mountain, the tallest, sitting between two others. It was unusually quiet with Michael and Ed still "bringing up the rear." Tommy and Bruce joined them. Bruce cautiously handed Tommy and Ed each a joint that he won playing "Rat men." Ed lit up first, followed by Tommy, then Bruce as the three of them took hits while hiding the joints, cupping them in their hands.

"You know, Charlie is everywhere in this valley," Ed told Michael. "I know. Karese's turf," Michael replied.

"Then why are we following this rookie deeper into hell? Ed asked, "I think our career ladder soldier, here, may be leading us the wrong way. Weren't we supposed to head out thirty degrees north of east from our last position, not thirty degrees east of north? He might be leading us to China, and I don't think that will get him a promotion, being the girlfriend of some slant eyes freak in between breaks of being tortured. And I'm saving my tender butt for the running of the bulls with the babes back in Saigon."

Reynolds, a young man in his early-twenties, with a baby face look and complexion, raised his arm for everyone to stop.

"What now? Does he have to take a leak?" Ed asked.

"We'll find out," Michael said as both he and Ed approached Reynolds. "Sergeant Marina!" Reynolds shouted.

Tommy jogged, a little bit stoned by the pot, past Michael and Ed toward Reynolds. "Yes, sir," Tommy replied.

"Give me that map again," Reynolds ordered Tommy.

"Great. We're lost," Ed said to Michael as they both approached Reynolds and Tommy to see what was going on.

"You know where you're going, Sir?" Ed asked Reynolds. "Because if you ask me, I think we're going the wrong way."

"You what, Sergeant?" Reynolds angrily asked Ed.

"I think we're going the wrong way, sir," Ed replied, pointing to the map. "From our previous position we should have been heading more east, sir."

"We should have been heading more...east," Reynolds sarcastically repeated. "Yes, sir," Ed replied.

"What's that in your hand, Sergeant?" Reynolds asked Ed.

"A joint, sir," Ed replied, showing him, adding, "You want a hit?"

Reynolds turned to Michael while continuing to stare at Ed. "I don't know what kind of unit you ran before, Captain. But I'm in charge now. And there will be no drugs. Am I clear?"

Michael nodded. Ed looked away, took a final hit, then tossed the joint to the ground.

When Ed turned back, Reynolds was nose to nose with him.

"Where did you graduate from?" Reynolds asked Ed. "Haddonfield High back in Maryland," Ed answered.

"At Haddonfield High how many map reading classes did you have?" Reynolds asked. "Well, none, sir," Ed answered with a confusion and a pause.

"At West Point I had the highest grade point average in my class. So who do you think is more qualified to read a map?" Reynolds asked Ed.

Turning toward Michael, Reynolds said, "Do you believe I'm going the wrong way too?" Michael did not answer. "Good," Reynolds said, "Let's keep moving. We should be at our ordered position by dusk. We'll meet up with wolf pack there. My buddy, Teddy, from the Point is in command of that unit." Reynolds, with a smile and nod, put the map inside his shirt.

"Did he have the same map class?" Ed asked under his breath as he, Michael, and Tommy went back to the rear where Bruce handed him another joint.

"Who does that baby face, lily-white butt rookie think he is? He probably doesn't like me because I'm black," Ed said.

"Try not to piss him off again," Michael said, adding, "When we get back, I'm sure it will only take one call to his uncle to set you up for another two-year tour of duty here."

"If we get back," Ed added, taking another hit of the joint, this time a slow deep one, holding his breath.

After marching a couple of miles deeper into the valley, Reynolds signaled again with his arm. Taking binoculars from one of the rookie soldiers, Reynolds looked out toward a river.

"You see anything, sir?" The rookie asked Reynolds. "A hut," Reynolds replied.

Ed, hearing this, sarcastically told Michael, "Alright. Now we're getting somewhere. The new captain has found a hut."

"Should we call it in, sir?" *the rookie a*sked Reynolds. Ed laughed. Reynolds replied, "No. Nothing can be transmitted while we're in this valley."

Ed, holding back more laughter, whispered to Michael, "They're thinking about calling in air cover to blow up a hut?"

When they arrived at the river's bank, some of the soldiers stood with their backs to the water, their weapons aimed outward in a semi-circle, as Reynolds, Ed, and Michael cautiously approached the hut. Tommy and Bruce, by the edge of the river, suddenly heard someone scream, "No!" As Michael and Ed stood at the doorway of the hut, they watched as Reynolds was on his hands and knees throwing up. On a table above him was a cut off head with the headless body a couple feet away, stretched out spread eagle on the ground with the hands and feet bound with ropes to stakes. The upper torso, bare, had deep gashes, as if a sword had sliced it up like lunch meat.

"Let me guess. Your buddy from the Point?" Ed asked Reynolds. Reynolds, wiping the spit up off his chin, followed with a nod.

"Well, there's two more years you've just enlisted for," Michael said to Ed.

"You know what? I don't give a..." Ed replied, grabbing the cut off head by the hair. Holding it up, he shouted at Reynolds, "Did he have the same map reading class as you?" Ed then tossed the severed head out the window.

Tommy, seeing this, said to Bruce, "Well, they finally killed Reynolds." Feeling sudden remorse, Ed went out and retrieved the head, came back into the hut, and gingerly placed it next to the body. "I'll bury him," Ed said to Reynolds, adding, "I'm sorry about your friend."

"I want to bring him back," Reynolds said. "We were roommates our first year. From the first day we hit it off. He even introduced me to my wife."

Michael helped Reynolds up. A bit shaken, Reynolds took deep breaths, regaining himself.

"That's what Charlie does after he tortures you. He cuts off your head. He believes once your head is cut off, your spirit will never rest," Michael said. "Ed will take care of him."

Reynolds wiped his chin again. "Alright. Let's move out," he said as Ed began wrapping up the body.

"Captain!" Tommy called out from a small dock by the river's edge.

When they got to the dock, Michael, Ed, and Reynolds looked down at their rippling reflections in the river. Among their reflections were submerged bamboo cages, and inside, mutilated American soldier's bodies floating in red; their limbs eerily tossing with the tide as if passing through death. With the river a bright red, they had not been dead long. All of their heads had been cut off.

"I told you we're going the wrong way," Ed said to Reynolds. "I'll take your offer now," Reynolds replied.

"What?" Ed asked, adding, "Oh," realizing what he meant. Ed reached into his pocket and gave Reynolds a joint. "This is the good stuff," Ed said. Ed lit it for him.

"The sergeant's right," Reynolds said after a couple of puffs. "I screwed up. I don't have a clue where we are." Turning to Michael, he added, "Can you get us out of here and to our ordered position by sundown?" Michael nodded.

"Good," Reynolds replied. Taking the map out of his shirt, he handed it to Michael. "Lead the way." Michael handed the map back to him with a smile and said, "I know the way."

After Ed buried Reynold's friend, Michael took back the lead, marching them back into the jungle and away from the blue mountain. Ed, Tommy, and Bruce were still bringing up the rear. But this time, Reynolds was with them, sharing, taking hits off the "good stuff." It was not long before all four were stoned.

"You know, Captain," Ed said to Reynolds. "I can fix you up with a nice babe back in Saigon who would love to..."

"Don't talk to the Captain like that," Tommy said to Ed, then to Reynolds, "He knows a whore back in Saigon..."

"She's not a whore," Ed said, adding, "She's an angel of the night whose beauty can only be surpassed by her own whispering breaths upon a passing moon..."

"Like I was saying. Ed's whore is getting together a contest called the 'Running of the Bulls,'" Tommy said.

"Ah. Like a Hemingway novel," Reynolds replied, taking another hit. "Yeah. I guess. Who's Hemingway?" Tommy asked.

"He's one of the best writers of this century," Ed answered.

"Thank you, professor," Tommy replied sarcastically to Ed. "Anyway. This whore of Ed's is getting together a lot of other 'angels of the night' who will set up a gauntlet where about thirty of us will run through hallways and end up in a giant room decorated like a bull ring. We will run naked, of course."

"Of course," Reynolds acknowledged with a nod as Bruce jumped in, finishing explaining the game. "The first one to reach the golden ring without getting lanced in the butt by one of the girls is the winner."

"Where's the golden ring?" Reynolds asked.

"Between the legs of my fair-eyed vixen," Ed replied with a smile, adding, "Remember, bulls don't have hands. So the winner will have to remove the ring with his teeth."

"Oh," Reynolds said. "Well, that all sounds interesting, but I won't be able to participate because I'm married. And if I do, my wife will remove something else with her teeth," Reynolds added, staggering a bit.

"Try to stay on your feet, Captain," Tommy said, catching him by the arm, asking, "How will your wife know?"

"I'll know," Reynolds answered.

"You're a good man, Captain," Ed said, adding, "Like our Captain Kahn. He's in love too."

"Is he married?" Reynolds asked. "Only to his hope," Ed replied.

Joshua sat in the back of his physics class trying to figure out one of the physic's problems that Dr. Johnson had given them to do. "Everyone finished?" Dr. Johnson asked. "Alright. You should have come up with the resultant vector being the velocity of twenty-two meters per second at seventy-three degrees north of east," as he drew the resultant vector on the chalkboard. Everyone in the class was proudly nodding, affirming that they got the right answer. Everyone except Joshua. His resultant vector was pointing in the opposite direction at twice the magnitude.

"I think we're covered enough for the first day," Dr. Johnson said, adding, "The next time I see you, I want you to have completed problems one through fifteen in chapter three on pages..." Dr. Johnson paused as he leafed through the book. "...twenty-three to twenty-five. I'll see you Wednesday." Dr. Johnson quickly gathered up his things and left before the students.

Joshua was the last to leave as he tried to figure out where he went wrong while checking out the last problem written on the chalkboard.

Joshua's father, still sitting on the back porch, took the last sip from his bottle of whiskey, finishing it. Gazing out to the woods, Michael's letter from Vietnam fell from his hand.

1969. Vietnam. "Michael!" Ed shouted out.

Looking annoyed, Michael signaled for the unit to stop, after which, he went back and confronted Ed. "You're making a lot of noise back here, Sergeant."

"You can quit the sergeant bull crap. Reynolds is gone," Ed said. "What do you mean, 'He's gone?'" Michael asked.

"I mean, 'He's gone,'" Ed replied, adding, "He said he had to take a leak."

"Great," Michael said, adding with a hesitation, "Captain!" out into the jungle. The echo seemed to pass through time to the woods before his brother's pain-filled stare. "Alright. Pan out," Michael ordered his men. "Let's see if we can find him."

Hours seemed to pass as Joshua's father remained with his blank stare, sitting upon the back porch, as if lost somewhere inside of himself, somewhere in the past, somewhere in the darkness that had a grip over him and wouldn't let him go. The tops of the trees in the woods gently blew in the wind, fading to the jungle of Nam.

"This is unbelievable," Michael said to Ed as they walked carefully through the waist- high brush. "You lost the nephew of a general? In a combat zone? After, of course, you got him stoned." Michael paused. "It's a good thing you don't have kids."

"Should we radio it in?" Ed asked.

"Yeah.Right," Michael replied. Michael looked out to the sun, sinking behind a mountain. "Well? What do we do now?" Ed asked.

"We keep moving to our ordered position," Michael calmly replied, hearing explosions echo far in the distance beyond the blue mountain holding he setting sun.

"What about Reynolds?" Ed asked. "Someone will find him," Michael replied.

"Yeah. Charlie," Tommy replied, not wanting to move. "I think we should keep looking." "Thee captain knows our orders," Michael answered, signaling to the rest of the unit.

Michael and Ed again took the lead. Ed asked, "Do you think Charlie will find him?" "What do you think?" Michael replied.

"I think evil has a way of finding everyone," Ed answered. "You getting philosophical on me again?" Michael asked. "You can't change who you are," Ed said.

Joshua walked out of the physic's classroom and, after adjusting the physics books in his hands, looked down toward the end of the hallway. His heart suddenly beat faster as, surprised, he saw Nia, smiling, talking to a middle-aged black man wearing a white suit. After she gave Joshua a casual glance, Joshua took a step back. With his back up against the wall, he wondered if she saw him and recognized him from the night he was beneath her balcony as the "Naked Shakespeare." He looked down. When he looked up, she was gone.

Desperately wanting to see her, he quickly ran down the hallway, bumping into students along the way, down a staircase, and out into a courtyard onto the cobblestone. Looking right, then left, he saw her walking with the man in the suit toward a lunch truck. He followed, trying to be inconspicuous. When he got close, he turned his back toward her as she stood only a few feet away talking to the white-suited man in front of the lunch truck. He listened, trying to hear what they were saying.

"Are you still singing?" the man asked Nia.

"No. I gave that up," Nia answered. "I'm trying to get through school mostly now." "So you're out of entertainment all together?" the man asked.

"I dance a little," Nia replied. "Oh, where?" He asked.

"Thank you," Nia replied, taking a soft pretzel from a vendor, a man with hairy arms, handing it to her from behind a counter of the lunch truck. Nia started putting mustard on the pretzel from a large mustard bottle.

"Can I help you?" the vendor asked Joshua. Joshua slightly turned to look at him. "One pretzel," Joshua replied, reaching out to pay him and taking the pretzel, turned toward Nia.

"Our band is still together if you ever want to rejoin us. We need a lead singer. Someone incredible, like you," the man in the white suit said to Nia as Joshua reached up for the container of mustard Nia had just put down on the counter of the lunch truck.

"Maybe, like I said..." Nia said as the white-suited man interrupted her, "You're involved with school. I understand." He paused, then asked again, "So, where you dancing?" He looked down at Nia's cleavage in her red halter-top that barely covered her breasts, with her nipples visible through the sheer fabric, leaving her firm, slender stomach and belly button, with a belly button ring in it, exposed.

Joshua, clutching the mustard bottle, squeezed harder because nothing was coming out. He didn't know that he had to twist the top nozzle of the mustard bottle counter clock wise to open it. With Joshua's tightening grip, the mustard bottle exploded.

"Hey!" the man shouted with mustard shooting into his eyes, his white suit becoming covered in mustard.

"Sorry," Joshua replied, fleeing.

"You're the one who followed me," Nia said to herself. Turning back to her friend, she said, "Are you alright?"

The vendor handed him a stack of napkins. He began wiping off the mustard. "Yes. I'm fine. I must be the world's biggest pretzel," he said jokingly.

"Well, it was nice seeing you again," Nia said, briefly waving her hand and walking away.

"It was nice seeing you," he replied, wiping the mustard out of his eyes with a napkin, calling out, "Remember what I said! We need a lead singer!"

Nia didn't turn around. She just kept going. As he finished wiping the mustard away from his eyes, he could see part of her red thong sticking out from underneath very tight and low-cut white jeans, continuing to walk away in white high-heels, her hips swaying from side to side with without a single mustard stain upon her. He looked down at himself and saw that he was stained in yellow. She disappeared into the sun with Joshua secretly guarding her as she moved through the city's streets.

1969. Vietnam. With the sun shining as if with a last breath upon them, Michael and his unit had reached their ordered position. They were deep in the jungle atop a small ridge overlooking a different valley. Michael knelt down on one knee and took hold of the walkie- talkie with Ed by his side. The rest of the unit panned out into a small clearing.

"This is it?" Ed asked, looking around.

"This is it," Michael replied to Ed while holding the walkie-talkie. "You going to tell them about the captain?" Ed asked. Michael did not answer. "Sea Hawk. This is Romeo. Do you read me? Over. Sea Hawk. Come in. This is Romeo, we're in position. Do you read me? Over." There was a pause.

"We read you, Romeo. What took you guys so long?"

"We got diverted," Michael said, adding. "Copy the orders from this position Sea Hawk." Another pause.

"Captain Reynolds has the orders," Sea Hawk replied. "Oh great," Ed said.

"Sea Hawk. Captain Reynolds is…" Michael said, pausing, "Captain Reynolds wants me to verify our orders from this position."

"You are to head North West, point zero, eight, thirty-eight degrees west of your position," Sea Hawk said.

Ed started laughing.

"Did you copy, Romeo?" Sea Hawk asked. "Yes. Over," Michael replied.

"Why do we even bother talking to those guys?" Ed asked. "I told you. We should have just stayed where we were. Well, at least Mey Lee will be happy to see you again."

"All clear, sir!" Tommy called out to Michael.

"Alright. We'll break camp here. Tomorrow we'll head back home," Michael said, smiling to Ed.

Ed said, "On the way can we stop by a nice Christmas shop so I can pick up some gifts for the kiddies?"

"Sure," Michael answered. "Maybe we'll find a nice inn to stay at too." "Captain!" Bruce shouted.

"Now what?" Michael asked.

"You know every time they've shouted out 'Captain!' they've found something disgusting. It's like we're the parents and our children keep digging things up in the backyard," Ed said.

"Well. Let's see what the kids have dug up this time," Michael said.

Looking down into a vast pit, they saw the remains of burned bodies piled on top of each other, a hundred, maybe more. Ed reached down to pick up a skull.

"Who are they, sir?" one of the rookie soldiers asked Michael.

"Probably villagers," Michael answered, seeing the remains of women and children. "They kill their own people?" another rookie asked.

"Could have been us," Michael replied. "Us, sir?" the same soldier asked.

"You walk into an unknown village, everyone could be armed, even women and children.

The one thing you learn quickly over here is that you only trust your own. Everyone else is the enemy, or so, some of us believe..." Michael said, walking away with other soldiers following. Only the rookies remained standing in horror, staring down into the pit.

Ed brought the skull he was carrying over to where Michael was sitting upon a rock drinking out of a canteen. Ed sat down next to him as the others began breaking out food and taking turns drinking from passing canteens. Sitting atop this ridge, Michael and Ed could see down into the valley. It is quiet with no fighting.

"It's too quiet down there. I can feel him, though" Michael said. "Karese?" Ed asked. Michael nodded, glancing at the skull.

"You think he's this far east?" Ed asked. "I thought we just left his valley."

"He's all over the place," Michael said. "That pit, it's probably his." Ed gazed at the skull more intently.

"You're not going to start reciting Shakespeare, or anything, are you?" Michael asked Ed as Ed began running his hand over the ridges of the skull's top.

"Was it in MacBeth or Hamlet the guy was looking at Ophelia's skull?" Michael asked. "It was Hamlet," Ed answered. "And Ophelia was the babe. Yoric was the skull," Ed

added. "I wonder what Shakespeare would think?" Ed asked, still gazing at the skull. "About what?" Michael asked.

"About the horror," Ed said, carefully placing the skull down. "Back at that hut... How long do you think Charlie tortured them before they cut off their heads?"

"I don't know," Michael answered. "I try not to think about it."

"Do you believe in God?" Ed asked. Michael remained silent, gazing up at the sky above the blue-toned mountain.

"I'll take that as a, yes," Ed said, staring upward, too, at the mountaintop.

Chapter 10

Their father was back in his bedroom, standing before his bureau with the picture of his wife playing Juliet in his hand. Appearing intoxicated, he whispered something too soft to hear.

Joshua followed Nia all the way to her next class, whispering something to her just as she entered a classroom. He paused out in the hallway, peering in as Nia sat down at a desk in the back. Although not enrolled in this class, Joshua went in anyway and sat down at a desk on the other side of the room from Nia. When she noticed him, she smiled and whispered, "Is your dog alright?" She recognized him from the night beneath her balcony and Samson getting shot. Joshua waved, nodded, and smiled back.

In the front of the class on the wall, there was was a large poster of a little girl kneeling at the edge of a cliff looking across a star-filled sky up to a full moon. An elderly woman of tall stature, with glasses just about to fall off the edge of her nose, walked in and wrote, "*Dr. Silva*" on the chalkboard. "Hello, class. As you can see, my name is Dr. Silva, and this is Medieval Literature five-ten. If, by chance, you are not registered for this class, you can leave now, or you can stay. I hope, though, you stay." She smiled, raising her eyebrows theatrically and then lowering them compassionately as Joshua followed her every expression.

"Not only will we be studying Medieval literature, but also the times surrounding those tales of knights slaying dragons for fair maidens. I, personally, would like to believe that even today, somewhere out there, there is a knight trying to slay a dragon for a fair maiden," Dr. Silva said, looking at Joshua. "We shall begin with the tales of King Arthur, through the medieval times, all the way up to the Elizabethan Era, when a fine writer, you may have heard of him, Shakespeare lived. I would like, as an objective of this course, for most of you to be able to recognize the great authors from these time periods, and possibly even be able to recite segments and verses from works such as Shakespeare's," she said with a larger grin and her eyebrows raised even higher. Joshua's grin was just as large, smiling back at Dr. Silva, as Nia with her head down and a frown, leaning on her hand, began writing in her notebook.

Dear Shakespeare,

Who is this old lady, your mother? She acts like she was jilted long ago by some knight and is still waiting for him to show up and carry her off on his white stead. She looks like she hasn't gotten any in a long time too. I know I haven't, at least none that I've wanted. And what's up with that guy who followed me? Is he stalking me or what, or just trying to learn about how to slay dragons? I will enjoy studying about you, though, that is, if I can deal with your mother and the dragon slayer wannabe on the other side of the room.

Sincerely yours,
Your abused, but still loving fan, Nia

Nia looked up from her notebook and over at Joshua still staring at her. He quickly backed away from the doorway as Nia turned her attention back toward Dr. Silva.

"I hope that you enjoy the class. After all, literature is life. And the tales that we will be reading, some believe, in some way, may have really happened," Dr. Silva said. "I will let you go early so that you can secure your text." Dr. Silva smiled at one of the students sitting in the front. "May I," she asked the student as she reached for the text on this student's desk. The student nodded. Dr. Silva raised it up.

"This is it, *Past Miracles*. I'm very proud to say that I am the author.

Does everyone know where the bookstore is?" Dr. Silva asked. Everyone nodded, arising. "Well, then, I'll see you next class," she ended.

As the students began filing out, Dr. Silva smiled at each one, telling them how much she was going to enjoy getting to know them. Nia was the first one out and didn't say anything to Joshua or Dr. Silva as she passed. Joshua, however, as with his physics class, was the last to leave.

"Welcome," Dr. Silva said, extending her hand to Joshua. "I'm not registered for your class," Joshua said.

"Do you want to be registered for this class?" she asked.

Joshua nodded. She handed him a piece of paper from her desk. "Write down your name and social security number," she said. Joshua did what she said. "Well, you're now registered," she said to him.

"That's it. I don't have to get signatures and walk through lines or anything?"

"No, you don't. I'll take care of it. Consider yourself officially registered for Medieval Literature five-ten," she said, reaching out to shake Joshua's hand again. "Welcome again. Joshua smiled, slowly letting go of her hand, turned, and walked toward the door. Strangely, the touch of her hand seems familiar. "What's your major?" She asked as Joshua paused in the doorway. "Your field of study that you wish to pursue?" she followed.

"Engineering," Joshua replied.

"You don't look like an engineer," she said to him. You look like a..." She turned over the piece of paper he had written his name on. It had a picture of a knight riding a horse. "Well, I'll let you find that out for yourself." After Joshua left, Dr. Silva turned to look at the poster of the little girl on her knees looking up to the full moon, as momentarily, the face of Dr. Silva turned to that of the old woman who had given Joshua the rose. "You'll find out, Arthur," she said. You'll find out who you are."

1969. Michael and his men were getting ready to move out, to head back toward Mey Lee's village. "Captain! Over here!" a soldier screamed out.

"Oh, here we go again," Ed said.

On the other side above the pit, after parting the brush, the soldiers found a young Vietnamese woman who was still alive. She was naked from the waist up, tied to a tree with large gashes slashed about her body. The blood was still moist and dripping from her abdomen into a puddle of blood by her feet which were dangling, bound to the tree's trunk, just a few inches from the ground. With flies swarming around her as if vultures encircling a fresh kill, she could hardly open her eyes as the soldiers slowly turned her head to take a closer look at her.

Around her neck, encased in blood, was a necklace, a small gold cross. Cutting her down, she fell silently into one of the soldier's arms. The soldier was Ed. Ed held her close as he tried to stop her bleeding, applying pressure to her wounds with his shirt that he had quickly taken off.

"Get me that! That! Now!" Ed shouted, pointing to a canteen, holding her closer to his chest with her head falling back, her eyes partially open. Ed placed the canteen to her lips, but she could not swallow. The water just ran off the side of her chin. Fighting to look up at him, she said with her last breaths in Vietnamese, "Disciple of Christ. Thank you." She died in Ed's arms. The blood would remain on him for three days to come...

The old woman who gave Joshua the rose stood on a street corner of UCLA's campus watching Joshua walk toward Pierson Hall where the wrestling room was. Just as Joshua passed the large stone statue of a male gymnast holding up a female gymnast overhead, her toes pointing upward toward the sky, the old woman said, "Awaken, my son, for the time is upon you, for you to be Christ's knight."

Standing once again before the wrestling room's doors looking in, Joshua suddenly felt a hand placed upon him. "Jesus died for our sins," the wrestler, Doug, said with his hand on Joshua's shoulder. Doug then took hold of one of the doors and flung it wide open as Joshua felt the warm air from inside the wrestling room pour out as if past spirits flowing through him.

Sensing the smell of the sweat accompanied with the sounds of the blows, Joshua watched Doug enter with his arms raised up, calling out, "A Kahn returns!"

"Time!" Villecco called out. The thirty wrestlers wrestling collapsed in exhaustion onto their backs upon the three large red mats that were spanning the room. Eight had already quit. There were even more red mats encircling the room on the walls. To the wrestlers upon the mats on their backs, the lights in the low ceiling appeared hazy as Villecco called out, "Everyone up!"

Still gasping for air, some arose slowly with their hands on their hips, their chests heaving, pacing in circles, as if caged, underfed wolves at a zoo awaiting for the stick lanced with a chunk of meat to be rattled once again through the bars of their cage. Many who had already started to cut weight had dark circles under their eyes, especially Aikens, the "Good Ole Boy" from the South.

Joshua slowly entered, wearing his tee shirt that said, "You've Got to Believe" on it as Villecco stared at him as if he was the piece of meat on a stick being rattled into his cage.

"A Kahn returns," Villecco said with a sneer. "Alright! Pair up!"

The wrestlers began picking out their partners for the next set of wrestling scrimmages as Joshua remained just inside the doorway with his hands behind him, leaning up against one of the red mats on the wall. His hand fell into a crack between two mats. Joshua felt the hard, cold concrete as Villecco approached him.

"Hey, Joshua! Come with me!" Mikey called out.

Joshua tried to walk over to Mikey, but Villecco grabbed Joshua by his tee shirt and pulled him out to the middle of the center mat. "He's mine," Villecco said.

"Alright. Ready!" Villecco cried out as his positioned himself in a stance in front of Joshua. "Wrestle!" Villecco shouted. Everyone started wrestling. Villecco gave Joshua a push. Joshua fell down on his butt and stumbled back up to his feet.

"Keep your head up, Joshua!" Mikey called out while wrestling his own opponent, Aikens, from a standing position.

"Hey! Coach has a virgin," Aikens called out, seeing Joshua's fear on his face.

Face to face with Villecco, it was like the night facing his brother in the storm with swirling images of red, feeling as if he was running again from the breaths of a wolf. Taking a breath and shutting his eyes, Joshua shot in.

With the warmth of the wrestling room accompanied by a cool breeze of being thrown high through the air, Joshua felt the sudden sharp sting of landing hard down upon his back. His eyes opened. Villecco let him up again and again after repeatedly throwing him to the mat. He watched as Joshua staggered, dazed, back to his feet each time. Shooting in on Joshua, Villecco picked him up even higher over head and with a different move, slammed him harder to the mat. This time, Joshua didn't get up. Villecco pounced down on him as a wolf upon its prey, wrestling him. Riding Joshua's back, with Joshua trying to stay up on his hands and knees, Villecco pummeled Joshua on the side of the head and face with his forearms.

Joshua's nose started to bleed. It felt broken. With bits of blood spilling down on the mat, Joshua could not escape. Villecco was too strong, too fast. And as in the night of the storm with his brother, this battle seemed to be a long time coming, awaiting for a day such as this to reach out from some destined horizon's edge. Curling up on the bottom, just trying to survive Villecco's wrestling blows, Joshua struggled as a prey beneath a wolf clamped upon his throat, his upper torso, in vain, attempting feebly to escape with his legs frantically kicking to escape.

"I guess, 'The Kahn Returns' wears panties," Carmel laughed while wrestling his opponent, Tony, seeing Villecco beat up Joshua.

"Come on, Joshua! You can do better than that!" Mikey called out as Aikens hit Mikey's face and shot in. Mikey sprawled back, extending his legs and digging in the mat with his toes. With Aikens arms wrapped around Mikey's legs, he tried to pull Mikey in. Mikey called out once more to Joshua, "You're a Kahn! It's in your blood!"

From the bottom, Joshua sat out and twisted, using his hand inside Villecco's thigh as a lever to switch Villecco, reversing him and landing on top. Joshua started to pummel Villecco's head with his forearms.

"Easy, brother," Doug said to Joshua a few feet away while wrestling his own opponent. Villecco quickly countered him as Joshua found himself once again on the bottom, beneath Villecco, struggling. Villecco barred both of Joshua's arms behind his back and began stretching them up over Joshua's head, going against the joints. With his shoulders feeling as if they were being twisted out of their sockets, Joshua could feel his ribs begin to tear. The immense pain showed on Joshua's face as the blood dripped faster from his nose and his head tossed side to side. Joshua cried out in agony, "Stop! Please stop!" But Villecco wouldn't as his shoulders continued to dislocate and ribs stretched. Pinned to the mat on his stomach, unable to move, Joshua awaited the final bite of the predator to the jugular. There was a loud crack followed by a scream.

Cif was writhing in pain on the other side of the room, on his back, holding his knee up to his chest. A couple of wrestlers stopped wrestling and went to Cif's side. Villecco continued to apply pressure to Joshua with Joshua continuing to cry out, "Stop!"

"Let him go, Coach!" Doug shouted to Villecco, leaving Aikens and running over to help Joshua. "Coach, let go!" Mikey shouted, also going over to help. Villecco finally got off of Joshua.

"Get him out of here," Villecco said.

"My chest! I can't breath!" Joshua cried out still on his stomach, holding his left side in pain just below his chest. "What's the matter with you, Coach?" Doug asked Villecco while stooping down to help Joshua. "It's alright, Joshua. We'll get you help," Doug said.

"Get him out of here," Villecco said again. "What?" Doug replied.

"You heard me," Villecco replied.

"But we're not supposed to move anyone who is just injured,"

Mikey said. "Move him, now," Villecco said, going over to see what happened to Cif.

"Come on, Joshua. We'll take you down to the training room. Can you stand?" Doug asked, seeing that Joshua's ribs might be broken. Joshua nodded, appearing to be in pain.

"Help me, Mikey," Doug said as Mikey carefully helped him get Joshua to his feet.

Joshua winced intensely, arising with the pain as Villecco stood over Cif.

"What's the matter with him?" Villecco said, looking down at Cif holding his knee. "His knee popped again when Mitch shot in," Carmel replied helping Cif up, mirroring the same grimace as Joshua.

"Hey man, I'm sorry," Mitch, the 118 pound wrestler said, with a little bounce in his step. "Forget it," Cif replied with gasping breaths, cringing as Carmel and Tony each took an arm to help him up.

"Where do you think you're going?" Villecco asked Carmel with Tony holding Cif up under the other arm.

"We're taking him down to the training room," Carmel replied.

"No, you're not," Villecco said, turning to all the wrestlers. "Anyone who leaves through that door is through!" Villecco shouted while pointing toward the doorway as Doug, Mikey, and Joshua were just exiting.

"What about them?" Tony asked, gesturing with his head to the three leaving. Villecco didn't answer. He just calmly turned to Cif and asked, "You're knee popped again?" Cif nodded in pain with his arms still outstretched, one around Carmel, the other around Tony. Villecco stooped down, took hold of Cif's knee, and with a loud crack, popped it back into place. Cif's scream could be heard echoing down the dark hallway where Doug and Mikey were walking, helping Joshua. Cif suddenly stopped screaming. Examining his knee with his hands, Cif smiled, stood up, and tested it. With no more grimaces of pain, Cif said, "Thanks, Coach," while walking in circles, stopping every few steps to bend his leg, feeling once again strong.

"Come on, coach," Aikens said. "What are you, crazy? I hope you never pop me like that." Aikens turned and said to Mitch, "I knew I should have went to Virginia University."

"Alright! Listen up! Anybody else that gets hurt will just have to suffer! No one leaves!

Got it!" Villecco turned to Carmel. "Carmel. Go get Douglas and Mikey. Tell them they have two minutes to get their butts back up here."

"He's nuts," Carmel said to Tony, gesturing at Villecco. "You have a problem?" Villecco asked Carmel.

"You know, Coach, you're the one with the problem," Carmel replied, walking away. "So what? You want a piece of me too?" Villecco screamed at Carmel.

Carmel paused, then turned around. "Don't talk to me that way. I'm not that poor Kahn guy you just kicked the crap out of. I'll be treated with respect."

"If you want to be treated with respect, you have to finish better than second in the Easterns this year," Villecco replied.

"I can get respect other ways," Carmel said. "What's that supposed to mean?" Villecco asked.

"It means there is more to life than wrestling. We work out four times a day, starting at six in the morning until nine at night. It's not normal," Carmel said.

"If you want to win, you have to work hard, no matter what," Villecco responded. "That's just it. I do want to win. But you're killing us with all these practices and we haven't even begun the season," Carmel ended. Everyone else remained silent as Villecco looked about the room.

"Is that what everyone thinks?" Villecco shouted. No one answered.

"Fine. You don't want to work, don't work. All of you can just joke around, party, get laid, or whatever it is you do. I thought everyone here wanted to win. I guess I was wrong," Villecco said. He left, slamming the two doors.

"I've had it," Carmel added. "That's why everyone else who was recruited left. They transferred out of here as soon as they found out how nuts Villecco is. One minute he's joking around like one of the guys, and the next he wants to kill you."

"You won't quit," Michael said to Carmel while looking at himself in the mirror. "It's alright. You don't have any marks. Your modeling career is safe," Tony said to Michael.

Michael turned away from the mirror. "You guys always complain and threaten to quit but you always come back. And if I was getting a full scholarship like you and Tony, I'd put up with it."

"He's right," Aikens joined in. "You have to look at it as a business and Coach is our foreman. I've worked construction jobs down south in the summer where the foremen have been a lot meaner than Coach. If you talked back like Carmel did to one of them, you'd find your car with a two ton steel cable dropped on it."

"Coach does have a Dave Gable though," Mitch said.

"Who's Gable?" one of the other younger wrestlers, another lightweight, asked. "Probably the best wrestler ever. He wrestles one seventy-seven out at Iowa," Mitch replied, adding to the others, "I heard Gable even has work out equipment in his car in case his car breaks down and he wants to work out."

"No way," Cif said.

"Yeah. It's true. I have a friend at Iowa. I've heard he's even crazier than coach, practicing sit out turn ins in his bed when he's asleep. My friend rooms with him on away matches," Mitch replied.

"You think Gable can be the first one to win four national championships?" Aikens asked Mitch.

"No one has been able to stop him so far," Mitch said. "He's still undefeated in three years. I bet he works out at least four times a day. Mike's right. You guys are getting full scholarships to wrestle, so just wrestle."

"Weren't you just calling Coach the wicked witch?" Tony asked with a laugh.

"Don't listen to him. He probably said that because he looks like one of the munchkins," Carmel said. "Look, I don't care what anyone says. I'll find another school and another scholarship. You guys can keep getting tortured. But scholarship or no scholarship, I'm following the Yellow Brick Road out of here." Carmel headed toward the doorway.

Nia was at the registrar's office. She had her bill in her hand but no money. "Aren't there any scholarships or anything that I might qualify for to pay this?" Nia asked.

The woman behind the counter simply responded, "You have to check with the financial aid office on the fourth floor."

"I did," Nia replied looking down. "They said, my stepfather, makes too much."

"I don't know what else to tell you, honey. If you don't pay that bill, they'll wash you out of your classes. Don't you have a job or something you can do?" the woman asked.

Nia nodded hesitantly. "Yes, but I don't like it. It's hard and humiliating."

"Working here, always being told what to do, hours each day, is humiliating for me, too, honey. But, sometimes, sometimes we just have to do, what we have to do," the woman said.

In the training room, Joshua was on the table with Mikey and Doug by his side. Christine walked in wearing her short shorts and carrying an icepack in her hand. She gently helped Joshua take off his shirt and placed the "You've Got to Believe" tee shirt on a table next to him. On his ribs, she carefully placed the icepack at the base of his chest on the side. Although cold, Joshua sensed warmth with her touch.

Villecco reentered the wrestling room carrying several large forty-five pound single plates of metal weights. "Where's Carmel?" he shouted, tossing the weights one by one with a crash onto the mats.

"Everyone line up!" Villecco called out. "Since you guys want to dog it, we're going to do crunches. Let's go!" Villecco shouted, swinging his arms faster as a few weight lifters entered from the hall carrying more forty-five metal plates and tossed them down next to the others on the mats.

"Alright! Everyone get a plate!" Villecco cried out. "It's crunch time!"

"Yankees. Those big guys are always messing us up," Pale and emaciated, Aikens, the lanky middleweight with stringy blond hair said. Aikens, lifted the plate up and lined up at the end of the room with the others. "You guys couldn't keep your mouths shut," he said to Tony. "Hey, that was Carmel," Tony replied, getting into position, on his back, raising up on the back of his head and sprawling his legs, lifting up the metal plate away from his chest. Aikens, in the same position, said, "Yeah, but he's your boy."

"Ready! Go!" Villecco shouted as the wrestlers, in all kinds of strange positions, began to crawl upside down while balancing the heavy metal plates on their chests.

"What wrestler thought up this drill?" Cif asked, gasping, collapsing with the metal plate. "Probably Mitch's boy Gable from Iowa," Tony replied, collapsing too.

After the wrestlers completed one lap, from one end of the mat to the other, Carmel stuck his head through the doorway, smiling. "You guys done yet?"

"Get in here, Carmel," Villecco said. Carmel came in followed by Doug and Mikey. "Alright. We'll wait for the three Amigos to catch up," Villecco said. "Grab a plate.

The wrestlers lay on their backs, sweating profusely, gazing up at the ceiling with the large metal plates still upon them, rising and falling on their chests.

As Carmel grabbed a plate and got onto his back, Tony asked him, "I thought you were out of here?"

"I'll give Coach one more chance," Carmel said as he began the drill. "Yeah, right," Tony replied.

"Come on, Carmel. My grandmother does it faster than that," Villecco said. "Maybe coach's grandmother is Gable," Tony said jokingly to Mitch.

"Hey, coach. We work hard," Mitch said with short breaths, lying on his back. "Every day we work hard. The big guys mess around. But then the rest of us have to pay for it by doing crunches."

"I thought we were a team," Villecco responded. "I know what he's doing," Mitch said. "Coach is using psychology. He's trying to get us to come down on Tony and Carmel for doggin' it. Like a one hundred and eighteen-pounder can threaten two of the biggest, badasses on the team."

"Set, go!" Villecco shouted as everyone, including Carmel, Doug, and Mikey joined the team, crawling as fast as they could from one end of the mat to the other carrying the metal plates. They crawled forwards, backwards, side to side, and pivoted on their heads. They even clasped together in pairs, momentarily placing down the metal plates to toss each other again and again overhead, like a slinky going down steps across the red mats. Villecco screamed, "One more time!" All thirty-three wrestlers fought to line up on their hands and knees, barely able to pick up the metal plates with one arm.

"I'm going to kick your big Italian ass after practice," Mitch said to Carmel.

"Go ahead and try, little munchkin man," Carmel responded with a wink and a smile.

Downstairs in the training room, Joshua was sitting up on the training table, leaning up against a wall and holding the icepack on his bare chest.

"How does that feel?" Christine asked Joshua as she adjusted the icepack.

"A little better," Joshua responded, still wincing a bit. "It hurts though to breath."

"It will for a while," Christine said as she took the icepack away and gently touched his chest with her palm. "I don't think you broke your rib. You probably just tore one of the intercostals," she added.

"What are intercostals?" Joshua asked.

"They're cartilage between the ribs, like bone, but softer," Christine answered, caressing Joshua's chest with her hand in describing them. She softly patted his chest and put the icepack back on, turning her eyes away. "Tonight it will probably hurt more. I know of some athletes who had to sleep sitting up. It will probably also hurt to eat, even go the bathroom," Christine said sympathetically. "You think you'll be alright?" She turned back. Joshua nodded.

"Do you have someone who can take you home?" Christine asked.

Joshua paused. "My brother is picking me up. I'll be alright." Joshua winced sitting up.

He stared into Christine's eyes, startled, envisioning a war, carnage, and flames upon a rising sea. "You sure, you're alright," Christine asked. Joshua nodded and stood with a renewed strength.

Chapter 11

It was late afternoon with the sun half-way behind the mountain ridge when Nia walked into the strip club wearing a bright red halter top and tight, white, transparent pants with her red thong visible. Ms. Gongel sat by the door on a barstool sipping a drink as Nia approached her with a backpack draped over her shoulder.

"Well, look who's here," Ms. Gongel said as Nia entered.

"Look. I'm really sorry for walking out on you and Maribel," Nia said as Ms. Gongel reached out and began adjusting Nia's belly button ring. Nia asked, "Can I have the money?"

Ms. Gongel laughed then replied, "Sure. You earned it. Follow me." Getting off her barstool, with her drink still in her hand, she led Nia into the back where some of the strippers were changing, sitting on benches in front of the large rectangular mirror. A few of them had bare breasts, wearing only sequin bikinis, while others, totally nude, were meticulously applying makeup onto their eyes and lips while gazing at themselves in the mirror.

"Where have you been?" one of the strippers asked Nia. Nia did not answer. With her head down in silence, she continued following Ms. Gongel.

"Battle-ax Gongel sure has her by the short hairs," the same stripper said to another.

Standing in the doorway of Ms. Gongel's office, Nia watched Ms. Gongel go over to her large mahogany desk with a white marble top, put down the drink, and reach into a drawer. She pulled out a lot of cash and tossed it down on the desk next to the drink.

"Well. Come get it," Ms. Gongel said while picking up her drink and taking another sip. Nia hesitantly walked in and stood before the desk, looking down at the money. "Go ahead. Take it. You earned it. You performed brilliantly, I'd like to add," Ms. Gongel said with a slight gesture of her head. "Three thousand dollars," she added, "... all yours."

Nia paused before she reaching for the money. Finally, picking up the stack of fifties and one hundred dollar bills, Nia said, "Thank you," carefully placing the money into her backpack. As Nia flung the backpack over her shoulder, turning to leave, Ms. Google noticed her red thong through her see-through white pants.

"It looks like you've come ready to work," Ms. Gongel said with Nia pausing at the doorway. Ms. Gongel slammed down the drink and went up to her. She let out a gasp as Ms. Gongel reached down her pants and pulled up on the back of her thong, pushing down her pants, partially exposing her bare bottom.

"Are you here to work?" Ms. Gongel asked, pulling up harder on the back of her thong. Nia nodded with another gasp, her backpack falling from her shoulder. "Well, let's get you ready then," Ms. Gongel said, closing the door, pulling Nia back into her office by her hair.

Facing Ms. Gongel with her head down and her hands by her side, Ms. Gongel unbuttoned the top of her pants, and with one swift motion, pulled them down to her ankles.

"Step out," Ms. Gongel commanded.

Nia stepped out of her heels and her white pants. Standing bare footed in just her thong and halter top, Nia quietly watched Ms. Gongel toss her pants over the back of a chair behind the desk. Ms. Gongel then went over and picked up the backpack, taking out the money. "I'll keep this for you," she said, walking over and placing the money back into the drawer of her desk.

"You really need this money? Don't you?" Ms. Gongel asked. "Yes," Nia sighed. "Turn around," Ms. Gongel ordered as she came out from behind the desk. Nia turned around. Ms Gongel grabbed Nia's bare cheeks and began caressing them, slowly running her hands down the back of Nia's thighs, then back up to her stomach, around her belly button ring, up to her breasts, pinching Nia's nipples through the sheer halter top as Nia slowly began to writhe, uncontrollably.

Ms. Gongel took off Nia's halter top and began caressing her breasts. Suddenly, there was a knock at the door. "Come in," Ms. Gongel said, backing away, as Nia quickly covered herself with her arms over her breasts.

A man in a suit entered. "Well, hello," he said to Nia.

"We can talk accounting in a second," Ms. Gongel said to him as he still stared at Nia.

Ms. Gongel patted Nia's bare bottom, "Go on and dance, honey," she said, tossing her the red top. Catching it, exposing her breasts, Nia covered herself with her arms, again, and left.

"Dancers. They have to be coaxed sometimes," Ms. Gongel said to the accountant.

"Your last deposit, from the Asians, was quite substantial," the accountant replied to her as Ms. Gongel shut the door. Nia paused, listening through the door. "They're willing to pay even more if you get them the right girls again..." *Nia displayed a curious slight smile.*

Displaying a renewed determination and confidence, Nia, wearing only her red halter top and thong, walked bare footed out into the middle of the floor of the club among men who were sitting at tables. Most of them were drinking frosted mugs of beer as Nia climbed up on the bar and relieved another stripper who was just getting down. The music changed from a fast pace to a slow one with Nia in tune, beginning to dance seductively while swinging around a brass pole, swaying with her head back, her hair flowing, her back arched in a move of a gymnast.

Joshua sat on a cement bench beneath the statue of the gymnasts by the gym. He gazed out toward the city streets as the sunset behind the mountain ridge. Lights of the city became visible as the street venders packed up their trucks, becoming overcome by shadows of darkness. He wondered about the vision he had of a war in the future. He imagined a great army, approaching from the far edges of the horizon, across the sea, and toward land. He saw a Tree, standing atop a cliff, overlooking the sea, as if transcending time, from a moment long ago...

Nia climbed down from the corner of the bar as a bartender handed her a drink.

"Great job," the bartender said, helping another young woman up the small steps by the bar behind Nia.

"Yes, great job," another voice said as Nia held the drink to her lips. She turned, shocked.

Father Gabe was holding a beer, his collar of a priest visible.

"What are you doing in here?" Nia blurted out, clenching her drink. "I could ask you the same thing," Father Gabe said with a smile.

Nia grabbed a jacket on the back of a bar stool and put it on. "I don't feel comfortable being in front of you like this."

"Like what? You're working, right?" Father Gabe asked. "Yes," Nia replied, feeling confused.

"Well, the way I see it, there are many uniforms for many different occupations." "But, you're a priest," Nia said, covering herself up more.

"You say, I am," Father Gabe answered. "However, how do you know?" "Because of your collar..." Nia said.

"Anyone can wear a collar and... anyone can wear what you're wearing, or hardly wearing. It's like a half-glass, half-full kind of thing," Father Gabe said with a wider smile.

"Aren't you going to get in trouble being here?" Nia asked.

"Why would a priest get in trouble for being in a church?" Father Gabe replied, taking the drink from Nia as He looked more confused. "You see, I am... in a church," Father Gabe said, looking upward toward the ceiling. This use to be a church. Look around. The high ceilings, the arched windows. There used to be stained glass in those. The stained glass, or so the story goes, came from medieval times from England. Pictures of a knight slaying a dragon and riding a white-winged horse off into the sky were in the series of stained glass." Father Gabe looked back down at Nia, looking up. "So, the ancient story goes... There are many versions..."

"What do dragons and knights have to do with God?" Nia asked.

"Maybe, some day, we'll both find out," Father Gabe said, while Nia was still looking up, seeing windows she hadn't noticed before in all the times she danced... She looked down at him.

"I guess you priests like entertaining yourselves by telling each other about ancient myths and signs of the end of the world," Nia said as she glanced back at a window. For a moment, the stained glass appeared, turning to a knight, a dragon, and a white-winged horse. "What the..."

"Who said anything about the end of the world?" Father Gabe asked.

"Look," Nia replied, looking back down. "Thanks for coming and all. But I have to get ready. It's Tuesday," Nia said. Father Gabe looks puzzled. "I have to wrestle," she ended.

Nia took off the jacket and got up on the largest stage with a wrestling mat in front of a section of men sitting at tables. Another young woman, also completely naked, got up on the same stage as the crowd of men, sitting at the tables and bar, began to gather around them.

Father Gabe pushed his way to the front. Nia rubbed oil all over herself, standing on a large red wrestling mat on the stage that became illuminated with a bright spot light. The other young woman also rubbed oil on herself. She was a foot taller than Nia, with long red curly hair, lily-white skin, and freckles on her shoulders and the bridge of her nose.

"You're going down," the young woman said, pointing toward Nia, standing a foot above her, towering over her as the giant facing David.

One of the male bartenders jumped up on the stage to referee, helping Nia remove her top. "Who's the amazon woman?" Nia asked the bartender while gesturing over at her opponent. "A new girl. She just showed up today," the bartender replied. "They call her, Angel of Red."

Angel met Nia at the center of the mat as Father Gabe stood by the edge of the mat with Nia crouching down in a wrestling stance, face to face with her opponent, in just a thong.

"Wrestle!" the crowd of men cried out as the bartender blew his whistle. Nia and Angel collided, wrestling, each one having trouble keeping hold because of the oil, sliding off one another. On her hands and knees, from underneath, Nia fought her way in, squirming, grabbing hold of Angel's sprawled legs, pulling them in, and tackling her to the mat. The crowd cheered, including Father Gabe, with his fist raised toward the ceiling.

Wrestling from the top, Nia threw in a half nelson around Angel's neck, underneath her arm, and turned her over onto her back. As Angel struggled not to be pinned, Nia sprawled out on top of her, chest to chest, with her own legs spread out, digging her toes into the mat. The bartender got down on his hands and knees to see if Angel's shoulder blades were touching the mat. He raised his hand. The crowd cheered as he slapped the mat. Nia jumped enthusiastically in victory to her feet. The bartender raised Nia's hand. Angel was lying on her back upon the mat, gasping for breaths. A couple of men got up on the stage and helped her up as many strippers came out and began dancing throughout the club. Nia got down off the stage. Someone handed her a towel to wipe off the oil.

"Nice match," Father Gabe said, releasing his hold of the towel. "Not only are you quite a dancer, but you're a pretty good wrestler too." Father Gabe paused as Nia continued wiping off the oil. "That's the first time you've ever won, isn't it?" Father Gabe said.

"Yes. How did you know?" Nia asked.

"Just a guess," Father Gabe said, smiling. As Nia tried to wipe her back, Father Gabe helped her wipe the oil off. "Thanks," Nia replied as Father Gabe moved the towel up and down her back softly, with a gentle touch she had never before felt. Down the back of her legs, and even up over her bottom, the touch was a comforting one. After Father Gabe patted her back, the bartender handed her, her red halter top. Nia took it and started to walk away.

"Wait," Father Gabe called out to her. Nia turned, a few feet from him.

"Father. I don't mean to be rude or anything, but I don't really feel right being naked in front of a priest," Nia said to him, covering herself with her halter top.

"Oh. I see. I guess I've been too busy looking into your eyes, the windows of your soul, to notice," Father Gabe replied, adding, "What?"

"My father used to say that to me," Nia paused.

"I know," Father Gabe answered as the windows throughout the club turned to the series of stained glass.

"What's going on?" Ms. Gongel said, noticing the glass changing.

"I am not sure," Nia responded. She turned toward Father Gabe, smiling, gesturing to Ms.

Gongel. "This is my friend. He's a priest..." "What priest?" Ms. Gongel said, sternly. "Are you seeing things?" With that... Father Gabe appeared to vanish before Nia... as if he was never there. "He's not real?" Nia said to herself as the stained glass changed back to darkness. Nia went backstage to Ms. Gongel's office to get her pants with Ms. Gongel following. As she entered the office, she put her halter top back on and picked up her pants on the back of the chair behind the desk. Ms. Gongel watched, still affirming her control. "Well, that was a first. You're usually the one squirming on your back. Congratulations on your win." After stepping into her pants and pulling them up, Nia finished buttoning her halter top while adjusting her pants. "Thank you." Nia said with a downward cast of her eyes. "You're very welcome, my love" Ms. Gongel responded. "I have a lot of, let's say, creative ideas how you can make money." "I'd love to hear them, sometime," Nia said as she searched for her heels. Finding them, she began putting them on. Suddenly, Ms. Gongel grabbed Nia's arm. She brought Nia close, forcibly kissing her on the lips, gently touching her breasts.

The kiss and the touch caught Nia off guard, becoming aroused, excited by the moment. Her heels dropped from her hands. Ms. Gongel unbuttoned Nia's top, lifted her up, and stretched her out upon her back on her desk. Slowly, she pulled off Nia's pants, tossing them back over the back of the chair. Ms. Gongel began to slide down Nia's red thong panties...

"I am sorry," Nia said, stopping her, adding, "I have to go." Nia got off the desk and quickly got dressed with Ms. Gongel confused, standing in silence. "As I said, I'd like to hear more about how I can make money. But, I have to learn to trust you, first. You took back what I earned. So, until I regain that trust. I will only be... available after the deal is complete," Nia said, completely dressed, in a defiant stance similar to the one she took with the senator.

Ms. Gongel paused, then broke out into a sinister laugh. "Wow. You've come so far, my love. You're even sexier, now, than before. It will be fun reconquering you..." Ms. Gongel turned, took the stack of cash out of her desk drawer, and tossed it to Nia, adding, "As long as we both make money, right my love?" Nia nodded with a coy smile, staring directly into her eyes.

Nia began to leave. "Wait," Ms. Gongel said.

Nia paused before the open door. "You know what you did with Maribel, we could also explore," Ms. Gongel said. "I very much enjoy hunting... prey. I'm sorry about that persnickety accountant interrupting us before. You seemed to be getting into it just as you were, right now... I'm looking for a new girl, love. But, I both understand and admire your new line in the sand for reciprocity, now, along with your new found awareness of your true value. It's all about power. Isn't it, my love. Something, I believe you just discovered. It must have been that win out on the mat. Yet, fair warning, love. I am not a red headed Irish dancer. I am more like a classical one, one with a fire in her belly and a thirst for the expensive fine arts. You know, like Impressionist Painters, Van Gough, Monet, Renoir, Degas, and you will become my work of art, of sorts. I'll very much enjoy... painting you, now, that I appreciate your true value... Did you know Van Gough could not sell a single painting when he was alive? And, yet, now... now they're worth millions. I look at you differently, now, my love."

Nia put the money back into her backpack, threw it over her shoulder, turned and left. As she walked through the club, she saw shadows of images of demons dancing, becoming visible as pieces of light of the sun cascaded down upon her as a waterfall, feeling the cool water's mist. She paused as she passed by the "center wrestling mat."

Momentarily, she saw an Angel in White appear, with large spanning wings, wearing a white robe. He had blond hair and carried with him a large sword - with a golden dragon handle.

"Good match, Nia," the bartender said as the image faded away. Nia nodded and left the club, walking across the parking lot toward her motorcycle.

Outside, Father Gabe was waiting by Nia's motorcycle beneath a flickering street light. Angel of Red, appearing in the night's dew, dressed in a medieval long white gown and sandals, moved toward him as if floating on air. "You owe me big time, Gabriel," Angel said. "Our leader, Michael never asked me to do anything like that."

"I know. I really appreciate you helping me out, and I'm sure you helped Nia's confidence," Father Gabe replied. "Pointing her toward her destiny," Father Gabe added, glancing upward across the parking lot toward the sign - *Destiny's Club*.

"I wouldn't have mind so much. I mean, I did fight in many battles during the Holy Wars.

But, what's with being naked? And that oil..." Angel said. "Come on. What's the purpose?" "It's part of a larger purpose. You know," Father Gabe said. "But, I don't understand human nature much. I'm still learning how to be an angel..." Father Gabe added with a smile. "Before I forget. Michael wants to know if they'll be ready. He said, the time, the hour is coming soon," the Angel of Red said, her hair becoming inflamed with an unusual light.

"I'm trying," Father Gabe replied, adding, "I'm trying..." "Have you made contact with Joshua yet?" Angel asked.

"Not yet. But I'm hoping Nia will lead me to him," Father Gabe answered with a sound of a trumpet somewhere far off in the distance.

"I have to go. They're calling me," Angel said as she backed away and slowly vanished upward with a puff of mist. Silence. Just the flickering street light... Nia stood by club, watching Father Gabe. She moved slowly toward him, wondering. Standing before him, gripping her backpack tighter, tossing it farther over her shoulder, she said, "Are you real, this time?"

"As real as your motorcycle," Father Gabe replied, placing his hand upon the handle bars. "I always wanted a motorcycle. I believe they are symbols of... Freedom."

"What kind of Freedom?" Nia asked, moving closer.

"The one you're searching for," Father Gabe said, backing away. "Go ahead. Get on." Nia placed her backpack on the back of her motorcycle and got on it, gripping the clutch on the handle bars. "I feel like I know you from somewhere," Nia said.

"I bet a lot of people tell you the same thing," Father Gabe responded. Nia started her motorcycle. "So, do you enjoy being a dancer?" Father Gabe asked.

"What?" Nia asked over the loud sound of the motorcycle.

"Do you enjoy being a dancer!" Father Gabe said, again, louder.

"Sometimes," Nia replied, lowering the accelerator, looking over at the church. "I hope you know that you are always welcome over there," Father Gabe said. Nia paused. "I don't feel right."

"About what?" Father Gabe asked, staring at the church. "Doing what I do and then going to church," Nia replied.

"What you do isn't who you are, Nia. I know God would like very much for you to visit," Father Gabe said, gently touching her on the shoulder. Nia's motorcycle suddenly became silent.

"What? Do you know God personally or something?" Nia asked.

"You could say that," Father Gabe. "Come..." Father Gabe vanished again as church bells sounded out. Confused, Nia dismounted her motorcycle and walked toward the church.

The bells of the church tower sounded out louder with the echo of the trumpet approaching in the distance. Nia paused, gazing upward toward the sky, fast passing clouds covering the stars, birds as dark shadows, moving in unison above her as if her soul flew across a night's sky within her...

Inside a chapel attached to the large church, Nia stood just in front of a medieval- looking door with a large black iron handle. "Come. All are welcome in His house," Father Gabe, appearing by the door said to her as she entered. The chapel was mostly made out of stone with a few pews and small altar in the front. On the altar was the Eucharist. Nia walked down the aisle and sat down in one of the pews in the back. Father Gabe sat down beside her.

"What are you?" Nia asked him, touching his shoulder. "You seem real."

"You wouldn't believe me," he said. "Besides, it doesn't matter in the grand scheme of things. You're not afraid of me. So, that's a start."

"I have more things to be afraid of," Nia replied, staring toward the altar. "Things, things you wouldn't believe."

"Touche'. I guess we're somewhat the same," Father Gabe staring toward the altar. "Did you help me? With that match? I never win," Nia said, turning toward him. He turned toward her, stared into her eyes, and said, "Well, maybe it's time for you to start winning."

"You know what's funny. When I was naked before you, you just kept looking into my eyes, like now. It's as if you can see, what's inside me," Nia replied. "And in a way, I feel more naked, now, than before.

Nia looked toward the altar. Slowly, she got up and stood before it. Feeling *naked before God, fell to her knees, stretched out her arms, and gazed up at the Cross,* as if she had kept her eyes away from it, deep within the sky of *her soul,* like a blinding sun during the passage of dark clouds across the echoes of time. Somehow, especially in these past years, she had preferred the shadows, remaining naked within the darkness, alone, with her pain amidst silent screams not heard, fading across an empty and endless sea, far off toward the horizon's edge... As Nia knelt before the Cross, *the Large Oak Tree* stood atop the cliff, overlooking *an arising turbulent sea. In a rolling wind she heard, "Ana wa a wa..."* Nia gazed up. *The Angel from the club stood, hovering off the side of the cliff before her in the vision. Nia arose. The Angel Vanished.*

Chapter 12

Joshua sat in the chair by the open window of the Victorian Home with streaks of red passing before an opening moon, as if it was beginning... *The birth of a Blood Moon*. As if in a trance, gazing out the window at the moon, Joshua said, "And I beheld when he had opened the sixth seal, and, lo, there was a great earthquake; and the sun became back as sackcloth of hair, and the moon, the moon became as blood..."

"What happened to you?" Tim said as he entered through the front door, seeing Joshua wincing, holding his chest by the open window where his mother once told him stories. Joshua turned toward him, away from the past, away from the pain... as his soul bled with the memory of his mother's death, her love echoing through time...

"I don't know. Something happened, to my ribs," Joshua answered a question from another time, still carrying the images of the dark night of the *dragon eating the moon*.

"What happened?" their father asked, entering, going up to Joshua.

"It looks like he broke his ribs," Tim said. "Did you do it wrestling?" Joshua nodded. "Are you alright?" their father asked Joshua, stooping down. Joshua did not answer. "The dragon is eating the moon," Joshua said, staring out the window, holding his ribs, barely able to breathe.

"Joshua," their father said as Joshua came out of his trance. "Get me an ice pack. There's one in the freezer," their father said to Tim. Tim left to retrieve the icepack.

"Joshua. What do you mean, the dragon is eating the moon?"

"I don't know why I said that. I guess, I'm just in a lot of pain," wincing louder. Tim re- entered and handed their father the ice pack.

Lifting Joshua's shirt, "Believe," he gently placed it on Joshua's side. "Thanks, dad," Joshua said, glancing back out the window... at the moon.

In a trance, gazing out the window looking at the moon, Joshua said... "And then a great wonder appeared in heaven: There was a woman who was clothed with the sun, and the moon was under her feet. She had a crown of twelve stars on her head. She was pregnant and cried out with pain because she was about to give birth...

1969. A Full Moon above a Vietnamese village. Ed was only a few inches away from the lips of a Vietnamese women's, her legs wide apart. She was in agony, having a baby.

"You can do it!" Ed shouted, his hands becoming engulfed with blood, flowing over the dried blood of the child who died in Ed's arms. "You can do this! Push! Push!" Ed shouted, going between her legs to deliver the baby.

Michael and Tommy were standing in the doorway of the hut. The woman was screaming. Then, the sound of a baby's cry... Ed held the newborn in his arms, the blood of life replacing the one of death.

"Congratulations, Uncle Ed," Michael said, walking further in.

Ed reached up and handed the newborn baby girl to her mother. Sweat and tears were running down the mother's face, still trying to catch her breath.

"Congratulations, mom," Ed said to her in Vietnamese. "A baby girl."

"What are you going to name her?" Michael asked the mother in Vietnamese. The mother replied, "Hope." They nodded and smiled.

Michael and Ed went outside the hut. They saw one of the soldiers approach a little boy, who was carrying a large brown sack over his shoulder.

"What is he doing?" Michael asked Ed with a shrug of his shoulders. Suddenly, gunfire.

Michael and Ed ran over to the little boy on the ground with the soldier standing over him. "What did you do?" Michael asked the soldier, getting down on his knees to cradle the little boy. The little boy coughed out blood. "I saw a weapon inside that sack, like what we were told to watch out for." Ed lifted up and unraveled the brown sack. Corn fell out.

The little boy gazed up at Michael, coughed out his last gush of blood, and died. Ed turned toward the soldier, breaking down in tears, with just a stare. "Forgive them Father, for they do not know what they do..." Ed said, walking away, looking up at the sky.

Joshua stared at the moon in the chair before the open window. He envisioned his mother's story of a great knight slaying a dragon for a fair maiden, carrying her off upon his white winged stallion to the horizon that meets the sea...

Nia was kneeling in the small chapel off to the side of the church. Father Gabe stood in the back by a doorway. He faded away as Nia bowed her head and prayed...

1969. Vietnam. Michael's battalion watched villagers burying the little boy. One woman approached Michael and began shouting at him, pointing her finger.

"What's she saying?" Michael asked Ed with an old woman standing before him, a few inches away, shouting. She was short, barely coming up to Michael's chest, as she stood with her toes in her sandals touching the tips of Michael's bloodstained boots.

"I don't know. She's talking too fast," Ed replied.

The old woman took hold of Michael's arm. Still shouting, she shook it.

Michael tried to pull away but she wouldn't let go of him.

"I don't think she wants us to leave," Michael said to Ed.

"We have to go. No, we can't stay," Michael said to the old woman loudly and slowly while trying to pull his arm free. "What's the sign for go?" Michael asked Ed.

"She's not deaf," Ed replied. Michael signaled with his free arm for the rest of his unit to head toward the jungle as the old woman continued to hang on.

"You can talk to thirty kids in Vietnamese, but you can't tell me what this one old woman is babbling about, Uncle Eddie?" Michael asked Ed again.

"No. She's much too fast. Her words are overlapping. She sounds really pissed," Ed said as the woman took hold of Michael's arm with both her hands.

Michael tried to pull away. "Tell her we can't stay." "I don't think she wants us to," Ed replied.

"Then why won't she let me go?" Michael asked. Michael looked into the old woman's eyes. He saw tears and pain. "Marina!" Michael called out to Tommy as Tommy was following the unit toward the jungle.

"That's it, get a Hispanic guy, who's speaks Spanish, to translate," Ed said.

Tommy came back. The old woman dug in further into Michael's arm, still shouting as the villagers had their heads bowed *in prayer* at the end of the village with the little boy buried.

"What's going on?" Michael asked Tommy while gesturing to the old woman. "Well, she's telling you off, sir," Tommy replied.

"Told you," Ed said.

"No, you didn't," Michael replied, adding, "You told me she was pissed at something." "Same thing," Ed said as Tommy started translating. "Silver planes killed her husband

and oldest son. You're a dirt bag or something like that. I don't really know the translation for that one; maybe more like you're a scum bag, sir." Marina said. The old woman's words began to slow. She started to cry. Tommy looked up at Michael.

"The little boy we killed was her grandson," Tommy said.

Michael looked over up at the Vietnamese as they were walking away from the little boy's grave. He handed Ed his weapon. "Hold this," Michael said.

"Where are you going?" Ed asked. Michael did not answer. He continued walking toward the little boy's grave followed by the old woman still on his arm.

"You can't go over there! We're the ones who killed him!" Ed shouted. But Michael did not turn back. He continued heading for the grave.

Ed watched as the old woman's hands fell from Michael's arm and he moved on ahead of her. The old woman struggled to catch up, running, taking little shuffle steps. When she did,

Michael was already standing in front of the little boy's grave. The old woman, alone, stood by Michael's side. As Michael drew her close to his chest, she pounded him with her fists, but then her arms fell down by her side. Ed could hear her crying. Comforting her, Michael slowly let her go and got down on his knees with his head bowed as if praying. He raised his head and arms upward toward the sky. Ed watched, remaining where he was, holding onto Michael's weapon and awaiting his return. Across the sky, the clouds were moving swiftly as if death was passing with the coming of the night. Ed knew that it wouldn't be long until another child was killed, more blood shed, more cries echoing through the valley up to the mountaintops.

The sun was brightly shining as Joshua sat on the front porch step, holding his side with Samson next to him. He looked out toward the valley, toward the canvas draped over Tim's secret project. He stood, moved toward the edge of the front yard, and raised his fist, then turned back toward the house, appearing determined, moved, with a rising spiritual wind...

Nia stood on the balcony in jeans and a tee-shirt, looking out, holding the closed locket between her fingers. Her mother walked out and stood next to her, holding a suitcase. "I wanted to apologize, for putting you in this position. It's not your fault, any of this." "It's okay, mom. I know. Everything will work out. You'll see..." Nia said, turning to hug her. "I'll call you when I get back to New York. Are you sure you don't want to come?" Nia shook her head. They hugged.

"I'm worried about you, Nia. You can't stay here."

"It's okay, mom. He won't do anything to me, now. It won't want to jeopardize his election. Everything is about power with him," Nia said, glancing back toward her bedroom.

"That's what I'm worried about. But, you know, I have to leave." "I know, mom. It's okay, really."

Her mother picked up her suit case, slightly turned and said, "I love you, Nia."

"I love you, mom. Don't worry. I'm going to use their own power against them. I have a plan," Nia said, clasping her cross.

"Them? Be careful, Nia. Sometimes the best plans can turn into a... well, a war... one in which you become something you're not. I hope you find what you're looking for."

The senator entered and walked toward them out on the balcony. "So this is where everyone is. I was wondering." The senator got closer to Nia as she took a guarded step back. "Did you tell her?" he asked Melinda. "Yes," she answered, gripping her suitcase.

"You're mother and I decided with all the drama, recently, that she go back east until the election is over. You're welcome to stay, here, of course, that is if you don't pull anymore of your emotional episodes," the senator said touching, brushing back Nia's hair.

"I understand... perfectly," Nia simply said.

"Actually, everything worked out. I got a great news cycle about my risqué, beautiful, and exotic stepdaughter and her open empowerment and courage. You've really become the talk of the town, in a good way, for my message about strength," he said, pulling his hand away.

"Come. I'll drive you to the airport," the senator said, turning, and taking Melinda by the arm. "I'll call you, Nia." After they left, Nia went into her bedroom and pulled out her back pack from underneath the bed. She began packing her clothes from her bureau drawers... "I'm out."

Tim walked through the Victorian house, noticing the door open to the basement. "Joshua!" Tim shouted down the steps through the darkness of the stairwell.

Tim slowly and cautiously walked down the basement steps trying to feel his way along an old, dusty, wooden banister as he could hear rustling on the other side of the basement. When he got to the bottom of the steps, he reached up, searching for a light. Finally, he found one with a small chain hanging down from it. Pulling the chain, one light bulb turned on. The socket was held by only one wire dangling from the low basement ceiling. A medieval-appearing door, to the right, was torn open. "Joshua?" Tim said as he entered.

Joshua was stretched out on a weight bench, preparing to lift - bench press - 250 pounds on a long bar with 45-pound metal plates. Joshua readjusted his grip beneath a flickering, swaying light. "What are you doing?" Tim asked. "Lifting," Joshua simply responded as Tim looked around this part of the basement from the "middle ages when darkness reigned. Past the rusted weigh bench cobwebs hung above a small red wrestling mat, spanning twelve by twelve feet with old rusted metal weights strewn about. Beyond the edge of the mat was a cold, hardened, exposed stone floor.

"Do you want me to spot you?" Tim asked, approaching him as Joshua took a deep breath. Tim got behind him and placed his hands underneath the long bar. "Are you sure you want to do this with your ribs injured and all?" Tim leaned over the bar and looked down to him.

"Okay, if it hurts, I'll catch the bar before it falls," Tim added. "Ready, one, two, three," Tim said, helping Joshua lift the bar with the weights up off the iron posts, arms extended.

Joshua bench-pressed the weights seven times with his brother spotting him. On the seventh time Joshua had a little trouble. Tim helped him complete the last rep by tapping the bar from underneath in the middle with his fingers on both hands. With Joshua's elbows locked and arms extended upward as far as they could go, Tim grabbed the center of the bar and helped Joshua put it back onto the iron posts.

"Not bad. Two hundred and twenty-five pounds. How do your ribs feel?" Tim asked.

With sweat falling from his brow, Joshua, taking deep breaths, slowly sat up holding his side. "It's really strange. It doesn't hurt that much now," Joshua said as he stood up.

"Why are you doing this?" Tim asked.

"I'm trying to get in shape, to wrestle," Joshua answered, turning away.

"That's a part of it. But, there's... there's something else. I can see it," Tim said. "I saw that girl, again," Joshua said, turning back.

"The one at the club?" Tim asked.

"Yeah... I ran into her at school. I don't know. There's just something about her," Joshua said, holding the side of his chest. "I didn't get a chance to talk to her, though."

"Well, next time you see her, why don't you try to?" Tim asked going up to him and placing his hand on his brother's shoulder.

"It's hard for me. I'm not as confident as you when it comes to girls. You know..." "Joshua. You just benched pressed 250 pounds with broken ribs. I think you can talk to a girl. Who knows, she might want to talk to you, too. Doesn't hurt to try, right?" Joshua nodded his head and smiled as Tim looked around the basement. "Man, I forgot all of this was down here. It's been such a long time." "Too long," Joshua countered. "I've waited enough..." Tim appeared curious what he meant as Joshua stopped the swaying light and turned it off.

When they got to the top of the basement stairs, their father was waiting for them. "What are you boys doing?" "Joshua was just working out." "So, you're really doing it? You're going to wrestle again?" their father asked Joshua. "Doesn't hurt to try, right?" Their father smiled.

Joshua remembered when he was three. His father was out in front, his mother right behind him. They were running together as fast as they could, trying to get the kit to fly as he and Tim held on to the end of the string. With an arising wind along the beach from across the lake, it seemed at first that it was going to fly. "You have to try! Hang on! Hang on!" his other cried out to them with the strong wind blowing back her hair. But the kite came crashing to the ground, and their mother fell to her knees. It was the last time the four of them would be together at this lake before her death. He could remember now how their father stood holding the kite while looking up to the sky. It was as if he thought God had let them down, as if he, and even

God, had given up. He remembered now, he remembered as the wind, remained still, unmoving within the unrelenting hidden storms of a forgotten time...

Nia pulled into the parking lot of the strip club and parked her car. The church bells were ringing. Briefly glancing up to the church's tower, she picked up the small plastic bag on her car seat and opened it. Taking it out, she held it up. It was a sheer, silk one-piece, tiger-striped body stocking. She brought it to her chest, held it to her legs, and stretched it out.

"This will work," she said to herself with a smile."

There was a sudden knock on her window. It was Ms. Gongel. Nia quickly put the body stocking back into the bag and behind the car seat. Ms. Gongel knocked again. Nia rolled down her window only a few inches.

"What are you doing? What do you have there in the bag?" Ms. Gongel asked. "Nothing," Nia replied.

"Do you want to model it for me?" Ms. Gongel asked again, with a wink. "I'm glad you could come in on such short notice." "No problem," Nia replied. Not realizing that her car door was not locked, Ms. Gongel opened the door. Nia, startled, looked up at her as she stooped down as Nia nervously remained in the car; she reached up, stroking Nia's cheek, gently brushing back her hair.

"You look afraid," Ms. Gongel said to her. "There's nothing to fear," she added. Slowly rising and leaning into the car, she softly kissed Nia on her lips as Nia let her.

"Now, wasn't that nice?" Ms. Gongel asked.

She kissed Nia again. This time Nia kissed her back as Ms. Gongel was stroking her hair.

Nia gently pushed her away with the sounding of the church bells. "No. I'm sorry. I changed my mind. I can't do this," Nia said.

"Yes, you can," Ms Gongel said as she took Nia's hand and helped her out of the car. "Come. I've set something else up with Maribel,"

Ms. Gongel added as she shut Nia's car door and led her by the hand across the parking lot toward the strip club.

Nia looked at the parking lot and saw something strange that she hadn't noticed when she pulled in. The parking lot was empty except for a couple of cars in front of the club.

"Where is everyone? I thought I had to do my shift," Nia asked while still being led by the hand.

"I gave everyone the day off. It will be alright. Don't worry. You'll still do your shift," Ms. Gongel replied as she opened the club's door. The bar was empty and dark as the door closed behind them.

"What are you going to do to me?" Nia nervously asked.

"Relax. I just have a little surprise for my favorite girl," Ms. Gongel replied with a laugh as she led Nia through the club and toward the stage.

"Sit here," Ms. Gongel gently directed Nia while holding out a chair for her by a table in front of the stage.

Nia sat down, trying to see what was on the stage. She could see someone, but because of the darkness, she couldn't see whom.

"I'm going to teach you how to really perform," Ms. Gongel said to her with a final stroke of her hair. "You will obey me, right?" Nia nodded, her eyes cast downward.

Ms. Gongel went over and turned on a switch. A light beamed onto the stage. On the stage, next to a chair, Maribel was submissively kneeling, wearing a tank top and thong, her bottom resting on the back of her heels.

Ms. Gongel got up onto the stage, stood over Maribel, and said, "I call this performance 'Ms. Gongel's Opus.' Now watch."

"Kiss my feet," Ms. Gongel ordered Maribel.

Maribel lowered herself and kissed Ms. Gongel's black spiked boots. Maribel paused, looking over at Nia.

"Get up," Ms. Gongel commanded while lifting Maribel up by her hair. Maribel winced as she stood. Ms. Gongel sat down in the chair and forcibly guided Maribel, face down, over her lap.

"Some musicians play a piano or a guitar. I play, well, you'll see," Ms. Gongel said with a fading smile and more stern look toward Nia.

Ms. Gongel began spanking Maribel; Maribel's feet were kicking up in the air. Amidst Maribel's gasps of "ow" in harmony with her spanking, Ms. Gongel bragged, "You see, Nia. This eventually will be you. I'm looking for a new instrument, a new sound..."

Ms. Gongel tossed Maribel to the floor. Nia got up and ran for the door. The door was locked as she frantically pulled on it trying to get it open. She looked back. Maribel was again submissively kneeling by the chair as Ms. Gongel moved determinedly toward Nia.

"You don't have to be afraid, my love," Ms. Gongel said as she caught up with her.

Nia tried to open the door again but couldn't. Nia then turned and tried to run but there was nowhere to go. Ms. Gongel cornered her by the side of the bar.

"Please, don't hurt me," Nia said as she cowered down.

Ms. Gongel bent down and gently kissed Nia on her lips. Nia's lips were quivering as she kissed Nia again, a long, deep, tender kiss. Nia started to kiss her back, putting her arms up around Ms. Gongel's back. Ms. Gongel raised her up by her shoulders while still kissing her and turned her away from the bar. Maribel suddenly appeared, standing behind Nia. Forcibly, Maribel took hold of Nia's arms and pulled them away from around Ms. Gongel. As Maribel held Nia's arms behind her back, Ms. Gongel slowly began unbuttoning Nia's blouse, exposing Nia's black lace bra.

"Please. I'm ready to do this," Nia said as Maribel pulled Nia's blouse down off of her arms and the blouse fell to the floor. Ms. Gongel took both of Nia's wrists and pressed them together in front of Nia's chest. Maribel, reaching around from behind, undid Nia's skirt. It, too, fell to Nia's feet.

"Come," Ms. Gongel said to Nia as she led her by both her wrists.

Maribel stooped down and held onto Nia's shoes as she stepped out of them in sheer black stockings and out of and away from the skirt.

She was led toward the stage wearing only her black push up bra, black lace thong panties, and the sheer stockings that rose up to the upper part of her thighs. Maribel obediently followed them from behind.

Before they got to the stage, Ms. Gongel stopped and let go of Nia's wrists. She walked over and turned on another light. Nia remained quietly standing by a large glass table.

"Lie down on top of it," Ms. Gongel ordered while gesturing with her head to the table. "What?" Nia asked with a slight gasp.

"Lie down on top of it," Ms. Gongel said again. "Face down," she commanded.

Nia slowly leaned over the table. Maribel went to the other side and pulled Nia's hands as she slid outstretched on her stomach across the glass table. Maribel, getting down on her knees and looking upward through the glass, grabbed hold tightly to Nia's wrists.

"You see, Nia, I know you want to obey me," Ms. Gongel said as she slowly took off Nia's stockings, gently sliding them down and off her legs.

With Nia's legs completely bare, Ms. Gongel undid Nia's bra. She pulled the bra away by its strap, flinging it to the other side of the bar. Nia remained in position on her stomach, being held to the table by Maribel. Nia felt the coldness of the table with her bare breasts, now just in her panties. The sensation of the glass turned to warmth as Ms. Gongel ran her hands down Nia's back, tenderly massaging her over her bottom and down the back of her legs to her feet.

"Just relax," Ms. Gongel whispered to her as Maribel held tight to her wrists, unmoving, and without a spoken word.

Ms. Gongel massaged Nia's feet, back up her legs and her bottom. Ms. Gongel paused seeing the branded Mark of the Dragon.

"What's this?" Ms. Gongel asked her, surprised, touching it.

Nia did not answer. Ms. Gongel paused, tracing with her finger the lines of the mark. "Interesting. I've seen this somewhere before," Ms. Gongel said. "You little whore. You should have my name tattooed on your butt," she angrily said, giving Nia's bottom a hard slap.

Nia winced. Ms. Gongel smiled, running her hands over the red mark she had just made. "There. That's my mark," Ms. Gongel whispered to herself. "You can get up, now."

Nia got up off the table. She glanced over at Maribel who was submissively kneeling.

"What were you planning on doing with that body stocking?" Ms. Gongel asked Nia with her hands on her hips. "The one in the bag in your car." Nia, startled, didn't know how to reply. "I've never seen you wear a body stocking. Tell me. Where were you planning on wearing it?"

"It's nothing," Nia replied to her while trying to turn away. Ms. Gongel pulled her back by her arm.

"Tell me," Ms. Gongel said sternly.

"I'm not going to do it now. It was a crazy idea. I'd be too embarrassed to wear it," Nia paused.

"I said, 'Tell me,'" Ms. Gongel said again sternly while gripping Nia's arm.

"I was going to wear it to embarrass my stepfather..." Nia said. Pausing, she added, "...at his fundraiser Friday night at a congressman's house."

Ms. Gongel laughed. "Well, you are a little whore." "But, I'm not going to now," Nia said.

"Oh, yes you are," Ms. Gongel replied.

Stunned, Nia looked confused as she continued. "You are going to wear it and I'm going to accompany you. I've never been to a congressman's house and this can be our coming out party. So I can show off my new girlfriend." Ms. Gongel put her arm around Nia, adding, "I can't wait to see the look on their faces when you strut around in your little outfit with me by your side."

"No. Please don't make me do this," Nia said. "My stepfather, he's..." "You said that you would obey me," Ms. Gongel responded.

"I know. It's just that—" Nia started to say.

"That you aren't ready to be humiliated by me in public?" Ms. Gongel asked, adding, "Look. You know you want to strut your little bare ass in front of everyone," Ms. Gongel said while giving Nia's bottom a slap.

"And you know that, deep inside, you want me to force you to do it." Ms. Gongel kissed Nia on the side of her neck while gently caressing Nia's breast. She suddenly grabbed hold tightly onto Nia's crotch.

"Ow," Nia gasped.

"You will do it. Right?" Ms. Gongel barked while still holding tight.

"Yes," Nia whispered, wincing while being pulled up and rising on her toes.

Ms. Gongel let go and said, "Good. I'll meet you here Friday night at eight. Don't be late." Ms. Gongel started to walk away. She turned back. "Oh. And don't forget to bring your outfit. I want you to look sexy for our first date." Ms. Gongel exited the stage, leaving Nia standing alone in the spotlight covering her chest with her arms. Slowly, she sat down on the stage, crossing her legs, bringing her knees up to her chest into a fetal position like Joshua did in the basement against the wall. She bowed her head. The church bells could be heard ringing louder outside...

Chapter 13

Dark gray clouds began to cover the late afternoon sky with soft rumbling of thunder in the distance. With drizzling rain, Joshua walked to his art class, which he discovered, by asking other students along the way, was across an open grass lot in an old building that looked like a converted barn next to a large stone house. This barn had small, rustic-looking windows on a second floor just beneath the overhang of a green, copper-shingled roof. As he approached, he saw young women carrying in giant canvasses through a large, open, side doorway as the barn's door, paint chipped and old, looked like it was left flung open. Upon entering, a couple of female students attempted to close huge wooden door with a black iron latch. Yet, they found that it would not remain shut, continuing to fling back open on its own.

Hesitantly, Joshua walked toward the open doorway. When he entered, he saw twenty young women getting into a semicircle, preparing to draw. Before them was a large, white, rectangular, stage-like object that was a few feet wide and high. Full length mirrors encircled the walls like the red mats in the wrestling room as a wooden gymnasium type floor spanned before him. In addition to being an art studio, the old barn was a dance studio with a bar running about waist high along the length of the encircling mirrors. Sarah and Maurine, the students from the bookstore, looked up at him as he entered. Both were smiling. Maurine's hair was unbraided, her long black hair flowing down past her shoulders to the center of her back. She flung her hair back with a sound of the barn's door hitting loudly against the outside wall in an arising thunderstorm. In her hand she gripped several pastels. She made marks onto her canvass, testing them. Sarah's hand was shaking a bit as she set up her canvass, as if excited, anticipating what was about to happen while glancing over at Joshua. Joshua looked at Sarah. Behind her in the corner was a CD player on the floor. It was not on.

"All guys are pigs," Maurine said. "You've got that right," Sarah confirmed.

Maurine continued, talking to everyone. "I mean, I don't care who the guy is. If some amazon walks by, you know the type, showing off her legs with her skirt almost pulled up to her crotch, the guy will look."

Others joined in. "Yeah."

"What is their problem? What is it, a genetic defect, or something? And when they look, they can't just give a discrete glance? They have to gawk like they've never seen a butt before."

Another student added with a laugh, "I know what you mean. Every time I put on a dress and heels I feel like I might as well put a sign on my back, 'Stare at my legs.'" Everyone laughed except a small young Asian woman who was meticulously setting up her easel and aligning her pastels in the corner, not speaking a word...

All the wrestlers were warming up on the mats in the wrestling room for their "volunteer practice," one of three each day. Villecco was not there yet.

"Girls love it when you check them out," Mitch said, adding, "That's why they dress the way they do."

"Yeah. Why do the babes wear practically nothing if they don't want to show it off," Tony said, adding, "You don't see us walking around in miniskirts."

"At least not in public," Carmel said with a smile.

"Alright! Everyone up!" Villecco shouted entering the wrestling room.

As Joshua stood in the middle of the studio, everyone became quiet upon noticing him. Another student finally said while looking over at Joshua, "I think we should start gawking at them. See how they like it."

"You're right. We should," another student replied while checking out Joshua. She added with a smile to Joshua, "Alright. Strip."

With a crash, a small rickety door which led to the second floor at the other end of the studio slammed open. Barely holding on, with its few remaining bowls clinging to their rusted hinges, a tall, slender woman, stern looking, pushed the door all the way open. In her hand was a large paintbrush. She had short black hair and a pale complexion. As this woman walked through the studio, the images of black and white returned to Joshua. She was dressed entirely in black with a long sleeved, wool turtleneck blouse and baggy pants that were tucked into the tops of her high heeled, knee-length black leather boots. Everyone immediately became silent.

"Good afternoon, Ms. Dominique," one student said to her as Ms. Dominique replied in a slight nod. She stared over at Joshua. She smiled. Joshua remained still. Ms. Dominique approached him as Sarah and Maurine snickered. She reached out her hand with the paintbrush as welding a whip, as Joshua nervously backed up toward entrance with the echoes of falling rain and approaching rumblings of cracks of thunder.

"I'm Ms. Dominique," she said with any affirmative, confident tone to Joshua. Joshua slowly reached out and shook her hand. She had a strong grip, with the paintbrush, as she stared and smiled. "Are you the model?" she asked.

"I—" Joshua started to say.

"Yes. He is," Sarah and Maurine simultaneously answered for him.

"Good. Come," Ms. Dominique ordered, still having hold of Joshua's left hand with the paintbrush, her symbol of control, embedding into it. "Class. We will return in a minute," she said, looking up at the clock at the base of a cathedral ceiling. Joshua glanced up, too, seeing all the wooden beams. "We will begin exactly at five after four, so be ready," she commanded.

She led Joshua over toward the small doorway at the other end of the studio. After walking up a narrow circular stairwell through darkness, they got to the top. At the top of the stairs, still holding his hand, she reached up and pulled a chain, turning on a light. It was suspended from a low ceiling of this attic, like his basement. The attic was a large, musty room with only a desk covered in papers, a bare wooden floor, and a coat rack at the other end with leotards and other women's dancewear hanging on hangers. A few boxes were at the side of the desk. A few feet away from them was a full-length mirror that was dusty with cobwebs upon it. She let go of Joshua's hand.

"Have you ever modeled before?" she asked. "No... I wanted to draw," Joshua replied.

She paused. "You will. But for now you will be our model. Take off your clothes," she said abruptly and sternly.

"What?" Joshua asked.

"Take off your clothes," she snipped again. Joshua slowly began taking off his clothes. He stripped down to his tee-shirt and underwear. "Everything," she added with a smile. He took off his tee-shirt and underwear and stood naked before her. She examined him. "Walk over there," she ordered, pointing toward the boxes by her desk. Joshua turned and walked naked over toward the boxes. "Good," she said. "You have nice buns. A very nice body," she added.

"What are in the boxes?" Joshua asked.

"Just costumes. Some from plays of previous years." "Oh," he responded as he turned and walked back to her.

"When I put you in a pose, you will hold that pose without moving for up to forty minutes. Can you do that?" she asked with gentle pat to his bare bottom.

"I think so," he answered.

"Good. You will get a five minute break at the end of each pose. You'll see. Come," Ms.

Dominique said, leading Joshua by the hand back down the stairway.

When they entered, Ms. Dominique let go of Joshua's hand and gestured toward the white platform. Walking across the studio naked, his bare feet felt the roughness of the wooden floor and a breeze of rain from the open doorway. In front of the twenty young women, he stepped up onto the platform with Ms. Dominique by his side. "Alright. We will do four poses, two standing and two lying down," she said to the entire class. She looked up at Joshua. "Stand like this," Ms. Dominique said, placing her arms behind her back and clasping her hands. Joshua got into the pose as she helped him with her one hand on the right cheek of his bottom and her other tapping the inner part of his left thigh. "Move your legs wider apart. That's it. Now, don't move. Alright, class. Can everyone see?" A few answered, "Yes." They began to draw, some at first looking up at Joshua's face, while others began at his legs.

Joshua looked into the mirrors. Standing atop the platform, he felt strange being nude in front of all the young women. With his hands clasped tightly behind his back, resting just at the top of his bottom, he felt embarrassed. He tried to think of something else. He began thinking about the time when Timmy, his father, and he went on a fishing trip at a lake near the bottom of a mountain years ago. The lake was on of their favorite spots." Joshua and Tim had learned to swim there on family picnics. On the beach was where his father and mother had tried to get the kite to fly. Joshua remembered now. Years later, they went back to the lake for another fishing trip. He was eleven then, and although they would return to the lake to go camping, that would be their last fishing trip.

Years Before... "Dad! Look what I caught!" Timmy screamed out while leaning over the side of the row boat, pulling up the line and lifting out a large catfish. The catfish was flopping about the boat, struggling to survive. Tim reached for a club to hit it. As he raised the club, Joshua screamed out, "No! Don't kill him!"

"What?" Tim replied while trying to steady the squirming catfish with his other hand. "Don't kill it," Joshua repeated again.

"He has to, Joshua. That's our dinner," their father replied with a chuckle. Tim raised the club and hit the catfish. Joshua screamed out, "No!"

"Alright, time!" Ms. Dominique called out like Villecco. Joshua looked up at the clock.

Forty-five minutes had passed. "You can take a break now," she told Joshua.

Joshua stepped down off of the platform but he didn't know where he could go. Some students had put down their pastels and were brushing off their hands as others continued working on their drawings. The silence slowly faded into talking and laughing as Joshua walked over to a small open window and leaned on the dance bar, looking out. He watched the rain falling, the wind moving the trees, the few aligning the open lot.

Joshua remembered when he was three. His father was out in front, his mother right behind him. They were running together as fast as they could, trying to get the kit to fly as he and Tim held on to the end of the string. With an arising wind along the beach from across the lake, it seemed at first that it was going to fly. "We're going to do it! Hang on! Hang on!" his mother cried out to them with the strong wind blowing back her hair. But the kite came crashing to the ground, and their mother fell to her knees. It was the last time the four of them would be together at this lake, before her death. He could remember now how their father stood holding the kite while looking up to the sky. It was as if he thought God had let them down, as if he, and even God, had given up. He remembered now, he remembered as the wind, remained still.

Out of the small window, the trees were bending with the winds of the storm as Joshua turned and saw Sarah and Maurine standing behind him.

"Hey sexy," Sarah said. "Nice bod," Maurine added.

"Girls! Leave my model alone!" Ms. Dominique called out.

"Her model? Wow. She's already claimed him?" Sarah said under her breath to Maurine as they went back to their easels and canvasses.

"Alright. Next pose," Ms. Dominique called out after leading Joshua back up on the platform. "Stand like this," Ms. Dominique whispered to Joshua, raising her hands, folding them up behind her head with her elbows out. Joshua did as she said. Ms. Dominique circulated the studio, helping the students as they all remained quiet, transfixed on their own creations as if the stillness of that wind from long ago had returned. Joshua looked over toward the open doorway. The rain was coming down much harder, draped in darkness.

He remembered the dinner, eating the catfish. "Pass the ketchup," Tim said as they were sitting around the dining room table. Tim and their father were digging into the catfish. Joshua sat with just vegetables on his plate.

"Aren't you going to have any?" Tim asked.

"No," Joshua replied, adding, "You shouldn't have killed it."

"Where do you think steaks come from, Joshua, or chicken sandwiches or pork egg rolls?

You eat all of them," Tim said.

"I'm sorry," Joshua said, getting up and leaving the table. He walked out and sat on one of the steps of the front porch. He looked out to the night's sky.

"Time!" Ms. Dominique shouted. Joshua stepped down off of the platform and went over to the open doorway. Folding his arms in front of him, he watched the rain coming down. Sarah came over to him as the other students were taking their break.

"Maureen and I are sorry about busting on you. But you are really cute," Sarah said. "That's alright," Joshua replied. "Do you have a girlfriend?" Sarah asked. Joshua did not answer. He partially turned as lightning cracked across the sky. The light passed across his face.

Maurine came over, too, and examined him, looking up and down. "Your body is really sexy. You have nice legs. So you know that?" she asked.

Joshua walked away and went back and sat down on the platform, his legs wide apart, his elbows on his knees, watching and listening to all the young women talking about various aspects of their lives. Some were talking about boyfriends, others about classes, and still others about dreams. Joshua felt he didn't have a life except for the one he was trying to start now with school, the one he still didn't feel a part of. Whether it was the wrestling room with mats on the walls or the art studio with mirrors, gazing at himself, he still felt like an outcast, someone to be mocked, naked and vulnerable to mean-spirited whims, whether it be Villecco's rage or...

Ms. Dominique came up to him. "This time we will do two poses lying down. She turned and walked back over to the other side of the studio. She picked up a long mat and slid it to the platform in front of him. Joshua picked up his feet. "Lie down on it," she said.

With everyone still on a break, Joshua lied down on his back on the mat. "Put your right arm up over your head. That's it. Now spread your legs. Good. Move up your right leg. Bend the knee. That's it. Good," Ms. Dominique said to him. "Alright, girls, lets get started again," she called out.

The students went back to their canvasses and began drawing. Joshua, spread out on the floor, tried not to move as he looked eye level at everyone's feet. The mat was spongy. It felt like the same mat he slept on when his father, Tim, and he went on the camping trip. He was twelve, a year later, after the catfish "got it." Though he told his father that he was going to boycott any future family fishing trips, he thought he would give camping one more shot. It was night. The moon was full and he could hear a wolf's howl in the distance. He got up out of the tent and walked to the edge of the lake. He could see the reflection of the moon bright and clear. He looked up at the sky. He saw a shooting star. He made a wish. Years later, he was still waiting for it to come true.

"Alright, time!" Ms. Dominique called out.

Joshua quickly got up and walked back in front of the small open window off to the side. Ms. Dominique followed him as the other students looked away, taking their break. Joshua and Ms. Dominique both had their backs toward the students, both looking out the small window.

"Are you alright?" she asked, as if concerned, standing slightly behind him. "Yes," he replied, looking out to the swaying trees, the rain.

Ms. Dominique went back to help a student with her drawing. As he continued to look out, he wondered if his life would ever be clear again, if light would ever be seen again reflecting in his soul.

"Alright, last pose!" Ms. Dominique shouted. "Lie face down," she said to Joshua. "Lift one leg up. Point the toes. Good," she added. Joshua was lying on his stomach with his right leg raised, resting up on his elbows with his head bowed. "Raise your head," Ms. Dominique called out to him. Joshua raised his head. "Alright. Hold that. Is that good for everybody?" Ms.

Dominique asked the class. They all responded, "Yes," beginning to draw on yet another canvass. From this position, in the mirrors Joshua could see the many different images of himself, the many perceptions of the artists in the room. Some were drawing him exactly as he was, others, a fantasy picture of possibly what he could become. He was intrigued by all the drawings, all the images of himself from the different poses, as if coming to a realization for the first time that there was much more to himself than he had ever known, as if he was beginning to see who he could become as the colors of the pastels to his vision returned. One drawing, resting off to the side on the floor at the feet of the quiet Asian student had him standing dressed as a knight, muscular, with a sword raised high after slaying a dragon.

"Alright! That's it, girls!" Ms. Dominique called out.

Everyone finished their drawings, some making last minute touches by smearing and reapplying their pastels to the canvasses. Others placed their pastels back into their boxes. Joshua remained where he was, not knowing if he was allowed to move.

"Good job," Ms. Dominique finally said to him, gesturing with her head that he could get up. Joshua got up and walked toward the small upstairs' doorway.

"Wait!" Ms. Dominique called over to him. Joshua stopped and turned. "I want you to put all the easels in that corner," Ms. Dominique said to him pointing to the other side of the room.

One of the students pushed her easel toward Joshua. Joshua took it, folded it, and carried it to where Ms. Dominique pointed. One by one he folded up and carried everyone's easel as the students continued packing up their things. Sarah and Maurine intermittently stared at him with smiles. "Let the games begin," Maurine said to Sarah.

Ms. Dominique approached Maurine and whispered something to her. Everyone else left out through the large barn doorway with the rain still coming down hard, covering their heads as they did. Sarah and Maurine, though, remained sitting on a long bench against the wall, as if waiting for a show to start. Joshua stood in the center waiting too.

"You're going to have to clean up. That's part of the model's job. Here," Ms. Dominique told him, handing him a broom. "Well, I'm waiting," she added. Joshua began sweeping up some of the chips from the pastels that had fallen to the floor. He looked over at the bench. Sarah was still there watching him, but Maurine was gone. Suddenly, the small rickety door flung open and Maurine walked out. In her hand she was holding a brown shopping bag looking like it was filled with something. Ms. Dominique smiled at her. Maurine returned the smile.

"Ready?" Maurine said to Sarah. Sarah arose and nodded.

"We'll see you, Ms. Dominique," Maurine called back as they prepared themselves to make a run for it in the downpour.

"Bye, girls. And thank you, Maurine, for taking care of that for me," Ms. Dominique said. "Take care of what?" Sarah asked as they stood barely inside in the doorway with the rain falling partially down upon them. Maurine opened the bag. Joshua's clothes were inside. Sarah let out a laugh, glancing back at Joshua still sweeping the floor. Maurine whispered to Sarah, "I better get an A for this." They both dashed out into the rain laughing, both letting out a scream as they became soaked. Joshua finished sweeping and looked up. There was silence except for the steady pulse of the rain. Ms. Dominique and he were facing each other, alone.

She went over to a closet, opened it, and disappeared slightly inside. Joshua heard a bucket fall and then water running. It sounded like she was filling up a bucket in a sink. Seconds later, Ms. Dominique came out of the closet carrying the bucket full of soapy water. "Here.

Come get this," she said. Joshua carefully placed down the broom and went over to get the bucket. Inside it was a scrub brush. "You're going to have to scrub the floor too," she said, adding, "There is a dance class here tomorrow morning, and they like the floor to be clean. They're starting early this year practicing for the school's spring show. It's always an event, and the Art Department always provides the props. This year it's a play, one of Shakespeare's, but with a twist." "Which play…" Joshua began to ask. "Just don't stand there. Start scrubbing," she said. Joshua hesitantly got down on his hands and knees. "Now," she added. Taking the scrub brush from the bucket, he began scrubbing the floor as Ms. Dominique supervised. "'Romeo and Juliet,'" she finally replied.

"I didn't know there were dancers in 'Romeo and Juliet,'" Joshua said as he paused from scrubbing. Ms. Dominique raised her hand. He suddenly felt a sting from the slap on his bare bottom. He flinched. "Did I tell you to stop?" she asked. Joshua glanced up at her. He continued scrubbing.

"It's a modern version of the play," Ms. Dominique said. "All the actors and actresses will be dressed in Elizabethan garb, but the dancers will be adding a number from the former Broadway play, "Cats" dressed, of course, as cats right after Juliet kills herself. It's sort of like Shakespeare meets Broadway kind of play. That's why the dancers and the drama club need all school year to prepare. And that's why you'll have to keep this floor clean, all year, just like this."

"Can I get dressed yet?" Joshua asked as he continued to scrub across the floor while crawling on his hands and knees.

"In a minute," she replied, walking over and standing over him as he paused again; she gently touched his toes with the tip of her boot. He felt another sting from a slap on his bottom.

"Do you like that?" Ms. Dominique asked. "Answer me," she commanded, giving him another spank as Joshua winced. She stood back with her arms folded. "Well, do you?" she asked. Joshua stared up at her. "Do you like doing this?" she asked again.

"I don't know what you mean," Joshua said.

"I pride myself on knowing...who likes a certain lifestyle. And I sensed from you, from when I first saw you, that you would like to be dominated," she said.

"What's that?" Joshua asked.

"You're kidding? You don't know?" she asked, adding, "Then why are you doing this?" "Doing what?" Joshua replied.

"Why are you...obeying me?" she asked.

"You're my teacher, and I want to learn. Get an education," Joshua replied, adding, "I've heard about hazings in fraternities and sororities. I figured that this was like that."

She looked away. She turned back. "You must have heard about S and M," she said with a somewhat sympathetic look.

"Sarah and Maurine?" Joshua asked. "Unbelievable," Ms. Dominique replied. "You're different, aren't you?" she asked.

Joshua stood and tossed the scrub brush into the bucket. "Yes. I am." he said, adding "I'm not doing this any more..."

"It's alright. Calm down," she said as she approached him and tenderly touched his shoulder.

"My brother warned me about women like you."

She kissed him. Joshua did not kiss back. She gently caressed his chest. "I shouldn't have to your... hazing," Joshua said, turning away.

She ran her hands down his chest to his tight muscular stomach, feeling the moisture of his sweat in the ripples of his perfectly toned body. She encircled a drop with her forefinger around his belly button. "You know, you want to be... hazed. Don't worry. Relax. I won't tell anyone. We all have our own little secrets." She paused. She slowly took her hand off his stomach and walked a few feet away. "Don't you understand? I am trying to give you an education, not just in Art but, also, sexuality... which, in a way, is Art, something to be created, grasped upon and explored... and I'm willing to help you. I'm willing to help you discover things that you've probably never even been aware of—fantasies just awaiting to erupt inside of you..."

Joshua turned back. "There's nothing inside of me," he said to her.

"A lot young men, would like to be in the very position you're in. To be mentored, to be trained, to be—"

Joshua paused again. He raised his head upward toward the wooden beams and called out, "Or not to be," interrupting her. He turned around, facing her, adding, "'Whether tis nobler in the mind to suffer the slings and arrows of outrageous fortunes or to take arms against a sea of troubles...'"

"Very good," she said. "Do you know a lot about Shakespeare?"

"My dad gave me a book about Shakespeare. It was my mom's," Joshua replied.

Joshua gazed at her stance, her feet wide apart, a message of control, confidence, and strength. With her hands were on her hips, her eyes slightly narrowed, her chin began to rise.

"A little," Joshua answered, nervously, beginning to feel submissive in her spanning shadow. She nodded. He knelt down before her as she lowered her chin, her narrowed cast eyes widened with a smile. She waited a few seconds, then approached him and gently placed her hand down back on his chest and began caressed him all over his upper torso as a sculpture sculpting her masterpiece, paying attention to every molded detail. He remained still, as if bound, his muscles tensing, his eyes closing to her seductive soft and gentle touch...

"Do you like me being in control... Say it," she commanded. Suddenly, Joshua shook his head and rose. "No. This is wrong," he said pulling away. "I'm sorry. But I'm not going to be a part of your hazing, fantasy, or whatever it is. I don't want to hurt God," Joshua ended.

"Fine. It's your decision," she snipped. "But you're giving up on wonderful education," she said with a pat on his chest. "And you do have quite a bod," she added with another smile.

Joshua turned and walked back up the spiraling staircase. When he got to the top in the musty attic, he could not find his clothes.

He came back down to ask her to help him, but Ms. Dominique was gone. After going again back upstairs, he went up to the full length mirror and began gazing at himself, his body. Covering himself with his arms, his hands touching his shoulders, he went over to the boxes next to the desk. He opened one up. After reaching in, he pulled out a costume. He began putting it on - *a purple robe...*

33 A.D. "Do you want me to release for you the King of the Jews!" Pilate shouted as he stood atop a stone platform called in Hebrew, "Gabbatha," before the angry crowd upon this early morning. "No! We want Barabbas! Barabbas!" the crowd shouted back. It was the day of preparation for the Passover. And Pilate, because of the festival, was going to release one prisoner. Pilate, not knowing what to do, looked back at his guards, the crowd before him growing angrier. He waved his hand in a command to two of the guard clasping their spears. The two soldiers left as Pilate turned and met them behind a large pillar about twenty feet away from where he stood before the crowd. Another man, along with the guards, was there, a short elderly man with no really recognizable features, at least not to Pilate.

"We cannot let this go on. We have to quiet this crowd," the man said. "But this Jesus, he has done nothing wrong," Pilate replied.

"He has incited the crowd, his own people. And if nothing else, he is, at the very least, crazy. Who will miss him? He thinks he is the King of the Jews. And listen, listen to them. He is not their king," the man said as the crowd grew louder, shouting. Pilate leaned up against the stone pillar as the two soldiers remained silent, awaiting his order.

"So you and everyone else want me to release a murderer, a killer, rather than someone who is innocent, someone who may just be crazy?" Pilate said to the man. "Do you really think he is crazy?" Pilate asked.

"Do you think he is the King of the Jews?" the man replied, adding, "Son of their God?" Pilate did not answer. He paused, hearing the crowd even become angrier. Pilate turned.

"What if, by some bizarre chance, he is some God's son," Pilate said. "Then, upon ordering his death, I will become forever known as the one who sentenced the 'Son of God' to death. Think about it. What if we are the ones who are crazy, the ones who..." Pilate said.

"Surely, you're joking. You can't believe for one minute that the man that was brought to you, a pauper, is the son of some god? And don't you think if he was, his father would have come and saved him? He would strike us down now as we speak! Crush us into the ground! But I don't see any god. I don't see, therefore, I don't believe," the man replied.

"But what if all of this was supposed to happen? What if we are merely being used for some Divine destiny," Pilate said.

"Then it is your duty to fulfill that destiny, to play your role," the man answered sternly. "You can't push this onto anyone else. Herod even returned him to you. This is your decision and your decision alone. So fulfill your destiny, Governor. Make your decision. Put him to death."

"You speak as if you know. Do you know about this destiny?" Pilate asked.

"I am merely trying to help you with your decision. I have been a consort to many a governor, and it is my duty to advise you as such," the man answered.

"It's strange. Until you arrived here, I'd never heard of you, and now you stand before me, trying to persuade me on probably one of the most important decisions of my life," Pilate said.

"Not persuade nor influence, my esteemed Governor. Merely... helping," the man replied, adding, "And I am well known." The crowd shouted louder its anger. "For it is only you who seems not to know me now." He paused. "This is not the most important decision of your life.

Conquering cities, ruling thousands, combating the trials of land and sea, those are your legacies. Not one pitiful man who doesn't even fight back. A pauper, no less! Not a king! You, Governor, represent Rome, having walked with emperors! Don't torture yourself over the lowly, for you are among the high."

"I thought you said this is my destiny. How can it not be the most important decision of my life and yet be my destiny? I think you lie..." Pilate said, pausing, "It's strange. I forgot your name."

"I go by many names, Governor," the man answered, adding, "And I do not lie. I am your friend. I speak the truth from my heart."

"So, you speak the truth. Then answer me this. Do you think a son of a god would come to us as an emperor?" Pilate asked, adding, "Why not a pauper?"

The crowd became violent as people screamed out, fighting.

"You must do something," the man insisted, "or they will tear down the whole city." Pilate looked at the two soldiers then back to the man. "Save your legacy, Governor, or you may be next. Someone even higher may decide your fate," the man said.

"Take him then. Flog him. Rip his flesh. If that's what everyone wants! So be it! Then bring him back here," Pilate ordered. The two soldiers left.

"Are you going to release Barabbas?" the man asked. "Not yet. First, let's see if shedding his blood satisfies their rage, their sick, misguided thirst." Pilate began to walk away. The man pulled him back on the arm. "You must kill him, you know. It's the only way. It must be," the man said.

"Why do you hate this man so?" Pilate replied, adding, "Do you know him?" The man let him go and remained silent. Pilate walked back out before the crowd. He raised his arms. The crowd became quiet as soldiers broke up the remaining fights.

"People of Judea! Your self-proclaimed king, will be flogged!"

"But we want him crucified!" the crowd shouted back. Pilate raised his arms again. He signaled to more soldiers arriving to encircle the crowd. "It is by my order as governor that he be flogged forty times! After it is done, I will bring him back before you," Pilate said. "It is so ordered!" Pilate shouted, making a fist with his right hand in the air, turning and walking angrily away. The rest of the crowd started to chant, "We want Barabbas! We want Barabbas!"

Jesus was dragged to a post where he was tied and his clothes ripped from his back. A large, muscular soldier stood over him with a whip that had a number of leather thongs with jagged edges of sharp metal. The soldier reached back, raising his arm. The crack of the whip was heard. Flesh was ripped, lacerating Jesus' back. Blood poured out. The whip continued to sound.

Art studio. Remembering Jesus, Joshua arose before the full length mirror.

33 A.D. Jesus was curled up on the ground in agony with his back profusely bleeding from the deep lacerations. A soldier went over to him and raised him up by the arms. Another soldier ripped his clothes all the way off of him. They dressed him in a purple robe. A crown of thorns was embedded into his scalp. Blood ran down his face, the thorns coming just above his tensed brow, mixing with his tears of pain. The soldiers spat on him and mockingly bowed down to him as Jesus was barely able to stand.

"All hail the King of the Jews!" one of the soldiers cried out.

Art Studio. Joshua was looking at himself in the mirror. He was dressed as a medieval knight wearing a two piece gray body suit covered with small, braided steel wires. It looked like he was wearing a long gray sweatshirt with a hood that came down to the upper part of his thighs and tight gray sweatpants that extended down. Both garments, though, were covered with the finely braided steel wires as atop the gray a purple cloak with a picture of a lion on the back was draped over him. The cloak was long coming down to just above his knees with a two-piece golden belt wrapped around his waist. One piece was empty but hung down to hold a sword.

33 A.D. Jesus was before the crowd in his purple robe and crown of thorns with blood still running down his face and into his eyes, the gashes still fresh and deep, seeping with red. The crowd was cheering and screaming, "Give us Barabbas!" as Barabbas stood on the other side of Pilate, on his left, with Jesus on his right.

"People of Judea! Here is your murderer!" Pilate pointed to Barabbas. "And here is your king! Pilate shouted, pointing to Jesus.

"Away with him! Away with him! Crucify him! Crucify him!" the crowd shouted at Jesus.

"Is this not enough!" Pilate shouted back, walking over and turning Jesus slightly around, pointing at Jesus' wounds from the scourging, adding, "Shall I crucify your king!" Barabbas looked over at Jesus as he turned back toward the crowd. Jesus remained standing with his head bowed. Pilate said to Jesus, "Who are you? Now is your chance to speak. Speak to your people. Now is your time. Save yourself. Say something." But Jesus remained silent with his head still bowed. "How do you expect me to save you if you won't even save yourself? Please, say something. Tell them that you were wrong, that you're not their king. Do you want to die?"

Pilate asked Jesus. But Jesus still remained silent. Pilate looked back out to the crowd. He raised his arms. The crowd became silent too. Soldiers were everywhere, encircling the crowd, carrying spears, and on top of walls with arrows ready to be poised.

"He has done nothing wrong, your king!" Pilate called out to them.

"He's not our king!" a woman shouted back. The rest of the crowed joined in. Pilate turned away from Jesus and looked back to the pillar. The man was standing there behind him, the man with no recognizable features. The man nodded to Pilate and then leered at Jesus.

Mother Mary and Mary Magdalene pushed their way through the crowd. "Save Jesus!" they cried out. The crowd pushed them back. "No! Crucify him! Give us Barabbas!"

Even though it was light, with blue seen in the sky, there was heard a rumbling of thunder in the distance. The crowd became silent as Pilate walked back to the middle in between Jesus and Barabbas. "It is your Passover! If you want a murderer to be freed, so be it! I wash my hands of this! It shall be done! We'll crucify your king!" Pilate shouted, turning and looking sympathetically over to Jesus. Jesus raised his head gazing out to the crowd with the thorns embedded deep in his scalp just above his brow. The crowd cheered. Mary and Mary Magdalene cried out, "No! Please! Save Jesus!" Barabbas raised his arms and cheered, too, being guided off by some of his friends with their arms around each other. Jesus was taken by the soldiers. They took off his purple robe and gave him back his torn clothes that barely covered him. They took him out to be crucified.

Art Studio. Joshua was standing in the large doorway downstairs looking out to the night. The rain had stopped. The sky began to clear with stars beginning to be seen. Mysteriously, the speaker in the corner came on by itself. "All Along the Watchtower," Jimi Hendrix's song from Woodstock was playing.

In the wrestling room, the wrestlers were practicing hard as in each corner of the room stereo speakers blasted out the same Jimi Hendrix song. They were doing a drill where they ran in place, pounded their feet, then sprawled to the mat onto their bellies and then back up again, back to their feet, pounding, on Villecco's command. The sounds were loud and furious with "All Along the Watchtower" echoing out of the room and down the dark green hallway.

The wrestling room doors flew open. The wrestlers poured out, huffing and puffing, sweating profusely. They marched, staggering down the green hall, toward the weight room. Each one got on a weight station; Carmel on the bench, Tony on the curl machine, Mitch reaching up to pull down a bar on the universal for lats. Cif, standing with his arms out stretched, took hold of two metal handles high above him a few feet away on each side to do butterflies.

Douglas, standing, placed his shoulders underneath a large bar with a lot of weights braced on a tall rack to do squats. All the others got on other stations. "Alright! Ready!" Before Villecco could shout, "Go," each wrestler started doing reps. The stereo in the weight room began playing a song from "Jesus Christ Superstar." Douglas's face was red as he struggled to do squats with the bar on his back, looking as if he was carrying a cross for Jesus. Villecco called out, "Switch!" The wrestlers switched stations.

"Who put this station on?" Tony asked.

"Probably Douglas," Cif replied going to the bench.

"Set! Go!" Villecco shouted. Everyone started lifting. Carmel, while continuing to lift, began to sing, "Jesus Christ Superstar, are you who what they say you are..." One by one, wrestlers, while also continuing to lift, joined in, singing, each on their own weight machine. The weight room echoed, "Jesus Christ Superstar!" with weights clanging and sounding out...

33 A.D. "Do you want me to release for you the King of the Jews!" Pilate shouted as he stood atop a stone platform called in Hebrew, "Gabbatha" before the angry crowd upon this early morning. "No! We want Barabbas! Barabbas!" the crowd shouted back. It was the day of preparation for the Passover. And Pilate, because of the festival, was going to release one prisoner. Pilate, not knowing what to do, looked back at his guards, the crowd before him growing angrier. He waved his hand in a command to two of the guards clasping their spears.

The two soldiers left as Pilate turned and met them behind a large pillar about twenty feet away from where he stood before the crowd. Another man, along with the guards, was there, a short elderly man with no really recognizable features, at least not to Pilate.

"We cannot let this go on. We have to quiet this crowd," the man said. "But this Jesus, he has done nothing wrong," Pilate replied.

"He has incited the crowd, his own people. And if nothing else, he is, at the very least, crazy. Who will miss him? He thinks he is the King of the Jews. And listen, listen to them. He is not their king," the man said as the crowd grew louder, shouting. Pilate leaned up against the stone pillar as the two soldiers remained silent, awaiting his order.

"So you and everyone else want me to release a murderer, a killer, rather than someone who is innocent, someone who may just be crazy?" Pilate said to the man. "Do you really think he is crazy?" Pilate asked.

"Do you think he is the King of the Jews?" the man replied, adding, "Son of their God?" Pilate did not answer. He paused, hearing the crowd even become angrier. Pilate turned.

"What if, by some bizarre chance, he is some god's son," Pilate said. "Then, upon ordering his death, I will become forever known as the one who sentenced the 'Son of God' to death. Think about it. What if we are the ones who are crazy, the ones who..." Pilate said.

"Surely, you're joking. You can't believe for one minute that the man that was brought to you, a pauper, is the Son of some God? And don't you think if he was, his father would have come and saved him? He would strike us down now as we speak! Crush us into the ground! But I don't see any god. I don't see, therefore, I don't believe," the man replied.

"But what if all of this was supposed to happen? What if we are merely being used for some Divine destiny," Pilate said.

"Then it is your duty to fulfill that destiny, to play your role," the man answered sternly. "You can't push this onto anyone else. Herod even returned him to you. This is your decision and your decision alone. So fulfill your destiny, Governor. Make your decision. Put him to death."

"You speak as if you know. Do you know about this destiny?" Pilate asked.

"I am merely trying to help you with your decision. I have been a consort to many a governor, and it is my duty to advise you as such," the man answered.

"It's strange. Until you arrived here, I'd never heard of you, and now you stand before me, trying to persuade me on probably one of the most important decisions of my life," Pilate said.

"Not persuade nor influence, my esteemed Governor. Merely... helping," the man replied, adding, "And I am well known." The crowd shouted louder its anger. "For it is only you who seems not to know me now." He paused. "This is not the most important decision of your life.

Conquering cities, ruling thousands, combating the trials of land and sea, those are your legacies. Not one pitiful man who doesn't even fight back. A pauper, no less! Not a king! You, Governor, represent Rome, having walked with emperors! Don't torture yourself over the lowly, for you are among the high."

"I thought you said this is my destiny. How can it not be the most

important decision of my life and yet be my Destiny? I think you lie..."
Pilate said, pausing, "It's strange. I forgot your name."

"I go by many names, Governor," the man answered, adding, "And I do not lie. I am your friend. I speak the truth from my heart.

"So, you speak the truth. Then answer me this. Do you think a Son of God would come to us as an emperor?" Pilate asked, adding, "Why not a pauper?"

The crowd became violent as people screamed out, fighting.

"You must do something," the man insisted, "or they will tear down the whole city." Pilate looked at the two soldiers then back to the man. "Save your legacy, Governor, or you may be next. Someone even higher may decide your fate," the man said.

"Take him, then. Flog him. Rip his flesh. If that's what everyone wants! So be it! Then bring him back here," Pilate ordered. The two soldiers left.

"Are you going to release Barabbas?" the man asked. "Not yet. First, let's see if shedding his blood satisfies their rage, their sick, misguided thirst." Pilate began to walk away. The man pulled him back on the arm. "You must kill him, you know. It's the only way. It must be," the man said. "Why do you hate this man so?" Pilate replied, adding, "Do you know him?" The man let him go and remained silent. Pilate walked back out before the crowd. He raised his arms. The crowd became quiet as soldiers broke up the remaining fights.

"People of Judea! Your self-proclaimed king will be flogged!"

"But we want him crucified!" the crowd shouted back. Pilate raised his arms again. He signaled to more soldiers arriving to encircle the crowd. "It is by my order as governor that he be flogged forty times! After it is done, I will bring him back before you," Pilate said. "It is so ordered!" Pilate shouted, making a fist with his right hand in the air, turning and walking angrily away. The rest of the crowd started to chant, "We want Barabbas! We want Barabbas!"

Jesus was dragged to a post where he was tied and his clothes ripped from his back. A large, muscular soldier stood over him with a whip that had a number of leather thongs with jagged edges of sharp metal. The soldier reached back, raising his arm. The crack of the whip was heard. Flesh was ripped, lacerating Jesus' back. Blood poured out. The whip continued to sound...

Jesus was curled up on the ground in agony with his back profusely bleeding from the deep lacerations. A soldier went over to him and raised him up by the arms. Another soldier ripped his clothes all the way off of him. They dressed him in a purple robe. A crown of thorns was embedded into his scalp. Blood ran down his face, the thorns coming just above his tensed brow, mixing with his tears of pain. The soldiers spat on him and mockingly bowed down to him as Jesus was barely able to stand...

"All hail the King of the Jews!" one of the soldiers cried out.

Jesus was before the crowd in his purple robe and crown of thorns with blood still running down his face and into his eyes, the gashes still fresh and deep, seeping with red. The crowd was cheering and screaming, "Give us Barabbas!" as Barabbas stood on the other side of Pilate, on his left, with Jesus on his right.

"People of Judea! Here is your murderer!" Pilate pointed to Barabbas. "And here is your king!" Pilate shouted, pointing to Jesus.

"Away with him! Away with him! Crucify him! Crucify him!" the crowd shouted at Jesus.

"Is this not enough!" Pilate shouted back, walking over and turning Jesus slightly around, pointing at Jesus' wounds from the scourging, adding, "Shall I crucify your king!" Barabbas looked over at Jesus as he turned back toward the crowd. Jesus remained standing with his head bowed. Pilate said to Jesus, "Who are you? Now is your chance to speak. Speak to your people. Now is your time. Save yourself. Say something." But Jesus remained silent with his head still bowed.

"How do you expect me to save you if you won't even save yourself? Please, say something. Tell them that you were wrong, that you're not their king. Do you want to die?" Pilate asked Jesus. But Jesus still remained silent. Pilate looked back out to the crowd. He raised his arms. The crowd became silent too. Soldiers were everywhere, encircling the crowd, carrying spears, and on top of walls with arrows ready to be poised.

"He has done nothing wrong, your king!" Pilate called out to them.

"He's not our king!" a woman shouted back. The rest of the crowed joined in. Pilate turned away from Jesus and looked back to the pillar. The man was standing there behind him, the man with no recognizable features. The man nodded to Pilate and then leered at Jesus.

Mother Mary and Mary Magdalene pushed their way through the crowd. "Save Jesus!" they cried out. The crowd pushed them back. "No! Crucify him! Give us Barabbas!"

Even though it was light, with blue seen in the sky, there was heard a rumbling of thunder in the distance. The crowd became silent as Pilate walked back to the middle in between Jesus and Barabbas. "It is your Passover! If you want a murderer to be freed, so be it! I wash my hands of this! It shall be done! We'll crucify your king!" Pilate shouted, turning and looking sympathetically over to Jesus. Jesus raised his head gazing out to the crowd with the thorns embedded deep in his scalp just above his brow. The crowd cheered. Mary and Mary Magdalene cried out, "No! Please! Save Jesus!" Barabbas raised his arms and cheered, too, being guided off by some of his friends with their arms around each other. Jesus was taken by the soldiers. They took off his purple robe and gave him back his torn clothes that barely covered him. They took him out to be crucified...

As Jesus carried the cross, people aligned the way. Some stood in the back, jumping up and down, trying to see as Jesus passed. But those in the back could only see the top of the cross. Crying was heard as Jesus' mother and Mary Magdalene followed, trying to make their way through the crowd. "My son! My son!" Mary cried out in tears, weeping. Jesus, so exhausted from being beaten, fell to the ground with the cross tied to his back. Soldiers whipped him to get up. Jesus struggled to his feet, only to stagger and fall again.

"Get up!" a soldier shouted to Jesus, whipping him. With all his strength, Jesus got back to his feet. But after only three steps, he fell once again.

"You!" the soldier pointed to a man in the crowd. "Me?" the man asked.

"Yes. You," the soldier said again, signaling to another soldier to get him. The other soldier pulled him out of the crowd.

"What is your name?" the soldier asked. "Simon of Cyrene," he replied.

"Well, Simon of Cyrene. You will carry the cross for your king," the soldier demanded. "What? I..." Simon started to say. Two other soldiers held him as he tried to pull away.

Soldiers untied the cross, took it off Jesus' back, and placed it on Simon's. Simon looked over at Jesus, bloody and torn. Simon willingly and proudly carried it the rest of the way...

Jesus was raised up on the cross on a hill, "Golgotha, The Skull," with an inscription above his head, "Jesus of Nazareth, the King of the Jews." The chief priests had objected to this inscription saying that they wanted, "This man said, 'I am King of the Jews.'" But Pilate answered them, "What I have written, I have written."

Jesus hung in the middle with two others were on each side. Watching from the distance were his mother, his mother's sister, and Mary Magdalene. The pain was excruciating, the large iron nails through his wrists embedded into the splintered wood of the cross. He felt the splintered wood against his back as he inched downward. The iron nails, unmovable, penetrated through his soul. It was pain he could have never imagined; his chest, his ribs stretching, feeling as if his muscles were tearing from their bones and almost cutting off his breaths. The nail through his foot that had broken through many smaller bones anchored into the wood and held him from completely falling and his ribs completely cracking, being torn and piercing through his skin. With the nails in his wrists, the pain permeated down his outstretched arms. Yet, he said, "Father, forgive them; for they do not know what they are doing," as soldiers before the cross cast lots for his clothes. Some who passed shouted, "Save yourself! He saved others! But he can't save himself! Let the Messiah, the King of Israel, come down from the cross now, so that we may see and *believe!*" As Jesus hung on the cross, the thorns in his head could no longer be felt, overshadowed by the immense pain in his wrists and feet as he struggled to breathe with his heart feeling as if it were ready to burst. The two others by his side struggled for their breaths, too, as all three, from nine o'clock in the morning on, slowly began to suffocate...

Three hours later, Mary, her sister, Mary Magdalene, and John appeared beneath the cross being held back by the soldiers with only a few people remaining and watching. When Jesus opened his eyes and saw his mother standing there next to John, he said to his mother, "Mother, here is your son." He then said to John, "Here is your mother." It was noon, and darkness suddenly came over the land...

Three o'clock. With all his remaining strength, Jesus raised his head to the sky and called out, "Eloi, Eloi, lema sabachthani... My God, my God, why have you forsaken me?" Someone shouted, "Listen, he is calling for Elijah." Someone else ran and filled a sponge with sour wine. He put it on a stick and gave it to Jesus to drink. But others said, "Wait, let us see whether Elijah will come to take him down."

Jesus said, "Father, into your hands I commend my spirit." He took his last breath and died. Suddenly, the curtain of the temple was torn in two from top to bottom. A centurion who stood facing him said, "Truly this was the Son of God."

Since the Jews did not want the bodies left on the cross during the sabbath, they asked Pilate to have the legs broken and bodies removed. Even though they broke the legs of the other two, when the soldiers saw that Jesus was already dead, they did not break his legs. One soldier, instead, pierced his side with a spear. Blood and water came out. According to medical people, when blood collects in the pericardium, the lining around the wall of the heart, it divides into a bloody clot and watery serum. During Jesus' intense pain and the pressure of his raging blood, his heart ruptured, bursting open. Jesus died from a broken heart...

In the weight room, the wrestlers were lying on their backs drenched in sweat, exhausted to the point of death and struggling to breathe. No one was able to stand. Only some were able to barely move, *Villecco stood in the corner, silently, watching...*

Father Gabe entered the church next to the strip club. He looked up toward the balcony.

Children were gathered by an organ. They were the choir.

"Up here, Father!" a boy, twelve years old, called down to him.

"Oh, there is everyone," Father Gabe replied. He went over and searched for a light switch. Finding one, the balcony became lit as a stage as all the children, ages seven to eighteen, were ready, holding their songbooks. All were handicapped or sick. One boy was in a wheel chair. Another girl was blind. The others, twelve of them, each carried their own cross, whether it was deafness, blindness, missing limbs, Multiple Sclerosis, or terminal cancer.

"How did everyone get up there?" Father Gabe asked. The boy, seven years old, in the wheelchair replied, "We just did it."

The blind girl, fourteen years old, sat at the organ. She began to play and the children started to sing.

"Wait a minute!" Father Gabe called up to them. But they continued singing. Father Gabe ran up to the balcony. "Hold up! Hold up!" Father Gabe cried out. He got up to the balcony. "Here, we're going to sing this one first," he said as he handed out sheets of a song. He whispered the song to the blind girl at the organ. A little girl with no legs tugged on his pants.

She asked him, "I thought we were going to sing gospel hymns." He looked down to her. "What, can't a priest like rock and roll?" Father Gabe replied to her.

"This is really more like Motown, from the sixties," the boy in the wheelchair said. "What are you? Some kind of wise guy?" Father Gabe asked him.

"Can we sing something about Jesus?" a little girl asked.

"Sure," Father Gabe answered, adding, "That's what this one is about." "It is?" the boy in the wheelchair replied.

"Yes, Joey. It is," Father Gabe said to him. "Let's do it everyone!" he shouted. He leaned over and whispered again into the ear of the blind organist. She giggled. "Just as we practiced it," he said to her.

"Father? Isn't this a song by Diana Ross?" Joey asked.

"So? You have a problem with that?" Father Gabe answered him.

"Sorry I asked," Joey replied back to him, adding, "I like old people songs."

"Listen, everyone! We have a few songs to learn that aren't the usual church stuff. But these songs are special, especially this one. We have to be ready to sing this song when it is time," Father Gabe said to them.

"Time for what?" Joey asked. Father Gabe did not answer. "I liked our other Father better. He knew church songs," Joey added.

"Yeah," the little girl with no legs added.

"Look, kids. I don't care what your previous priest taught you. I'm telling you we have to learn this song first. So sing," Father Gabe said. He turned toward the organist. "Betsy?" Betsy began to play. The children, hesitated but started to sing, "Ain't No Mountain High Enough," out of tune.

Nia pulled into the parking lot of the strip club and parked her car. The church bells were ringing. Briefly glancing up to the church's tower, she picked up the small plastic bag on her car seat and opened it. Taking it out, she held it up. It was a sheer, silk one-piece, tiger-striped body stocking. She brought it to her chest, held it to her legs, and stretched it out.

"This will work," she said to herself with a smile. There was a knock on her window. It was Ms. Gongel. Nia quickly put the body stocking back into the bag and behind the car seat. Ms. Gongel knocked again. Nia rolled down her window only a few inches.

"What do you have there in the bag?" Ms. Gongel asked. "Nothing," Nia replied.

"Do you want to model it for me?" Ms. Gongel asked.

Nia lowered her head and did not answer. Not realizing that her car door was not locked, Ms. Gongel opened the door. Nia, startled, looked up at her. Ms. Gongel stooped down as Nia nervously remained in the car; she reached up, stroking Nia's cheek, gently brushing back her hair.

"You look afraid," Ms. Gongel said to her. "There's nothing to fear," she added. Slowly rising and leaning into the car, she softly kissed Nia on her lips as Nia let her.

"Now, wasn't that nice?" Ms. Gongel asked.

She kissed Nia again. This time Nia kissed her back as Ms. Gongel was stroking her hair.

Nia, gently pushed her away with the sounding of the church bells.

"No. I'm sorry. I can't do this," Nia said. "Yes, you can," Ms Gongel said as she took Nia's hand and helped her out of the car. "Come. I've set something else up with Maribel," Ms. Gongel added as she shut Nia's car door and led her by the hand across the parking lot toward the strip club.

Nia looked at the parking lot and saw something strange that she hadn't noticed when she pulled in. The parking lot was empty except for a couple of cars in front of the club.

"Where is everyone? I thought I had to do my shift," Nia asked while still being led by the hand.

"I gave everyone the day off. It will be alright. Don't worry. You'll still do your shift," Ms. Gongel replied as she opened the club's door. The bar was empty and dark as the door closed behind them.

"What are you going to do to me?" Nia nervously asked.

"Relax. I just have a little surprise for my favorite girl," Ms. Gongel replied with a laugh as she led Nia through the club and toward the stage.

"Sit here," Ms. Gongel directed Nia while holding out a chair for her by a table in front of the stage. Nia sat down, trying to see what was on the stage. She could see someone, but because of the darkness, she couldn't see whom.

"I'm going to teach you how to perform at a higher level," Ms. Gongel said to her with a final stroke of her hair...

Ms. Gongel went over and turned on a switch. A light beamed onto the stage. On the stage, next to a chair, Maribel was submissively kneeling, wearing a tank top and thong, her bottom resting on the back of her heels.

Ms. Gongel got up onto the stage, stood over Maribel, and said, "I call this performance 'Ms. Gongel's Opus.' Now watch."

"Kiss my feet," Ms. Gongel ordered Maribel.

Maribel lowered herself and kissed Ms. Gongel's black spiked boots. Maribel paused, looking over at Nia.

"Get up," Ms. Gongel commanded while lifting Maribel up by her hair. Maribel winced as she stood. Ms. Gongel sat down in the chair and forcibly guided Maribel, face down, over her lap. "Some musicians play a piano or a guitar. I play... a different kind of, well, instrument," Ms. Gongel said with a fading smile to Nia.

Ms. Gongel began spanking Maribel; Maribel's feet were kicking up in the air. Amidst Maribel's gasps of "ow" in harmony with her spanking, Ms. Gongel bragged, "You see, Nia. This eventually will be you. I'm looking for a new... instrument."

Ms. Gongel tossed Maribel to the floor. Nia got up and ran for the door. The door was locked as she frantically pulled on it trying to get it open. She looked back. Maribel was again submissively kneeling by the chair as Ms. Gongel was moving toward Nia.

"You don't have to be afraid, child," Ms. Gongel said as she caught up with her.

Nia tried to open the door again but couldn't. Nia then turned and tried to run but there was nowhere to go. Ms. Gongel cornered her by the side of the bar.

"Please, don't hurt me," Nia said as she cowered down.

Ms. Gongel bent down and gently kissed Nia on her lips. Nia's lips were quivering as she kissed Nia again, a long, deep, tender kiss. Nia started to kiss her back, putting her arms up around Ms. Gongel's back. Ms. Gongel raised her up by her shoulders, while still kissing her, and turned her away from the bar. Maribel suddenly appeared, standing behind Nia. Forcibly, Maribel took hold of Nia's arms and pulled them away from around Ms. Gongel. As Maribel held Nia's arms behind her back, Ms. Gongel slowly began unbuttoning Nia's blouse, exposing Nia's black lace bra.

"Please. I'm ready to do this," Nia said as Maribel pulled Nia's blouse down off of her arms and the blouse fell to the floor. Ms. Gongel took both of Nia's wrists and pressed them together in front of Nia's chest. Maribel, reaching around from behind, undid Nia's skirt. It, too, fell to Nia's feet.

"Come," Ms. Gongel said to Nia as she led her by both her wrists.

Maribel stooped down and held onto Nia's shoes as she stepped out of them in sheer black stockings and out of and away from the skirt. She was led toward the stage wearing only her black push up bra, black lace thong panties, and the sheer stockings that rose up to the upper part of her thighs. Maribel obediently followed them from behind.

Before they got to the stage, Ms. Gongel stopped and let go of Nia's wrists. She walked over and turned on another light. Nia remained quietly standing by a large glass table.

"Lie down on top of it," Ms. Gongel ordered while gesturing with her head to the table.

"What?" Nia asked.

"Lie down on top of it," Ms. Gongel said again. "Face down," she added.

Nia slowly leaned over the table. Maribel went to the other side and pulled Nia's hands as she slid outstretched on her stomach across the glass table. Maribel, getting down on her knees looking upward through the glass, grabbed hold tightly to Nia's wrists.

"You see, Nia, I know you want to obey me," Ms. Gongel said as she slowly took off Nia's stockings, gently sliding them down and off her legs.

With Nia's legs completely bare, Ms. Gongel undid Nia's bra. She pulled the bra away by its strap, flinging it to the other side of the bar. Nia remained in position on her stomach, being held to the table by Maribel. Nia felt the coldness of the table with her bare breasts, now just in her panties. The sensation of the glass turned to warmth as Ms. Gongel ran her hands down Nia's back, tenderly massaging her over her bottom and down the back of her legs to her feet.

"Just relax," Ms. Gongel whispered to her as Maribel held tight to her wrists, unmoving, and without a spoken word.

Ms. Gongel massaged Nia's feet, back up her legs and her bottom. Ms. Gongel paused seeing the branded Mark of the Dragon. "What's this?" Ms. Gongel asked her, surprised, touching it. Nia did not answer. Ms. Gongel paused, tracing with her finger the lines on Nia's bottom. "Interesting. I've seen this somewhere before," Ms. Gongel said. "You little... You should have my name tattooed on your butt," she angrily said, giving Nia's bottom a hard spank.

Nia winced. Ms. Gongel smiled, running her hands over the red mark she had just made. "There. That's my mark," Ms. Gongel whispered to herself. She turned away from Nia. "Lesson over. You're dismissed," Ms. Gongel added to her, nodding toward Maribel...

"Alright. Let's do it right this time," Father Gabe said in front of the children. "Come on, Joey. Put some heart into it." Joey rolled his eyes but started to sing along with the other children.

Joshua, riding Bud, rode into the parking lot of the church. Pulling up on the reins, he looked up at the high steeple. The church bells were ringing. Nia pulled into the same parking lot and got out of her car. She had a long white coat on. It was Friday night.

"Why am I doing this?" she asked herself, adding, "Because Ms. Gongel has control over me and there are no knights in shining armor anymore, that's why."

Startled by a horse whinnying, she looked over her shoulder. She saw Joshua dressed as a knight atop Bud. They were a few yards away. She smiled, recognizing him. "You again. Are you acting out something from our Medieval lit class, some kind of assignment?" she asked.

The children continued to sing, "Ain't No Mountain High Enough," inside the church as the song echoed out to Nia and Joshua.

Nia turned away after shaking her head in disbelief with a wave and walked toward the strip club. Joshua dismounted Bud and walked toward the church...

33. A.D. Mother Mary cradled Jesus' bloody body in her arms. His head was back, his arms and legs dangling lifeless upon her. "No!" She screamed out. "My son! My son! Please, help us! God, help us! My son. My son." Tears gush down Her cheeks.

Joshua went into the church. The children saw him, as he appeared walking in the center aisle beneath them. They slowly stopped singing.

"Who is he?" Joey asked. Father Gabe leaned over the balcony. "It's alright. He's someone God has sent. A knight," Father Gabe said with a slight turn of a smile.

Joshua walked over to a large replica of the Pieta. He knelt down in front of it. Tears were in his eyes as he gazed at the statue of Mother Mary holding Jesus. Father Gabe turned back to the children. "Alright. We're going to sing a gospel hymn. Open your books." He whispered to Betsy and raised his hand to lead. The children started singing a beautiful hymn as Joshua remained kneeling in front of the Pieta.

Nia was sitting at the bar waiting for Ms. Gongel. The bar was filled with customers and dancers before them as the music of the children's hymns were drowned out by the loud music of the strip club. Christine was waiting on a couple of tables as Ms. Gongel approached Nia. "Are you ready?" Ms. Gongel asked her as she parted Nia's coat. She saw she had on the tiger body stocking underneath along with matching high heels. "Oh. You got heels to match," Ms. Gongel said with a smile. Nia nodded, putting down her drink on the bar.

"Come. I want to talk to you alone in the back first," Ms. Gongel said as she took Nia by the hand and led her to her office. As soon as they entered the office, Ms. Gongel pushed Nia up against the wall, kissing her. Nia did not resist, her arms down by her side. Ms. Gongel slid off Nia's coat, lifted her up in her arms, and carried her over to the marble desk. She laid Nia gently down upon it, running her hands slowly up and down the tiger body stocking over Nia's body.

She kissed her again, licking Nia's lips.

The children were singing another hymn. Joshua was still kneeling in front of the Pieta.

Father Gabe was standing behind him. "Are you alright?" Father Gabe asked him. Joshua did not turn or answer. Joshua was crying. Father Gabe knelt down by his side.

"I messed up, Father," Joshua said. "I sinned." "We all have," Father Gabe said.

"But I sinned a lot," Joshua said, wiping away a tear from his cheek.

"That's why he died for us," Father Gabe said.

"But I don't want him to have died for what I did," Joshua said. "I'm sorry for what I did. I'm just so lonely, Father. I've always dreamed that I would meet someone nice and fall in love. But..."

"What?" Father Gabe asked.

"No one can love me. I don't know why. I guess they can't see who I am," Joshua said. "Who are you, Joshua?" Father Gabe asked. Joshua paused. "I don't know yet," he

answered, adding, "How do you know my name?" "You look like a Joshua," Father Gabe replied, adding, "Do you know what the name 'Joshua' means?"

"No," Joshua answered.

"It means God of Salvation." Father Gabe paused as he gazed at the statue with Joshua as the children continued to sing the hymn. Father Gabe continued, "I will love You. O Lord, my strength. The Lord is my rock and my fortress and my deliverer."

"I'm not a God of Salvation," Joshua replied, looking into Father Gabe's eyes. "Your Father is. And you are His son," Father Gabe answered.

"And he went through all this because of me?" Joshua asked, looking back at the statue. "Not because of you," Father Gabe replied, "For you. For all of us." Father Gabe patted Joshua on the shoulder, arose, and started to walk away.

"I'm sorry, Jesus, "I'm sorry, Father." Joshua said, continuing to gaze at the statue of Jesus lying with his head back in his mother's arms. Joshua could see the holes in Jesus' hands and feet as blood suddenly appeared running out of them. One of the children stopped singing and screamed. Father Gabe looked up at the balcony and then turned back to Joshua. He saw the blood pouring out onto the floor of the church around Joshua, kneeling with his arms and head raised. "Jesus! Father! Forgive me! Forgive us!" Joshua called out.

The children became quiet, watching. Father Gabe looked up toward the cathedral ceiling of the church. "What's going on? Peter? Michael? What's going on?" He looked back down. The blood continued to pour out. But Joshua was gone. Father Gabe reached down and touched the blood. It was real. Joshua was walking across the parking lot.

"Please help me, Father," Joshua said. He stopped in the middle of the parking lot. He raised his arms and head again up to the sky.

"I want to love! Father! I want to love! I need love, Father, please! I need love!" Joshua screamed out.

The two men Christine waited on walked out of the strip club. They heard Joshua. "So do we, brother," one of the men said to Joshua with a laugh. He pointed back to the strip club. "Maybe you can find love in there."

Nia walked out with Ms. Gongel. Joshua saw her. He remained still, gazing at her as she glanced over at him back on Bud. Ms. Gongel opened the car door for her. Seeing Joshua, too, Ms. Gongel said, "I have to get better security for this parking lot. Now we're being invaded by knights." They drove away.

When Nia and Ms. Gongel arrived at the fundraiser at the congressman's house near the bay, people were dressed in tuxedos and gowns as they walked up high rising steps, past pillars, and into a mansion. A giant chandelier hung high overhead in the white marble foyer with a spiraling staircase and mahogany handrail. The senator was greeted by Congressman Sanders and his extremely handsome, dark haired, twenty-two-year-old son. "You know my son, George Junior?" Congressman Sanders said, introducing his son to the senator.

"Why, yes. I do," the senator replied, shaking George Junior's hand, adding with a smile, "We met last year, election night, I think it was, at the mayor's house." The senator partially turned. He saw Nia standing just inside the doorway, wearing her long white coat with Ms.

Gongel dressed in a blue gown by her side.

"Would you excuse us," the senator said to George Junior, who nodded in reply.

The senator took Sanders by the arm. "Our problem has just walked through the door," the senator whispered to him, gesturing over to Nia and Ms. Gongel. "We have to take care of this now," the senator added.

"Two of my men are waiting outside. The ones I told you about," Sanders replied. "What about your butler?"

"He knows what to do," the senator answered. "So do my men," Sanders added.

One of the servants, a middle-aged woman with dark hair, offered to take Nia's coat. Nia politely refused to give it up.

"Nia! How are you, hon?" Sanders asked with a large grin, giving Nia a kiss on the cheek. The senator remained silent behind them.

"I'm Ms. Gongel," Ms. Gongel said, reaching out her hand to Sanders. Sanders hesitated to shake it. "I'm Nia's escort this evening and you must be Senator Stanworth. I've seen you on Various News Channels," Ms. Gongel said as she reached out to shake the senator's hand. Nia nervously stood clutching her coat, keeping it closed, not knowing if she really wanted to go through with this. The senator reached out and took Ms. Gongel's hand. "That's a little hard, Senator," she said as she tried to pull her hand away. But he began squeezing it tighter and pulled her close, swiftly taking her by the arm, and leading her back out the door like a bouncer. Nia tried to intervene, but she was pushed aside with one brush of the senator's arm.

"It will be alright, Nia. Just do what we planned," Ms. Gongel shouted back to Nia. George Junior, upon seeing Nia, came quickly over to greet her. "Nia, this is my son,

George Junior," Sanders said, introducing him.

"Hi. I'm Nia," Nia replied as she glanced back over her shoulder, wondering what was happening to Ms. Gongel.

"I'll leave you two alone," Sanders said and went outside. He saw two large, young Italian men in tuxedos, his men, approach the senator and Ms. Gongel by a limousine. The butler was standing by the side of the limousine, holding the door open. Pulling her arm away from the senator, it looked like Ms. Gongel was arguing, starting to shout.

"Get in," the senator said to her.

"Where are you taking me?" Ms. Gongel asked.

"Back to your club. Now get in or I'll have them shove you in," the senator said with the two Italian men beside her.

"I haven't gotten this much attention in years," Ms. Gongel replied, getting in. The young men got in the back on each side of her. Maurice got in the front behind the wheel and drove away.

"Can I take your coat?" George Junior asked Nia. "Not yet," Nia hesitantly replied.

"Mint?" one of the young men said to the other, reaching past Ms. Gongel. "No. That stuff upsets my stomach," he replied.

"Everything upsets your stomach," the first young man said. He offered a mint to Ms. Gongel. She hesitantly took it and put it into her mouth. "Hmm. Peppermint," she said while sucking on it.

"This is my brother, Joey. I'm Paulie," the first young man added as he put a peppermint into his mouth.

"What are you doing?" Joey asked him.

"I thought we should introduce ourselves," Paulie answered. "You're unbelievable," Joey said.

"Well, at least I can ride in the backseats of cars," Paulie said as Joey looked uncomfortable, starting to sweat.

"What's the matter with him?" Ms. Gongel asked Paulie.

"He gets…" Paulie started to reply to Ms. Gongel. "What are they called?" Paulie added, asking Joey.

"Panic attacks," Joey replied angrily. "Yeah. Panic attacks," Paulie answered.

"Do you have to tell her our whole medical history now too?" Joey asked, sweating more, starting to hold his chest.

"What? We can't be polite or make conversation when we do this?" Paulie asked. "Do what?" Ms. Gongel asked.

Joey pounded on the glass of the limo behind Maurice. "Pull over!" Joey shouted.

Maurice did not answer at first. Finally, Maurice slid the glass open in the middle. "Yes, sir?" Maurice asked. "I said, 'Pull over,'" Joey said again.

"Oh, here we go," Paulie said.

"Shut up," Joey said back. Maurice pulled over and Joey got out, opening the driver's door.

"Get out. We're switching," Joey said to Maurice. "What?" Maurice asked.

"You heard me. Get out," Joey said again to Maurice.

"But I'm the only one who is supposed to drive this car, sir," Maurice said. "Are you going to get out, old man, or will I have to drag you out?" Joey asked.

"Just get out, man!" Paulie shouted to Maurice. Maurice got out. "You don't want to mess with him when he gets his panic attacks," Paulie said to Ms. Gongel.

"Is that what this is?" Ms. Gongel sarcastically replied. Maurice got into the backseat next to Ms. Gongel. Joey drove away.

The senator reentered the house back in the foyer. Sanders intercepted him and whispered into his ear. Nia was standing right underneath the large, bright chandelier with a drink in her hand next to George Junior, who was flirting with her. Many guests filled the spacious foyer with others entering the dining hall. Nia saw the senator staring at her. The same servant who had offered to take her coat before passed.

"Excuse me," Nia said to her, adding, "But could you please take my coat now?" Nia handed her drink to George Junior. With the senator watching in the middle of the crowded foyer, Nia took off her coat and carefully handed it to the servant. When she did, George Junior dropped his glass. The glass broke. Everyone looked over at Nia. Silence. The senator's eyes turned to rage.

"Wow," George Junior said, looking at her.

Everyone resumed talking. Nia gave an angered glance back to the senator and another servant came over to clean up the broken glass and wine on the floor.

"I'm sorry. That was clumsy of me," George Junior said to Nia as he stepped out of the way to allow the servant to clean it up. "That's quite an—"

"Outfit," Denise, a political leader in her red gown said as she approached. "Nia, I wish I had enough courage to wear something like that," she added as she checked out Nia's tiger skin outfit. It was sheer and tight with the tiger stripes covering her nipples, crotch, and part of her bottom. Nia looked like she was naked but with stripes, like a tiger. Her hair looked wild, too, her spiked heels raising her seemingly off the ground.

"Well, if I had your body. I might," Denise laughed. She added, "You've got quite a build, girl."

"You do look really...amazing," George Junior said. A servant offered him a glass of wine on a tray. He took it.

"Why, thank you," Nia replied tossing back her hair, taking the glass as George Junior offered it to her. He grabbed another glass of wine off the tray for himself. They both took sips while gazing into each other's eyes.

"Don't look now, but I think you're in trouble, hon," Denise whispered over to Nia as the senator and Sanders came toward them through the crowd. "When I was your age, if my father ever caught me wearing something like this..." Denise started to say.

"Excuse me," the senator said pushing his way through with Sanders right behind him. "Don't worry. I'll back you," George Junior whispered to Nia, seeing her worried look.

When the senator got to Nia, he immediately took hold of her arm. In a soft but stern tone, he said to her, "Nia. I think this is inappropriate. You remember our conversation," he said.

The senator turned to Sanders. "George. My daughter seems to have gotten a little carried away with her wardrobe. Is there something one of your daughters might possibly have upstairs that Nia can slip on?" the senator asked.

"Nonsense," George Junior replied while gently taking hold of Nia's other arm. "I think she looks stunning. I wouldn't change a thing."

The senator let go. Sanders patted the senator's back. "Ease up, Justin. We live in L.A., remember? A lot of the young people wear this kind of...thing," Sanders said as he, too, was staring at Nia.

"Dinner is now being served!" a servant called out to the rest of the guests in the foyer from the entranceway of the dining hall.

"Shall we?" George Junior asked Nia, extending his arm. Looking away from the senator, Nia held George Junior's arm as he escorted her in.

"What was that all about?" The senator asked Sanders. "What?" Sanders replied.

"My daughter comes half naked to my fundraiser and you..." the senator started to say. "Well, at least she's not totally naked," Denise said.

"Look, she's alright. She looks great, like a rock star," Sanders said to both of them adding to the senator, "What? You think it will hurt you? Is that what you think? That's what you're thinking isn't it, that it will hurt you."

"Not me. Not me, George," the senator responded to Sanders as he turned to greet some guests as they all began to enter into the dining hall.

Joey was still driving along the mountain road with the ocean's night sky towering over them. There were only a few stars and a hidden moon.

"How long has your brother been having these panic attacks?" Ms.

Gongel asked Paulie. "Just a few years now. They don't know what causes it. Some doctors think it might be a change in his metabolism," Paulie answered.

"Well. I hope he is alright now," Ms. Gongel said.

"Yeah. He will be fine. He just has to drive," Paulie said, adding, "Some also think it might be some kind of mental disorder. He can't ride in the back seat of cars, amusement rides, things like that. Isn't that right, Joey?" Paulie said through the small opening in the glass. Joey reached over and closed the glass window.

"Well, I'm glad someone who is sane is driving," Ms. Gongel said as she looked over at Maurice.

"So, Maurice. Did you like the show Nia put on for you? You never did tell me," Ms. Gongel said.

"You two know each other?" Paulie asked.

"Why, yes. Me and Maurice go way back," Ms. Gongel answered. "Huh. So both of you are going..." Paulie started to say.

Joey slid the glass window back open. "Shut up, Paulie!" Joey shouted. "Both of us are going to what?" Ms. Gongel asks.

"You know what, Paulie? You're the one with the mental disorder!" Joey shouted as the car swerved a bit and a car, coming toward them in the opposite lane, sounded its horn.

"Hey! Mom said it was a learning handicap. Not a mental disorder. A learning handicap. I was diagnosed!" Paulie shouted back.

"You nervous, Maurice?" Ms. Gongel asked. "No," he answered.

"Then why is your hand shaking?" she asked. Maurice reached over with his other hand to steady it.

"That's how it usually starts, hand shaking, sweating, shortness of breath, and then..." Paulie said as Ms. Gongel interrupted him.

"How do you know so much about panic attacks, I mean, besides your brother?" Ms. Gongel asked.

"Don't say anything, Paulie. Just shut up. Shut up!" Joey shouted.

"What! I was just going to tell her I get a lot of practice, alright!" Paulie shouted back. "Practice doing what?" Ms. Gongel asked.

"Seeing people...you know..." Paulie said.

"I don't know," Ms. Gongel said. "Seeing people what?" she asked again. "Panic," Paulie answered.

"Great. Just great," Joey said under his breath. He looked at Paulie in the rearview mirror. "You know, Paulie, if you weren't my brother, I'd do you too. You know that?"

Ms. Gongel looked out the window. "Where are you taking me?" she asked.

Paulie took out a gun from inside his coat. He held it up to Ms. Gongel's head. "Now you shut up, alright," Paulie said to her.

"Easy, brother," Joey said.

"No. You told me to shut up. Now I'm telling everyone, everyone to shut the up! Alright?

Alright, brother!" Paulie shouted with hand tightly gripping the gun poised to Ms. Gongel's head.

"Alright! Alright! Take it easy," Joey said.

"Why don't you take it easy, Joey? You're the one with the panic attacks," Paulie said.

"Look, Paulie. You have to take it easy, alright. You can't splatter her brains in the car," Joey said.

"Why not?" Paulie asked. "Fine. Go ahead," Joey replied.

"Wait! Wait!" Ms. Gongel cried out. "I don't know what's going on here, but I have money, lots of it. Just get me back to the Doll House," Ms. Gongel begged.

"Money won't help you now," Maurice said.

"You know about all this, Maurice?" she asked him. Maurice nodded. "Why, you bastard," she said to him. She suddenly hit Paulie's hand away from her head with the gun and lunged over Maurice for the door. "Let me out! Let me go!" she screamed while trying to grab the handle.

"Get back!" Paulie shouted as he pulled her back.

The car swerved, then regained itself. She started to cry. "Please! Please!" She called out as her voice echoed in the distance as they drove around a bend along the mountain road, the spanning sea seen on one side, going toward the bay.

Nia was talking to George Junior inside the large dining hall. There was a buffet. Guests were in line, filling up their plates as, at one end of the hall, some of the guests were already eating at tables. Other guests were slow dancing on a dance floor in front of the tables. Nia and George got up to go to the buffet line.

"So. My father tells me that you go to U.C.L.A." George Jr. said to Nia. "Yes," Nia replied.

"So what are you going to do you when you get out?" he asked. "I don't know," she answered.

"What's your major?" he asked. "Teaching," she said.

"So, I guess you'll look for a job where you can...teach?"

"Yeah. That's pretty much it," she replied as their plates were full and they went back their table. He placed down his plate and held her chair out for her to sit down.

"Thank you," she said.

Congressmen Sanders was in front of a microphone on a small platform by the dance floor. He signaled to lower the music as guests on the dance floor slowly stopped dancing and turned listen.

"Ladies and Gentlemen, I wanted to take this time to thank everyone for coming this evening. I'd like to especially welcome two reporters, Carol Jackson from the Times and Benett Gathers from the Post." Carol and Benett were sitting together at one of the tables. After being introduced, they partially stood. Sanders continued. "Both of them are doing in depth stories about our campaign trail. Carol, you've been following us around for now, what, two months?" Carol nodded. "And you're still not sick of us?" Sanders added. Carol smiled.

"Benett. You're new, so Carol will have to fill you in on all the dirt," Sanders said with a laugh. The guests laughed too. Several photographers got close to the platform and took Sanders' picture. "Well, let me just say again, 'Thank you,' for everyone coming this evening. I would like to say that it has been truly and honor and a privilege to have worked with Senator Stanworth for these many years, and I can tell you that both in his professional and personal life there is not a more honest and dedicated man who cares more about family and the moral fiber that has made our great nation. While other politicians talk the walk, he walks the talk, finding solutions for this state's problems. It is with my pleasure to introduce my dear friend, with this being his fourth run for the senate..."

"You must be very proud of your father," George Jr. said to Nia as she was taking a bite of a potato skin. "As you must be with yours," Nia replied, putting the potato skin back down. She pushed it to the edge of her plate.

"Senator Justin Stanworth the Third!" Sanders called out. Everyone stood and applauded.

George Jr. and Nia remained sitting.

"I never did care too much about politics," George Jr. said as Nia stared at the plate before her.

"Are you alright?" George Junior asked. "Fine," Nia replied, raising her eyes to him.

"I would also like to thank everyone for coming here this evening," the senator said. "I am especially proud to have here tonight my daughter, Nia." The senator looked with a smile and gestured toward her. Everyone looked. Nia tried to cover herself with her arms.

"It appears that it's a little too cold in here for her this evening," the senator said. "George? Do you have the air conditioning on too high?" the senator asked, turning back to Sanders, smiling. "I'm sure, though, when we politicians get talking long enough, all the hot air will start to warm everyone up," the senator added. Everyone let out a laugh.

Nia reached out for two drinks as a servant passed with a tray and drank them quickly.

The senator continued. "It has, indeed, been my pleasure to have served this state as its representative to the United States Senate for the last few years. And I can promise you, that in the next six years, I will do my very best to continue to serve the State of California with honor and dignity, remaining true to my word..."

The limo pulled over to a desolate side of the road by the bay. They drove onto the beach. "Where are we?" Ms. Gongel asked.

"Everyone get out," Joey said.

Ms. Gongel struggled as Paulie and Maurice took her by her arms and led her across the sand to the water's edge. With the rippling tide, both Joey and Paulie shot Ms. Gongel in the head.

"You shouldn't have messed with Nia," Maurice said with a laugh as her body fell into the surf.

"That's right," Joey said, pointing the gun at Maurice and shooting him in the head, the blood washing up on the shore.

At the fundraiser, Nia was seductively dancing in her tiger outfit on the dance floor with George Junior. Other people were dancing around them, but all eyes were on Nia.

Joshua rode Bud up to his front yard. Many stars appeared above him with the awakening of a bright moon. Tim was just pulling in the driveway in his truck.

"What is going on now?" Tim asked, seeing Joshua. As Tim got out of his truck, their father came riding from around the side of the house on a mule dressed as King Richard the Third followed by Samson. "My son the knight!" Their father called out seeing Joshua dressed as a knight on the large white horse. Joshua dismounted Bud and their father dismounted the mule.

"Kneel my son," their father said to Joshua.

"I, King Richard the Third, hereby knight thee, Sir Joshua," their father said, knighting him on each shoulder with a sword. "Now rise, go forth, and be that knight I believed you could be." "This is unbelievable," Tim said. "Why can't I have a normal family."

Chapter 14

Nia was driving home along the mountain road overlooking the bay while still dressed in her tiger outfit and spiked heels. She had on her long coat. She reached over and turned on the radio. Searching for music, she heard a news cast. "Two bodies were found..." Her cell phone rang. It was her mother. "Nia. I'm finally leaving. You were right."

"Mom. Where are you?"

"I'm on a bus right now heading back east. Whatever you do, Nia, don't go back to the house."

"Mom. What are you talking about?"

"Something is going on. He's starting to..." her mother paused. "Who are you talking about?"

"The senator. I found Maria... He's starting to kill, Nia," she whispered and then began to cry.

Over the radio, Nia heard, "Senator Stanworth is being sought by local officials for questioning in these murders."

"Mom, I've got to go. I'll call you back," Nia said, flooring the accelerator and speeding to get home.

"Nia. Promise me you won't go back there." "I'll call you back in a little while, Mom."

Nia hung up and raced home along the mountain road. When she got to the mansion, she had to get out of the car after taking off her heels and push the large gate open by hand at the end of the driveway. Getting back in the car, she floored it, bare footed, up the driveway and across the front lawn toward the barn. Running into the barn, she found the old horse lying down, barely breathing.

"Get up! Get up! You can do it!" Nia cried, trying to lift him. The horse looked up to her as his eyes closed with deeper longer heavy breaths. "Please help him!" She screamed out, looking up. "Please help him," she whispered. The horse's eyes opened and he staggered with Nia's help to his feet. "Good boy. Good," she said as she gingerly led him by his bridle out of the barn and across the front yard toward the gate. "I'm going to find you a nice home. Somewhere where you will be taken cared of and loved," Nia said to him along the way. When they got just outside of the gate, the horse collapsed. Nia fell on top of him, crying. "Please don't die. Please," Nia pleaded. With Nia's soft touch, the horse raised his head one more time, gave her a kiss, then died. Crying, Nia took off her coat and placed it gently over the dead horse's body.

Bright headlights suddenly appeared coming toward her. It was the senator's limousine. It rode over her heels as it pulled up to the gate and came to a stop. The window slowly rolled down. "You're pathetic," the senator said to Nia as she was still crying. "Just like your mother.

I'm glad she left. I was hoping, however, she would have taken her her whore daughter with her. You're no use to me anymore, and you're not a threat. You're much too weak. You may go now just as you are." The senator gestured at her tiger outfit. "But if you come back here again, I'll kill you," he ended, rolling back up the widow and driving up the driveway. The gate closed on its on.

Nia wandered bare footed in her striped body stocking across the road and into the woods. She headed for the pond and the waterfall, still crying about the horse. Once at the side of the pond, she sat down in a fetal position and gazed up at the stars flowing down the waterfall.

When she did, the moon came out and the pond lit up to a beautiful blue. "I'm sorry," she whispered upward. "I couldn't save him. I can't even save myself."

"I'll save you," she heard as horse steps came through the woods.

Joshua rode out of the woods, still dressed as a knight, atop Bud, and up to her side. "What's with you? Why do you keep following me?"

she asked. "This is unbelievable." "Hi. I hope I didn't startle you. But I was just taking a ride and I heard you crying. I'm

Sir Joshua. My father just knighted me. I'm in your Medieval Lit class." "I know who you are," she said, looking up to him.

"Why you dressed as a tiger? That's alright. My brother knows a leopard woman. Come," Joshua said atop Bud, reaching his hand down to her. "I'll show you something that will make you feel better. She reached up and took his hand. Joshua lifted her up, sitting her atop Bud behind him.

Joshua, dressed as a knight, and Nia as a tiger, they rode Bud up a path to the top of the waterfall looking over the sea. Still atop Bud with Nia's arms around his waist, Joshua pointed out across the sea lit by the bright moonlight to the horizon.

"Out there. At the edge. That's where they go when they die," Joshua said. "But they are always with you. My mom whispers to me in the wind like an angel. She always believed in me, that I would be a knight some day, and someday your dream will come true."

Nia, after looking out across the beautiful sea to the horizon's edge, rested her head against Joshua's back and said, "My dreams are too far away to come true."

"But that's when they are the closest," Joshua said. "Just like the horizon."

Joshua kicked his heels gently on Bud as Bud carried them back down the path along the mountain road. Headlights again appeared as a car approached. Joshua pulled up on the reins.

Father Gabe got out.

"Nia. Are you alright?" Father Gabe asked.

"Yes. I was saved by this knight," Nia said with a smile and a kiss on the side of Joshua's cheek. Gently, Joshua helped Nia down off Bud. "Thank you," Nia said to Joshua. Joshua waved and road away back into the woods, into the moon.

"So. Do you need a lift, a place to stay?" Father Gabe asked.

"You know I do," Nia replied, getting into his car on the passenger side. "How do you know I know?" He asked, getting into the driver's side.

"You just do. You know everything. You're like an angel or something," Nia replied, shutting her door.

Father Gabe gazed out his windshield, watching Joshua disappear into the woods he whispered, "I'm not the only angel."

Inside the church, Nia was standing in her soiled bare feet and her outfit before the bishop in his office. The bishop had a stern look on his face as Father Gabriel was standing in support and silence behind her. The bishop, momentarily silent, looked up and down at her in concerned wonderment.

"Gabe. Don't just stand there. Get her something she can wear," the bishop said. "Yes, Bishop," Father Gabe replied, leaving.

"I'm sorry," Nia said, curling her toes and putting her right foot on top of the other with pieces of dirt falling to the floor.

"Well. I've heard quite a lot about you," the bishop said. "You're a dancer. But you want to be a singer." The bishop paused then asked, "Why are you dressed as a tiger?"

"It's a long story," Nia replied.

The bishop went behind his desk and sat down with Nia still standing before him. "So do you still want to be a singer?" he asked her.

Nia nodded and said, "Yes."

"Our choir is always looking for good people." "I'm not that kind of singer," Nia replied.

"Oh. Well, what kind of singer are you?"

"I don't feel comfortable with all this. Thank you for offering to help, but I better go," Nia said, beginning to leave.

"Wait," the bishop called out. "Do you like kids?" Nia paused, then said, "Yes. Why?"

"We have a choir with a lot of handicapped children. They've been walking all over Father Gabe lately. It would really help us out if you could spend some time with them. In turn, we'll give you a place to stay."

"I don't know," Nia replied.

"You can wear whatever you want. If you want to come to church dressed as a lion, go for it. What do you say?" the bishop asked with a smile.

"Alright. That would be nice. Thank you," Nia responded as Father Gabe came back with clothes in his hand.

"A couple of the sisters got together a few things," Father Gabe said, handing her the clothes.

"Good," the bishop replied, adding, "Father Gabe, meet the new director of our youth choir."

"Great. So am I relieved?" Father Gabe asked.

"No. You'll still help out. But Nia will be in charge," the bishop said, adding, "Why don't you take her to her room."

Father Gabe led her down a hallway adorned with many religious paintings. At the end of the hall, he opened the door for her.

"If you need anything, I'll be at the end of the hallway on the right," Father Gabe said. "Thank you," Nia replied, going in.

Inside the small room there was a bed, a desk, and a window. It was simple. She sat down on the bed, still holding the clothes, and looked above her. There was a cross. After making the sign of the cross, she got down on her knees and started praying.

Father Gabe went back to the bishop's office. He entered without knocking. The bishop was standing behind his desk looking out the window. He turned when Father Gabe came in.

"I think I need new glasses. I keep seeing that same dragon out there," the Bishop said. "Maybe you're stressed out because they're going to tear down this church," Father Gabe replied.

"You know about that?" the bishop asked. "Yes."

"Why am I not surprised," the bishop said, pausing. "Can you believe that the city is going to tear down this church to make room for a strip mall? Isn't that ironic, calling it a 'strip' mall. The strip club will still be here, but we'll be gone."

"I thought the parish was building another church?" Father Gabe asked.

"Where? There were plans and no one did anything about it. Right now we don't have anywhere to go," the bishop replied. "Like Nia."

"We have to help Nia, Bishop. A lot depends on it," Father Gabe said as the Bishop looked puzzled.

"For the girl's sake, you mean," the bishop responded, wiping his glasses.

"And for others," Father Gabe replied while looking past him and out the window, "many others."

"Who are you? I called the parish," the bishop asked Father Gabe. "I'm Gabriel..."

The bells in the church tower sounded above them. Nia got up from praying and looked out the window, past the strip club, and up the mountain across the bay. She whispered, "Thank you, Sir Joshua," as Tim and the construction workers were almost finished building the new arena, the Apollo.

Arising clouds from across the sea passed before the moon, encircling the bell tower of the church. In the days and weeks that followed, Nia would help the handicapped children at the church and become close friends with Joshua, who also helped the children, especially when they entered the Special Olympics. Joshua was their coach and would be waiting at the finish line to give them their hugs. Joshua and his father, in the days and weeks that followed, also became close, sitting at the dinning room table many a night with his father helping him with his physics class. Joshua studied hard in his history class about Vietnam as well, pausing as he passed his uncle's picture on the mantelpiece. Joshua, wanting his father to be proud of him, kept going back to the wrestling practices, too, although Villecco kept beating him up. And his Medieval Lit class? Well, he loved learning about knights. However, he didn't go back to the art class, although he did go to the disco dance class. Nia helped him with that one.

"Alright. You have to lead with your right foot," Nia said to Joshua, holding his hand in a dance position.

"I am leading with my right foot."

"No, you're not. You keep stepping on mine," Nia replied, adding, "Now concentrate. Ready..." They started to dance to disco dance music on the CD player across the wooden floor where Joshua modeled.

"Good. Just go with your feelings," Nia said. "Feel the music. That's it." "Who taught you to disco dance?" Joshua asked.

"I taught myself. When I was three," Nia replied, adding, "When my mother would go out on her dates."

"She left you alone when you were three?"

"No. She was there. On the other side of the door. I'd turn up the music so I couldn't hear. I started dancing." Nia stopped dancing. She went over and turned off the CD player.

"I'm sorry. Did I step on your foot again?" Joshua asked.

"We better get to our lit class. Dr. Silva is going to assigned research projects today instead of giving a midterm exam," Nia said.

Dr. Silva stood in front of the class with her smile and one eyebrow raised. She had just finished giving out the research assignments to the rest of the class when Joshua and Nia entered.

"I'm glad that both of you finally showed up. I was getting concerned. Please sit. I was just telling the class that each research assignment will count as a midterm exam. You will work in pairs. So Joshua, you, of course, will work with Nia. Both of you will do research and write a paper about whether or not there was really a King Arthur and a magical sword, Excalibur. I have included the research guidelines and database sources that can get you started." Dr. Silva handed Joshua and Nia a packet of information. "Alright class. Don't just sit there. Go do it," Dr. Silva said.

Joshua and Nia, still leafing through their packets, were the last to leave. Nia approached Dr. Silva. "I thought King Arthur was a myth passed on down through the centuries," Nia said.

"Ah. A myth," Dr. Silva responded, adding, "I guess you can write your paper right now then."

"That's alright. We'll go and do research first," Nia replied. "What happened to Excalibur?" Joshua asked, as if it was real.

"The Lady of the Lake supposedly got it when King Arthur died," Nia said to Joshua. "What lady? What lake?" Joshua asked.

"I'll fill you in. Come on," Nia said to him as Dr. Silva just smiled, turned, and gathered up her books.

Walking through the campus, Nia said to Joshua, "There is no lady or lake. It's like I said, a myth, a story. Supposedly, there was some kind of king like King Arthur that started the whole thing. But there definitely isn't an Excalibur. That was just part of the myth. It was added later to the story, along with Lancelot. The French did that part. And it was a story about Old England."

"How do you know so much about King Arthur?" Joshua asked. "I read a lot," Nia said as they approached the library.

Inside the library, Joshua and Nia did searches of the university databases. After finding codes, they searched the stacks of volumes of historical literature documents housed in the old section of the library that not many people had used before. Finding one dusty, large book, after brushing away the dust on its code number, Nia took it to a table with Joshua following. She opened the book and they saw pictures of what King Arthur and his knights looked like. There was also a picture of Guinevere.

"She's beautiful," Joshua said, adding, "I wonder what happened to her."

"You act like you knew her or something," Nia replied, turning the page. "Look, Joshua.

There it is, Excalibur."

"How are we going to prove it is real?" Joshua asked.

"You mean, how we going to prove it's not real," Nia said. "Let's just make some photocopies and..." Nia started to pick it up to take it to the copy machine. It was so old that it began to fall apart. "Alright. Let's just write some of this down, get quotes, page numbers, and the volume number so we can put it as a reference."

"There aren't any page numbers," Joshua said.

"What?" Nia replied, looking at the front cover and then inside the front page. "What are you looking for?" Joshua asked.

"A date," Nia replied.

"There it is," Joshua said pointing, "The year of our Lord—"

Nia turned to the back page and read aloud. "In the year of our Lord's return, Excalibur will be found by the leader of the new world, be raised up, and peace again will reign upon the land…"

"Well, this looks real to me," Joshua said.

"It can't be real. Maybe someone put this back there as a fraternity stunt. Otherwise, with no code or anything, how did it get back there?" Nia asked.

A librarian passed. "Do you need help?" the librarian asked them.

"Yes. This book…" Nia started to say with the librarian looking through it.

"Where did you find this?" the librarian asked. "Back there," Nia responded.

"Well. It's not ours," the librarian said. "I've never seen this before." "Joshua! Are you ready?" Tim called up the stairs of their house.

"He's not up there. He's around back feeding Bud," their father replied to Tim.

Tim went around to the back yard. Joshua had a bucket raised and was feeding Bud, who was in a small barn. Samson was by their side.

"Thanks for building Bud his house," Joshua said to Tim. "Come on, Joshua. Dad and I are ready to go."

Joshua put down the bucket, patted Bud, and walked with Tim and Samson to the truck out front. Their father was already seated in it. Samson jumped up in the back, and Joshua began getting in the passenger side.

"Wait a minute," their father said. "You can sit in the middle."

Joshua got in the middle and Tim pulled away. Joshua reached behind him and opened a sliding glass window so Samson could put his head through. Joshua petted him.

"Now this is a fishing trip, Joshua. Don't do what you did the last time," Tim said. "We're going to eat the fish. It's the circle of life."

"I know," Joshua said, still petting Samson.

"Maybe if we catch enough fish, we can have fish for Thanksgiving dinner instead of trukey," their father said as they drove down the mountain road toward the lake.

"Your line is too tight, Joshua," Tim said, seeing Joshua clutching his fishing pole, adding, "You're acting like you don't want to catch anything."

"I don't," Joshua replied.

"It's alright, Joshua. If you don't want to fish, you don't have to," their father said as they all sat in a boat in the middle of the lake. Their father and Tim recast their lines as Joshua pulled his in and just sat, watching.

"You know, Jesus went fishing," Tim said.

"I know," Joshua replied to Tim, adding, "Do you read the Bible?"

"I do," their father said.

"You do?" Tim asked their father.

"Yes," their father replied again. "You boys should too. We're only in this life a little while. That's why life is precious and God is forever."

"You're not going to die soon, are you, Dad?" Joshua asked.

"I'm not planning on it," their father said as his fishing reel bent. "I think I have something."

"Go for it, Dad! Bring him in!" Tim said.

Their father reeled in a large fish and Tim helped him bring it into the boat. It flapped about the bottom of the boat as Tim shouted, "Way to go, Dad!"

Their father looked over at Joshua. He wasn't smiling. Their father said, "Yeah. He's a big one," then, after feeling a deep-rooted pain within his chest and down his left arm, he picked up the fish and slowly lowered it back in the lake.

"What are you doing, Dad?" Tim asked.

"I told you, life is precious," he said with a shortness of breath..."even for this fish."

As their father's grasp slipped and the fist got loose, swimming away underneath the water's surface, the image of their father began to fade away upon subtle ripples of the lake's surface. Tim and Joshua's images crossed over that of their father's, that of a father's will.

That night, Joshua was sitting at the dining room table studying for his physics exam. His father came in and sat down next to him. "How are you making out?"

"Alright," Joshua replied. "I'm doing what you said. I'm writing down all the variables and what is given before doing anything else. Then I look on my card to see what formulas I should use."

"Good. Now remember to check answers by the units. You have on your card what a Newton is, right?" his father asked.

"Yes," Joshua replied, "it's kilograms meters per second squared." "Great. I think you're all set for your test."

"Did you know that Newton didn't get married, Dad? He was in love with a woman, but I guess he was too involved in his work." Joshua paused. "Do you think I'll ever get married, Dad?"

"I think with God all things are possible," his father replied. "I know I haven't told you this before, but I love you, Joshua, and I know that your dreams will come true, especially finding someone you love and getting married. If your wish is strong enough in your heart, then it's strong in God's too."

"You sound like Mom," Joshua said. "I guess I do."

"I love you too, Dad," Joshua said. "Thanks for helping me."

"Alright. You will have two hours and fifteen minutes to take this exam. When you are finished, please place your exams up here on my desk, and then quietly leave. Remember, others are taking the exam as well," Dr. Johnson said as he passed out the exam to his students.

Joshua was given the exam. "You may begin," Dr. Johnson told the class. Joshua turned the page open to the first problem. With the graphing calculator that his father gave him, he began solving the physics problems; every few minutes he looked up at the clock to see how much time he had left.

The clock said, 1:11 atop the scoreboard in the gymnasium as Joshua looked up to it. He was sitting in the stands alone, with about a hundred other students, watching a pre-season wrestling match between UCLA and Iowa. Doug passed Joshua as he came out of the locker room.

"Hey, Joshua. Keep the faith. Your day will come. You'll have a chance to wrestle," Doug said.

Villecco was at the bench screaming as Cif was struggling with his opponent. Cif's match went in overtime.

"My knee hurts," Cif said on the side of the mat to Villecco.

"You have to take this guy. It's our only chance to stay in this," Villecco responded.

"I don't think he should go on," Fanelli came up and said. "It looks like it's ready to pop again."

"Who's the head coach?" Villecco asked Fanelli, adding, "He keeps going. Cif, get back in there."

Cif walked back out to the center of the map. The referee flipped a disk. Cif won the choice. He chose to begin in the standing position. The referee blew his whistle and Cif's opponent shot in. Cif's knee popped. He collapsed onto the mat, writhing in pain. A couple of the wrestlers carried him off as the match continued. The team score was close, but when Dave Gable wrestled Tony at 177, he tossed Tony around as if he was nothing. Gable quickly pinned

Tony, hardly breaking a sweat. This put Iowa ahead to later win the match. When the referee raised Gable's hand, he briefly looked over at Joshua in the stands. With Gable's stare, Joshua thought he was looking directly at him, as if challenging him. Joshua looked back up at the scoreboard. One of the bulbs was out, making the number three appear like a two. Briefly, Joshua saw different colors of the lights.

When Joshua got home, there were different colored lights atop the ambulance that was parked in front of his house. He ran up to the house as they were carrying his father out on a stretcher. Tim was already there.

"Dad! Are you alright?" Joshua asked him.

"He's had a heart attack," Tim said to Joshua. "They're taking him to the hospital. Come on, Joshua. We'll follow them." Joshua ran to Tim's truck, got in, and followed.

"I don't want Dad to die," Joshua started crying.

At the chapel inside the hospital, Joshua and Tim were kneeling next to each other in prayer. "If Dad makes it through this, I'm going to go on more fishing trips with him," Joshua said. "And I'm going to wrestle, for him." Tim still remained silent. A doctor approached them in the chapel.

"He wants to see both of you," the doctor said.

"Dad," Joshua said, trying to awaken his father, as he remained still, his face turned away, eyes closed.

There was barely a heartbeat as both Joshua and Tim were watching their father slip away. Joshua was crying.

"Dad," Joshua said again.

The doctors and nurses in the room said that their father was in a coma and would not awaken. Then, miraculously, their father turned his head, opened his eyes, and reached up his hand to Joshua's brow.

"Believe, Joshua. Believe," their father said to him.

Taking his last gasp of life, eyes glazed over, and their father died. In the hospital's chapel, the single candle that burned before the altar went out. Joshua's echoes of his cries resonated through the marble of the chapel long after they left. Slowly, the trees upon the mountainside turned to those colors of a golden brown of fall—the winter before them, their father fast asleep.

Days later, as Carmel was passing the dark wrestling room hours after the last practice, he heard someone in there. Peering in and opening the door, he saw Joshua wrestling himself across the mat. He stood there watching Joshua for a few minutes before Joshua noticed him.

"I didn't see you," Joshua said, standing up. "What are you doing?" Carmel asked. "Practicing," Joshua replied.

"But you're wrestling yourself," "I know,"

Carmel went over to turn on a light. Joshua told him not to. "I want to stay in darkness until I'm ready," Joshua said. "You're different, aren't you?" Carmel said.

"I'm not crazy,"

"I think all wrestlers are crazy," Carmel said. "And if you're a wrestler, then crazy is a good thing. The crazier you are, the better you're a wrestler."

"My brother must think I'm a great wrestler then," Joshua said. "So why you doing this?" Carmel asked again.

"I told you, I'm practicing,"

"But you don't even wrestle. There's no spot on the team for you," Carmel said. Joshua at first didn't answer. Then he said, "My father died."

"I know. I heard. I'm sorry," Carmel replied.

"I want him to proud of me and see me win nationals,"

"Win nationals. You are crazy," Carmel said, adding, "I haven't even gotten close to the finals of nationals. And you think you can?" Carmel paused. He looked over at a poster on the wall from the 1970's of a five-hundred-pound heavyweight named Chris Taylor from Iowa wrestling in the Olympics against an East German. The East German had lifted Chris up from behind, although he could only get his arms around part of him, and was arched backwards, carrying Chris's massive girth, his head only a couple inches away from the mat. The move back then was called a "souffle," before that, the "straight back salto."

"I guess, anything is possible. Miracles can happen," Carmel said while staring at the poster. He then added, "Alright. I'll help you. First of all, you have to work on your stance. Stand like this with your arms here. That's it. You have to be able to defend yourself before shooting in. Let's try a few take downs..." Carmel, in the darkness, began teaching Joshua how to wrestle.

Each night, Joshua and Carmel would wait until everyone left, go into the wrestling room, and practice.

"Joshua. You have to remember one thing," Carmel said, "Whatever dream is inside of you, it is still there. A dream placed by God cannot be lost." Carmel turned on a speaker...

Songs from the 70's. Journey. "Don't stop believing, hold onto that feeling..."

"Let's do it, Joshua," Carmel said to him, gesturing to practice takedowns.

"Alright. You let them shoot in, go ahead, Joshua, shoot in," Carmel said. Joshua shot in on Carmel's legs. "Then you keep your left arm over his shoulder like this, cross face the face, then.   " Slam! Carmel tossed Joshua onto his back hard.

"There," Carmel said, adding, "That's how you do it. Now you try it   "

Slowly, Joshua became better at his takedowns—especially Carmel's move—escapes, and riding using pinning moves from the top. Carmel praised him. "You're the man, Joshua," Carmel would often say, adding, "UCLA's first national champion. " amidst songs from the 70's.

Thanksgiving day, Joshua was in the kitchen, struggling, trying to make dinner. There were two places set at the table.

"What are you doing?" Tim asked.

"It's Thanksgiving. I'm making us dinner. What does it look like I'm doing?" Joshua replied.

"This isn't going to bring Dad back, Joshua."

"Where are you going?" Joshua asked as Tim turned to leave. "To have a few beers and watch the games," Tim replied. "But what about dinner?" Joshua asked.

"Joshua, I haven't nor will I ever eat something you cooked," Tim said and left.

Joshua put the turkey back into the stove and sat down alone at the dining room table. He looked out the window and remembered wrestling when he was young, his father in his corner. His father's image in the corner faded as it started to rain. There was a knock at the door.

"What did you do, forget your key? Joshua asked, thinking it was Tim as he opened the door.

"Hi," Nia said, standing in the doorway, partially wet. "How did you find out where I live?" Joshua asked.

Tim's truck rode back up as Nia remained on the porch. Tim got out and walked up to them. At first Tim didn't say anything. "I forgot my money," Tim finally said while gazing at Nia. "Hi. I'm Tim. The Naked Chef here's brother."

"Hi, I'm Nia," Nia said extending her hand. "Joshua and I are in the same Medieval Lit class. We're working on a project together. We're also disco dance partners, right, Joshua?"

"Disco dance?" Tim asked, looking at Joshua, "Well, I'll let you two practice your disco dance routines," he added passing, retrieving his money from his room and leaving again. "It was nice meeting you," Tim said. "Joshua, are you going to invite her in or what?" Tim took hold of her hand again. He reached up and for a brief moment touched her hair. "You have nice eyes," Tim said to her.

"Come on in," Joshua said to Nia, trying to interrupt them gazing at each other.

"It was nice meeting you too," Nia said to Tim. She walked in and stood next to the dining room as they heard Tim drive away. "It smells like you're cooking something," Nia said.

"It's supposed to be a Thanksgiving dinner," Joshua said, "but, I think I'm burning everything. Where are you going for Thanksgiving?" Joshua asked.

"I helped out at the church the morning, but I was thinking about you so I thought I'd stop by. I hope you don't mind," Nia said.

"No. I'm glad to see you," Joshua said, "Do you want me to get you something to change into? I can't believe that I said that."

"It's alright. That would be nice. Thank you. I just need an old shirt or something. How about if you let me cook and we can have Thanksgiving dinner together?" Nia asked.

"I don't have a lot of utensils or anything," Joshua replied.

"That's alright. I'll consider it a challenge," Nia said, going into the kitchen and beginning to prepare dinner.

Joshua went down into the basement. He went to the large pile of clothes next to the washer and pulled out a white dress shirt. It was his father's. He took it to her.

"Here you go," Joshua said to her, handing her the shirt in the kitchen as she was bent over checking out the turkey.

"Thank you," she replied, taking it. "Why don't you go in and watch the football game or something. Let me do this," she said.

"Okay," Joshua replied. After he went into the living room and began watching the football game on a small TV that his brother had won in a poker game, the burnt smell turned to one of a nice one. It reminded him when his grandmother cooked Thanksgiving dinner for the family.

"Do you have a dryer to put these in?" Nia asked with her clothes in her hand, wearing his father's dress shirt, which came down to the middle of her thighs. She stood in the center of the small foyer just at the bottom of the stairs. Joshua stared at her for a moment. She was so beautiful. Her long brown hair flowed down her shoulders, her smooth olive complexion, her deep, beautiful eyes of brown.

"Yes. I do," Joshua said, arising. He took the clothes from her hand while still gazing at her. "Dinner's almost ready," she said.

Joshua went and put the clothes in the dryer. From upstairs, as he saw Samson sniffing at the windows of the basement, he heard, "Joshua! Do you have a serving platter?"

"A what!" Joshua called back.

"A large dish!" she replied.

"In the cabinet by the stove!" He shouted up to her as Samson let out a howl. Back upstairs, she said to him, "What's that howl?"

"That's my dog, Samson," Joshua replied.

"Why don't you get him? He can have dinner with us too," Nia said. "He's not allowed in the house," Joshua replied.

"Why don't you let him in the house?" Nia asked. "My father..." Joshua paused. "I'll go get him."

When Joshua returned with Samson, Nia was bringing food in and setting it on the table. "Dinner is served," she said.

Joshua sat down and Samson obediently sat down next to him. Nia went back into the kitchen and came back in carrying a bowl of mashed potatoes. She sat down with them. "Do you want to say grace?" Nia asked him.

Joshua bowed his head. "Heavenly Father, we thank you for being our Father, Lord, we..." Joshua paused.

"Why don't you just use your own words," Nia said.

"Thank you, God, for Nia and Samson, for letting them be in my life and be my friends," Joshua said.

"Amen," Nia said, starting to serve Joshua, filling up his plate. After she did, she put some turkey into a bowl with mashed potatoes for Samson and put it down on the floor for him. She filled her own plate.

"That book we found was pretty amazing, wasn't it?" Nia said as they ate. "Oh wait. We need something," she said. She went back into the kitchen, found a candle, brought it into the dining room, placed it on the table, and lit it. "There. We have to have a candle."

"Do you believe there is an Excalibur still somewhere?" Joshua asked her. "And there was really a King Arthur?"

"I guess if someone finds Excalibur, that will prove that there was a King Arthur and the story was true," Nia said. "We only have a couple of weeks left to get our paper into Dr. Silva."

"Thanks for helping me and for dinner," Joshua said to her.

"Thanks for being my friend," Nia said, reaching over and petting Samson. "You know, in medieval times they used dogs as napkins," Nia said with a laugh. Samson barked.

"I think Samson wants you to use the napkins though," Joshua said with a smile.

As the continued eating dinner and talking, the rain gently came down without thunder or lightning. At the end of dinner, Nia took the plates into the kitchen and cleaned up. She insisted that Joshua and Samson go into the living room and watch more football as she did. After she cleaned up in the kitchen, she asked Joshua to go and see if her clothes were dry. Joshua went into the basement and opened the dryer...

"They're still wet," Joshua said to her in the living room. "I had it on air instead of heat," Joshua added. "I'm sorry."

Nia was looking out the window at the rain. "That's alright. Let's go for a walk," she said. "But it's raining," Joshua said.

"It will be fun, Joshua. Come on," she said, going out the front door. Joshua followed with Samson. They walked around the back past Bud. She stopped to pet him in the barn that Joshua's brother had made for him and fed him some oats.

"Come, Joshua," she said, taking his hand, walking bare footed in his father's white dress shirt that was becoming transparent with the rain. She had nothing on underneath. They went to the side of the pond. It was warm as they gazed up at the waterfall. Nia reached out with her arms, closed her eyes, and let the rain fall softly down upon her. "Let's go to the top," Nia said, taking again his hand with Samson following. They went to the top of the waterfall and, standing next to the large old oak tree, looked out across the sea. "The horizon's edge. I remember when you told me about that," Nia said, looking out. "Do you still have your knight's outfit?" she asked. The rain, falling down upon them, gently turned into snow.

"I'm not a knight," he replied.

"I think you are," she said, mesmerized by the falling snow. Turning to face him, Nia appeared naked, completely wet, draped in a soft white unusual spiritual glow. She reached over and gently opened his clasped hand. Inside was his mother's heart-shaped crystal necklace.

Through the tiny glass, a small rainbow appeared, a small image of hope, and the colors in Joshua's life finally returned. Gently, he placed the crystal in her hand and closed it as he put his arm around her, as if he was about to lead her in a dance. With the touch, they kissed. The falling crystals from the sky echoed a voice of faith from long ago.

At a local bar Tim went up to a dusty old music box, put in coins, pushed "G-777," and gave it two hits. With spiders running down the side, Donna Summer's song, "Last Dance" started to play as Tim sat back down at the bar and picked up his mug of beer.

Nia and Joshua danced atop the cliff overlooking the sea as if they could hear the song. The song faded. Facing each other again, this time in each other's arms, they passionately kissed as the snow, turning back into rain, slowly stopped. As the clouds parted, one by one, stars began to fill the sky. The moon, too, came out, shining down upon them as Joshua carefully began unbuttoning her shirt. The shirt fell to her feet. Silence, just the sounds of the waterfall and the sea.

Another song at the bar was loudly playing from Stevie Nix, "Landslide," while Nia and Joshua fervently made love. On the TV, muted, was a replay of the UCLA vs. Iowa match. Gable was wrestling Tony. Tim slowly finished his beer, watching the match.

After making love atop the cliff overlooking the waterfall and the sea, Nia and Joshua were lying naked beside each other on their backs atop the cliff looking up at the stars. A Dandelion "wish" floated by above them. They both gently took hold of it, made a wish, and blew on it. It floated upward, away into the sky. "Do you believe dreams can come true, Joshua?"

"Yes," Joshua replied, gazing up at the sky while holding her hand. "My mother told me that for every shooting star, there is a dream that comes true." Joshua helped Nia up. They kissed again as thousands of shooting stars shot across the sky above them, their reflections spanning across the blue sea in a rainbow and through the image of the moon...

Chapter 15

1969. Vietnam. Michael was making love to Mey Lee with the gray mountain skyline in the distance. The sun was setting behind the largest mountain as Mey Lee collapsed into Michael's arms. Michael held her close, caressing her hair, for he did not know when he would see her again. She, too, had waited so long to feel his hand, his touch upon her lips, for she was the one he loved.

"I love you," he whispered to her. The whisper faded into the night awakening in a shout arising in a new day.

"Uncle Eddie!" Hoa Sung shouted running to Ed's awaiting arms. Ed picked her up and held her up over his head making airplane sounds as she let out giggles that turned into laughter. He put her down. "I have something for you," he said to her, taking out a small book with a picture of a dragon on its cover from inside his shirt.

"She's only three. I don't think she can read yet," Michael said, coming out of a hut followed by Mey Lee.

"Do you mind? This is between me and my girl," Ed replied, taking Hoa Sung by her hand and walking her over to the stone fountain in the center of the village. Sitting on its edge, he lifted her up onto his knee and began to read to her. "This is a story, a story that happened a long, long time ago, when knights slew dragons for fair maidens, carrying them away into the night, and riding white-winged horses off into the sky..."

Several army trucks, jeeps, and American soldiers from other units began coming into the village. In the distance, Michael was talking to an officer as Ed continued reading the story to Hoa Sung. "Once upon a time there lived a princess. She was so beautiful with long, dark hair," Ed touched her hair gently with a smile, "the brightest brown eyes, and the cutest nose above her soft, soft lips. She dreamed of the day she would meet her valiant knight, how he would come riding out of the forest upon a white stallion and bring to her..." Ed paused. He reached down by the side of the fountain and found a small rosebud. "Bring to her a rose..." Ed said, giving her the rosebud.

"We have orders to evacuate everyone," the officer said to Michael, adding, "There's movement coming this way."

Mey Lee came up to Michael. "What's going on?" she asked him.

"We have to get everyone out of here," Michael said, walking over to Ed. "Bruce! Get everyone on the trucks!"

Bruce acknowledged Michael with a wave and then shouted to the other soldiers in Michael's unit to help get the villagers onto the passing trucks and jeeps. The villagers started running in a panic, hearing gunfire and explosions coming closer. Ed and Hoa Sung continued to be transfixed on their story while still sitting on the edge of the fountain although chaos was occurring around them.

"We have to get everyone out!" Michael shouted over the gunfire going up to Ed. Ed looked up from the book. "What?" Ed asked.

"Take Hoa Sung over to that truck! Now!" Michael shouted to Ed amidst the explosions hitting the village. As the ground shook, the book with the dragon on its cover fell from Ed's hands to the ground by the side of the fountain. Michael picked up the book as Ed carried Hoa Sung over to one of the trucks and into the awaiting arms of a soldier. Mey Lee threw her arms around Michael and kissed him good-bye with Hoa Sung calling out from the back of the truck as it began to pull away. Hearing her daughter's calls, Mey Lee turned and ran toward the truck, to her daughter's outstretched arms, frantically calling out, "Wait! Wait! My baby!"

Another explosion. Mey Lee fell to the ground. Michael and Ed ran over to help as, looking up, Mey Lee saw Hoa Sung's truck had been hit and was engulfed in flames. With the truck ablaze, everyone in it was dead except for Hoa Sung. She was thrown from the truck, clinging to life, gasping with shortened, shallow breaths. Her mother picked her up in her arms and cried out, "Don't die. Please don't die. Please. My baby. My precious baby..." to her in Vietnamese while explosions erupted around them. Reaching up with her little bloody arm and with her tiny finger, Hoa Sung touched her mother's lips. And with the touch, in the silence, she said good-bye to her mother's heart as the small rose bud fell out of Hoa Sung's hand to the ground.

The fighting erupted in the village, blowing up the stone fountain, as Hoa Sung's body remained lifeless in her mother's arms. With Mey Lee's high-pitched cries being drowned out by the gunfire, Ed forcibly pulled Mey Lee away from her daughter and lifted her up to a passing jeep as two American soldiers grabbed her, disappearing into a haze. The rest of Michael's unit fought their way back into the jungle as the other American soldiers and villagers made their escape down the dirt road. Ed picked up the rose bud and carried Hoa Sung's body amidst the gunfire out of the village and into the jungle followed by Michael.

Once deep enough in the jungle, far away from the gunfire, Ed gently placed the tiny, lifeless body down on the ground. He patted his shirt, searching for the book he was reading to her by the fountain. Michael, knowing what he was looking for, tossed it to him. Ed read the ending of the story over Hoa Sung's body "...and as the knight knelt down over her, he reached down with a rose," Ed placed the rosebud on her, "held it to her chest, and it slowly melted and became her heart."

Suddenly, gunfire rained down upon them. It looked like heavy snow as Michael, Ed, and the rest of the unit had to take cover. They watched as the little girl's body was ripped apart by the gunfire. There wasn't much left. The gunfire stopped. But Ed, angered, kept firing back.

Michael calmed him down. Bruce, after making his way through the jungle, came up to Michael and said, "Everyone got out safely including Mey Lee."

"What are we going to tell her about her daughter?" Bruce asked.

"That we buried her," Michael replied, signaling with his hand to move on.

Michael and Ed, days later, caught up to Mey Lee at one of the main army camps south near Saigon. She ran and threw her arms around him again upon seeing him. "Everything is set. All the paperwork is done," Michael told her, turning to Ed he added, "Tell Jerk Hawk I owe him one."

"Congratulations. You're a beautiful bride," Ed said. "Next time, invite me to the wedding."

"When we get back home, I will really marry you," Michael told Mey Lee. "Now, you have my brother's address?" Mey Lee nodded. "Oh. Could you give him this when you see him?" Michael said, giving her a small wrapped package.

"What is it?" she asked.

"It's for him. I just bought it. He will know what it means," Michael replied.

"I want you to have this," Mey Lee said, taking off her gold cross from around her neck and placing it in his hand.

They kissed good-bye and waved as Mey Lee joined a group of Vietnamese heading toward Saigon being escorted by American soldiers. She held up the cassette tape, showing him that she had it, and smiled.

"So, she's going to the states," Ed said.

"That's what Jerk Hawk supposedly set up," Michael replied, adding, "She's a United States citizen now, my wife."

"Did you phone your brother and tell him she's coming?" Ed asked.

"Yeah. Back in the jungle over there," Michael replied. "I told her what to say to him. He will know she's my wife when she gives him that tape."

"What's on it?" Ed asked.

"A song," Michael simply replied.

"What if she can't find your brother's house?" Ed asked with Michael walking away. "I gave her a map and directions," Michael replied with Ed trying to catch up to him.

"I know, but the states are a big place, especially L.A   " Ed said as they faded back into the jungle.

In the church in Los Angeles, Joshua and Nia were studying in the balcony where the children practiced singing. Joshua looked up from the open book before him and over to Nia who was reading.

"So, when are you going to sing in church?" Joshua asked. "Why?" She replied.

"It's your dream isn't it, to be a singer?" Joshua answered.

"When are you going to wrestle in a match?" Nia asked. Joshua remained silent then said, "I'm not on the team yet."

"You're not on the team? You go to practice everyday." "I'm not in the line up to start."

"But you're still on the team." "Not really."

"Why not?"

"The coach won't let me. He only lets me practice." "What, is mad at you or something?"

"I don't know. I think it has something to do with my brother." Joshua paused, then asked, "So, why are you afraid to sing?"

"It's hard for me in front of people."

"You danced in front of..." Joshua started to say. Nia got up and leaned against the rail of the balcony.

"You don't understand. When I sing, I feel more naked." "Why?"

"Because it's my deepest dream, I guess."

"If I make it to the national championships, will you sing a song for me in church?" Joshua asked.

"Is that your biggest dream, Joshua, to be a wrestling champion?" "No. It's my second biggest," Joshua answered.

"What's your first?" Nia asked. Joshua did not answer. He looked back down at his book and started studying again as the handicapped children began coming up the balcony stairs to practice singing.

Later that day, Joshua entered the wrestling room for practice. Everyone was already there, warming up, with Villecco standing in front of them going over the line up for the Christmas tournament a few weeks away. Joshua went directly up to Villecco and said, "I want to wrestle."

"There's no spot for you, and you're too old," Villecco replied.

Tony raised his hand. "I'm glad Joshua brought this up, Coach. I was going to tell you, but I have to go back home to New York that weekend. My grandmother is flying in from Italy and my whole is going to be there. They're coming from all over the country."

"Every year, you guys don't take this tournament seriously, and it's our Christmas tournament," Villecco said.

"That's because it's Christmas, Coach. We're thinking about other things," Mitch said.

"Like what?" Villecco asked.

Mitch added, "You know, hanging out with our babes..."

"...drinking eggnog, singing Christmas carols," Carmel said as everyone laughed. "Alright. If you guys don't want to put wrestling first..." Villecco started to say. "God's first," Joshua said.

"He's right," Doug added.

"Coach, why don't you give Joshua a chance?" Carmel asked. "He's been coming to practice everyday. He's ready. I've been helping him."

"Fine. Tony, you don't want to wrestle, then don't. Joshua. You're in. You can take Tony's spot, but only for the Christmas tournament," Villecco said.

"Alright!" Mikey called out. Others applauded and said, "You're the man, Joshua." Carmel was the loudest. "Joshua's my hero. He's going to be our first national champion ever." Joshua joined them in warming up.

"Yeah, right," Villecco said sarcastically beginning to warm up too. Villecco then shouted, "Alright! Everyone up! Get into your groups! Ready, wrestle!" Joshua wrestled Carmel.

Chapter 16

"This is unbelievable," Villecco said as he stood in the middle of a gymnasium where the Christmas tournament was to be held. Villecco was looking up at snowflakes hanging down from the ceiling over the two large wrestling mats. "Hey, Joe," Villecco called out to the athletic director as he passed. "What's all of this?" Villecco pointed up.

"There's a dance here tonight as soon as the tournament is done," Joe replied.

"It wasn't my decision."

"You can't even see the scoreboard and clock," Villecco said.

"Well, if you want to cut all of them down, go ahead. But the Alumni Association are the ones who decorated. 'Memories of Snow' I think they're calling it."

"Couldn't they have their dance somewhere else?" Villecco asked. "They wanted a gymnasium."

"What about the basketball team and their gym?" Villecco asked.

"How many national champions have we had in wrestling?" Joe asked, adding, "Look.

When the Apollo is finished in a couple of months, you won't have this problem. Oh, by the way. It looks like we will be able to host the nationals this year."

"At the Apollo?" Villecco asked.

"That's what I'm being told," Joe replied. "It would be nice if one of our guys made it to the finals, don't you think? We haven't had anyone since Tim Kahn, have we?"

"Alright, Joshua. Remember what I taught you. Just have confidence.

You can do it," Carmel said, sitting on a bench in the locker room as they were getting dressed to wrestle. Joshua nodded. Carmel started to sing, "My pants are systematic...go, go, grease lightning." Mitch went up and turned on a radio. Rap music.

"What is this stuff?" Aikens said.

"You have a problem with my music?" Mitch said. "What kind of music do you listen to, Southern boy?"

Aikens went up and smashed the radio. Silence. "I guess you haven't made weight yet," Mitch said.

"I haven't eaten in three days or drank anything in two. I had to drop eight pounds of sweat in our last practice and still not be able to take one drop from the water fountain. So you tell me if I'm in the mood to listen to some punk spit out songs," Aikens replied while taking off a rubber suit, sweat pouring out to the floor.

"Aikens!" Villecco called out with a wrestling official along side of him. Aikens followed them to the scale. Naked, Aikens stepped on it. He was a pound over. "Damn!" Aikens cried out. "That's it coach. He forfeits," the official said. Aikens immediately went up to the water fountain and began drinking. He punched the water fountain and went into the bathroom. It sounded like a door got smashed.

"Alright, guys. Could you gather around?" the official said as the UCLA wrestlers came over to him. "I've already talked to the other teams. We have ten schools here, right, Coach?" Villecco nodded. "All the rules are the same as with all the other tournaments I've officiated. I know most of you. Just make sure you allow your opponent to get set on the bottom position before getting on. I'll give you one warning, then it's a penalty point. Do you understand?"

"Yes," some of them said.

"If I think you're stalling, I'll call that to. If you want to defer until the next period, you have to tell me loudly and immediately." The official then turned to Villecco, "Coach, if you have any questions about a call, go to the table. They'll call me over. Alright. Good luck, guys."

"Carmel. Take them out and warm up, our usual drill," Villecco said.

Carmel led the team upstairs and into the gymnasium where the wrestlers from the other schools were warming up too. Joshua was overwhelmed by all the wrestlers from the other schools and the crowd that was beginning to fill the stands. There were several tables by the mats with a lot of people organizing score cards and sounding loud buzzers, practicing. The tournament began. Two mats had wrestlers competing simultaneously. As the clock on the scoreboard at each end of the gym ticked down, students went out onto the mat to tap the officials with a rolled up towel to tell them time was up when the buzzers, drowned out by the loud crowd, went off. Both the wrestling mats were roped off with security people keeping spectators on the outside and in the stands. Carmel sat on a warm-up mat next to Joshua the end of the gym. Joshua, watching the wrestlers go out one by one, was practicing, mimicking their moves, looking like he was wrestling himself. He did flips, kicks, and sit out turn ins. "Alright, Joshua. Just relax, will you. It's only a Christmas tournament. Calm down," Carmel said. Joshua sat down next to Carmel.

"It's pretty amazing all of this, isn't it?" Carmel asked. "Like modern day gladiators. Do you believe in reincarnation? I bet long ago we fought together at the Coliseum in Rome."

"There's your guy," Carmel pointed over to a large wrestler with huge biceps. "He looks good," Joshua said.

"I wrestled him last year. You can take him," Carmel said. "Can you imagine what it's like to win the Eastern Championships like I did last year..."

"Next, on mat one from UCLA, Joshua Kahn, and from Tennessee" was heard echo loudly over the intercom. Joshua got up and took off his warm-up suit. "Let's go, Joshua," Coach Fanelli said. "We're up next on mat one."

Joshua put on his headgear and jumped up and down outside the ropes with Carmel at his side. Villecco was coaching Doug on the other mat. The match before Joshua's on mat one ended quickly in a pin. Joshua was up. He had trouble getting over the ropes and tripped on the mat walking out to the center. An official handed him a red Velcro ankle marker to put on. Joshua bent down and put it around his ankle. He got up, shook hands with his opponent, and the official blew the whistle. Joshua's opponent immediately shot in and took him down. Joshua had no trouble escaping back to his feet, but his opponent continually took him down each time. At one point Joshua was struggling on his back with the TV camera at the corner of the mat zooming in on him with the red light going on. Joshua turned his head away because he didn't want to be seen close up.

At the local bar, Tim was watching Joshua almost getting pinned. He paid the bartender before Joshua's match was over and left. "Have a merry Christmas," the bartender said, adding, "If I don't see you."

"Oh. Yeah. Right," Tim replied walking out the door. Tim wandered a bit down the city's street, pausing for a moment at a display of New York City. When he got home, he went up to his secret project, lifted the canvass, and said, "Well. I'm almost done. There isn't anything to keep me here anymore." He went inside and out onto the back porch next to his father's chair.

When Joshua got home, Tim was watching TV. "How did you do?" Tim asked.

"I didn't get pinned," Joshua replied. "Look. I got my grades in the mail."

Tim looked at them. All A's. "I knew you could do it, Joshua. See. You are smart." "Do you think dad is proud of me?" Joshua asked.

"I know Mom is," Tim replied.

"I mean, if I don't do very well wrestling, do you think he will still be proud of me?" Joshua asked.

"Sure. He will be proud of you no matter what you do. And besides, you haven't wrestled in a while in a match. You'll get better."

"I'm not allowed to wrestle again. That was it, the one match," Joshua replied. Joshua paused, then said, "Can we do something for Christmas?"

"Like what. Christmas is only a few days away."

"I'll think of something," Joshua said, adding, "But when I do, do you promise you'll do it?"

"Fine. Whatever. Yeah, I promise," Tim replied. "Can we get a tree and decorate too?" Joshua asked. "Joshua, you can do what ever you want to."

1969. Vietnam. In May Lee's village, there sat a woman working with sweat pouring down her face as her hands shined a golden pot a foot high. A wasp flew by and her hands swatted it away as it again and again came back. Angrily, she arose and went into a hut to get a broom. A little boy just barely over a foot high strutted naked over to where the pot was. Looking one way and then the other, the little boy turned around and sat his bare bottom in the pot and proceeded to go the bathroom. The woman coming out of the hut saw a look of alarm come over him as he cried out jumping up with a scream. Holding his bare bottom in pain, he ran to the woman, who was his mother, as a wasp flew out of the pot. Running into his mother's legs, the little boy disappeared under her long dress as Michael and his men came marching into the village...

"What's going on?" Tim asked, coming in the front door.

Joshua had all kinds of boxes he had gotten out of the attic spread out all over the living room floor. "You wouldn't believe what I found in the attic," Joshua said, taking out Christmas ornaments and showing Tim.

"What are you doing with all of this?" Tim asked.

"It's Christmas Eve. I'm decorating like you said I could." "Decorating what?" Tim asked, seeing no tree.

"I was going to get a tree to surprise you, but I didn't want to kill one. So I got a better idea. I've been working on it all day since you left for work until now. What time is it?" Joshua asked.

Tim looked at his watch, "Seven," he replied.

"I ran out of lights, so I had to keep going back to the store for more. Christine helped me all day too. She just left. Come. I'll show you," Joshua said, leading him to the back porch by their father's chair. Stepping on a lot of wires, Tim hesitated before looking down.

There were about a hundred entangled green cords with Christmas lights coming out of what looked like surge protectors or some type of transformers going from the back porch and fading into the darkness of the backyard.

"Unbelievable," Tim said, adding, "I hope you know an amazing electrician... Joshua.

What are you trying to do? Light up the whole back yard?"

"You'll see. Watch," Joshua said, taking a plug of an extension cord that led into all the others and putting into a socket just inside the living room. Nothing. "Wait. I know," Joshua said. "Ready?" Joshua asked with his hand poised on a light switch.

"Go for it," Tim said, trying to hold back laughter. Joshua flipped the switch as both of them gazed into the backyard. Still nothing.

"I don't understand," Joshua said.

"Joshua. You probably have a bulb that is no good somewhere. So that means you have to find it and replace it with a good bulb."

"You're kidding. Who thought of that stupid idea?" Joshua asked.

"Well, most people don't search for the one bad bulb but instead go out and buy a whole new set of lights. Get it?" Tim paused, and then asked, "So how many lights did you buy?"

"Enough," Joshua simply replied.

"Enough to light up the backyard?" Tim asked.

"Enough to light up the entire city of Los Angeles," Joshua replied. Joshua paused, then said, "I have another surprise for you. What you promised..."

1969. Vietnam. As Michael and his men passed through the village, the woman with the long dress just stared. Ed was right behind Michael. "I don't like the feeling I'm getting," Ed said to him. Michael held his weapon tighter as the rest of his men were passing through. There were about twenty or so huts with a few women and children. But it was quiet, too quiet...

"I can't believe that you talked me into this," Tim said after ringing a bell as he and Joshua stood on a doorstep in the ghetto section of the city. It was dark as a large African American woman peered out her window through a curtain. "What do you want?" she asked.

"We're Christmas carolers," Joshua replied.

"Just a second," she said. They could hear several locks opening, then the door. She had a shotgun in her hand. She pumped it twice.

"I'll give both of you ten seconds to get out of here," she said. "Who's there?" a man's voice from upstairs called out.

"I'm handling it!" the woman called back, gripping the gun, and aiming at Tim and Joshua.

"Alright, lady, we're leaving," Tim said.

Joshua began singing. "Oh, Holy night..." The woman slowly lowered the gun.

Inside the strip club next to the church, strippers were seductively dancing atop the bar and on the stage with others lap dancing on top of men in the shadows. Although it was Christmas Eve, the club was packed with men drinking beer amidst loud music and heavy smoke.

It was almost midnight as Christine, "Believer in Christ," was leaning up against a table in the strip club, looking out across the smoke-filled room, counting her tips. She had been waiting tables for the past five hours after she left Joshua's, having worked late into the night the past seven days. She wondered how her three-year-old daughter, Crystal, was doing. She worried that Crystal was growing up much too fast with so little precious time to spend with her. She reached into her pocket and pulled out a photograph of Crystal stumbling along in the park in her Tiger costume. Being a single parent had been hard. Money always seemed to be spent faster than she could make it. Having to pay for a babysitter, rent, utility bills, food, clothing, etc., every penny for every month was already accounted for. If something happened, she didn't know what she would do. She had already gotten behind in the rent and the phone company had temporarily disconnected her phone. This proved to be almost fatal the time when Crystal fell out of her bed and severely hit her head in the middle of the night. Christine couldn't call an ambulance, so she had to rush Crystal to the hospital herself in a car that had broken down several times.

Suddenly, the music stopped and the lights went out. "What's going on?" Someone called out in the lap dance section. The Christmas caroling became louder, coming down the city's street toward them as the stained-glass windows came to life in light from the moon with knights, white-winged horses, and dragons. Christine was waiting on tables again while looking up the clock because she wanted to go home and see her daughter.

Joshua, Tim, and the large black woman were leading hundreds of people down through the streets holding lit candles. "Silent Night. Holy Night..." They began gathering in the parking lot, still singing. Nia came out of the church with the handicapped children huddled behind her. The caroling got even louder as one of the dancers went and opened the front door. Hundreds were in the parking lot. "Oh holy night the stars are brightly shining. It is the night of the dear Savior's birth.

1969. Vietnam. The child underneath his mother's dress lifted it above his head. Peering out from underneath it, Ed could see that the little boy had eyes like Hoa Sung's, a look of innocence. Ed waved to him. The little boy waved back. His mother raised her dress further and took out a weapon. Before Michael could shout, the woman fired, and bullets ripped Ed apart. Michael fired back, killing the woman and her little boy. The rest of the women and children took out weapons and began firing into Michael's men. Everyone of Michael's men, although trying to fire back, began to fall...

The carolers were singing, "...fall on your knees, hear the angel's voices..."

All of Michael's men were killed except for he and Ed. While firing back at the villagers, Michael dragged Ed's body back through the jungle. Ed's legs were gone, and his blood was gushing from his body.

"Hang in there buddy!" Michael shouted, still dragging him.

"Don't leave my body over here," Ed managed to say as he spit out blood.

"You're not going to die. Don't die!" Michael shouted. Michael got to the edge of a cliff. He stood over Ed's body. "Don't leave my body over here..." Ed said, as his breathing shallowed.

"Don't die on me, Uncle Eddie. Santa Claus doesn't die," Michael said, taking out some rope. He tied it around both stumps of what was left of the top of Ed's legs to stop the bleeding. Ed's eyes closed.

In Vietnamese, Michael heard, "Take him. He's ours." Michael looked up. It was Karese.

Michael was captured, and Ed was left to die on the side of the cliff.

Oh Christmas tree, Oh Christmas tree..." The caroling continued as bright lights came on in the club. Nia entered the club, followed by Father Gabe. "I heard she's a nun now," one of the dancers said. Everyone in the club was quiet as the carolers sung softer.

Father Gabe raised his arms. "You don't have to do this. God loves you," he said. Some of them laughed. Nia got up on top of the bar and said, "Listen to him. You're wasting you lives here and what God gave you. All of you are better than this."

"You danced here for two years and now you've found God?" one dancer asked.

"I believe in God. I believe in Jesus," Christine said, adding, "I think Nia's right. We shouldn't be doing this."

"Well, I'm not going to be preached to by a priest or a nun," still another dancer said, "not unless it's in church."

"You're all welcome," Father Gabe said.

"Turn the music back on! Start dancing!" the men began crying out. One grabbed Nia's bottom. "Come on, baby," he said to her. Nia took his arm, twisted it, and shoved him off his seat and to the floor.

"Man. You've learned to fight since you've become a nun," a dancer said.

The lights went out again. Silence, even the carolers. They just stood with their lit candles in the parking lot. The stained-glass windows exploded open. Some people began to panic.

"Sit down!" Father Gabe called out. They listened to him. Joshua entered holding a single lit candle. He got up on top of the bar, next to Nia, and started to sing as he did when he was three in front of the church. Everyone listened, captured by his angelic voice. After he was finished, the people from the parking lot entered and led the men and dancers out while holding the lit candles. The carolers started singing again. This time, the men and the dancers joined them. They all went into the church, leaving Tim and Joshua alone to walk back down the city streets.

"I didn't know you could sing like that," Tim said to Joshua. "Neither did I," Joshua replied.

Christine got into her car after praying that it would start and turned on the radio as she drove away. A song played about an angel who gave up eternity to spend one moment holding the woman of his dreams. The song, "Iris" played as Joshua paused to look up at the sky. "And I'd give up forever to touch you. And I know you feel me somehow. You're the closest to heaven I'll ever be... I just want you to know who I am..." Nia was looking up to the cross inside the church as everyone was singing except her. Christine wondered if there were really angels, and if one could ever love her. He would be good and pure in heart, "the man." Christine started to cry. She hoped one day to be held by the man, the angel, of her dreams. Yet, how can you touch the sky? Joshua reached up his hand toward the sky.

When Christine arrived home, she found her daughter asleep, curled up underneath the covers in her bed. Just her daughter's face could be seen as she leaned over and kissed Crystal on the cheek. Crystal's eyes slowly opened. Reaching up, Crystal hugged her mother and said, "I love you, Mom."

"I love you too. Merry Christmas," Christine whispered back., "Happy Birthday, Crystal."

Tim opened the book with a picture of the dragon on its cover after reaching into a box at home. "I wonder where Mom got this," Tim said.

"Don't you remember?" Joshua asked, adding, "A man in a wheelchair gave it to her when he came to the house that day looking for dad. You know, the day before Christmas Eve, the day before Mom," Joshua paused. "But dad wasn't here. And the man, he didn't have any legs. But you were here. Mom gave you that book and you hung it on our Christmas tree.

Remember?"

"I do," Tim said, adding, "I hung it next to the pegasus with green sparkles." "What's a pegasus?" Joshua asked.

"It's a mythological white-winged horse." "Like the one I dreamed about?" Joshua asked.

"Yeah. I guess. It was supposedly in many ancient wars, a favorite of Zeus, bringing him the thunder and lightning during all the battles. Oh, and it had a horn, I believe," Tim replied, adding, "That reminds me." Tim went out on the front lawn and looked underneath the canvas that was still draped over his secret project. Joshua stood and watched him from the porch. "Is it alright?" Joshua asked.

"Yeah. I just have to add something, then it will be finished," Tim called back. "Then I'll know what it is?" Joshua asked.

"Everyone will," Tim answered with a rumble of thunder in the distance.

Chapter 17

Joshua was at the school store looking for a card to get Nia. It was late afternoon. After going through what was left, he decided to write his own. So he went outside, sat beneath the bell tower by the library, and began writing. The bells sounded above him simultaneously with the church bells.

"Where's Kahn?" Villecco asked in the wrestling room at practice with the wrestlers warming up.

"Why?" Carmel asked, adding, "You don't let him wrestle."

"He wrestled at the Christmas tournament and blew it," Villecco replied.

"It was his first match. Like no one in here has ever lost before," Carmel responded. "Coach. How come you don't give us Valentine's Day off?" Mitch asked.

"He didn't give us Christmas off, why Valentine's Day?" Aikens said. "Is there any holiday we can have off?" Mikey asked.

"Yeah. The day after Easter," Villecco said, adding, "After someone in here wins the nationals."

"The finals are on Easter this year?" Doug asked. "So. You have a problem with that?" Villecco asked.

"It's the most sacred day for Christians," Doug replied, adding, "The day Jesus rose from the dead."

"I don't believe in that. Once you're dead, you're dead," Villecco said. "You don't believe in heaven?" Mikey asked.

"Where does your dog go when he dies?" Villecco asked. "In a hole in the backyard," Aikens responded.

"Right," Villecco said, adding, "And so do we. We end up in a hole."

"Thanks for cheering us up," Carmel said to Villecco. "You going to write that down on your Valentine's Day card to your wife?"

"Alright! Everyone up!" Villecco called out.

Joshua put what he was writing in his pocket and went to practice. The bells above him stopped. Practice went into night, later than usual.

On the porch of Joshua's house, Nia walked up and knocked, wearing a long jacket over her tiger skin body stocking and flip-flops. She had a card in her hand. As she peered in the windows to see if anyone was home, Tim pulled up in his truck next to Nia's car. Nia turned. Tim got out carrying a suitcase and walked up to her, not saying anything.

"Is Joshua home?" Nia asked.

"He's still at wrestling practice," Tim said, adding, "Can I help you with something, honey?"

"I just wanted to give him this card," Nia replied, covering up. "I would have mailed it, but I wanted to give it to him in person."

Tim checked her out and looked at it. He knew it was a Valentine's Day card.

"Joshua has never gotten a Valentine's Day card from anyone before." Tim paused. So what? Are you boyfriend girlfriend now, Tiger Lady?"

"We're friends," Nia replied, adding, "I was in a hurry and I didn't have anything else to wear."

"Great, the 'friend' word," Tim said. "What's that supposed to mean?" she asked.

"Never mind. I'll give it to him," Tim said, taking the card out of her hand and starting to pass by her. "Where are you going in such a hurry?"

"Away. Where are you going? Are you moving in?" Nia asked. "No, out," Tim replied.

"Where?"

"You ask a lot of questions, you know that," Tim said. "New York. But don't tell Joshua.

I don't want him to know."

"You're just going to leave him alone and not tell him?" Nia asked, getting in front of him.

"Something like that. Like you," Tim said, putting down the suitcase, not knowing the card fell out of his hand. "Look, is there something else I can help you with, sex kitten?

Otherwise, I'd appreciate it if you got your little butt out of my way." "You're a real jerk," Nia said, leaving.

"Who are you to criticize me?" Tim shouted from the porch, pointing as she continued walking away. "You don't know what I had to put up with for years!"

Nia stopped and turned. She said, "Yeah. Well. We all had to put up with something," and began getting into her car. Tim shouted, "Wait!" ran up to her and added, "I'm sorry," before she could close the car door. Tim stooped down and looked up to her. "Forgive me," he said, gently touching hair.

"Forget it. I've got to go," Nia said.

Tim stood up. "How about joining me on one last night out on the town?" Nia didn't answer. "Alright. I'll tell him," Tim said.

"Where?" She asked.

"I guess here," he replied.

"No. I mean, where do you want to go out on the town?" "I've never been to the zoo," Tim said.

When they pulled up to the zoo in Tim's truck, Nia said, "It doesn't look like it's open." Tim got out and went up to the gate. There was a custodian putting on the final locks.

"Can I help you?" the custodian asked. "You open?" Tim asked.

"No. We closed a couple of hours ago."

"Look. I wonder if you can do me a favor. I promised my girl, here, that I'd take her to the zoo. If you just let us in for about, let's say, a half hour, I promise we won't do anything to the lions," Tim said, holding up a roll of twenty-dollar bills.

"Sorry, buddy. I don't think so," the custodian said with a laugh.

Tim went back to the truck and got in. "So I'm your girl now," Nia said sarcastically. "I just said that to get us in. Well, it worked in the movie *Rocky*." Nia looked confused.

Tim added, "When Rocky took Adrian to the skating rink." "So now you're calling me retarded."

"What?"

"In the movie Rocky, Adrian was retarded." "No, she wasn't."

"When he took her to the skating rink, she was."

"Look. I'm not calling you retarded." Tim paused. "What do you want to do?" "You're the one who invited me out, remember?"

"Alright. We'll break in." "What? Are you crazy?"

"It will be alright. What can they do to us? It's not like we're going to steal anything, like a monkey or something. Come on, you'll see," Tim said, backing up the truck and pulling away. He drove up to the other side of the zoo into a dark alleyway leading up to a fence.

"Now what?" Nia asked as Tim turned off his truck. He looked around. "Come on," he said, getting out. Nia followed. They stood by the large fence. There was a dumpster next to it. "We'll use that to get over," Tim said.

"I'm not stepping in trash," Nia replied.

"You won't. That's if you don't fall in. Come on," Tim said. He helped her up on top of the dumpster. "Stay here," he said. He went to the back of his truck and lifted out a rolled-up rug.

"What's that, your magic carpet to fly over?" she asked. "Something for us to sit on," Tim said.

"Most people use blankets," she replied.

"It's all I have," he said, tossing the rug over the fence, adding, "I got it from the last job I did." He began climbing the fence. Once over, he called for her to follow. She did, slipping, but catching herself as she climbed. As she came over on the other side, he helped her down by taking her around her waist. She slid into his arms. Nose to nose, he said, "See. I knew we could do it. Come on." He led her by the hand, the rug underneath his other arm, through the dark paths with some of the animals calling out.

"I feel like I'm in a jungle," Nia said. "You're not afraid, are you?" Tim asked.

"No," Nia replied, adding, "I was a tiger once." "Really. A tame or wild one?"

"I little of both," Nia responded.

Tim took her to a top of a hill overlooking the zoo and rolled out the carpet. They sat down close to each other and looked out into the night with some of the animals still rustling.

"It was nice of you to get Joshua that Valentine's Day card," Tim said.

"Is it really his first card, you know, from a woman?" Nia asked. "Probably. Joshua keeps a lot of things secret though..."

"Like what you're building on your front lawn," Nia replied. "How do you know about that?" Tim asked.

"Joshua told me."

"I told him not to tell anyone," Tim said, a little angry. "You know Joshua writes poems.

He hides them under his bed."

"Really? What are the poems about?"

"About love. He writes them to girls he falls in love with, but he never gives them to anyone. Instead, he hides them. I bet he wrote one for you," Tim replied.

"Why?"

"Because he probably fell in love with you," Tim answered. "But I told you we're just friends," Nia said.

"Did you tell Joshua? To him you're the girl of his dreams," Tim said with a laugh. "I'm going to have to talk to him," Nia replied.

"Don't do that," Tim replied, adding, "It won't change anything. Believe me. I know. It's just better if you don't say anything to Joshua. Besides, he has always had trouble with girls. I keep telling him to go with the flow instead of trying to paint a picture; let the picture paint itself."

"So who's the better artist, you or Joshua?" Nia asked.

"It depends on what you like. Joshua is more like a painter who uses long, bold, romantic strokes. Whereas I prefer to sculpt in a rhythm with a more forceful. deeper penetration around the curves."

"Is that why you want to go all the way to New York, to be an artist?"

"I want to go all the way to find another part of the world, something I've never seen before."

"What part are you hoping to find?" he asked as he got close to her lips.

"The part that every man dreams about," he said as he guided her to her back, kissing her, stretching out her arms over her head. The flip-flops slipped from her feet. A tiger in a cage peered out with a growl and a slap of the bars with her paw.

At wrestling practice, the wrestlers were stamping their feet in unison, hitting the mat and then back up again on Villecco's command as a song from the movie, *Rocky* played, Eye of the Tiger."

As Tim continued to make love to Nia on the carpet, another song from the musical group *Stepenwolf* began playing, "Magic carpet ride..." Joshua jogged in place, covered in sweat.

Covered in sweat, Nia lied naked next to Tim looking up at the sky. "What's the matter?" Tim asked her.

"It's my birthday."

"Happy Birthday," he replied. "There aren't any stars," she added. "So."

"Every birthday I look for the largest star and make a wish." "You're kidding," Tim said with a laugh.

"No. I'm not," she replied.

"Just because you can't see something doesn't mean it's not there," he tried to reassure her. "Go ahead. Make a wish."

"On what?"

"Go ahead. Make a thousand wishes on those thousand stars you can't see."

She smiled. "Alright," she said, sitting up and closing her eyes. "There, I did it." "That was fast."

"I have only one wish," she said, her smile fading, brushing back her hair. "What did you wish for?"

"It has to stay secret," she replied, adding, "In order for it to come true."

"My brother is always reaching for stars. But he is always disappointed. It's like he reaches for a star in the sky that doesn't exist anymore, only its light—like you. He loves you, you know.

"We better go," she replied with a roar of a lion indicating someone was coming. Nia left her jacket behind.

Tim pulled up to the house and looked over to Nia. Nia was looking straight ahead, leaning on the truck's door. "Thanks for going with me," Tim said. Nia was silent. Finally, she asked, "Do you have Joshua's card?" Tim began looking for it. He couldn't find it. "Maybe I left it on the porch," he said.

"Great," she replied, getting out and going up to the porch wearing her tiger body stocking and bare-footed. On the first step she found it. She picked it up and turned. Tim was right behind her. He took her again into his arms and passionately began kissing her. Nia didn't fight back. The card fell from her hand. As it hit the ground, there was a bark. Still in each other's arms, they saw Joshua a few feet away, standing next to Samson.

"No!" Joshua screamed. "That's it. I'm out of here," Tim said, going into the house and into his room to get his things.

"Why did you do this to me?" Joshua asked Nia.

"Joshua, we're just friends..." Nia started to reply as Joshua ran into the house. "Joshua!" she called out.

As Tim was coming down the staircase, Joshua charged and tackled him. At first, Tim didn't fight back. But then, the remaining rungs of the staircase became broken. As they fought to the bottom of the staircase and out onto the front porch, falling against the wooden post, Nia tried to break up the fight but was shoved aside. Samson kept barking.

Joshua finally let go. Tim got up and went to his truck and drove away. "Don't leave me!" Joshua cried out, watching Tim's truck for the final time drive down the long mountain rode.

Joshua turned toward Nia.

"He's not coming back," Joshua said, crying.

"Neither am I, Joshua," Nia replied, adding softly, "Neither am I." She started walking to her car as Joshua stood on the porch calling out, "But I love you!"

Before getting in and driving away, she replied, "I'm sorry, Joshua. But you can't make someone love you. I'm sorry."

"But you do! You do love me! I know it! It was meant to be! It was in the stars!" Joshua called out as she began to drive away.

"There are no stars, Joshua!" she called back, driving away. "Stop reaching for something that doesn't exist!"

He remained leaning against the porch post, not moving, until there was complete silence.

Then, he sat down on the first step with Samson by his side and, while reaching down with his open palm, found Nia's card. He opened it. "Happy Valentine's Day Joshua, Love, Nia," his mother's heart shaped crystal taped to it...

A couple of weeks later, Joshua sat seemingly alone on the first row of the bleachers in the gymnasium along with a sparse crowd watching UCLA's wrestling match against Iowa State. Tony was warming up behind the bench as the other wrestlers each awaited their turn to go out and wrestle. Some, who had already wrestled, were joking around as Villecco continued to shout out moves to his wrestler upon the mat, clearly being heard along with others calling out from the stands. The buzzer sounded loudly. Tony was next. Tony went out onto the mat and shook hands with his opponent and began wrestling, as Villecco's calls along with the crowds seemed to echo into a silence. Joshua sensed something was happening. Suddenly, the calls returned, accompanied by a loud slam. Tony was hurt. Villecco ran out onto the mat with Coach Fanelli and knelt down over Tony as he writhed in pain holding his chest. Villecco looked over to Joshua in an angered stare. Joshua looked up at the scoreboard's clock - 1:11.

It was the day of the wrestling Championships in the old arena with the Apollo almost ready. During weigh-in, The wrestlers waited to hear their names and weight class called out by the coaches and officials standing by the scales. After his name was called, Joshua stepped up on the scale. He was exactly 177 pounds. He made weight, went to the back of the locker room, and began putting on his uniform.

Nia stood by the open window of her room in the rectory of the church looking upward toward the mountaintop. She wondered how close she was to her dream as she knelt down and began to pray.

Joshua was on his knees praying in the locker room dressed in his uniform. He arose and sat along side Carmel.

"This is it, Joshua. This is where it all begins," Carmel said, adding, "You keep winning, you keep going."

"How far have you gotten?" Joshua asked him.

"Second round of nationals. I've won this tournament twice," Carmel replied, "But that doesn't matter now. It's a new battle. You have to take each match one at a time. I've seen national champs get upset in the first round. Anything is possible. You just have to believe.

Alright. We can do this." Carmel stood up. Joshua followed. When they got upstairs to the gymnasium, they began warming up on one of three mats with the other wrestlers. Music was playing loudly from Guns and Roses, "Welcome to the jungle..." as thousands of fans began filling the seats. All the other wrestlers were warming up with their teams on various spots on the mats. Some, pausing, waved to friends in the stands. Joshua, seeing this, looked in the stands, hoping to see his brother or Nia. But he had no one to wave to.

"You looking for somebody?" Carmel asked him, noticing. Joshua shook his head and kept warming up, going through a few moves at a slow and gentle pace with Carmel. A large buzzer sounded. It was time. The lightweights would be first.

Mitch had no trouble taking care of his opponent, hardly breaking a sweat as he threw him onto his back and pinned him in only a few seconds. Most of the other wrestlers made it easily through the first round. Joshua, however, had to wrestle the number one seated wrestler in his weight class because Joshua only had a 0-1 record. As Joshua prepared to go out onto the mat, Villecco was standing by his side in silence. Coach Fanelli, though, was giving Joshua instructions along with Carmel. A couple of other Wrestlers, Mikey and Doug, were sitting in Joshua's corner.

"This should be quick," Villecco said to himself as Joshua walked out onto the mat. "Maier's a three time champ," Doug told Mikey talking about Joshua's opponent, adding,

"And he placed third in nationals last year."

Immediately after the official blew the whistle to begin, Maier shot in on Joshua, lifted him up, and threw him down hard to the mat. As Maier began to bar Joshua's arms and turn him over, Villecco reached down for the water bottle and towel, sensing Joshua was going to get pinned. "I'm going down to get ready for Carmel's match," Villecco told Fanelli, gesturing to the other end of the arena. "You coming? You know you're up next," Villecco said to Carmel as Carmel's name was announced as being on deck on mat one.

"I'm staying here with Joshua," Carmel replied to Villecco. Carmel then shouted, "Come on, Joshua! Don't give up!"

Joshua was on his back, bridging up like he did when he was three with his Dad shouting from his corner. With Joshua's neck being stretched, Maier began bouncing up and down on Joshua's chest to push Joshua's shoulder blades, clinging to a two-inch space, to the mat. Joshua could hardly breathe as he saw the lights high above him in the arena becoming blurry. He struggled to turn his head, and when he did, he saw in the stands that someone was there for him. Nia was sitting in the first row by the corner, just inside the doorway.

"Come on, Joshua! You can do it!" Nia shouted.

Joshua bridged up on his head, flipped to his stomach, fought to his knees, stood up, and broke free. Villecco looked back at Joshua as Carmel, Doug, and Mikey were screaming, "Alright, Joshua!" The official signaled one point escape.

"Now go after him! Take down that chump!" Carmel shouted.

Joshua shot in. Maier sprawled back. Joshua shot in again. Again, Maier countered. From the standing position, head to head, Maier shot in on him. This time, Joshua clasped his arms around him and threw him to the mat onto his back. Maier struggled with Joshua on top of him not to be pinned. Most of the crowd that was watching the other matches all turned to Joshua's.

"I can't believe Maier's getting pinned. Didn't he take third in nationals last year?" Someone asked another in the stands while looking at the program.

"What's that other guy's record?" the other person responded. "Unbelievable," he added as the official slapped the mat. Joshua pinned Maier. His first win. Carmel, Doug, and Mikey went nuts. They ran out on the mat, lifted up Joshua, and carried him off the mat. Coach Fanelli patted Joshua on the head and said, "That a boy. Now you're wrestling like a Kahn."

"I can't believe I won," Joshua kept saying. Villecco didn't say anything. He signaled to Carmel that he was up. Carmel hesitated but then went down to his end of the mat. He didn't have any trouble with his opponent.

Walking down to watch Carmel's match, Joshua went up to Nia. She ran to him and hugged him. "Nice match," she said, "I heard that guy you wrestled was really good."

"Are you going to come see the rest of my matches?" Joshua asked, "That is, if I keep going."

"I'm sure you will keep going, Joshua. But I came here to tell you I'm sorry. I didn't mean to hurt you. And I want you to know that I will always be your friend, your best friend." She gently touched his arm and then turned to walk away.

"So are you going to watch me wrestle?" Joshua asked her again. She turned back. "I've come to say good-bye, Joshua. I'm going back east to be with my mother."

"But I love you," Joshua said, adding, "You're all I've got."

Nia came closer to him. "I know you do. Thank you. But I have go after my dream, too, Joshua. I want to try to make it as a singer back in New York. My mother found someone who can help me, a producer."

"That's where my brother went. Isn't it?" Joshua asked.

"I don't know. I haven't talked to your brother, Joshua," Nia replied. She paused, then said. "Now you go on and win the nationals. Your second biggest dream. What's your first?"

"I don't want to tell you," Joshua said as they both opened their arms and hugged each other tight.

"I'll miss you, Joshua." "Don't leave me, Nia."

"It will be alright, Joshua," Nia said, brushing away tears on Joshua's cheeks. "I'll always be there for you. How's that song go? Ain't no mountain high enough..." Nia started to sing softly to him, and then she told him, "Win nationals, Joshua. Do it for your mother, your father, me, but most importantly do it for yourself. You can do it, Joshua. I believe in you." Nia walked away.

After this, his opponents, including the one in the finals, didn't have much of a chance. Joshua, in a turbulent rage, beat up each one. So it was on to Nationals. Joshua would be seated higher since he was the Champion. The other wrestlers who made it and would go on with Joshua to the nationals were Carmel, Doug, and Mikey, the ones who had cheered for him in his corner. All the others, including Mitch, Cif, and Aikens, had been eliminated. It was as if God had chosen Joshua's closest friends to go the rest of the way with him on his journey, although he still wished with all his heart that Nia would be with him too.

Chapter 18

Inside the wrestling room Joshua was doing shadow wrestling moves alone. The room was dark as Joshua's image appeared intermittently as light cascaded in through the narrow slits of glass of the doors. Glancing in, Carmel caught Joshua's image passing back into the darkness.

"Yo, Joshua. Is that you?" Carmel asked, opening the door. Joshua stood up in the light. "What, are you practicing alone again?"

"I just wanted to work on some things," Joshua replied. "You want me to help?" Carmel asked.

"That's all right," Joshua answered.

"Come on. I'll help you," Carmel said, getting into a wrestling stance from his feet.

Joshua got in a stance too. "Here. Let me teach you a new throw," Carmel said. "You have to get underneath both arms like this and then you—" Carmel threw Joshua.

"Let me try it," Joshua said. Joshua threw Carmel. "Like that?"

"Yeah," Carmel moaned from his back. Joshua helped Carmel up. They gently went through motions of takedowns.

"You know. You're getting a lot better," Carmel said performing a wrestling move.

Joshua countered. "It's like you had it in you all the time," Carmel added as Joshua took him down and did a pinning combination move. Joshua got up off him and sat down against the wall.

"What's the matter?" Carmel asked.

"My whole life I've been dreaming of going to the nationals and it's finally happening," Joshua said.

"Yeah. So?"

"So. I wanted my dad, and" Joshua paused. "someone else, to watch me wrestle," Joshua said.

"I guess the someone else is a girl? I don't know what to tell you about that other than just have faith. That's what's life is about, right, having faith. I didn't know what faith was until my dad died. I was in high school," Carmel said, "He came to every one of my wrestling matches. The first thing I did when I came out into the gym was to look for him in the stands. The day after he died, I had one of my biggest matches against a guy who was undefeated. Out of habit, when I came out, I looked up into the stands. For a moment, I pictured him there. Then I thought that maybe he was. I beat the guy. Everyone was cheering. But I didn't celebrate at all. I just went up to where my father always sat and I opened my arms. It was strange, but I could feel him there."

"Do you believe when you die you can be with the ones you love in this world too?" Joshua asked.

"I believe with God all things are possible, even with your girl," Carmel replied with a smile, adding, "Isn't that what it says in the Bible? Where is Doug when you need him?"

"Thanks," Joshua said.

"Come on. Let's do a few more takedowns. I want you to make it through at least a couple of rounds of the nationals so I'm not by myself wrestling in the quarter finals," Carmel said as they both got up and started practicing again, their images passing through the light. "Remember. Move like the wind. Then you can touch the sky," Carmel added.

The bell tower above the church began to sound out in the distance as off, in the horizon, a fast shooting star moved across the sky. Nia went to her window as if called. She remembered the night on top the cliff with Joshua and wondered what he was wishing for as the same bell tower echoed into the night, ringing out - "Ava Maria."

Joshua now stood before his mother's grave, gazing again at the dried-up rose lying on it as he did the first night after his brother brought him back home. He picked it up and held the rose to his chest, looking with the same wish as Nia. He bowed his head and prayed...

"Mom. I'm sorry. I'm sorry for everything. I'm sorry for letting you down and other people in my life and not living up to what you wanted me to be. I know you wanted me to be a knight. But I'm not a knight, mom. I'm having trouble just being me. Please help me, mom. I love her so much and I don't know what to do. She's so beautiful and has so much love in her heart. I know God's with her. She's special to Him. I can feel it. And I don't know if I'm good enough to be with her. I don't know if I'm attractive enough or anything, like Timmy." Joshua knelt down, getting closer to the grave.

"You told me once to just be myself. You whispered it in my ear. I remember. But I don't know if I can do it, mom. I think God forgot about me, about my dream. And I always trusted Him that it would come true no matter how many years it took. But I think He forgot about me. Everyone left me, mom. I'm all alone, now. It took me my whole life to find the woman of my dreams. I found her, mom. I feel her in my heart so much it hurts. The love for her, it's deep inside here." Joshua pushed the rose closer to his chest.

"God ripped my heart out a long time ago. And now, he gave it back to me when I found her. I love her, mom. Please ask God to take care of her, for her to live a long life and have all her dreams come true. I think the time for my dream has passed. It's been too long. I hope you're still proud of me, though, of the things I've done right. I'm sorry my heart's going to die, mom." Joshua placed the dead rose back on the grave then took off his tee-shirt, "You've Got to Believe," and carefully placed it over his mother's grave. As he walked away in silence, the wind blew across her grave as if a breath from God and the rose came back to life.

"National Collegiate Wrestling Championships." The banner hung high up inside the new Apollo stadium as Joshua stood far below, beneath a large window, waiting in the shadows.

Then, suddenly, sunlight showered upon him as he looked up and envisioned his father sitting in the stands. Joshua charged out onto the mats as music blared out around the arena meeting Carmel, Doug, and Mikey.

"This is it, Joshua, what you've been waiting for," Carmel said to him.

The best wrestlers in the nation were all there, warming up with the ferocity of gladiators about to fight in the Coliseum. A feeling hung in the air that the greatest battles were about to begin. As more people entered, they paused to look up on the walls at the seating charts listing whom the wrestlers would be wrestling in each round. Joshua was seated fourteenth in the second seated bracket and would have to wrestle a champion out of the East from the University of Pennsylvania. Dave Gable in Joshua's weight class, 177 pounds, in the first seated bracket was seated first. Underneath the names on the seating charts were the wrestlers' records. Gable's was 33-0.

The first round of the nationals was about to begin, a round that many wrestlers were proud just to still be alive in, as horns blared, startling some, and referees walked out onto eight large mats and getting into their positions. Everyone was ready. It was finally time; a time Joshua had been waiting for his entire life, from the first moment his father put headgear on him and sent him out onto the mat to wrestle when he was three. Joshua glanced back up into the stands. The vision of his father was still there. Joshua strapped on his headgear. He was ready.

Nia was ready, too, as she stood in front of the fountain in the courtyard of the chapel next to the church. Flowers were beautifully in bloom all around it, the sun glistened in the colors of the rainbow upon the water flowing from an angel's hand in the fountain's center as Father Gabe led an older priest out of the chapel toward her. The priest was silent for a moment and then whispered, "Nia. My beautiful daughter." He opened his arms and she ran to him. They hugged, tears streaming down their cheeks. Gently brushing back her hair, he looked into her eyes and began to say, "I'm sorry I—" But she interrupted him, replying, "You have nothing to be sorry about." She took him by the hand and walked with him up to Father Gabe.

"Thanks, Gabriel. I don't know what to say," Nia's father said. "Just take care of your daughter," Father Gabe replied.

"I know this is sudden and all, but I'm going to Rome next month and would really like for you to come with me," Nia's father said to her.

Nia turned. "I'm sorry. But I'm going to New York."

"So this is it, then. We say hello and then immediately good-bye?" Her father asked, adding, "I guess you just can't walk into someone's life and expect them to drop everything for you, even your daughter's."

"I'm sorry," Nia said.

"You have nothing to be sorry about," her father replied to her. They hugged again. He kissed her cheek.

Father Gabe said, "Your father is going to say mass here this Easter Sunday."

"Will you sing for us at mass?" her father asked her, adding, "Is that still your dream, to be a singer?" Nia nodded. He raised her chin softly and looked at her neck. "Do you still have the locket I gave you?"

Nia started to nod again, and then paused. She said, "I have it, somewhere, but I do have it."

"That's alright," he replied, adding, "I didn't really expect for you to keep it for all these years. Well, I'm looking forward to hearing you sing on Easter. She has a beautiful voice, Gabriel."

"I know," Father Gabe replied, adding while looking up at the sky, "So I've heard."

"Do you know what you would like to sing?" Her father asked her.

"Yes, she does," Father Gabe answered for her. "Something for a friend of yours, right?" "How do you know?" Nia asked.

Writing on the seating charts using markers, students wrote in the names of the winners and the scores from each round. It was the fourth round. Carmel's winning scores were 7-1, 8-2, and 9-0. Joshua's were 2-1, 3-2, and 4-3. Gable didn't have scores. Under his name were just the times that he pinned each one of his opponents, 2:19, 1:20, and 3:16. In the locker room below, Doug was reading from the Bible as Carmel and Joshua, in their uniforms, had their heads bowed with Doug and Mikey, in street clothes, were next to them, all praying. "God so loved the world that he gave His only begotten son.   " All the other wrestlers in street clothes joined them.

Joshua and Carmel were in the arena of the Apollo together, side by side. It seemed bigger, with more people packed into the stands and standing around the mats behind the ropes. Officials attempted to keep the crowd back, but there were too many of them, and some climbed over the ropes and huddled at the edge of the mats. Joshua and Carmel had to make their way past all the people to get their bands from the officials. They had to put the bands around their ankles. They were about to wrestle on two mats next to each other. Villecco went with Carmel, Fanelli, with Joshua. All the time Carmel was wrestling, he was keeping his eye on Joshua.

Joshua had a former national champion who wrestled another weight class the year before. He immediately put a headlock on Joshua and threw him onto his back. Joshua struggled not to be pinned as the official raised his hand a couple of times to slap the mat. Carmel screamed over to him while sprawling back on his own opponent. "Joshua! Don't give up!"

Carmel cross faced his opponent, pancaked him, and quickly pinned him. He then ran to the edge of the mat and screamed to Joshua, "Hang in there! Twenty seconds!" Joshua's opponent did everything he could, but Joshua didn't give up. The buzzer sounded as a young female student with a towel tapped the official to signal it was time. Because of the loud noise, it was hard for the officials to hear the buzzers, let alone know which buzzers signaled which.

The official tossed the large green and red disk as Joshua was on one knee gasping for breath. It came up red, the color around Joshua's ankle. Joshua chose top and got into position on top of his opponent. The official blew the whistle. Joshua tried to ride his opponent, but he quickly escaped. "Do what I taught you!" Carmel screamed out.

When Joshua's opponent shot in, Joshua got underneath his arms and did Carmel's throw. He slammed his opponent down onto the mat. The official raised his hand and slapped the mat. Joshua rolled over exhausted onto his back in victory. Carmel and the other wrestlers ran out and helped him up. "What happened?" Joshua asked.

"You won," Carmel replied, adding, "You're in the finals. Just like your brother was. We both are."

"Unbelievable," Villecco said.

"I believed," Fanelli said. "So did I," Christine came up to them, affirming.

"Well, congratulations, Coach," Joe, the athletic director, said to Villecco, adding, "You have not one, but two in the finals."

A loud scream echoed over all the buzzers, and the crowd became immediately silent. Gable had just broken the arm of his opponent, simultaneously pinning him. The bone broke through the skin. In the courtyard of the church, the water of the fountain turned red, flowing from the angel's hand passing over a reflection of the moon. Beneath Gable, blood gushed out all over the white mat. Joshua looked up.

"So that's the guy I have to wrestle next?" Joshua asked Carmel. "Sorry," Carmel replied. "Remember what I said though." "What's that?" Joshua asked.

"With God all things are possible," Carmel said.

"Just believe, Joshua. You can do it," Doug said to him.

"That's right. You can do it, Joshua," One by one, each wrestler reassured Joshua as they all gazed at Gable standing in the center of the mat. Gable didn't even look like he was breathing hard. After walking over to the corner of the mat and wiping what little sweat he had on his brow off with a towel, he pointed over at Joshua.

"You're next!" Gable called out.

"He knows who I am?" Joshua asked.

"A lot of people do now," Carmel replied as a student wrote Joshua's name using the marker in the finals of the 177-pound seating chart, "Joshua Kahn."

One person looking up at this chart said, "I wonder if he is related to Tim Kahn.

"Man, that was some match years ago in the finals," another man added. "That Tim Kahn should have won. He was winning and his opponent used an illegal move and broke his arm. Tim Kahn was the best wrestler I ever saw."

"Even better than Gable?" another person asked. "He was twice as good as Gable."

"How do you know?"

"Gable's father was the guy he wrestled. He used an illegal move to break Timbo's arm. But if this guy, Joshua Kahn, is related to Timbo, that means it's in his blood. He's a Kahn. And it would be big time payback for the family."

Joshua and Carmel carried out the wrestler with the broken arm, still bleeding. Some of the blood got on them. "I'm dead. He's going to kill me," Joshua said to Carmel while wiping off the blood.

"So you've come this far just to give up, to let him kill you?" Carmel asked. Joshua paused then answered, "I need my brother. I need him to be here with me." Villecco heard him. "And I need..." Joshua paused again.

"Who?" Carmel asked, adding, "Oh, the girl."

"We have to be here 5:30 on Sunday for weigh-ins," Villecco said to Joshua and Carmel. "We're all going to go to church together Sunday, Coach. Do you want to come?" Doug asked Villecco as all the wrestlers nodded, adding, "It's Easter."

"I'll see," Villecco replied. "We'll all see... what happens. Won't we?"

On the back porch, Joshua sat on the step by his father's chair with a partially filled glass by its side. He sat curled up, his knees to his chest, watching Samson play in the backyard like he was chasing something invisible. Suddenly, Samson paused, looked up, and came running toward Joshua.

"He's not going to attack me, is he?" Carmel asked, petting Samson when he came running up to him.

"What are you doing here?" Joshua asked.

"I just came to visit. Do you mind if I sit down?" Carmel asked, starting to sit in the chair. Joshua stopped him and gestured for the step. Carmel sat down next to Joshua, continuing to pet Samson. "You finally got your confidence. Look. You're in the finals of the Nationals."

"Thanks to you. So, what now? Do you think I can do it? Beat Gable?" Carmel gazed out toward the valley. "Well, David beat Goliath. Right?"

"He was chosen by God."

"And what about you..." Carmel got up, looked down at Joshua with a smile, turned, and walked off, disappearing into a veil of a mist.

Joshua remembered the small stone church, when he was standing in front of the children singing, holding up the candle. He remembered what his mother said with a mysterious wind.

"Now you're going to be out in front, the lead one. I want you to raise your candle high to the sky and then call out Jesus' name as loud as you can..."

Joshua got up, and with Samson by his side, he walked toward the edge of the front yard, gazing at the valley below...

"So you're really going back to New York?" Father Gabe asked Nia as she was packing a few things in her room of the church.

"I have to go, Father. Thank you for all that you did for me and believing in me." "Did you pack your tiger outfit?" Father Gabe asked her with a whimsical smile.

"I'm leaving that for you. Something to remember me by," Nia replied with a smile back. "I'll always remember you, Nia," Father Gabe replied, adding in a soft tone, "wherever

you may go." He wasn't smiling. He slowly opened his arms as she paused before hugging him. She wondered what he meant. He kissed her on the forehead and whispered something in Latin in her ear.

"What does that mean?" she asked.

"You'll find out, Nia. God's Hand is moving the stars..."

Villecco stood in the middle of the empty gymnasium of the Apollo gazing up at the ceiling. Fanellie walked across to meet him. As he walked, there was an echo, as if something was calling out from the past.

"I always dreamed I would be here one day wrestling for the national championship," Villecco said still looking up.

"Well, now you have two wrestlers in the finals," Fanelli replied, adding, "I think it's better to help others obtain their dreams than yourself. Don't you?"

Villecco looked back down and at Fanelli. He nodded and then said, "I hope he does it, for his brother, for his family, for himself. I'm sorry I was so hard on him. You're right. I took out my lost of hope on him. Time passes, then it's too late."

"It's not too late for Joshua," Fanelli said to him.

"Maybe this is my redemption, my chance, to help a Kahn win nationals," Villecco said with a smile, raising up his arm, his hand in a fist. Fanelli gave the thumbs up...

Early Easter morning, Joshua fed Bud out of a rusted bucket in the backyard in the small barn his brother had built for him as Samson playfully ran by the windows of the basement. It was like the day Joshua had went into the basement after hearing his brother's hammering to build his secret project to get clothes for a new day. But now, the new day had finally come.

Joshua patted Bud on his nose as he ate his oats and then went back into the house and out onto the front porch. He sat down, placing his gym bag next to him, alongside Samson. As he waited for Doug to come pick him up to go to church, he looked and saw a car approaching. But it wasn't Doug's. It was an old car, looking like something from the 1960's. The car pulled up right next to Tim's secret project, still covered by the canvas. The car's door opened and an Asian woman got out, holding something in her hand. She stood gazing up at the house as if Joshua were not there. She looked down at a worn piece of paper and back up at the house. She slowly walked toward Joshua and Samson.

"Can I help you?" Joshua asked.

"I'm looking for a Mr. Kahn," the woman softly said. "I'm Joshua Kahn."

The woman smiled and said, "I'm looking for a Mr. Kahn much older than you." She handed him the worn piece of paper.

"My father died," Joshua said, giving her back the piece of paper.

"Oh. I'm sorry," she said, adding, "I wanted to give this to him. It's from his brother." "My uncle died in Vietnam a long time ago," Joshua said.

The woman's face turned pale. She gasped for breath and almost fainted. Joshua caught her, sitting her down on the porch step.

"I'm sorry. I don't even know if this is the right house. I would have done this years ago, but I just couldn't bring myself to because I was afraid to hear—what you just told me. I waited until my children were grown before I could do this. I'm sorry," she said.

"I have a picture of my uncle if you want to see it," Joshua said. The woman paused, then nodded. Joshua went into the house and got the picture of his uncle from the mantle. He came back out and handed it to her. She smiled. "Michael," she whispered. She tried to give the picture back to Joshua but he didn't take it.

"You can keep it," Joshua said. "He would probably want you to have it."

"Thank you," she replied, getting up to leave. "Oh, I was supposed to give this to your father years ago." She gave him the small wrapped package.

"What's in it?" Joshua asked. "I never opened it," she replied, leaving.

Nia couldn't find her locket anywhere. She searched in her room at the church and in her car. The only place she thought she might have left it was in her room back at the mansion, but she didn't want to go back there.

"What's your name?" Joshua asked the woman as she walked away.

"Mey Lee," the woman said. Joshua followed and helped her into her car. After shutting the door, she said to him, "You seem like a fine young man. I'm sure your mother is very proud of you." As she drove away, the canvas over Tim's secret project arose a little in a wind. Joshua went back to the porch step as Doug pulled up and beeped. Joshua picked up his gym bag and got in.

"What's that?" Doug asked Joshua, looking at the small package. "I don't know. Something that my uncle gave to my father." "You going to open it?" Doug asked.

"Not now," Joshua replied, putting it in the backseat of Doug's car.

When they got to the church, all the other wrestlers were waiting there, but the church was empty except for Father Gabe, who opened the door for them.

"When is mass, Father?" Doug asked.

"We're not having mass until this evening," Father Gabe replied. "Easter mass at night?" Doug asked.

"It's a special mass this year," Father Gabe said, adding, "Candlelight." "Who thought of that?" Carmel asked.

"Actually, it was my idea. I know. I've been hearing about it from all the parishioners," Father Gabe replied.

"But tonight" Doug looked at Joshua and Carmel.

"I know. Both of you are wrestling in the finals of the national championships," Father Gabe said, looking at Joshua and Carmel.

"You know?" Joshua asked.

"I'm a fan," Father Gabe said, adding, "I was a fan of your brother's too. You can come in anyway."

"You want to go to another church?" one of the wrestlers asked.

Doug looked up, hearing the bells. "This is the one," Doug said, adding, "This is the one we're supposed to go to."

All the wrestlers quietly entered, sat down in the same pew, and kneeled, praying. Joshua went up to the front by the altar. Gazing up at the cross, he opened his arms and started to speak a strange dialogue like he had when he came to this church with his brother. One by one the wrestlers looked up.

"What is he, an angel or something?" they whispered.

Father Gabe, standing in the back of the church, answered, "Yes. The Seventh." But no one heard him.

The church doors opened and Villecco and Joshua's brother, Tim, walked in side by side.

Joshua turned around. "Timmy," he said, getting up. Joshua hugged him.

"Why does he always have to do this," Tim said, having trouble breathing as Joshua hugged him like the time he came to bring him home from the hospital.

"So are you ready?" Tim asked him.

"I've been waiting a long time for this moment," Joshua replied as he did to him in the hospital. Joshua nodded.

Then let's do it," Tim said as all the wrestlers joined them, putting their hands together high up in the air.

Tim remembered what the doctor told him when he picked Joshua up at the hospital. *"So.*

Any instructions or anything?" Tim asked her. "Like I said, 'Just be a brother.'"

Father Gabe gazed up at a statue of Archangel Michael. "I'm ready, too, my brother."

At the Lady of Lourdes psychiatric hospital, the old woman, Silvia, tied in her wheelchair, gazed out a window and began screaming, "He's coming! He's coming! Jesus is coming!" As Joshua had done with her once before, freeing her from her bonds, she was mysteriously freed as Mr. Jeffreys again came to her side. "It's almost time, Cinderella. I'm going to take you to the ball," he whispered to her as they both gazed out the window at the clouds passing fast across the blue sky.

Easter night candles aligned the church, flickering upward and lighting up the stained glass windows. The parishioners began filing in and filling up the pews as across town in the Apollo arena, the fans began filling the stands. As they entered, they fought the winds of an apparent oncoming storm.

High above the lights of the city below, Samson barked frantically as Tim's secret project began to come to life. With a large gust of wind, the canvas was completely torn from it and Tim's secret was finally revealed. Samson became quiet, staring at it as Bud, breaking out of the barn, trotted and joined him. Its wings spanned twenty-one feet and it was eight feet high, eleven feet long. It was white, sturdy, and strong. Gazing at it in awe, Bud nudged closer, but as it began to move again, Samson resumed barking. The Pegasus from Tim's heart was finally free. Here was the love he had for his mother, the memories he carried of her Christmas stories about dreams coming true. Tim had built the white-winged horse for Joshua, a giant kite, like the one they tried to fly with their parents when they were children.

When Tim walked down the stairs and entered the locker room, he saw Joshua sitting alone in the corner. Joshua appeared upset. Tim sat down next to him and put his arm around his shoulder. "Who am I," Joshua asked. "My brother," Tim answered with a smile.

"I'm still trying to catch my dreams... but they seem so far away."

"Well, one is right in front of you," Tim answered, adding, "Right outside that tunnel." "And the other?"

"You know how many people would want to be in your position, right now? A chance to win a national championship?" Tim said.

"Gable seem unbeatable. Not many want to wrestle him," Joshua answered hesitant. "You're not many... This is your moment, your time, your destiny. Don't let it pass," Tim said, getting up, lifting Joshua up by the arm. "You're a Kahn. Remember our uncle, what he did. You have something Gable doesn't have..."

"And what's that?"

"You'll find it out there..." Tim pointed toward the tunnel. "I'll be our there for you."

Tim walked away and through the tunnel. The crowd began to chant and have a roar like a lion, as Gable emerged out into the arena, moving toward the mat to warm up, leading a large group of wrestlers who were in the finals.

Joshua stood, remaining in the tunnel, appearing lost.

"Are you coming, Joshua?" Doug asked, approaching him.

Joshua remained silent. Doug stood facing him. "You don't have to be afraid, Joshua.

God is with you. Come, we'll walk out, together." Joshua walked with Doug through the tunnel and out into the large spanning, high, arena with over 5,000 spectators. "God gave you this day, Joshua. Seize upon it... for Him. Hear His Voice." *An Angelic Voice echoed within an ancient wind... Ana wa a wa... Ana wa a wa... Ana wa a wa...*

Joshua paused. "Did you hear that?"

"Yes. What does that mean?" Doug replied. "I could clearly hear it. Like someone...

All the wrestlers from several different teams were lined up facing each other on either side of the one mat that remained for the finals. A spotlight shined upon it, suspended from the ceiling high above. Some of the wrestlers bounced up and down, swinging their arms, and kicking out their legs, ready to begin. The handicapped children that Father Gabe tried to teach came in and sat in the stands, appearing in awe of everything that was happening. An announcer read the wrestlers' names as they ran out to shake hands with their opponents at the center of the mat. As Joshua's name was called, Tim whispered, "I can't believe this." Villecco, sitting next to him, replied, "You better start. Your little brother is about to wrestle in the battle of his life." The whistle blew. The finals began amidst thousands of screaming fans and an unseen spiritual swirling wind.

"Are you ready, Nia?" her father asked, as he stood about to enter the church. They looked in. All the candles were flickering and the people were singing.

"Yes," Nia replied.

"Then let's do this," her father strongly affirmed with a nod of his head.

Nia held the Bible high in the air and followed the children carrying the cross down the center aisle of the church up toward the altar. Her father sung out loudly, following her, as everyone sung out a hymn. Nia softly sang the closer she got to the altar. Once there, Nia opened the Bible. Her father greeted the congregation as Father Gabe was about to leave through the chapel. "I finally figured out who you really are," the bishop said to him, emerging from the shadows of the garden.

"Bishop? Oh, it's you," Father Gabe replied, acting startled.

"You can drop the facade. I don't think I can startle an Archangel. I continued to attempt to find out, you know, where you came from, but no one had a record of you, anywhere. So..."

Father Gabe transformed into Archangel Gabriel and approached the bishop.

"I always wondered what you looked like," the bishop said with a slight gasp as Archangel Gabriel approached, closer. "I didn't think Archangels could lie."

Archangel Gabriel stood before him, towering over him, casting a shadow toward the statue of Archangel Gabriel next to Archangel Michael's in the garden.

"We don't lie. I am... Gabe. And any... misdirection was part of my cover.

"I see. Well, the kids really like you. Maybe you have a calling to be a teacher."

"A teacher?" Archangel Gabriel laughed. Archangel Gabriel turned away and moved toward the fountain, gazing down at a reflection of a Seven-Headed-Dragon, hovering in front of the club. "I'd rather deal with fighting demons." Archangel Gabriel moved his hand in the water, swirling away the image...

"That may be. But, you *are* a good teacher... I never met an angel before. Tell me, do you really have wings?"

"Not the kind you're thinking of. But, yes, we do." "If I may ask, why are you here?"

"It's almost time." "For what?"

"For Armageddon." Archangel Gabriel turned back with a powerful stare. "It's all part of the plan," Archangel Gabriel said, adding, "You must keep who I am a secret."

"Does Nia have something to do with... *the plan?*"

"You know, one of the most precious people I met down here has been Nia. It's easy to see why Joshua loves her so," Archangel Gabriel said. "Who's Joshua?" the bishop asked.

Archangel Gabriel paused, then said, "The Seventh Angel, in the Book of Revelation."

"How..." the bishop began to ask.

Gabriel looked up at the sky at the fast passing clouds of an oncoming storm and smiled. The bishop looked up too. When he looked back down, Gabriel was gone. After hearing a sound like the sounding of a trumpet, the bishop looked over at the fountain. The water turned red as the a BLOOD MOON EMERGED.

Apollo Arena. NCAA National Championships. "Alright, Joshua. This is it," Carmel said, to him in his corner as he was about to go out and wrestle Gable. Gable stood in his corner, staring over at Joshua, swinging his arms, warming up. Both Tim and Villecco were silent by his side. Joshua, with his hands shaking, had trouble putting on his headgear as he looked out of the corner of his eye and saw Gable charge out onto the mat.

"Here. Let me," Tim said, strapping on the headgear for him. He added, "Remember, Joshua, with God all things are possible, even beating this chump. So, kick his butt."

Joshua nodded and ran out to the center of the mat. After the sound of the whistle, Gable shot in, and with one swift motion, Joshua threw him using Carmel's move. Joshua had Gable on his back and was pinning him. The stands erupted in cheers with people almost throwing Doug and Mikey from their seats in the middle of the crowd. The official was on his stomach looking to see if Gable's shoulder blades were touching the mat. He started to raise his hand to slap it, but Gable roared out like a lion and flipped Joshua over. Gable was now on top. Joshua struggled to break free as Gable pummeled his head like his brother did. Blood started to drip from Joshua's nose. Gable cross-faced Joshua again. Blood spouted from Joshua's mouth. The official signaled time. Joshua went over to his corner so that Fanelli could try to stop the bleeding. The score was 5-2. Joshua was winning.

"Alright. You have to keep moving," Carmel said to Joshua. "When you get out, toss him again with the same move." The bleeding stopped. "Go get him, Joshua," they all cried out.

Joshua started from the bottom position and exploded up onto his feet and broke free of Gable's grip. This time Joshua shot in and lifted Gable up, taking him to the mat.

"Joshua never shoots in," Tim said, surprised.

Joshua was on top but only for a few seconds. Gable escaped, took Joshua down using a headlock, and was now pinning Joshua.

"Don't give up, Joshua!" Carmel and the other wrestlers cried out as Joshua struggled to breathe, gasping for breath, trying to keep his shoulder blades off the mat. Joshua held on, but barely, as the first period ended. Joshua staggered to his feet. The disk was tossed. The official signaled that Joshua would have choice. He chose top. The whistle blew. Gable quickly escaped and took Joshua down. Joshua, exhausted, fought to keep off his stomach as Gable worked pinning combinations using legs. Joshua was being stretched and could feel his ribs starting to tear again. Joshua screamed out in pain, but the official just said, "Keep wrestling." There was a crack. Joshua's ribs broke. The official signaled time for the injury clock as Joshua was writhing in pain. Tim came out to see him in the center of the mat.

"Are you alright, Joshua?" Tim asked.

"My ribs. They tore again," Joshua cried out. Tim and Carmel helped Joshua to the side of the mat as Gable strutted on his side taking hits out of a water bottle.

Bulldozers began to tear down the church across the club from the strip club.

"We need to help Joshua," Doug said to Mikey. Mikey replied, "How?"

"I figured it out," Doug replied. "Come with me.

"You did really well, Joshua," Villecco said to Joshua, getting ready to signal the match was over.

"What are you doing?" Fanelli said to Villecco.

"He can't go on. Look at him. His ribs are probably broken," Villecco said.

"Don't give up on him yet," Fanelli said as they both looked back over at Joshua, who was walking to the center of the mat. Joshua got into position. Gable spit out the water in his mouth and got on top. The whistle blew. Joshua exploded out from the bottom and escaped.

"I haven't seen one of these in decades," the announcer said to Doug looking at the eight- track tape Doug had just given him.

"Can you play it?" Doug asked.

"Now? While they're wrestling? And how?" the announcer asked.

"Yes, now," Doug replied. "Don't you want to see Gable get his butt kicked?"

"I'll see what I can do," the announcer said, putting the tape into a dusty old machine underneath an old tattered blanket overtop a series of antique music machinery.

"People thought I was crazy for keeping this," the announcer said, pushing a button.

Nothing happened. "Sorry. It's too old, a forgotten piece of time..."

For the rest of the second period the gladiators fought, taking turns, shooting in, doing throws, and escaping. When it came to the third and final period, Joshua could barely breathe or stand; Gable chose top. Putting his hands on Joshua's back, he let Joshua escape and then took him down quickly. From the top, Gable did tilts and built up the points as Joshua could barely fight back. Villecco looked over at the scoreboard. The score was 15-7. Gable was winning and there was about a minute left in the match. Then, there was a loud crack and Joshua screamed. Villecco looked back. Gable had broken Joshua's arm just as he had done to Tim's. Tim and Carmel ran out again to the center of the mat as Joshua rolled over onto his injured arm. The official couldn't see if it was broken. Tim and Carmel helped Joshua to the side of the mat, this time hiding the injury. Joshua was screaming in pain. When the water bottle was offered to Gable, he slapped it away and raised both his arms as if in victory.

"Timmy, he broke my arm," Joshua cried out with blood spurting out where the bone had broken through the skin.

Tim turned to Fanelli. "The answer is yes,'" Tim said to him. "What?" Fanelli asked.

"Yes. I would have continued if I knew about my arm," Tim said. "Let's tape him up." "Do you think we should do this?" Fanelli asked.

"You heard me. Tape him up!" Tim shouted.

Fanelli nodded and opened the training kit box, taking out the tape. Still writhing in pain on his back, Joshua looked over and into a mirror inside the top of the box. He saw himself. He was forty-eight-years-old. He did not look away this time. He accepted who he was.

"I think this is yours," Fanelli said to Tim, reaching into his pocket and handing him the Mary Mother Medal he held on to for Tim for years.

"Coach, can your wrestler continue?" the official asked, trying to see. But the rest of the wrestlers joined Carmel and stood around Joshua, hiding what was going on. "You have thirty seconds to decide, Coach," the official said as Villecco considered what to do. Gable raised his arms again, roaring back at the crowd.

"Hurry up!" Tim screamed at Fanelli over the chanting of the crowd.

"Joshua! Joshua!" Some of the wrestlers got started, including the handicapped children from the church who just entered. Fanelli took tape and starting taping over the blood and covering up the broken bone through the skin.

"Joshua! Joshua!" the crowd continued to call out as Gable paced back and forth on the other side of the mat ready *to finish the kill.*

At the church, Nia got ready to sing. Her father was by her side and said, "It is my honor to introduce to you Nia, my daughter, who will be singing for you." Some in the congregation started whispering but became quiet as Nia's father handed her the microphone. Silence.

Nia stood before them. Taking a breath, she looked over to a stained glass window of an angel and whispered, "For Joshua."

Nia started to sing, "Ain't no mountain high enough..."

As the crowd around Joshua parted, he staggered out to the center of the mat in an image of who he was, feeling like he was forty-eight years old. Years had seemingly passed, a lifetime, in just a few minutes, wrestling Gable upon the mat. Both Joshua's arms were taped from the wrists up to the shoulders. Gable couldn't remember what arm he had injured.

Joshua started from the bottom position, exploded out of it, and tossed Gable again with Carmel's move to the mat. Time was running out as Gable fought to his knees. There were only eleven seconds remaining in the match, and Gable was still winning. Nia continued to sing even louder.

Seven seconds. As he had with his brother, Tim, Joshua did the move that his father taught him, a cross face cradle. Tim was the first one to scream out in a cheer, realizing what Joshua was doing, as Joshua cross-faced Gable and locked his fingers together with his left arm, the injured one, in agony. As Joshua lifted Gable, outside the city and high above the mountain, Samson was barking and Bud whinnying. The Pegasus was being lifted up with the wind. Joshua did a double backflip and pinned Gable in the cradle as Gable kicked his feet and legs frantically to break free. The Pegasus broke free from the mountain and flew away high into the sky. The official raised his hand. Two seconds. The hand hit the mat. The buzzer sounded. Joshua won!

Rolling over onto his side, covered in blood, Joshua got to his knees and then to his feet.

Taking off his headgear, disoriented, he raised his head toward the ceiling.

Christmas Eve. The day of his mother's death. Joshua, just three years old, silently stood inside at the front of the stone church holding up a candle as high as he could. All the children, including Joshua, were dressed as angels. "Silent Night" echoed through the crowded church as Joshua's mother, in a small room off by the side, frantically tried to get a group of children in costumes ready to go out and perform their Christmas play.

Joshua raised his hands, as if cupping a candle, high overhead. Finally, after forty-five years, he called out Jesus' name like his mother told him to.

"Jesus... Jesus... Jesus!" Joshua cried out...

Silence. The cheering stopped. Joshua realized that he was in front of the wrestling crowd and not in the church when he was three. Suddenly, everyone looked up as part of the ceiling of the Apollo flew off first and snow came cascading down upon them. Slowly, the walls began to fall away - revealing a medieval style church. Tim and his workers had unknowingly been used by God to build His house. It had not been torn down, like the bishop thought, just transformed, like Joshua.

Snow! All over Los Angeles, the City of Angels, it was snowing. Tim ran to Joshua's side. He took him under his arm and held him around his waist.

"Unbelievable," Tim said. "Joshua, do you remember when you asked me if I believed in God and I said, 'Sometimes?'"

"Yes."

"Well. I think I believe now."

Doug cheered, breaking the silence, pounding his fist, hitting the machine on the announcer's table. The eight-track tape that Michael had gotten for his brother, Joshua's father, and Mey Lee had given to Joshua, began to play as Tim helped Joshua toward the winner's stand. "He ain't heavy... He's my brother..." through the falling snow.

"Well, you were right, Joshua. The snow did come," Tim said. "So that's what you were building," Joshua said, looking up.

"I guess I was," Tim replied, his white-winged horse still flying across the sky. "Do you think Dad saw me win?" Joshua asked.

"I think he did and Mom too," Tim replied. "How do you know?"

"I feel them helping us, like the time they tried to help us fly the kite when we were little." The white-winged horse flew higher off into the sky, carried by the wind through the falling snow over the sea.

Carmel came up to Joshua. "Great job, Joshua. I knew you could do it," he said. "Oh. Thanks for tearing down the place. I was supposed to wrestle next." Carmel smiled with an affirming nod and said, "I knew you could touch the sky."

The crowd began to call out amidst the miracle, each one in their own faith, "Allah! Yahweh! Jehovah! Jesus!" like Joshua had as other miracles began to occur throughout Los Angeles; people were becoming cured from life-threatening illnesses, prisoners were being released, forgiving, and helping each other—everyone's dreams were coming true. Thousands were drawn to synagogues, mosques, and churches as the snow continued to fall amidst newscasts from all over the city, each one reporting another special miracle.

The older couple at Lady of Lourdes hospital was alone by a window, watching the snow come down. He was standing with his hand on her shoulder while she sat, smiling, looking out the window in her wheelchair. She reached up with her hand and touched his.

"Well, Mr. Jeffreys," she said. "You see. Miracles do happen."

He got down on one knee and, after gazing into her eyes and gently brushing back her hair, he kissed her. As they continued to kiss, the snow came down harder in a blinding sheet of white.

"Can I help you?" one of the doctors said to the couple. "With what?" Mr. Jeffreys asked.

"Are you here to see someone?" the doctor asked. "Visiting hours are over."

The couple looked at each other in awe. They were both young again, in their twenties.

They briefly glanced at their reflections in the glass before the falling snow. Then Silvia stood up and they hugged.

"Thank you," Mr. Jeffreys replied to the doctor. "I guess we will be going now." They both laughed as the doctor looked on confused.

When Silvia and Mr. Jeffreys walked out the front door of the hospital, they playfully danced in the snow.

"Shall we dance, Cinderella?" "Why, yes, my prince..."

Nia's mother stood silently by the fountain next to the church that lay in rubble. Except for the rectory, the garden was all that remained. Construction workers were clearing away the debris.

"I've been waiting a long time for this moment," a man's voice said to Nia's mother, coming out from the shadows. It was Nia's real father.

They ran and embraced as a beautiful sunset arose around them amidst the falling snow. "Well, I guess miracles do happen. A Kahn finally won the nationals," Villecco said, reaching out to shake Tim's hand in the locker room.

Joshua, dressed in his street clothes, began to leave. "Where are you going?" Tim asked.

"To thank a friend," Joshua replied. "I'll meet you back at the house." "Aren't you forgetting something?" Tim asked.

"What?"

"Your arm. We have to get you to a hospital." Tim looked at Joshua's arm. It was healed. "What's going on?" Villecco asked.

"You wouldn't believe it if I told you," Tim said to Villecco, adding to Joshua, "I'll meet you back at the house."

Inside the rectory, Nia was saying good-bye to her father. "Thank you for coming and seeing me," Nia said to him as they hugged.

"When I get back, I'd like to see you again. I'll bring you a new locket," he replied. She nodded in tears. "Maybe I'll find the old one," she said.

"Someone else came to see you," her father said. Her mother walked out. Nia and her mother hugged.

The phone in the bishop's office rang. The bishop answered it. "Why, yes. She's still here," The bishop replied. Putting down the phone, he went to get Nia, but she was gone. "Do you know where Nia went?"

Nia's father replied, "To look for her locket at some mansion, and then she's catching a train to New York." The bishop got back on the phone. "I'm sorry, but she left. I don't know. But she mentioned something about a locket and a mansion, then New York."

"Thank you," the voice said.

"What's a matter?" Nia's father asked.

"I don't want her to go back there alone," her mother said.

Nia drove up to the gate of the mansion. There was a rose through its handles, the miracle rose Joshua had placed for her. She got out of the car and took it off the gate. Holding it to her chest, she saw a small, wooden, hand carved dragon on the ground beneath where the rose was on the gate. It was a gift Joshua had made for her. She looked up to the sky, holding the rose to her heart, and saw thousands of stars in the sky and the white-winged horse flying against the full moon, signifying dreams do come true. She looked back down and saw something else in the gate. An envelope. She took it out and opened it. She started reading it aloud, a story Joshua had written for her, while holding the rose.

"This is a story, a story that happened a long, long time ago, when knights slew dragons for fair maidens, carrying them away into the night, and riding white-winged horses off into the sky," he began in his mother's words—right before she was raped and murdered—then continued in his own, *"In a land of dragons, there once lived a knight from long ago, alone, high above in a tower...*

At a small, rundown veterans hospital deep within the city, an old, middle-aged black man with no legs sat in his wheelchair by a partially open window. Pieces of snow fell in upon him. As he reached out his hand to touch the snow before him, a nurse came up to him and said, "Do you believe it's snowing, Uncle Eddie?"

The man paused. "No one has called me that since..."

"I'm sorry. I don't know why I said that," the nurse replied.

As the snow continued to fall far off in a jungle near Vietnam, bamboo bars covered in ice lay across the ground over a hole. Reaching out through the bars, two emaciated hands and arms reached up to the falling snow toward the sky. In one hand was Mey Lee's gold cross.

Michael was still alive.

"God bless you, Michael. Wherever you are," Ed said looking out.

Standing before his mother's grave, Joshua said, "I won, Mom. I won." The only sound was the wind passing through the woods to where he stood. He could remember the Christmas carols more clearly now and the story his mother told him about someday becoming a knight. Yet, in his heart, he was still in much pain. He lowered his head and knelt down before his mother's grave. He placed upon it the medal he had won from the nationals. "This wasn't my real dream, Mom. You know what my real dream is. You're the only one who knows. I love her so much, Mom. Please help me. Please help her see who I am."

The wind blew back some of the snow to reveal the rose that was still alive. Joshua picked it up and held it to his chest, making a final wish looking skyward as the white-winged horse flew before a rising moon, the largest Joshua had ever seen. An old woman in white appeared by the grave.

"Nia needs you, Joshua. Go to her," the old woman said and then vanished in a wave of snow, as if a page was being turned.

Riding upon Bud, Joshua, dressed as a knight when his father knighted him, charged through the woods through the falling snow carrying the rose. Tim walked out onto the back porch calling out, "Joshua." He stepped on something. He looked down and saw one of the Christmas tree light bulbs that Joshua had tried to light up after decorating the backyard for Christmas with Christine. Tim stooped down and took the broken bulb out of the string of Christmas lights on the back porch that led into the woods of the backyard, cutting his hand. He looked over to an unwrapped package of bulbs, found one that wasn't broken, took it out, and screwed it in. When he did, not only did the entire backyard light up, but the entire forest was illuminated with ornaments leading to the tree atop the cliff as Joshua and Bud rode through the lights and snow.

High atop the tree on the cliff overlooking the sea, a star lit up as all the lights in the city by the bay went out. The star shined brightly across the sea, a lighthouse to guide something that was coming.

"Unbelievable," Tim said, still holding onto the electric cord.

As Joshua continued to ride Bud through the falling snow and Christmas lights, Nia's voice echoed what she had read...

...Although he prayed for years, longing to share love with the woman of his dreams, his wish had all seemed to be forgotten. Then, one day, the most beautiful princess he ever saw, with long brown hair and soft brown eyes, came riding into the courtyard below into the castle. Briefly looking up at him, she saw him. But she did not see within him who he was, a gallant brave knight, a hero in another time passed, for his armor was all rusted and worn. Yet, still deep inside of him, there beat his heart in the form of a rose.

As many suitors attempted to win this fair maiden's hand, all he could do was watch from high above while still praying for his wish to come true. Then, one night, he walked out of the tower, made one last wish, took his sword, and raised it high with lightning shooting across the sky. Standing on the edge, a bolt exploded into him, suddenly making his armor shiny and bright, strong once more, as a white-winged horse appeared coming toward him from a distant star. Flying off into the sky as the princess quietly slept with a wish of her own upon her lips, he vanished upon the white-winged horse silently into the night. After the storm passed and the stars returned, she opened her eyes, and there he was kneeling over her, protecting her. Gently, he reached down with the rose, taking it from his chest, and placed it upon her. The rose melted and became her heart.

Nia, I will slay this dragon and carry you off upon a white stallion into the sky...Joshua

"It's beautiful, isn't it, Crystal?" Christine asked her three-year-old daughter, who stood by a window mesmerized by the falling snow. Crystal turned to her mother and simply said, "He's coming."

Joshua, riding upon the white horse, Bud, passed the waterfall as Nia opened the door of the mansion. "Is anyone here?" Nia's call echoed. A few lights were on as she started up the stairs. Halfway up, she paused.

She thought she heard something. She looked back down the stairs and at the open door, then back up toward her bedroom. Reaching the top of the stairs, she moved quietly toward her bedroom. The door was open. She looked in. It remained as she had left it. Hesitantly, she went in and looked around. She got down on her hands and knees and looked underneath her bed for her locket.

"It's got to be here," she said, feeling around with her hand. As she did, she sensed there was someone standing in the doorway, watching her. She thought she saw a shadow. Startled, she turned and looked. But no one was there. She reached under the bed again. "Got it," she said, finding her locket. Suddenly, someone grabbed her around her waist from behind. She screamed as she was lifted up and thrown forcibly onto her back upon the bed, her blouse completely tearing from her as she fell. It was the senator.

"I've been waiting for you to come back," he said, wearing soiled riding boots, a riding crop in his one hand, and the dragon knife in the other.

Bud's eyes became wide as he carried Joshua through the mansion's gate.

"No, please," Nia pleaded as she tried to get up and break free. But he was too powerful, too strong as he took her and flipped her over hard onto her belly, like he did with Joshua's mother. Clasping the back of her head by her hair, straddling her, he made a cut with his knife aside her neck. After tasting her blood, he began to try to cut her tongue out, pulling back on her hair as if pulling back on the reigns of a horse.

Bud stood in the foyer as Joshua entered the doorway. Seeing Nia, he flashed back to the image of his mother's attack when he was three. This time, within his hand, like the rosebud he held before, the rose had bloomed and was now open.

"Never tell me 'No,' my sweet whore. Never tell me 'No.'"

The senator turned around. He saw Joshua. "Well. History does repeat itself, doesn't it?" the senator snarled, getting off Nia.

"Leave her alone."

"Or what? You'll beat me up?" the senator said with a laugh, "You remember what happened the last time you tried to stop me, the time your mother screamed out like a whore?"

Joshua rushed the senator and threw him up against the wall. The dragon knife fell to the floor. Taking the senator by the throat, Joshua lifted him up and pounded his head. Joshua squeezed harder. The senator could not breathe and blood began to flow from the side of his mouth.

"No don't, Joshua!" Nia shouted. "Don't kill him, or you'll be just like him. Joshua!

Don't! Let him go!"

Joshua let go slowly as the senator fell down to the floor, gasping for breath, wiping the blood away from his chin. Nia hugged Joshua and he handed her the rose. The senator stood up. Joshua quickly turned, picked up the knife, and stood in front of her to protect her. The senator moved closer.

"You wouldn't hurt me, Mr. National Champion. After all, how can a son hurt his own father?" The senator asked, adding, "You know how you won? You have my blood in you."

"What do you mean?" Joshua asked holding the knife poised.

"I'm your real father, Joshua. Didn't your mother tell you?" the senator asked.

"My real father is dead," Joshua said as both Nia and he backed up onto the balcony. "And so are you," the senator said, taking a gun out of his riding boot.

Nia screamed, "No!" and pushed Joshua aside. The gun fired.

Joshua looked over at Nia and then down at his stomach. There was blood. He fell to the floor. Picking up the dragon knife, the senator thrust it into Nia's side as Joshua tried to reach out and save her, but he couldn't. The senator laughed and tossed the dragon knife back in front of Joshua. Nia leaned over the railing of the balcony, bleeding, still clasping the rose, trying to find a way to escape, but there was nowhere to go. The senator stood before her. As he raised and aimed the gun at her head, she sank down, bringing her knees up to her chest, and held her wounded side with the rose. With her blood flowing upon it, turning its pedals into a bright red, he placed the gun softly against her lips and whispered, "Suck it." Slowly, she took the shaft of the gun and brought it into her mouth. Suddenly, Samson appeared and lunged, pushing the senator up against the balcony and the gun from his hand. Standing in front of Nia, protecting her as Joshua had done, Samson growled at the senator. The senator laughed, picked up the gun, and aimed it at Samson's head. "Don't hurt him," Nia pleaded for Samson.

"This time, I'm going to kill you," the senator said to Samson.

Tim's white-winged horse kite, the one with a horn, appeared from the sky and lanced the senator, impaling him through his back from behind. The senator's eyes bulged and blood spilled from his mouth. The wind shifted and the kite lifted the senator up off the balcony. Carrying him a few feet, the horn broke, dropping the senator onto the sword of the angel in the fountain of the garden below, as Joshua arose. The senator's eyes turned black as the last drops of blood flowed from his mouth. The kite flew back across the sea toward the horizon's edge and into the moon.

Joshua struggled to Nia's side. He tried to move her. "Joshua, you're hurt," she said, reaching out and touching his wound.

Joshua struggled to Nia's side. He tried to move her. "Joshua, you're hurt," she said, reaching out and touching his wound. "I'll get help," he replied, getting up in pain. But Nia pleaded, "Don't leave me, Joshua. Don't leave me. Just hold me." He put his hand on Nia's wound to try to stop the bleeding, and held her close with Samson by them.

"So you won nationals, your second biggest dream," Nia said. "Yes," Joshua replied.

"I knew you would. I had faith in you." She paused and then asked, "So what is your biggest dream?"

"You," Joshua simply replied. "My dad said that with God anything is possible. So will you marry me?"

"Is that what you wished for, that time we were atop the cliff?" she asked with fading breaths.

"That's what I've wished for with every breath I've taken, in every second of every day since I found you," he said.

"We made the same wish, Joshua. You're right. I do love you," Nia replied, then whispered something in Joshua's ear.

"Don't leave me, Nia," Joshua pleaded.

"I'll always be with you, Joshua..." Nia took her last breath... and the rose he had given her, melt and became her heart. "No!" Joshua cried out...

Against the light of a full moon, he carried her off, riding upon Bud with Samson running alongside of them, toward the cliff atop the waterfall, overlooking the sea. When he reached the top of the cliff, he gently took her body and held her beneath the stars.

"Come back... Don't leave... Come back! Make her alive again!" He cried out toward the sky. As his screams faded, he lowered her body slowly to the ground by the side of the old oak upon the mountain - standing before the sea... The star atop the tree flickered and went out as the rest of the Christmas lights and the stars in the sky followed as the lights in the city below slowly returned. He sat there awhile with Samson and Bud. Praying, he kissed her, tears falling down upon her... Miraculously, with his power from God, his wound was healed again, but he could not bring her back. No one could; she was gone. Samson gazed up at the tree, howling deep into the night as Joshua used the dragon knife covered with Nia's blood to carve into the tree, "I do too," what Nia had whispered in his ear... Crystal, Christine's little girl, stood in her bare feet on a front porch in her nightgown looking up toward the mountaintop. The snow had stopped. Raising her hand, she made a fist...

Chapter 19

Years later... On the mantlepiece above the fireplace next to Joshua's mother's diploma—Elizabeth Prather Kahn. Master's Degree, Medieval Literature—were three other diplomas. Joshua Kahn. Bachelor's, Masters, and Ph.D., all in education.

"Yes, Crystal," Joshua called, standing in front of his high school class as Crystal raised her hand.

"Doctor Kahn. Shouldn't the resultant vector be thirty-three degrees north of east?" Crystal asked as Joshua stood before the chalkboard with vectors drawn all over it.

"Yes. You're right. I just did that to see if you were paying attention."

The class laughed. Crystal replied, "Yeah. Right," adding, "Did you even take physics in college?"

"What are you trying to say, that I don't know what I'm doing?" Joshua joked. "Did you want to be a physics teacher?" Crystal asked.

"I wanted to teach," Joshua said. "But I really wanted to be a writer. I used to write poetry."

"Then why don't you?" Crystal asked.

"I don't know. I guess that dream died a long time ago," Joshua answered.

"But you're still alive. Didn't you tell us that all we have to do is believe in ourselves and that with God anything is possible?" Crystal asked. "So why don't you go after your dream?"

So I did...

As I am writing this story, the candle is lit on the bedroom floor where I left it years ago, although the path through the woods to the waterfall is much overgrown now. I haven't been able to go to the old oak tree in a while. The climb up there has become too much for me. Yet, I still frequently visit the graves of my mother, my father, my brother Tim, who died in a car accident a couple of years after I won nationals, and yes, Samson finally left me as well. I'm all alone now, except for Bud. He is still with me. And although we are both older now, we still take walks together to the edge of the woods and wonder what dreams, what stars falling from the sky, lie in some distant hidden moon beyond. I'll never forget the darkness of that night when my mother told me that the dragon was eating the moon. But I'll also never forget how the rose upon her grave came back to life beneath the largest moon I have ever seen and how Nia told me that she loved me...

Although I have been alone through all these years and have trouble getting around now, I still love teaching high school students and being around them. They are filled with so much hope and have so much faith in their dreams. I try to help all of them so all of their dreams can come true. And I know it may sound crazy, but, as I look out into the woods, sitting in my father's chair, holding his empty glass, I'm still hoping that my biggest dream with Nia will come true. After all, my father said, "With God all things are possible." I know now why my father held this glass so tightly. It held all of his dreams.

For now, I am just writing this book and thinking about all the love that I shared with Nia, my mother, my father, my brother Tim, and Samson. The parts about my Uncle Michael I got from the letters he sent to my father and the stories Mey Lee told me before she, too, died. She came to see me a lot, even bringing me dinner at times.

I wonder what heaven is like. Will I see all of them again, even Samson? Will I look like when I was young... when I wrestled? I hope so. And I hope all of them are happy and with me somehow. Nia told me that she always would be with me. I don't really know how to end this book. I guess I'll leave it open. That's what life is about, right? Always being open. Always new surprises, new life.

Although I am unable to go to her grave, I go to church every day and pray for Nia. I pray that all of her dreams came true, wherever she is, and to let her know how much I love her. I've never loved anyone in this world as much as I love her.

The wind is growing again, that strange wind from years ago. I don't know what is going on, but I sense something is happening. God is willing it. The glass! There is something in it! It looks like red wine. Tasting it, it tastes like blood. That moon, it's back. That's strange. I hear children singing—a Christmas carol, the song my mother sung to me as a child. It echoes from the old, abandoned stone church nestled in the woods. Overgrown with trees and brush, my moment of raising the candle for God transcends time across the rippling pond unmoved with the reflection of the moon.

"Oh holy night the stars are brightly shining. It is the night of the dear Savior's birth...fall on your knees, hear the angels' voices"

"Dr. Kahn!" Someone is coming.

The glass falls and shatters with blood oozing from refractions created by the broken glass, carrying the moon, spilling out into transformed yet rigid crevices of the back porch's decaying splintered wood. Then, within opening crevices of some lapsed splinter of time, someone seeps out from a predestined past and appears as if a shadow from the future approaching from out front. Walking out onto the front porch to meet an image of a woman walking out of a mist, I once again fall against that same wooden porch post that I did years ago. It is even more brittle with more chipped paint upon it, still seemingly to exist only with no support or purpose.

"Hi, Doctor Kahn."

"Crystal. You're all grown up. What are you doing here?" I ask, picking off a paint chip from the post of the past and flicking it into the coming wind.

"Doctor Kahn. A man in the city has been looking for you. He said that it is time and to show you this," Crystal replies to me, handing me a locket. The locket is a brilliant silver, reflecting in a bright full moon. It has swirling, outstretched vines holding roses.

"Nia's," I whisper, giving her back the locket. "What did this man look like?" I ask. "He was about six feet tall, had long brown hair, a beard, and bright blue eyes. A lot of

people were with him calling him Savior. They said he was doing miracles, helping people. Oh, and he had a nice smile. He told me to find you and that you would know where to meet him."

"Thank you, Crystal. But you better get home now, a storm is coming, the storm, and soon you will know who you are."

"What do you mean?"

"I don't know why I said that."

"Dr. Kahn, I always remembered what you told me about believing in your dreams. Do you think mine can come true too?"

"I don't know what your dreams are, Crystal, but I do know that in order for your dreams to come true, you have to follow your heart. Just follow your heart, Crystal."

We hug. She cries in my arms. "I'm pregnant. My boyfriend doesn't want the baby but I do. There are complications. What should I do?" Crystal asks.

"You know what to do. Everyone does, to make their dreams come true." "Follow my heart?" Crystal asks, holding the locket to her chest.

I nod with a smile. She kisses me on the cheek. "Bye, Doctor Kahn."

"Bye, Crystal. Be careful and take care of your daughter." "How do you know?"

"I just do sometimes," I whisper to myself.

As I watch Crystal drive away, I can see the lights fading in the city below. I remember Timmy and me, the time we tried to hold down the canvas over his secret project, and that wind, that strong wind as if God sent. I don't know why life is so hard at times or why some people seem to suffer more than others do. I guess it's just like wrestling. There are only a few who win and are champions, but in a way we all are. We all are given a gift, life. And no matter how difficult times may seem, it's when it is the darkest, having taken that last step, when God surprises you. I was surprised so much in my life. After all,

I would have never thought I would fall in love with a beautiful girl who was dressed as a wolf in the middle of the night by the side of a pond or see my father knight me dressed as King Richard the Third. I guess Shakespeare is right, "Life is a play."

I didn't know it at the time, but I have lived such an interesting life. I thank God for that and all the people I have met in my journey along the way, especially my mom. She always believed in me and that all my dreams would come true. Somehow her faith always carried me. I wish I could have helped her that night and that she could have finished the story she was reading to me beneath the light of the moon. Yet, in a way, she did. My life was her story, and now I feel the final page being turned with another wind, growing strong and unraveling from God's palm.

I walk toward the woods in the backyard. Bud tries to go with me, but I tell him to wait here. I go into the woods alone, making my way through the brush, finding the old path. I stop by my mother's grave by the old abandoned church. Pushing away the soil, my old tee shirt is still there, keeping her safe. "You've Got to Believe" it still says.

With a renewed strength, I climb up by the waterfall and to the tree atop the cliff as the growing winds begin to raise the sea. Then, with the whisper of a hidden angelic woman's voice, the Christmas lights leading through the forest to the cliff and the star atop the tree mysteriously light up. The whisper turns into a lion's roar... *They were looking intently up into the sky as he was going, when suddenly two men dressed in white stood beside them. 'Men of Galilee,' they said, 'why do you stand here looking into the sky? This same Jesus, who has been taken from you will come back in the same way you have seen him go' (Acts. 1:11).*

"Doctor Kahn should have this," Crystal whispers, still holding the locket, returning to the house.

On top of the cliff the wind is strong. I have to steady myself against the old oak tree.

Beneath my hand I see that what I wrote on the tree is still there.

Then, something strange happens. I see myself on the ground. It looks like I am dead, but my body—I look like what I did when I wrestled.

"I told you I would always be with you, Joshua."

I turn around. Nia stands before me. She hugs me. "I love you, Joshua."

"I always keep my promises. You will never be parted again," a man says, the man with the bright blue eyes. He adds, "Come, Joshua. Doctor Kahn. It's time. Your brother and family are waiting to fight in the war alongside you, and where would I be without my Seventh Angel?

He takes me by the hand and walks with Nia and me off the cliff and over the rising turbulent sea. "Is this the end of the world?" I ask.

"It is just the beginning," he replies, adding, "I've always seen the love you have for her in your heart and that's why I've joined your heart with hers."

Crystal appears as if coming out of the clouds riding Bud up to the cliff by the old oak tree. Suddenly, the tree is hit by lightning, breaking it in half and causing it to fall into the sea. There, embedded in its trunk, is King Author's sword, Excalibur, from long ago. Crystal goes over and clasps her hands upon it. With lightning and thunder shooting across the sky above her, she draws out the sword and raises it high above her head. She sees us walking out above the sea, disappearing into the night. As a rush of lightning shoots through her hand, Crystal feels the sword's power.

Music on Tim's radio by the side of the house again mysteriously comes on for one last time. The song is from Elton John, "Lean On.

"And the New York Times said God is dead and the war's begun" as the archangel weathervane atop the house swirls, this time clockwise in the wind pointing east.

Sounds of battle. The moon in red. Armageddon.

"Where will we build our house?" a little girl asks, looking up at Crystal, riding Bud.

Crystal, at the edge of a small town being constructed, sits upon Bud with a heroic, yet battle worn look with Excalibur draped around her waist. Gently, she reaches down and helps the little girl up with her in front of her on top of Bud. With her arms securely around the little girl, Crystal begins to ride toward the center of town where men, women, and children are building new homes similar to how the Apollo was built. One young man screams out at his younger brother, a lot like Joshua, about ruining a wall. "I told you to hold it up. When are you going to wake up? Would you hold it up! Hold it up!" the older brother screams.

"I'm sorry," his younger brother meekly replies.

"Go. Just go! You're crazy. You know that?" his older brother shouts back at him. "I'm not crazy."

As the younger brother starts to climb down, Crystal says to him, "Get back up there and try again. Don't give up. You've got to believe," she adds with a smile, pointing Excalibur at the young man's shirt. He has a tee shirt on like Joshua's. The older brother nods his approval.

Reaching out his hand, he patiently shows his little brother how to do it—teaching him.

With the new buildings beginning to form, they appear to be made of an unusual wood and brick as people are riding horses down a dirt-covered street while others are walking, greeting each other with a smile like the man with the beard and piercing blue eyes. The little girl continues to ride with Crystal as others come up to greet her with a hero's welcome. Crystal looks up toward the mountaintop. She points to where Joshua's house used to be and whispers to the little girl, "Up there on the mountain, that's where we will live."

Atop the mountain Joshua's house is gone, but the front porch and that old paint-chipped porch post that didn't seem to have any support or purpose is still standing. The screen door is also there, left alone and silent. Nothing else. All that is left are remnants of what use to be; Tim's canvas of his secret project, half covered in soil, Samson's doghouse with the shingles missing, Bud's stable, barely standing, and their father's chair, near Samson's doghouse with the POW flag draped upon it. The chair—it suddenly starts to move. Tim's radio.

371

Static. Then, the first song of the new world. "When there's no one else, look inside yourself...and find the strength... Young girl, don't cry. I'll be right here when your world starts to fall." Christina Aguilera.

"Why up there?" The little girl asks Crystal.

"Because that's sacred ground" Crystal replies, adding, "and that's where he lived." "Who?"

"Someone who didn't believe in himself. Someone who felt God had forgotten about him. Someone who God had chosen and eventually helped all his dreams come true. He was my teacher and my friend."

All the people in the town are standing around Crystal, looking up at the mountaintop. Smoke is seen in the distance beneath it, still arising from pieces of still smoldering ashes from the war. People just outside town are burying the dead. One is a child, a little girl, like Hoa Sung. Her mother weeps over her grave as they lower her lifeless body into it. The men are in tattered clothes, their hands bleeding with blisters from the intense digging, tightly gripping their shovels.

"Is the war over?"one man asks another standing over the graves, seeing the smoke in the distance beneath the mountaintop.

"Yes," Crystal whispers at the center of town, a few hundred yards away from the gravesites and these men, as if hearing him, gripping her sword tightly, with blood still upon it.

"Yes," a very old man echoes back at the gravesites, looking like a soldier from long ago.

He tosses down his rifle by the side of the child's grave. "Who are you?" one of the men asks this old man.

The old man begins to answer, "Captain..." But then remains silent. He sits down and takes off his boot, shaking it. A small snake that had been hiding beneath his foot during all the fighting begins to slither out. "It's safe to come out now, little guy," the old man says, standing up and looking ahead toward the center of town.

"Do you think we can live like God wants us to now?" a man asks Crystal.

"That's up to us," Crystal replies, adding, "With God all things are possible, but it is up to us to fight and to believe with all our hearts no matter what happens so that our dreams can come true."

"Did your dream come true, Mom?" the little girl asks Crystal.

"Yes. I have you, Hope," Crystal replies, hugging her. She takes off Nia's locket from around her neck and places it in her daughter's hand. "And one day you will be the new leader, just as the descendants of King David. But this time, Crystal gets off Bud and looks to the people around her. Her daughter opens the locket.

The Sacred Heart of Jesus.

"We will live as He wants us to," Crystal says. "How?" a different man asks.

"We will love one another. We will simply love one another," Crystal replies, reaching out her bloodstained hand toward him. One by one, the people in the town all join hands, except Crystal's daughter, who is still on Bud.

With both her hands Hope leans over Bud and lifts Excalibur from her mother's waist and holds it up. "Mom, look what I can do," she says. The sky brilliant, the sun draped in the colors of a dawn.

Outside of town the old man leans over into the child's grave and places in the dead little girl's hands a small rosebud, like the one Nia gave Joshua when, the one Ed placed in Hoa Sung's hands when she died, and the one Hoa Sung was growing for Michael. He gently places the small rosebud in her hands. He whispers to her "...and as the knight knelt down over her, he reached down with a rose. She held it to her chest, and it slowly melted and became her heart."

Atop the cliff, a piece of the old oak tree that survived Armageddon is on the ground where Joshua laid Nia's body, the piece that has carved in it, "I do too." Someone picks it up. He holds it to his chest, looks out across the sea, smiles, and says, "I didn't forget about you, Joshua. I was just waiting for you to come to me." The man is Jesus...